GNOSIS AND HERMETICISM
FROM ANTIQUITY TO MODERN TIMES

SUNY Series in Western Esoteric Traditions
David Appelbaum, editor

GNOSIS
and HERMETICISM
from ANTIQUITY *to*
MODERN TIMES

edited by
Roelof van den Broek
and Wouter J. Hanegraaff

State University of New York Press

In chapter 4 the *Gospel of Truth* is quoted from the translation by
H. W. Attridge and G. W. MacRae, in *Nag Hammadi Codex I,*
vol. 1, ed. H. W. Attridge (Leiden, 1985), with permission
from Royal E. J. Brill, Leiden.

Published by
State University of New York Press

© 1998 State University of New York

For information, address the State University of New York Press,
State University Plaza, Albany, NY 12246

Marketing by Dana Yanulavich
Production by Bernadine Dawes

Library of Congress Cataloging-in-Publication Data

Gnosis and hermetism from antiquity to modern times / edited by
    Roelof van den Broek and Wouter J. Hanegraaff.
        p.   cm. — (SUNY series in western esoteric traditions)
    Includes index.
    ISBN 0-7914-3611-X (hardcover : alk. paper). — ISBN 0-7914-3612-8
(pbk. : alk. paper)
        1. Gnosticism—History. 2. Hermetism—History. I. Broek, R. van
den. II. Hanegraaff, Wouter J. III. Series.
    BT1390.G485   1998
    299'.932—dc21   97-26329
                                                                       CIP

1   2   3   4   5   6   7   8   9   10

TABLE OF CONTENTS

Preface   vii

1 ❧ *Roelof van den Broek*
   Gnosticism and Hermetism in Antiquity:
   Two Roads to Salvation   1

2 ❧ *Jean-Pierre Mahé*
   Gnostic and Hermetic Ethics   21

3 ❧ *Johannes van Oort*
   Manichaeism: Its Sources and Influences on
   Western Christianity   37

4 ❧ *Jan Helderman*
   A Christian Gnostic Text:
   The *Gospel of Truth*   53

5 ❧ *Gilles Quispel*
   The *Asclepius:* From the Hermetic Lodge
   in Alexandria to the Greek Eucharist and
   the Roman Mass   69

6 ❧ *Jean-Pierre Mahé*
   A Reading of the *Discourse on
   the Ogdoad and the Ennead*
   (Nag Hammadi Codex VI.6)   79

7 ❧ *Roelof van den Broek*
   The Cathars: Medieval Gnostics?   87

8 ❧ Antoine Faivre
Renaissance Hermeticism and the
Concept of Western Esotericism 109

9 ❧ Cees Leijenhorst
Francesco Patrizi's Hermetic
Philosophy 125

10 ❧ Karen-Claire Voss
Spiritual Alchemy: Interpreting
Representative Texts and Images 147

11 ❧ Joscelyn Godwin
Music and the Hermetic Tradition 183

12 ❧ Roland Edighoffer
Hermeticism in Early Rosicrucianism 197

13 ❧ Arthur Versluis
Christian Theosophic Literature of the
Seventeenth and Eighteenth Centuries 217

14 ❧ Wouter J. Hanegraaff
Romanticism and the
Esoteric Connection 237

15 ❧ Jos van Meurs
William Blake and His Gnostic Myths 269

16 ❧ Daniël van Egmond
Western Esoteric Schools in the Late
Nineteenth and Early Twentieth Centuries 311

17 ❧ Joscelyn Godwin
Stockhausen's *Donnerstag aus Licht*
and Gnosticism 347

18 ❧ Wouter J. Hanegraaff
The New Age Movement and
the Esoteric Tradition 359

List of Contributors 383
Indexes 385

PREFACE

It is still often regarded as self-evident that western culture is based on the twin pillars of Greek rationality, on the one hand, and biblical faith, on the other. Certainly, there can be little doubt that these two traditions have been dominant forces in cultural development. The former may be defined by its sole reliance on the rationality of the mind, the latter by its emphasis on an authoritative divine revelation. However, from the first centuries to the present day there has also existed a third current, characterized by a resistance to the dominance of either pure rationality or doctrinal faith.

The adherents of this tradition emphasized the importance of inner enlightenment or gnosis: a revelatory experience that mostly entailed an encounter with one's true self as well as with the ground of being, God. In antiquity this perspective was represented by Gnostics and Hermetists; in the Middle Ages by several Christian sects. The Cathars can, at least to a certain extent, be considered part of this same spiritual tradition. Starting with the Italian Renaissance of the late fifteenth century, the newly discovered "Hermetic philosophy" rapidly spread all over Europe. It found many adherents, in particular during the sixteenth and the first half of the seventeenth century. This so-called Hermeticist tradition and its later developments—the whole of which may referred to as "western esotericism"—was characterized by an organic view of the world that assumed a strong internal coherence of the whole universe, including an intimate relationship between both its spiritual and its material elements.

The scientific mechanization of the world, the doctrinal consolidation of Reformation and Counter-Reformation, and the rationality of the Enlightenment of the eighteenth century made the Hermetic philosophy, with its strong connections to alchemy, magic, and astrology, scientifically backward and religiously suspect. Nevertheless, the hermeticist current took on new forms in Rosicrucianism and Christian theosophy, and continued to flourish in secret associations such as Freemasonry. Thus, it continued to have a strong impact not only on philosophers, mystics, and occultists, but on many writers, painters, and musicians as well.

In our own time many people, disappointed in the perspectives on humanity and the world offered by either rationalism or traditional religion, turn again to the basic principles of Gnosticism and Hermeticism, often integrated with some kind of New Age thinking.

The academic study of these developments is a comparatively recent phenomenon. Most literature about the various aspects of "western esotericism" has traditionally been of an apologetic or polemic nature: a debate, basically, among believers and their opponents. Academic researchers generally tended to avoid an area of cultural expression that was widely regarded as inherently suspect; openly to express interest in these traditions might too easily endanger a scholar's prestige among colleagues. During the last few decades, the realization has been growing that this attitude has little to commend it from a scholarly point of view, and may on the contrary have blinded us to important aspects of our cultural past. Even more importantly, it has become increasingly clear that the scholarly recovery of "esoteric" traditions may eventually force us to question basic received opinions about the foundations of our present culture.

These considerations apply most directly to those movements that developed in the wake of the Hermetic revival of the Renaissance period. The scholarly study of ancient Gnosticism and Hermetism has been accepted and taken seriously for much longer. This should not surprise us, if we take into account the battle between doctrinal Christian theology and Enlightenment rationality that began around two centuries ago. An impartial—instead of polemic—historical study of Gnosticism was potentially dangerous to the self-understanding of traditional Christianity and its modern representatives. It held little threat, on the other hand, to the liberal theologians, Bible critics, and religious historians who increasingly came to dominate the academic study of Christianity. On the contrary: the historical study of Gnosticism could serve these scholars as a useful means of undermining the claims of their more conservative colleagues.

The situation was entirely different with respects to post-Renaissance "Hermeticist" movements. Not only were these less distant in a strictly chronological sense, they were also much closer in spirit. Having flowered in the same period that saw the emergence of modern science and rationality (and having been, as we now know, crucially involved in that emergence) they evidently touched upon the very roots of modernity itself. If Gnosticism had traditionally been perceived as the enemy of established Christianity—exemplifying what were regarded as essentially pagan temptations—modern Hermeticism held a comparable position in relation to the newly established rationalist worldview. To the intellectual heirs of the Enlightenment, it appeared very much as Gnosticism had appeared to the early church fathers: as a collection of archaic and potentially dangerous superstitions. They were regarded as the epitome of those kinds of error from which human reason had now finally managed to free itself.

However, one openly fights an enemy only as long as one fears that he still might win. In this respect as well, history seems to repeat itself. Like the Christian Church before it, modern rationalism, once safely consolidated, could afford itself the luxury of exchanging active combat for a more comfortable (and perhaps more effective) solution: silence. Believing in the inevitable progress of human rationality, one could simply ignore esotericism, in the confident expectation that its still surviving remnants would eventually wither and die by itself.

However, even if one avoids the use of currently fashionable labels (most of which seem to begin with "post-" and to produce book titles beginning with "Beyond"), it is clear that the optimistic self-confidence of Enlightenment thinking is no longer widely shared. Together with growing doubts about the doctrine of human progress through science and rationality, we witness a new interest in historical alternatives to the dominant components of western culture. It is only natural that the study of Gnosis and Hermeticism profits from this widespread reorientation. It is the conviction of the editors of this volume, nevertheless, that in this newly emerging domain scholars should try to avoid repeating the mistakes of the past. Even if the academic study of "Gnosis and Hermeticism" (in the comprehensive sense employed here) may gratefully ride the current wave of a popular search for alternative sources of meaning, it should not once again allow itself to be put into the service of covert religious or ideological warfare. It is the task of historical scholarship faithfully to describe and interpret "what has been," as well as "what is." It should not see it as its calling, however, to prescribe "what should be." Accordingly, this volume intends to introduce the reader to what has sometimes been called "the third component of western culture," leaving it to that reader to make up his or her own mind about its inherent merits, or about its possible contemporary relevance.

The chapters of this volume originated as lectures given at the Amsterdam Summer University in August 1994. In line with the historical orientation of the book, we have attempted to arrange the different contributions so as to produce an unbroken chronological story, in which each chapter builds upon and develops from preceding ones. At the same time, the volume as a whole definitely intends to be more than just introductory. All the contributions are based on new and original research, which not seldom happens to challenge accepted interpretations and to propose new directions for future research.

R. van den Broek
W. J. Hanegraaff

CHAPTER 1

GNOSTICISM AND HERMETISM IN ANTIQUITY
Two Roads to Salvation

ROELOF VAN DEN BROEK

It is impossible to give a short and clear definition of Gnosticism and Hermetism in antiquity. In both movements there is a strong interest in knowledge, *gnosis*, of the divine world and in the final bliss of the soul. The Greek word *gnosis* means "knowledge," indeed, but the knowledge proclaimed by the Gnostics and Hermetists was not obtained by the accepted rules of methodical reasoning but by divine revelation. Their knowledge was a saving knowledge, which means that it was basically of a religious nature. Those who had gnosis knew the way to God, from our visible material world to the spiritual realm of divine being; its final goal was to know or to "see" God, which sometimes went as far as becoming united with God or being in God.

However, these characteristics are not specific enough. For this kind of knowledge is also found, for instance, in the Gospel of John and the works of non-Gnostic Christian authors such as Clement of Alexandria and Origen. It is also insufficient to say that the gnosis of Gnostics and Hermetists was a deep personal conviction of the fundamental identity between God and man, that is to say, man's soul or mind. It is true that this idea was cherished by Gnostics and Hermetists alike, but it was also characteristic of all Platonists, from Plato himself to the late Neoplatonists of the fifth century A.D. Actually, both in Gnosticism and Hermetism there is a strong philosophical influence, though in the latter this lies much more on the surface than in the former. A short discussion of the relationship between philosophy, on the one hand, and Gnosticism and Hermetism, on the other, will give a better understanding of the characteristic features of these movements.[1]

1

GNOSTICISM

In the middle of the third century A.D. there was in Rome a group of Christian Gnostics who had close connections with the school of the great Neoplatonic philosopher Plotinus.[2] They were interested in philosophical questions and attended the lectures of Plotinus, but their Gnostic inclinations led them to views that completely differed from those of the master. Some of them even belonged to the inner circle of the Roman Neoplatonists, for Plotinus himself says that some of his own friends "happened upon this way of thinking before they became our friends, and, though I do not know how they manage it, continue in it."[3] As Porphyry in his *Life of Plotinus* tells us, they were of the opinion that "Plato had not penetrated to the depths of intelligible reality," and in support of their views they appealed to "Revelations by Zoroaster, Zostrianus, Nicotheus, Allogenes, Messos, and other people of the kind."[4] About 265 Plotinus took the offensive against these Gnostics: he not only wrote a full treatise against them himself[5] but also induced his most faithful pupils, Amesius and Porphyry, to do the same.[6]

What is most interesting is that at least two of the Gnostic books mentioned by Porphyry have been preserved in the codices of the Nag Hammadi Library, found in 1945, viz., *Zostrianus* (Codex VIII, 1) and *Allogenes* (Codex XI, 3). Porphyry informs us that Amesius wrote forty treatises against *Zostrianus*. Unfortunately, not a single one of them has been preserved.

It would take us too far to discuss here the complicated problem of the relationship between these texts and Plotinus's refutation of the Gnostics. There is no doubt, however, that Plotinus read *Zostrianus* or a work that contained the same ideas, such as the so-called *Untitled Gnostic Treatise* of the Codex Brucianus.[7] I mention only one instance of the many identical ideas that can be noted. In his *Against the Gnostics*, Plotinus attacks the Gnostics' complete rejection of the visible creation and the earth on which we live and their idea that there is another, new earth to which the Gnostic will ascend. In that connection he says that they introduce strange hypostases such as "Exiles" *(paroikèseis)*, "Antitypes" *(antitypoi)*, and "Repentances" *(metanoiai)*.[8] These views are also expressed in *Zostrianus* and in the *Untitled Treatise* of the Bruce Codex. In

Zostrianus, the visionary of that name ascends to heaven on a great light-cloud, first to what is called the airy earth, then, successively, to the "Antitypes" of the Aeons, to "Exile," and to "Repentance."[9] This passage of *Against the Gnostics* shows us in a nutshell Plotinus's main objections against the Gnostics: they introduce a great number of levels of being, whereas he accepts only three (the One, the Mind [*Nous*], and the Soul), and they affirm that the world and its creator are bad, whereas he holds that the world is good and beautiful, originating from the divine World-Soul.

Plotinus makes it completely clear that Gnosticism is something quite different from philosophy. His Gnostics were interested in philosophy, but they proved themselves to be charlatans since their claims were not based on solid philosophical reasoning. He wrote indignantly, in *Enneads* 2.9.6:

> If they wish to disagree on these points, there is no unfair hostility in saying to them that they should not recommend their own opinions to their audience by ridiculing and insulting the Greeks but that they should show the correctness on their own merits of all the points of doctrine which are peculiar to them and differ from the views of the Greeks, stating their real opinions courteously, as befits philosophers, and fairly on the points where they are opposed, looking to the truth and not hunting fame by censuring men who have been judged good from ancient times by men of worth and saying that they themselves are better than the Greeks.[10]

With respect to the numerous hypostases introduced by the Gnostics on the basis of their revelations, Plotinus observed with some bitterness in the same section:

> And by giving names to a multitude of intelligible realities they think they will appear to have discovered the exact truth, though by this very multiplicity they bring the intelligible nature into the likeness of the sense-world, the inferior world.[11]

According to Plotinus, the Gnostics were not philosophers at all; and he was right. Gnosticism is not even a depraved form of philosophy. It is something quite different, though the Gnostic writers often made use of philosophical ideas.

A notorious, but unsatisfactory, attempt to formulate a generally accepted definition of Gnosticism was made at the 1966 Messina Conference on the Origins of Gnosticism.[12] Its starting point was the distinction between Gnosis and Gnosticism. Gnosis was defined as "knowledge of the divine mysteries, reserved for an elite," which implies that all kinds of esoteric doctrines and mystic experiences can be labeled Gnostic. This makes the term Gnosis so vague that it loses all concrete substance. The Messina colloquium reserved the term Gnosticism for the Christian-Gnostic systems of the second and third centuries. We should not forget, however, that this term Gnosticism, with a pejorative connotation, was coined in France as late as the eighteenth century. In antiquity, both Gnostics and their opponents only used the term gnosis. The writer of 1 Timothy (6:20) warns against "the falsely so-called gnosis," a term adopted by the antiheretical church fathers to describe what we call Gnosticism. It was in agreement with this usage that Clement of Alexandria could exalt his super Christian as the "true Gnostic," in opposition to the "false Gnostic," the adherent of forms of gnosis not accepted by the early Catholic Church.

With regard to the precise character of Gnosis and Gnosticism, A. D. Nock noted in 1936, in his review of the first volume of Hans Jonas's now classic *Gnosis und spätantiker Geist:* "I am left in a terminological fog."[13] Sixty years later, and with much more original Gnostic treatises at our disposal, we are still groping in the same fog. Since the discovery of the Gnostic writings of the Nag Hammadi Library we now see even more clearly that the borderline between Gnostic and non-Gnostic texts and ideas is less easy to draw than was thought in the thirties. In the following I shall use the term Gnosticism to indicate the ideas or coherent systems that are characterized by an absolutely negative view of the visible world and its creator and the assumption of a divine spark in man, his inner self, which had become enclosed within the material body as the result of a tragic event in the precosmic world, from which it only can escape to its divine origin by means of the saving gnosis. These ideas are found in most of the original Gnostic writings that have survived, for the greater part in the Nag Hammadi Library and in the systems described by the antiheretical church fathers such as Irenaeus, Hippolytus, and Epiphanius.

HERMETISM

In a number of specific Hermetic writings the influence of Greek philosophical ideas is very conspicuous, much more than in the Gnostic treatises. However, there is here also a serious problem of definition: What do we exactly mean when we speak of Hermetism? Formally speaking it is easy enough, for everything ascribed to Hermes Trismegistus, the ancient Egyptian sage, or to his first pupils (his son Tat or his associate Ammon in particular) can be said to be Hermetic. Thus there are philosophical, magical, astrological, and later also alchemical writings ascribed to Hermes, but these writings have so much in common with others that do not bear his name that the term Hermetic becomes almost meaningless. When I speak about Hermetism here I primarily have in mind the teachings and doctrines found in the so-called philosophical Hermetica. To these writings belong the seventeen treatises of the *Corpus Hermeticum* (henceforth abbreviated as CH), the Latin *Asclepius*,[14] the Armenian *Hermetic Definitions*,[15] and the Coptic Hermetica found at Nag Hammadi, of which the new treatise entitled *The Eighth and the Ninth Sphere* (Codex VI.6) is the most important.[16]

These writings show a strong philosophical influence, in particular of Stoicism and later Platonism. In their teachings about God, the cosmos, and man the Hermetists made use of all kinds of views developed by Greek philosophy and science. It is even possible to write a commentary on these Hermetic tractates almost exclusively based on the Greek philosophical traditions found in them.[17] But then one is missing the point, for the central concern of these writings is not philosophical but religious. Their authors were convinced that, in the end, it is not philosophical reasoning but divine revelation that leads to the truth. The philosophical Hermetica teach a way by which the soul can ascend to the divine realm above the sphere of the fixed stars from which it has originally come down. There it mingles with the divine powers, comes to "see," that is, to know God, which means to become absorbed in God. As the *Poimandres* puts it: "This is the final good for those who have received knowledge [*gnosis*]: to be made god" (CH I.26). This deification will be fully attained after death when the soul ascends to God, but it can also be an inner experience during this earthly life, at the end of a process of Hermetic instruction culminating in mystical initiation. The ascent to the divine realm after death is described in the *Poimandres* (CH I.24–26), the inner experience in CH XIII, called *On being born again and on the promise to be silent*, and in the *Eighth and the Ninth Sphere*.

As indicated above, the Gnostic and in particular the Hermetic texts of antiquity cannot be fully explained without reference to Greek philosophical traditions, but their main argument is distinctly religious. They both claim to have received their knowledge of the divine world and the fate of the soul from divine revelations. As we saw, the Gnostics of Rome appealed to revelations ascribed to visionaries such as Zostrianus, Allogenes, and the like. One of the basic texts of second-century Gnosticism, the *Apocryphon of John*, is put into the mouth of Christ himself, albeit only secondarily. The Hermetic *Poimandres* (CH I) claims to be a revelation by the Supreme Divine Mind to a unnamed pupil who already in antiquity was identified with Hermes Trismegistus.[18] In CH XIII and in the *Eighth and the Ninth Sphere* Hermes is the mystagogue who reveals the divine mysteries. This attribution of essential teachings to divine revelation characterizes Gnosticism and Hermetism as basically religious movements. With respect to the soul's final state of bliss as well there is not much difference between Gnosticism and Hermetism. The salvation of the soul consists in its deliverance from the bonds of the body and its return to its divine origin. The indispensable prerequisite for this return, and at the same time its instant realization, is a spiritual understanding *(gnosis)* of the nature of man, of the cosmos, and of the divine world. It seems that the Hermetists put much emphasis on a systematic instruction in "the way of Hermes," leading up to a final initiation into the Hermetic mysteries that they described as a mystic experience. In Gnosticism there is less interest in the intellectual aspects of the way to gnosis, all emphasis being laid on the gift of gnosis as the direct experience of salvation and enlightenment. But both in Hermetism and Gnosticism the basic idea is the fundamental identity between the soul and the divine and in both movements the final goal is the return of the soul to its origin, its reunion with God.

However, these similarities cannot conceal the great differences that separate Gnostics and Hermetists with respect to three fundamental issues—namely, the doctrines of God (theology), of the visible world (cosmology), and of man (anthropology).

GOD

At first sight the Gnostic and Hermetic doctrines of God have much in common, since both start from a theological concept that was widespread in the classical world. It is the idea that God is so transcendent that he can only be described in the terms of what we call "negative theology": he is ineffable, invisible, incomprehensible, unbegotten, without beginning and without end, incorruptible, immeasurable, invariable, unnameable, etc.[19] This view is found among pagan philosophers, Christians theologians, Gnostics and Hermetists. There is a difference, however, for the philosophers and some early Christian theologians as well said that, though it may be true that God is unknowable in his essence, he nevertheless can be comprehended by the human mind *(nous)*, through philosophical reasoning and through contemplation of the cosmic order. This emphasis on the human nous as a useful, though imperfect, instrument for the knowledge of God is also found in the Hermetic texts, but never in those of the Gnostics: in their view, the supreme God was inaccessible to the human mind. However, like the Platonic philosophers of their time, the Gnostics felt no difficulty in combining this negative theology with positive qualifications of the ineffable God.[20] A few lines of the *Apocryphon of John* may suffice to give an impression of this kind of theology:

> He is neither perfection, nor blessedness, nor divinity,
> but he is something far superior to that.
> He also neither infinite nor limited,
> but he is something superior to that.
> He is neither corporeal nor incorporeal,
> he is neither large nor small,
> he has neither quantity nor quality,
> nor is anybody able to know him.
> He is in no way anything that exists
> but he is superior to that,
> not simply superior but wholly being on his own.
> He does not share in eternity, time does not belong to him.
> . . . .
> The immeasurable Greatness,
> the Eternal One, the giver of eternity,
> the Light, the giver of light,
> Life, the giver of life,

the Blessed One, the giver of blessedness,
Knowledge, the giver of knowledge,
the One who is always Good, the giver of goodness . . .
Mercy which gives mercy,
Grace which gives grace,
the immeasurable Light.[21]

It is interesting to see how in this passage the philosophical terminology of negative theology passes into a hymn on the Supreme God as the abundant source of all good.

The Gnostics spoke the language of the philosophers only as long as they tried to describe God's absolute transcendence, but they switched over to the language of mythology as soon as they came to speak about the divine world, which they described as the self-realization of God. According to the *Apocryphon of John*, the Unknown Father saw himself mirrored in the light-water that surrounded him, he recognized himself, and immediately his thought became an independent female entity, Ennoia (Thought). Together they proceeded to bring to actuality a number of other male and female divine aspects, which again formed pairs and brought forth a whole world of divine powers and attributes. This divine world is in fact an extension and actualization of the nature of God; it is called the Pleroma, the "Fullness" of God, and its powers are called *aeons*. These aeons constitute at the same time the various levels of being in the supreme world; the last and the least of them is Sophia, Wisdom, who disturbs the serenity of the Pleroma and becomes the cause of a cosmic tragedy. All Gnostics seem to have indulged in aeonic speculations of this kind, which led to considerable differences between the various Gnostic systems with respect to the number and names of the aeons.

Nothing of all this is to be found in the Hermetic texts. It is true that the *Poimandres*, a key Hermetic text, also has a mythological story, but its doctrine of the divine world has nothing to offer that could be compared with the Gnostic speculations about the Pleroma. I will come back to these mythological aspects of Gnosticism and Hermetism in due course. The Hermetic doctrine of God kept close to that of the Greek philosophers, but it was not a philosophical but a religious doctrine and, therefore, the Hermetic God is often more personal and less abstract than the First Principle of philosophy. That will become clear if we turn now to the difference between Gnostics and Hermetists with respect to cosmology.

THE WORLD

For the Gnostics, the cosmos is the bad product of an evil creator. Our world is the result of a tragic split within the divine world or even within the godhead itself, since the Pleroma is only the extension of the nature of God. According to several Gnostic systems, the first step in this downward development was the wish of Sophia to become equal to God by producing something on her own. However, since every thought in the divine world, even a sinful one, becomes an independent entity, she brought forth a ghastly monster that eventually became the creator, the demiurge, who made the bad world of matter after the image of the spiritual realm. As a result of Sophia's insolence, the soul, which is of divine origin, became incarcerated in the body. The Gnostic view of the world is anticosmic; the material world was only devised to be the prison of the soul. Since Plato it was usual to see the celestial bodies as divine living beings, visible gods. But the Gnostics considered the planets and the signs of the zodiac as evil powers, which the soul on its way back to its origin could pass only if it had true gnosis.

If we now turn to Hermetism, the picture becomes quite different. It is true, the views exposed in the Hermetic texts are sometimes at variance with each other, just as in the Gnostic writings. Some treatises contain doctrines that come close to the negative worldview of the Gnostics. Then the difference between the good of the divine world and the evil we encounter during our earthly life is pressed to the utmost. A striking example of this negative view is found in the sixth treatise of the *Corpus Hermeticum,* entitled *That the good is in God alone and nowhere else:*

> With reference to humanity, one uses the term "good" in comparison to "evil." Here below, the evil that is not excessive is the good, and the good is the least amount of evil here below. . . . The good is in God alone, then, or God himself is the good. Therefore, Asclepius, only the name of the good exists among mankind—never the fact. (CH VI.3).[22]

The cosmos is good "in that it makes all things" (CH VI.2), but it is also called "a plenitude *(plèroma)* of vice, as God is a plenitude *(plèroma)* of the good or the good of God."[23]

As matter of fact, it would be strange if there had not been intermediate forms between radical Gnostic and authentic Hermetic ideas. Another of these forms we find in the *Poimandres* (CH I). I will return to that. But here it must be emphasized that nowhere in the Hermetic texts do we find the idea that the cosmos is bad, or that it had been created by an evil demiurge. On the contrary, the cosmos is God's beautiful creation, his first son and his first image (man is his second). God is invisible, but we can know him through his creation. This is, for instance, the theme of CH V, entitled *That God is invisible and entirely visible.* God has ordered the cosmos, and that order *(kosmos)* is beautiful (CH V.5). The human body is not the soul's prison devised by the bad demiurge and his evil powers but it is "a beautiful and divine image" (CH V.6), representing the utmost of God's creative power. God is continuously creating all things,

> in heaven, in the air, on earth, in the deep, in every part of the cosmos, in every part of the universe, in what exists and in what does not exist. For there is nothing in that whole universe which he himself is not. He is himself both the things that are and those that are not. Those that are he has made visible; those that are not he encloses within himself. This is the God who is too great to have a name; this is the invisible one and the entirely visible one. He who is contemplated by the mind can also be seen by the eyes. He is bodiless and many-bodied, or rather all-bodied. There is nothing that he is not, for whatever exists that is he too. (V.9–10)[24]

That contemplation of the cosmos gives us an impression of the creative power of God, and so of God himself, was a well-known Stoic doctrine. Their opinion could not be better formulated than it was done by Saint Paul in his Epistle to the Romans, where it is said of God (1:17): "His invisible attributes, that is to say his everlasting power and deity, have been visible, ever since the world began, to the eye of reason, in the things he made." But in Hermetism this originally philosophical doctrine became the core of a cosmic religiosity, which could lead to the mystical experience of falling together with the universe, that is to say with God himself. In CH XIII.11, the initiated pupil exclaims with a certain astonishment:

> I am in heaven, in earth, in water, in air; I am in animals, in plants, in the womb, before the womb, after the womb, everywhere![25]

It is absolutely inconceivable that a Gnostic would have had this experience. For him the world was not transparent toward God and essentially divine; he could only see it as the work of God's great opponent, the power of darkness.

MAN

This view of the material cosmos also determined the Gnostic's understanding of man. The split in the divinity that initiated the birth of the demiurge and the making of the world finally also led to the creation of man. Man is a stranger in a hostile world. His soul or mind or divine spark—in any case, his inner self—originally belonged to the divine world but it got trapped in this material world, incarcerated in the body and enslaved to the passions. As a result, it completely forgot its divine origin. It can only be saved from its prison if it receives gnosis. Against this background the famous definition of gnosis by Theodotus, a second-century Christian Gnostic, becomes perfectly clear: Gnosis is the knowledge of

> who we were and what we have become, where we were and into what we have been thrown, wither we hasten and from what we are redeemed, what is birth and what rebirth.[26]

The Hermetist's positive view of the world did not imply that he was optimistic about the fate of the soul in its earthly existence. He too knew of the passions of the body and the allurement of the senses, which continuously threatened to pull down the soul to a state of deadness, forgetfulness, sleep, or drunkenness, and obscured its awareness of its divine origin. The message of the Hermetist to people who were in this state was to wake up and to raise up their minds to the world of incorruptibility. Listen for instance to what Hermes says in the *Poimandres:*

People, earthborn men, you who have surrendered yourselves to drunkenness and sleep and ignorance of God, make yourselves sober and end
your drunken sickness, for you are bewitched in unreasoning sleep.
Why have you surrendered yourselves to death, earthborn men,
since you have the right to share in immortality? You who have journeyed with error, who have partnered with ignorance, think again:
escape the shadowy light, leave corruption behind and take a share in
immortality. (CH I.27–.28)[27]

This view could lead to a depreciation of the body that came close to
that of the Gnostics, for instance in CH VII, where the body is called
"the garment of ignorance, the foundation of vice, the bonds of corruption, the dark cage, the living death, the sentient corpse, the portable
tomb," etc.[28] But we should realize that this view of the dangers of the
soul during its earthly existence in the body was far from being solely
Gnostic or Hermetic. It was also shared by all Platonists since Plato (and
before him by the Orphics), by Stoics like Seneca, and by all non-Gnostic Fathers of the Church. I only call to mind the observation with which
Porphyry opened his *Life of Plotinus*: "Plotinus, the philosopher of our
times, seemed ashamed of being in the body."[29] But a Gnostic could
never have said of man that he is a *magnum miraculum*, a most astonishing being, as he is called in the *Asclepius* (chap. 6), that compendium of
Hermetic lore.[30]

The Hermetic way implied instruction in the nature of the cosmos
and of man. In that process of instruction use was made of all kinds of
human knowledge, theories of space and movement, the science of astronomy and astrology, medicine, and also, sometimes, magical practices. But the purpose of all this was to make the world transparent toward God. The Hermetic way finally led to initiation in the divine mystery, to knowledge of God, to God himself as the source of being. With
respect to the ultimate goal of their quest for knowledge, Gnostics and
Hermetists had much in common, but as to the way to get there, they
differed profoundly.

MYTHOLOGY

There is another difference between Gnosticism and Hermeticism: their
use of mythology. The Gnostic writings abound with myths, mostly of

an artificial character, carefully constructed to be the vehicles of Gnostic ideas. As said above, the heavenly world, the Pleroma, is densely populated with divine powers and attributes, bearing their own often abstract or Semitic-sounding names and constantly mingling with each other in order to produce new ones. The same holds for the lower world of the demiurge and the powers of evil, his satellites, who are identified with the twelve signs of the zodiac and the seven planets (which include sun and moon). To get an impression of Gnostic mythology one has only to read the first part of the *Apocryphon of John*, which in an impressive myth describes the development of the divine world, the Fall, the Creation, and the beginning of redemption by a divine power called "luminous Epinoia." In works like *Zostrianus* or *Allogenes* we meet some of the basic entities of the *Apocryphon*, but on their journey to the highest heaven these visionaries also meet a great number of previously unknown aeons.

There is in fact only one Hermetic text that contains a revelation in the form of a myth describing the acting characters and events that led to the creation of world and the birth of man. That text is the *Poimandres*. True, there are also a few other texts that contain elements that could be called mythological, but only the myth of the *Poimandres* can be compared with the great Gnostic mythological narratives. The myth of the *Poimandres* is not completely coherent. An analysis of its contents shows that the author has made use of sometimes conflicting or even mutually exclusive traditions and that he was unable to combine the elements he used in such a way as to avoid inner contradictions. Thus, it is said in chapter 8 that the *Boule* of God, his active will, having received the Logos into her womb and contemplating the beautiful spiritual cosmos, made a material copy of that cosmos. This would imply that the *Boule* of God, being pregnant by the divine sperm, the Logos, gave birth to the world. A closely related view is found in the Alexandrian Jewish writer Philo, who goes as far as saying that God in a nonhuman way had intercourse with his knowledge *(epistèmè)*, which from his semen brought forth "his only perceptible son, this cosmos" (*De ebrietate* 30). But in the *Poimandres* this idea is not worked out further, apparently because the author felt it was in fact incompatible with the main line of the creation story.

The difference in appreciation of the planets can be mentioned as another example of this lack of inner coherence in the *Poimandres*: chapter

9 relates that the highest androgynous god, the Mind, who is life and light, brought forth a second Mind, the demiurge, who as a god of fire and spirit made seven Rulers, i.e., the sun, the moon, and the planets, who encircle the visible world. There is not a single indication that the demiurge or the celestial bodies made by him are bad. But in chapter 25 it is assumed that these seven rulers exercise an unfavorable influence on man: during its ascent to the eighth and the ninth spheres the soul leaves at each planet the bad characteristics it had received from that planet. The idea that the soul on its descent to earth receives all kinds of personal qualities from the celestial bodies is well known from Gnostic, Middle Platonic, and Neoplatonic sources.[31] But it was typically Gnostic, because of their negative view of the cosmos and its creator, to say that the planets only could give *negative* qualities of character. The author of the *Poimandres* incorporated traditional, Gnostic-colored materials without adopting their presuppositions and implications. His work has a Gnostic flavor, but it remains an authentic Hermetic work.

To illustrate this, I will end this article by comparing the myth of the creation of man in the *Apocryphon of John* with that in the *Poimandres*.[32] According to the Gnostic apocryphon, the demiurge, having just created the cosmos, heard a voice from the Pleroma saying: "Man exists and the Son of Man." And immediately there shone a light over the water of chaos, which formed the lower part of the cosmos, and in the water the satellites of the demiurge saw the image of Man. Then they decided to make a man after the image of the heavenly Man they had seen, and created Adam in a psychic body.[33] But they were unable to raise it; it remained inactive and immovable. Then the Unknown Father intervened by sending five aeons, disguised as servants of the demiurge, who advised the creator: "Blow into his face something of your spirit and his body will arise." By this divine trick, the spirit of the demiurge, which is the power of Sophia, came into man and thus man became a living being. That is the reason why man has a divine soul. Moreover, the father sent to the soul a helper, called "luminous Epinoia," who informed man about his descent from heaven and the way to ascend to his place of origin. Adam's knowledge proved to be greater than that of his creators and out of jealousy they made from the elements a material body in which Adam's psychic body was locked up, and so he became a mortal human being.[34]

If we compare this story with that of the creation of man in the *Poimandres*, we see that the author of the Hermetic text has made use of a tradition that was closely related to that of the *Apocryphon of John*, but that the final result is something quite different. Both texts know the important notion of a heavenly Man—a notion that has to be explained through its Jewish background. This is not the place to discuss that in sufficient detail. I only call to mind that the prophet Ezekiel (1:26) saw the Glory of God in the shape of a man: the first manifestation of the transcendent God appears in human form. This and a specific interpretation of the creation of man in Genesis eventually led to the myth of the heavenly Man.[35] In the *Poimandres* God is the Supreme Mind *(Nous)* and is androgynous, being life and light. From himself he engendered a second, demiurgic Nous who made the seven Rulers, the planets, and put them into an eternal rotation. The revolution of these celestial gods brought forth fish from the water and birds from the air, it separated water and earth, and the earth produced all kinds of living animals (CH I.9–11). There is not the slightest indication in this story that this creation is bad; it is only said that the animals are without reason since the divine reason had been united with the demiurgic Mind. In Gnosticism the creation is bad, in Hermetism it is not. Then, the *Poimandres* continues, the Supreme Nous, who is life and light, engendered a heavenly Man, who was equal to him and very beautiful, because he was made in his Father's image. The Father handed over to this son everything he had made: Man became the lord of the cosmos. Having complete authority over the world, Man broke through the vault of heaven, bent down through the framework of the spheres, and showed the beautiful form of God to downward-tending nature. Nature saw his beautiful form mirrored in the water and his shadow on the ground and she smiled with burning desire. Heavenly Man, for his part, saw his own reflection in the water, fell in love with it, and wanted to reside there. And so Man came into the irrational form, and nature received him, and they had intercourse, for they were lovers. For that reason man on earth has a twofold nature, mortal because of his body, immortal because of the true heavenly Man (CH I.12–15). The sexual union of nature and Man wrought, as the *Poimandres* says (CH I.16), "a most amazing miracle," a *thauma thaumasiotaton* (which seems the Greek background of the famous *magnum miraculum est homo* of *Asclepius* 6). The amazing thing was the birth of seven human beings, whose nature corresponded to that of the seven Rulers, and who were androgynous and went upright. The life and the light of the heavenly Man became the soul and the mind of earthly man. These men remained immortal and androgynous for seven generations, but then these androgynous beings were parted in two and became males and females, in accordance with God's will. And God said (CH I.18):

> Increase in increasing and multiply in multitude, all you creatures and craftworks, and let him who is mindful know that he is immortal, that desire is the cause of death and let him know everything.[36]

The last words reflect a Hermetic saying that is inter alia preserved in the *Hermetic Definitions* (9.4): "He who knows himself, knows everything." In the context of the *Poimandres* the implication is: you really know yourself if you know that you are of divine origin and that sexual desire is the cause of death.

The foregoing has made clear that the *Poimandres*, just like the *Apocryphon of John*, knows of a divine being called Man. In the *Apocryphon* the demiurge and his daemons created a human being after they had seen a reflection of heavenly Man's shape in the waters of chaos. In the *Poimandres* divine Man himself falls because of a narcissistic love for his own beautiful shape, which he sees reflected in the waters below. The human body is not devised by an evil demiurge to incarcerate the soul but it is simply the material and mortal part of man. And man's mortality is due to his sexuality: as long as he remained an androgynous being he was immortal; the separation of mankind into males and females introduced death. If there is a sin in the *Poimandres*, it is sexual desire (CH I.19):

> [B]ut the one who loved the body that came from the error of desire goes on in darkness, errant, suffering sensibly the effects of death.[37]

It is the old and very widespread idea that the senses, and sexual desire in particular, draw the soul deep into the world of matter and make him forget his divine origin—an idea that was found among pagan Platonists, Christian theologians, Gnostics, and Hermetists alike. But in sharp contrast to the Gnostics, the author of the *Poimandres*, as all Hermetists, was convinced that matter, the cosmos, and the human body were not bad in themselves. According to him, the origin of evil—original sin, we might say—was sexual desire. That makes him an ascetic Hermetist, not a Gnostic.

Our brief survey of the similarities and differences between Gnosticism and Hermetism leads to the conclusion that radical Gnostics and Hermetists had more that separated them than they had in common. The similarities are due to the fact that both movements originated and developed in the same time, in the same oriental part of the Mediterranean world, Egypt and Alexandria in particular, and in the same spiritual climate. They both answered to a deeply felt spiritual need: the restoration of the original integrity of man, the return to the source he came from, through a personal experience of the ground of being, the transcendent God. But with regard to such fundamental issues as the nature of God, the cosmos, and man, they were separated by a deep cleft. Both offered a road to salvation, but this led to two different religious systems.

NOTES

1. There exists an extensive literature on both Gnosticism and Hermetism in antiquity. I only mention here some basic studies and text editions. *Gnosticism*: H. Jonas, *The Gnostic Religion*, 3d ed. (Boston, 1970); K. Rudolph, *Gnosis: The Nature and History of Gnosticism* (San Francisco, 1977) (German: *Die Gnosis. Wesen und Geschichte einer spätantiken Religion*, 2d ed. [Göttingen, 1980]). The Coptic texts found near Nag Hammadi in Egypt (1945) are being published in two great international projects: *The Coptic Gnostic Library*, in the series Nag Hammadi (and Manichaean) Studies (Leiden: Brill) and the *Bibliothèque Copte de Nag Hammadi*, Section "Textes" (Québec: Université Laval). English translations of the Coptic texts from Nag Hammadi in J. M. Robinson, ed., *The Nag Hammadi Library in English*, 3d ed. (Leiden and New York, 1988); some of these and other texts in B. Layton, *The Gnostic Scriptures: A New Translation with Annotations and Introductions* (Garden City, N.Y., 1987). *Hermetism*: A.-J. Festugière, *La révélation d'Hermès Trismégiste*, 4 vols. (Paris, 1942–53); G. Fowden, *The Egyptian Hermes. A Historical Approach to the Late Pagan Mind* (Cambridge, 1986); J.-P. Mahé, "La voie d'immortalité à la lumière des *Hermetica* de Nag Hammadi et de découvertes plus récentes," *Vigiliae Christianae* 45 (1991): 313–26, and Mahé's fundamental studies and editions mentioned in notes 15 and 16 below. The Greek texts were edited, with a French translation and commentary, by A. D. Nock and A. J. Festugière, *Corpus Hermeticum*, 4 vols. (Paris, 1945–52; English translation by B. P.

18 ❧ *Roelof van den Broek*

Copenhaver under the title *Hermetica. The Greek Corpus Hermeticum and the Latin Asclepius in a New English Translation, with Notes and Introduction* (Cambridge, 1992).
    2. See C. Elsas, *Neuplatonische und gnostische Weltablehnung in der Schule Plotins* (Berlin, 1975); for a still fundamental discussion of Plotinus and the Gnostics, see H.-Ch. Puech, "Plotin et les gnostiques," in: *Les sources de Plotin*, ed. E. R. Dodds et al., Entretiens Hardt 5 (Vandoeuvres and Geneva, 1960), 161–90 (revised version in H.-Ch. Puech, *En quête de la Gnose* [Paris, 1978], 83–109).
    3. *Enneads* 2.9.10. The *Enneads* and Porphyry's *Life of Plotinus* are quoted here after the Loeb edition by A. H. Armstrong, *Plotinus, with an English translation*, 2 vols. (London and Cambridge, Mass., 1966).
    4. Porphyry, *Life of Plotinus*, 16.
    5. *Enneads* 2.9: *Against the Gnostics.*
    6. Porphyry, *Life of Plotinus*, 16.
    7. The classic edition, with German translation, of the Bruce Codex, which contains the *Books of Jeû* and the *Untitled Gnostic Treatise*, is that by C. Schmidt, *Gnostische Schriften in koptischer Sprache aus dem Codex Brucianus* (Leipzig, 1892). Schmidt's translation was edited separately in his *Koptisch-Gnostische Schriften*, vol. 1 (Leipzig, 1905), fourth edition by H.-M. Schenke (Berlin, 1991), 254–367. Schmidt's edition was reprinted, together with an English translation, by Violet MacDermot, *The Books of Jeu and the Untitled Text in the Bruce Codex*, Nag Hammadi Studies 13 (Leiden, 1978), 225–77. The first English edition of the *Untitled Gnostic Treatise*, with translation and commentary, was that by Charlotte A. Baynes, *A Coptic Gnostic Treatise contained in the Codex Brucianus* (Cambridge, 1933). All desirable information on the Bruce Codex can be found in M. Tardieu and J.-D. Dubois, *Introduction à la littérature gnostique*, vol. 1, *Collections retrouvées avant 1945* (Paris, 1986), 83–97 (by M. Tardieu).
    8. *Enneads* 2.9.6.
    9. *Zostrianus* 4.20–5.29, 8.10–8.20 (translated in Robinson, *Nag Hammadi Library in English*, 404–6); slightly different in the *Untitled Treatise*, 136ᵛ (ed. Baynes, 180, with commentary; ed. Schmidt-MacDermot, 263).
    10. *Plotinus*, ed. Armstrong, 2:246–47, lines 43–53.
    11. Ibid., 244–45, lines 28–31.
    12. U. Bianchi, ed., *The Origins of Gnosticism: Colloquium of Messina 13–18 April 1966*, 2d ed. (Leiden, 1970), xx–xxxii, xxvi–xxvii in particular.
    13. A. D. Nock, in *Gnomon* 12 (1936): 605.
    14. For the standard edition of these texts by Nock and Festugière and Copenhaver's English translation, see note 1 above.
    15. Edition of the Armenian text, with French translation by J.-P. Mahé, *Hermes en Haute Egypte*, vol. 2, *Le fragment du Discours Parfait en les Définitions hermétiques arméniennes*, Bibliothèque copte de Nag Hammadi, Section "Textes," 7 (Québec, 1982), 273–481. Some Greek fragments in J. Paramelle and J.-P. Mahé, "Nouveaux parallèles grecs aux Définitions hermétiques arméniennes," *Revue des Etudes Arméniennes* 22 (1990–91).
    16. Edited by J.-P. Mahé, *Hermès en Haute-Égypte: Les textes hermétiques de Nag*

Hammadi et leurs parallèles grecs et latins, vol. 1, Bibliothèque copte de Nag Hammadi, Section "Textes," 3 (Québec, 1978), and by P. A. Dirkse, J. Brashler, and D. M. Parrott, in *Nag Hammadi Codices V, 2-5 and VI with Papyrus Berolinensis 8502, 1 and 4,* ed. D. M. Parrott, Nag Hammadi Studies 11 (Leiden, 1979), 341–73. See also Mahé's "Reading of the Discourse on the Ogdoad and the Ennead (Nag Hammadi Codex VI.6)" elsewhere in this volume.

17. As was done in the Nock and Festugière edition and in Festugière's *Révélation*.

18. First identification in CH XIII.15; see Nock and Festugière, *Corpus Hermeticum*, 2:215–16 n. 65.

19. See R. van den Broek, T. Baarda, and J. Mansfeld, eds., *Knowledge of God in the Graeco-Roman World* (Leiden, 1988).

20. For an explanation of this phenomenon, see J. Mansfeld, "Compatible Alternatives: Middle Platonist Theology and the Xenophanes Reception," in ibid., 92–117.

21. Translation of the short version as found in the Berlin papyrus 8502, p. 24, 9–25, 3, and 13–22, edited by W. C. Till, in *Die gnostischen Schriften des koptischen Papyrus Berolinensis 8502*, ed. H.-M. Schenke, 2d. rev. ed. (Berlin, 1972), 88–91.

22. CH, ed. Nock and Festugière, 1:73–74; translation Copenhaver, *Hermetica*, 22.

23. CH, ed. Nock and Festugière, 1:74 and 1:76–77 n. 17 (on *plèroma*); translation Copenhaver, *Hermetica*, 22 and 144 (note on "plenitude of vice").

24. CH, ed. Nock and Festugière, 1:63–64; cf. Copenhaver's translation, *Hermetica*, 20, which I have only partly followed here.

25. CH, ed. Nock and Festugière, 2:205; Copenhaver, *Hermetica*, 51.

26. Clement of Alexandria, *Excerpts from Theodotus*, 78.2 in *Clément d'Alexandrie: Extraits de Théodote*, ed. F. Sagnard, Sources Chrétiennes 23 (1948; reprint, Paris, 1970), 202–3.

27. CH, ed. Nock and Festugière, 1:16–17; Copenhaver, *Hermetica*, 6.

28. CH, ed. Nock and Festugière, 1:81; Copenhaver, *Hermetica*, 24.

29. *Plotinus*, ed. Armstrong, 1:3.

30. CH, ed. Nock and Festugière, 2:301: "magnum miraculum est homo, animal adorandum atque honorandum."

31. See E. R. Dodds, *Proclus: The Elements of Theology*, 2d. ed., (1963; reprint, Oxford 1964), 313–321, appendix 2: "The Astral Body in Neoplatonism"; A. Kehl, "Gewand (der Seele)," *Reallexikon für Antike und Christentum*, vol. 10 (Stuttgart, 1978), 955–62; R. van den Broek, "The Authentikos Logos: A New Document of Christian Platonism," *Vigiliae Christianae* 33 (1979): 260–66.

32. A recent discussion of the origins and early history of the Gnostic and Hermetic Myth of Man is to be found in J. Holzhausen, *Der "Mythos vom Menschen" im hellenistischen Ägypten*, Theophaneia 33 (Bodenheim, 1994).

33. There are two creations of Adam: in a spiritual and in a corporeal body. On Adam's spiritual body, see R. van den Broek, "The Creation of Adam's Psychic Body in the Apocryphon of John," in *Studies in Gnosticism and Hellenistic Religions,*

Presented to Gilles Quispel on the Occasion of his Sixty-Fifth Birthday, ed. R. van den Broek and M. J. Vermaseren (Leiden, 1981), 38–57.

34. At this point there is not much difference between the long and the short version of the *Apocryphon*. See the translation of the long version in Robinson, *Nag Hammadi Library*, 116.

35. See G. Quispel, "Ezekiel 1, 26 in Jewish Mysticism and Gnosis," *Vigiliae Christianae* 34 (1980): 1–13; also Holzhausen, *'Mythos vom Menschen'*, 104–8.

36. CH, ed. Nock and Festugière, 1:13 and 1:23 (commentary); Copenhaver, *Hermetica*, 4 (who is only partly followed here).

37. CH, ed. Nock and Festugière, 1:13; Copenhaver, *Hermetica*, 4.

CHAPTER 2

GNOSTIC AND HERMETIC ETHICS

JEAN-PIERRE MAHÉ

Every student of ancient Gnosticism is acquainted with Irenaeus's famous charge of immorality against the Valentinians:[1]

> They maintain that good works are necessary to us (psychics of the Church), for that otherwise it is impossible we should be save. But as to themselves they hold that they shall be entirely and undoubtedly saved, not by means of conduct, but because they are pneumatic by nature. For, just as it is impossible that material substance should partake of salvation [. . .], so again it is impossible that pneumatic substance—by which they mean themselves—should ever come under the power of corruption, whatever the sort of actions in which they indulged. (*Adversus Haereses* 1.6.2)

As a result, the so-called perfect among the Valentinians are supposedly addicted to all kinds of forbidden deeds, like eating meat offered in sacrifice, taking part in the heathen festivals, yielding to the lusts of the flesh, etc.

Irenaeus's polemics aim at showing that, unlike the faithful believers of the great church, who seek perfection in performing good works and are mainly concerned with their moral praxis, the Valentinians rely on their spiritual nature and are mainly concerned with gnosis, i.e., esoteric knowledge. For them salvation does not depend on action but on speculation.

It has often been emphasized how cautious one should be about accepting such a conclusion. Irenaeus himself does not go as far as charging all the Valentinians with the different kinds of immorality he mentions. "Some of them" do this, "others" do that, he writes, but even if such cases are frequent, they are not necessarily representative of their whole congregation.

21

Moreover we might ask what kind of knowledge is gnosis. The form of the word, with the suffix -ti- or -si-, suggests some kind of dynamic process. Gnosis, we should assume, is anything but fixed learning, it is rather a research attitude, an active openness to divine intuition. Therefore, it cannot be merely intellectual; it must also be connected to some peculiar way of life and have a moral impact.

This assumption can be substantiated by considering the meaning of gnosis in Hermetic literature. There are three stages on the way to immortality. According to the Coptic *Prayer of Thanksgiving* these are intellect or mind *(noûs)*, discourse or speech *(logos)* and knowledge *(gnosis)*. Noûs is the highest degree and gnosis the lowest or at least the first one. In order to gain divine contemplation through the Noûs, we must *first* have gnosis, i.e., clear consciousness of what we are in search of, and logos, i.e., sound teaching concerning the existing beings. God proclaims this teaching by means of a herald to the hearts of all men; but some of them do not pay heed to the proclamation (CH IV.4)[2] or even mock the herald (CH I.29). They do not understand, because they are unbelievers (NH VI.68.36, 69.31–32). Though they have been endowed with the power of speech like other reasonable beings, they have sensations much like those of unreasoning animals, because they have not received the gift of mind (CH IV.4). Therefore, their words are mere noise. They can be compared with a crowd, which has only basic instincts and no reason (DH 5.3).

In fact, if we really are to understand divine teaching we need deliberate, active, and deeply personal involvement. We must resist the flood of drunkenness and ignorance. We must look up with the eyes of the heart (CH VII.1–2). Truly inspired and efficient as they may be, the words of Hermes are by no means magical spells ensuring automatic salvation. We cannot receive them passively; we rather have to use them as tools for our own research. The esoteric form of certain treatises is meant to stir up our curiosity and to arouse our desire to inquire into the truth (SH XXIII.4).

Precisely this desire has much in common with gnosis. Knowledge is the goal of science and learning (CH X.9); but we cannot even start to learn if we do not know anything at all about learning. Therefore, gnosis is first of all *aisthanesthai*, i.e., becoming aware of knowledge. It is some kind of sudden enlightenment (CH XIII.8) which brings us from ignorant indifference towards God to the firm belief that he exists and wishes to get known (CH I.31). Gnosis is like a sill or a doorstep (CH VII.2), an eagerness for spiritual life, which is one and the same as *eusebeia*, i.e. piety (CH I.27, VI.5, IX.4). For "*gnosis* is not a beginning of the good, but it furnishes us the good that will be known. So let us seize this beginning and travel further with all speed" (CH IV.9).

As a result, gnosis cannot be mere mental knowledge; it is closely connected with a *bios*, i.e., a special way of life. At the end of the Latin *Asclepius*, Hermes and his disciples pray to God with the following words: "We ask you only this, that you wish us to persist in the love of your *gnosis* and that we never be cut off from such a life as this."

What does this life consist in? We might be tempted to reply by quoting CH XIII.1: "You said you would deliver to me (the discourse on being born again) when you were about to become a stranger to the cosmos." *Kosmou apallotriousthai*, becoming a stranger to the cosmos in order to be born again, is the supreme goal of spiritual life, but it cannot be reached at once. The break must be cautious and gradual. We cannot suddenly become what we have never been before. We cannot simply reject social life and social order. We need special training so that we may learn like the Christians in the *Epistle to Diognetus* (5.5) how "to dwell in our own countries simply as foreigners sharing in all things with others, and yet enduring all things as if foreigners."

This can be exemplified by the Hermetic attitude toward traditional cults. Trismegistus often gives utterance to admiration for the cults and the godliness of Egypt "the holy land of our ancestors" (SH XXIV.13), "the abode of the Gods and the school of piety" (NH VI.70.30–32), a "country which is more pious than any country" (ibid.). He respectfully mentions mysterious inscriptions carved on steles and obelisks. He quotes the aretalogies of Isis and Osiris (SH XXIII.65–68) and sometimes paraphrases the hymns to Khnoum (CH V.6–7). He takes up the Egyptian theory of ensouled statues that foreknow the future, make people ill, and cure them (NH VI.69.33–70.2), and leave or rejoin their shrines by themselves in response to human behavior (NH VI.71.12, 73.4, 75.26–29).

This theory allows full justification of traditional cults that allegedly are necessary to the balance of the universe (NH VI.70.6–7, 73.12–22). These include the worship of Isis and Osiris (SH XXIII.64) as well as pharaohs, souls of the great men, and sacred animals (Ascl 37), the latter being a matter of scandal and derision to pagan Greek rationalism.

Therefore we may fairly assume that the disciples of Hermes Trismegistus would spend a great part of their time in or about sanctuaries (as they are depicted in the Latin *Asclepius*). They would also take part in the pagan festivals. Their piety would not consist in rejecting popular religion but rather in making it more complete, profound, and spiritual.

The most important point is to locate the different cults on the level they really belong to. In the *Perfect Discourse*, for example, there are three levels. The highest one is immaterial. It applies to the invisible, unbegotten God. The second level is the abode of the star gods, who are made out of a pure, imperishable matter and bound to eternal and inflexible trajectories (NH VI.67.18). The lowest level belongs to the earthly gods who live in the temples (NH VI.69.26). There is an analogy between the invisible God creating the heavenly images of the stars, and man, that privileged creature endowed with science and gnosis, who in turn models material images after the likeness of the heavenly gods.

For each of these levels there is an appropriate form of worship. Since the earthly gods are material they need a material cult. On the contrary, the heavenly gods deserve learned admiration.

> Pure philosophy that depends only on reverence for god should wonder at the recurrence of the stars, how their measure stays constant in prescribed stations and in the orbit of their turning; it should learn the dimensions, qualities and quantities of the land, the depths of the sea, the power of fire and the nature and effects of all such things, in order to command, worship and wonder at the skill and mind of God. (Ascl 13)

Finally, the Highest God must be given merely intellectual worship. He needs no sacrifices, even no burning of frankincense. "For he wants nothing, who is himself all things or in whom all things are [. . .] but he finds mortal gratitude to be the best incense" (Ascl 41). The most appropriate utterance of that gratitude is pure, silent prayer as described in the *Ogdoad and the Ennead* (NH VI.6).

What is true in the case of religion can also be extended to moral behavior. Hermetism does not reject or even criticize common morality; rather it aims at more consciousness and more spiritual depth. In the description of hell included in the *Perfect Discourse* we can read fairly hackneyed opinions, drawn from a Platonizing vulgate, about afterlife and the judgment of the souls. If the chief demon presiding over the court sees a soul "smeared with the stains of wrongdoing and dirtied with vice, he sends it tumbling down from on high to the depths below and consigns it to the storms and whirlpools of air, fire and water [. . .]. To escape this snare, let us recognize what we must fear, dread and avoid" (Ascl 28).

The most serious crimes we should avoid are "adulteries, murders, assaults on one's father, acts of sacrilege and irreverence, suicides by hanging or falling from a cliff" (CH IX.3). The main vices we should get rid of are ignorance, grief, lust, injustice, greed, deceit, envy, treachery, anger, recklessness, and malice (CH XIII.7). Common people vainly try to avoid these mistakes. But they hardly can be successful, as long as they do not have learning or understanding (Ascl 22). The best they can do is to abide by human laws. But this cannot possibly free them from fatality, because "there is a law in heavens, which is above fatality [. . .] and there is another law which has been issued according to human necessity" (DH 8.1).

"But if [. . .] anyone has a ray [of gnosis] shining upon him in the rational part [of his soul] [. . .] the demons' effect on him is nullified" (CH XVI.16). Thus he may be able to choose the better rather than the worse (CH IV.7); he becomes, blessed, good, pure, and merciful (CH I.22); he relentlessly fights the fight of piety (CH X.19). Piety towards God and love of humankind are one and the same thing, "for there cannot be any better form of piety, but understanding the beings and giving thanks for them to the Creator" (SH II.B.1).

However, this way of life normally implies some kind of retreat. The one who is in knowledge is "one who says little and hears little. For he fights with shadows [. . .] who wastes time on talking and listening to talk" (CH X.9). Therefore,

> those who are in knowledge do not please the multitude, nor does the multitude please them. They appear to be mad, and they bring ridicule on themselves. They are hated and scorned and perhaps they may even be murdered [. . .]. But all things are good to such persons, even things that others find evil. If they lay plots against him, they

refer it all to knowledge, and they alone make evil into good. (CH IX.4)

Does Hermetic withdrawal from the world also demand sexual continence? At first glance we seem to have evidence of the contrary. "Wise people regard the making of children as a duty in life to be taken most seriously and greatly revered" (CH II.17). For "the gods sowed the generations of humans [. . .] to be working witnesses to nature [. . .] to increase by increasing and multiply by multiplying" (CH III.3). Therefore,

> should any human being pass away childless, [we rightly] see it as the worst misfortune and ungodliness. After death such a person suffers retribution from demons. This is his punishment: the soul of the childless one is sentenced to a body that has neither a man's nature nor a woman's—a thing accursed under the sun. (CH II.17)

This Hermetic attitude toward sex rests on religious grounds. Even God is male and female, since he exists as life *(zoè)* and light *(phôs)* (CH I.9). "Completely full of the fertility of both sexes and ever pregnant with his own will, he always begets whatever he wishes to procreate" (Ascl 20). Therefore, procreation is a mystery of divine love, and the union of man and woman is an adequate picture of divinity (Ascl 21).

However, when we analyze Hermetic ideas, we should never forget that Hermetism is not a fixed system but a way, i.e., an evolution with several stages. Granted that sex be allowed or even compulsory in the early stages, what happens in the last one? Although our treatises give no direct answer to this question, I am inclined to assume that, once perfection has been reached by means of Hermetic initiation, sexuality is somehow overcome or superseded. Instead of being exterior, it becomes purely interior.

For the goal of Hermetic gnosis is to be born again in the Ennead like the first self-generated man, who was male and female (CH I.12). So were also all the antediluvian generations (CH I.16–17). It is only in a later stage that, "by the counsel of God, all living beings, that had been male-and-female, were sundered into two parts—humans along with them—and part of them became male, part likewise female" (CH I.18).

If Hermetic initiation enables us to reach the Ogdoad and the Ennead, as will be shown in my second contribution to this volume, then we have to become male-and-female in the process of being born again from the womb of divine wisdom, whereas "the seed is the true God," i.e., Intellect (CH XIII.2). This seems to happen in the Ogdoad, where souls are constantly associated with angels (NH VI.56.1–2, 58.18–20, 59.29–30). On a comparative mythological basis, we may fairly assume that the angels are the male partners of the female souls. Therefore the meeting of souls and angels in the Ogdoad brings about the reunification of primordial male-and-female humankind.

When we have gone through this process, we become able to beget spiritual children, like Hermes (NH VI.52.20, 52.26–27, 53.29–30). However, this peculiar way of begetting is different from normal procreation. It can be likened to divine sexuality: "God takes no pleasure in this work, nor does he have any partner in it" (CH IX.14).

Let us sum up the Hermetic attitude towards ethics. The Hermetic gnosis is deeply concerned with piety and morality. The disciples of Trismegistus accept common morals and common religion, but the farther they go on the way of knowledge, the more they aim at deepening and spiritualizing them. As to sex, continence is by no means a Hermetic virtue; on the contrary, procreation is a religious duty for every human being. Nevertheless after the spiritual rebirth of initiation, sexuality becomes something quite different. It no longer needs an exterior partner, since the human being has recovered primordial androgyny.

This position is in violent contrast with the strict sexual continence demanded by certain Gnostics. Let me adduce an extreme example: *The Testimony of Truth*, a Gnostic homily of the late second or the early third century, the Coptic translation of which has been preserved as the third writing of the ninth codex of Nag Hammadi.

The author of this text believes, as has been rightly pointed out by F. Wisse, that the only relevance of Christ lies in the fact that he has abolished carnal generation. This indeed is the only way of getting rid of the "old leaven of the Pharisees and the scribes," i.e., the defiled Law of the Archons and the Authorities, which "commands everyone to take a husband or a wife and to beget and to multiply like the sand of the sea" (NH IX.29.12–30.5).

This point is vividly illustrated by the interpretation of the descent of Jesus on the Jordan.

The Son of Man came forth from Imperishability, being alien to defilement. He came to the world by the Jordan river, and immediately
the Jordan turned back[. . . .]. Now the Jordan river is the power of
the body, i.e. the senses of pleasures. The water of the Jordan is the
desire for sexual intercourse. And John is the Archon of the womb.
(NH IX.30.20–31.5)

The opposition between John and Jesus, as representatives of the Law
and the Imperishable Light, is still emphasized by the contrasting description of their births.

John was begotten by speech through a woman, Elizabeth; and Christ
was begotten by speech through a virgin, Mary. What is the meaning
of this mystery? John was begotten by means of a womb worn by age,
but Christ passed through a virgin's womb, and when she had conceived, she gave birth to the Saviour, furthermore she was found to
be a virgin again. (NH IX.45.6-28)

As a result the author strictly rejects sex and procreation. He also con-
demns money, water baptism, and the false testimony of martyrdom.
All these interdicts are closely related to each other. For "he who is the
father of Mammon is also the father of sexual intercourse" (NH IX.68.6–
8). Moreover, the water of baptism is a symbol of lust and defilement.
Finally bloody martyrdom takes place in the presence of unrighteous
authorities, who are somehow similar to the unrighteous Mammon.

Consequently, humankind is divided into two parts: the "seed of
Adam" and the "generation of the Son of Man." The only criterion by
which this division can be ascertained is sexual behavior:

It is fitting that [the Christians] should become undefiled, in order
that they might show that they are from the generation of the Son of
Man, since it is about them that the Saviour bore testimony. But those
that are from the seed of Adam are manifest by their deeds, which are
their work. They have not ceased from wicked desire. (NH IX.67.3–
13)

Thus, praxis is crucial to the knowledge of Christ. "For no one who is
under the Law will be able to look up to the truth, since they will not be
able to serve two masters" (NH IX.29.22–25). Nevertheless, this praxis
can hardly be dissociated from Gnostic teaching or Gnostic understand-

ing of the New Testament: "This is what the Son of Man reveals to us: it is fitting for you to receive the word of truth, provided one will receive it perfectly. But as for one who is in ignorance, it is difficult for him to diminish his works of darkness" (NH IX.31.5–12).

Now, the correct interpretation of the Scriptures heavily depends, in the eyes of our author, on a Gnostic system very close to Valentinianism. I cannot dwell here on every detail concerning Christ and the Superior God. I will rather focus on anthropology, ethics, and spiritual progress.

Human being is constituted of three elements: (1) flesh or body, (2) soul, (3) mind or heart. These three elements are approximately equivalent to the Valentinian tripartition of body, soul, and spirit. Likewise, they are involved in two binary oppositions. Soul is opposed to body like right to left (NH IX.43.10–13), whereas mind is opposed to soul like male to female (NH IX.40.29, 44.2–3). These metaphors also occur in Valentinianism, as we can read in Irenaeus: "[A]ll that is material, which they also describe as being 'on the left hand' [. . .] must perish [. . .] and every Psychic existence, which they also denominate 'on the left hand' [. . .] is a mean between the spiritual and the material" (*Adv. Haer.* 1.6.1). On the other hand, according to Theodotus, "while the elected soul is asleep, the Saviour has laid in her a male seed" (*Excerpts from Theodotus* 2.1), whereas "males are the election and females all those who are called" (*Excerpts from Theodotus* 21.1).

The standing up of the Gnostic and his progression from left to right, and then further up to the truth, demands the purification of his soul, which depends on the latter's choice between life and death. Thus after he has condemned the error of the Archons "he has cleansed his soul from the transgressions which he had committed with an alien hand. He has stood up, being upright within himself, because this depends on everyone and everyone has death and life within himself or rather everyone is in the midst of both of them" (NH IX.43.1–9).

The Coptic word *efsoutôn* (NH IX.43.4, cf. IX.38.23), which describes this interior standing up, is a translation from the Greek *diorthoun*, a Valentinian technical term normally describing the cure of passions. As to the in-between position of everyone in this passage, it fits in with the Valentinian definition of the psychic nature, that "passes to the side to which inclination draws it" (*Adv. Haer.* 1.6.1). Therefore, anybody aiming at Gnostic perfection is deeply concerned with the moral choice made by his own soul, because his mind has to be formed in it.

Indeed, since the spiritual element is sent forth from heavens in a feeble and immature state, it must eventually be brought to perfection (*Adv. Haer.* 1.6.4). The Valentinians would distinguish two stages of spiritual formation: according to essence and according to knowledge. The first stage aims at bringing about awareness of the passions and giving an odor of immortality that may arouse a tendency to superior realities (*Adv. Haer.* 1.4.1). The second stage of formation aims at curing the passions by cutting them off (*Adv. Haer.* 1.4.5). These two stages also occur in the *Testimony of Truth* in nearly equivalent terms.

Refuting adversaries who expect a carnal resurrection (NH IX.36.30) on the last day (NH IX.34.27), the author describes the spiritual resurrection of the Gnostics:

> [They] stood [. . .] they asked what they have been bound with, and how they might properly release themselves. And they came to know themselves, as to who they are, or rather, where they are now and what is the place in which they will rest from their senselessness, when they arrive at knowledge. (NH IX.35.20–36.3)

The idea that true resurrection consists in gaining gnosis in this life is well ascertained in Valentinianism. The present passage describes only the beginning of the process, when one wakes up and becomes aware of the questions to be asked. These questions are mentioned in Valentinianism as typical of the contents of gnosis: "Who we were, and what we have become; where we were and where we have been cast, where we hurry, whence we shall be delivered, what is birth and what is rebirth" (*Excerpts from Theodotus* 78.2). However, gnosis itself and spiritual rest still remain to be reached.

This first awakening, which is most similar to the Valentinian formation according to essence, is followed by a deeper evolution, which can be likened with the formation according to knowledge:

> Like Isaiah, who was sawed with a saw and he became two, so also the Son of Man divides us by the Word of the Cross. It divides the day from the night and the light from the darkness and the corruptible from incorruptibility, and it divides the males from the females. But Isaiah is the type of the body. The saw is the word of the Son of

Man which separates us from the error of the angels. But no one knows the God of Truth except solely the man who will forsake all the things of the world. (NH IX.40.21–41.8)

This time we really have a separation, a cutting off of the passionate element of the flesh, i.e., night, darkness, corruption, female tendency. And this emancipation from carnal passions, this renunciation of the world, ends up in knowing the God of Truth. All of this fits in with the Valentinian formation according to knowledge. This formation brings about deeper understanding, as we can see from the numerous questions that are asked just after this passage. These questions are connected in antithetical pairs such as "What is the light, and what is the darkness? Who is the one who has created the earth, and who is God?" Thus they present the Gnostic with a choice, so that he may confirm the division that has taken place within himself through gnosis.

The instrument of that division is the "Word of the Cross." This reminds us of a Valentinian exegesis assimilating the Cross to Horos, the Aeon who contains the passion of Sophia (*Adv. Haer.* 1.2.2). Just as there are two formations of the Gnostic, this Aeon "has two faculties, the one of supporting and the other of separating" (*Adv. Haer.* 1.3.5). In our text, the "Word of the Son of Man" (NH IX.41.2), or "the Word of the Cross" (NH IX.40.25), is compared with the saw that divides Isaiah into two parts. In this respect, it is most similar to the Aeon Horos, whom the Valentinians would recognize in this statement of the Lord: "I came not to send peace but a sword" (Mt 10:34).

Not only can we assert that the author of the *Testimony of Truth* has been greatly influenced by Valentinianism, but we have every reason to conclude that his rigid moral standards and his demand for absolute sexual continence mainly derive from a radical interpretation of the Valentinian myth.

This does not mean that this kind of position was widespread among the Valentinians and typical of Gnosticism. In fact, we have some evidence of the contrary. First of all, our text itself contains a polemical development against Valentinus, his disciples, and other Gnostics.

Although this part of the papyrus is badly damaged, we may guess that they were severely criticized on moral issues. A first group of Valentinians are charged with celebrating an impure baptism of water in the Ogdoad, in order to receive salvation (NH IX.55.1–9). Instead of that archontic rite, which can only harm, they should rather aim at a good praxis, despite the presumably bad example provided by Valentinus himself (NH IX.56.1–2). One of the prominent Valentinian teachers is likewise accused of carrying on with the same licentious behavior. He also speaks about the Ogdoad, but his disciples leave the good and worship the idols (NH IX.56.1–9). As to Basilides and his son Isidor, they are said to have yielded to the deceit of the world (NH IX.57.2–3). Finally, a last group, maybe the Simonians, are blamed for taking wives and begetting children, along with other unspecified sexual practices.

Beyond these polemics, we may assume that the Valentinians were divided into two very different camps. Some of them may have given way to sexual excesses, like Marcus and his disciples (*Adv. Haer.* 1.13.3–6). Others appear to have been strictly continent. Due to the ambiguity of our sources, we do not know exactly whether Julius Cassianus—the alleged "originator of docetism," who had written a book *Concerning Continence and Celibacy*—had or had not been a Valentinian. But Tertullian reports that there were eunuchs among them.

As to the current position of the school, I think we can rely on Peter Brown's lucid analysis in his book *The Body and Society*.[3] According to the presumably Valentinian *Gospel of Philip*,

> The marriage in the world is a mystery for those who have taken a wife. If there is a hidden quality to the marriage of defilement how much more is the undefiled marriage a true mystery! It is not fleshly but pure. It belongs not to desire, but to the will. It belongs not to the darkness or the night, but to the day and the light. (NH II.82.2–10)

The marriage in this world is a defilement inasmuch it belongs to flesh and darkness. However, it is not totally blameworthy, since it is a mysterious image of the undefiled marriage.

As a result, we may understand that fleshly marriage can be tolerated for the psychics or, at least temporarily, for persons on the way to spiritual perfection. But the real goal to be attained is the undefiled marriage, i.e., the restoration of spiritual androgyny, very much like in Hermetism. "When Eve was still in Adam death did not exist. When she was separated from him, death came into being. If he again becomes complete and attains his former self, death will be no more" (NH II.68.22–26). Whoever reaches such a goal does not need sex any longer.

Thus Irenaeus's charge of immorality against the Valentinian *perfecti* seems to be a mere polemical argument. We hardly can believe that they would bluntly say that continence and good works were necessary for the psychics of the Great Church, whereas they themselves, the spiritual, would not need such a course of conduct at all, since it is not conduct of any kind that leads into the Pleroma but the seed sent forth from heavens (*Adv. Haer.* 1.6.4).

A major objection against this sharp contrast between the conduct of psychic and pneumatic individuals is that the three kinds of men— spiritual, material, and psychic—have only two kinds of souls: those who are by nature good, and those who are by nature evil: "The good are those who become capable of receiving the spiritual seed, and the evil by nature are those who are never able to receive that seed" (*Adv. Haer.* 1.7.5).

That the bad souls are material and the good ones psychic (eventually to become spiritual) is ascertained by Tertullian:

> They classify the souls, according to their nature, into two categories, the good and the bad ones, depending on their having the earthly constitution, as initiated by Cain, or the psychic one, as initiated by Abel. As to the spiritual element initiated by Seth, they add it only as an accident, for it is no natural gift but a grace, since Achamoth makes it rain from on high upon the good souls, i.e. those who belong to the psychic category. (Tertullian, *Adversus Valentinianos* 29.2–3)

In his celebrated study about the original doctrine of Valentinus,[4] Gilles Quispel has rightly emphasized the importance of Tertullian's testimony. The distinction between material and psychic individuals is nothing like that between psychic and spiritual persons. The former rests on nature, the latter on grace. The material men are mere material natures; the spiritual, at least as long as they remain in this world, are psychic natures who have been granted by grace a spiritual seed, i.e., a potentiality, a vocation for spiritual life.

Also with respect to efficacy, nature differs from grace. Nature works automatically, like some inescapable gravity. It yields assured but merely negative results. For example, material souls *cannot* possibly receive the spiritual seed; the psychic man as such *cannot* possibly perceive spiritual realities, and so on. On the contrary, grace is an opening up to the superior level. Far from limiting or suppressing liberty, it brings it to completion. Whoever has received a spiritual seed shall certainly be saved thanks to grace and free will, inasmuch as we simply cannot imagine that spirit might be totally captured or eliminated by matter.

However, this does not mean that the Gnostic shall be saved, whatever his praxis may be and even should he commit the most deadly sins. For he is perfectly free and, as we can read both 1 John 3:9 and in the Valentinian *Gospel of Philip*, "a free man does not sin" (NH 2.77.17). In this regard he is quite different from the psychic, since his liberty is infallible and absolute, whereas the latter's free will is fallible, so that he must relentlessly start again from the beginning to choose between good and evil.

Let us try now to imagine what these abstract principles really mean to concrete individuals in everyday life. The psychic element, i.e., free will and ethical discernment, is given at once to good souls in its entirety. You cannot possibly have half of a moral consciousness. As soon as you ask whether you have it, you are sure you have it. But you cannot be that sure as to the spiritual element. Since in the form of a tiny seed it is unconsciously insufflated into the soul by an ignorant demiurge, it remains unknown even to the consciousness of the Gnostic. It is revealed with some certainty only when it has been formed and educated within the soul. Now how can that happen if the soul itself does not decide to choose the good and avoid evil? No doubt a soul that contains such a seed must be naturally good. But we have no other means of ascertaining the presence of this seed and its growing up, but to observe whether a man is doing good or evil deeds.

In the visible conduct of their life, the Valentinian pneumatics would not necessarily differ from the psychics. Who can be sure he is really elected, but he who is really perfect and constantly performs goods works? Therefore, except for some cases of imposture and charlatanism, we may assume that the Valentinian pneumatics would be truly holy people.

We might conclude by saying that, contrary to the accusations of heresiologists, many Gnostics, far from having a dissolute way of life, were deeply concerned about morals. However, as we understand from the comparison with the Hermetic texts, their main purpose was to tread a spiritual path, i.e., to bring about mental transformation within the individuals.

For this very reason, their moral principles are in a way much more complex and may sometimes seem less rigorous than those of common Christianity. From the standpoint of the Great Church, the same moral rules apply to all Christians, regardless of their state of perfection. Such a rigidity sounds like nonsense to a Gnostic or a Hermetic teacher. For when you progress on the way of perfection you become a different person, depending on the stage you have reached. Therefore you must adapt your moral standards to your new condition.

Thence derives the charge of double morals against the Gnostics. Nevertheless, we have no reason to assume that making one step further toward spiritual regeneration would allow anybody to lead a loose life. On the contrary, the more one understands God and the universe, the wider and the deeper one's ethical principles become. But instead of being imposed from outside, they spring up from the innermost part of mind, the dwelling place of the Divine Intellect or the pneumatic seed. For discovering one's transcendent nature along with the gift of divine grace cannot possibly inspire an arrogant certitude of salvation. It is rather felt like an appeal, a challenge imposed on the soul with the awful strength of love and sweetness.

NOTES

1. Valentinianism is a Gnostic system that existed from the second century to the fourth century. The name refers to the supposed founder, but whether or not Valentinianism actually derived from Valentinus himself is currently a subject of discussion among specialists.

2. *Abbreviations*: Ascl = *Asclepius*; CH = *Corpus Hermeticum*; DH = *Definitiones Hermeticae*; NH = Nag Hammadi codices; SH = Stobaei Hermetica. For bibliographical details of the editions and translations of these texts, see the first note in Van den Broek's contribution entitled "Gnosticism and Hermetism in Antiquity" elsewhere in this volume. *Quoted translations* (with some minor changes): Ascl and CH: B. P. Copenhaver, *Hermetica* (Cambridge, 1992); SH : W. Scott, *Hermetica*, vol. 1 (London, 1924); NH: various translators in J. M. Robinson, *The Nag Hammadi Library in English* (San Francisco, 1977): NH II.3 *(Gospel of Philip):* W. W. Isenberg; NH VI.6–8 (*The Eighth and Ninth*; *Prayer of Thanksgiving*; *Asclepius* 21–29): J. Brashler, P. A. Dirkse,

D. M. Parrott; NH IX.3 *(The Testimony of Truth):* B. A. Pearson, S. Giversen. Irenaeus, Diognetus, Tertullian : various translators in the *Ante-Nicene Fathers,* vols. 1 and 3 (Grand Rapids, 1963, 1967). *Bibliography:* See our *Hermès en Haute-Egypte,* vols. 1–2 (Québec, 1978, 1982); updated in *Vigiliae Christianae* 45 (1991): 372–75; Claudio Gianotto, *La testimonianza veritiera* (Brescia, 1990) and our forthcoming edition of the same writing in the Quebec Series.

    3. Peter Brown, *The Body and Society* (New York, 1988).

    4. Gilles Quispel, "The Original Doctrine of Valentine," *Vigiliae Christianae* 1 (1947): 43–73.

CHAPTER 3

MANICHAEISM
Its Sources and Influences on Western Christianity

JOHANNES VAN OORT

In the context of this book, Manichaeism seems to be an excellent subject to illustrate what in fact Gnosis or Gnosticism was, and what it, perhaps, still can be.[1]

By late antiquity, Manichaeism had become a world religion. Actually, in its Manichaean form Gnosticism once was a real world religion, i.e., a worldwide and separate Gnostic community or church *(ekklèsia)* with its many thousands and, later on, even millions of adherents; its own leader, bishops, and priests; its own liturgy and rites; its own canonical scriptures; and even its own very attractive art. Once Manichaeism spread from southern Mesopotamia as far as the Atlantic in the West and the Pacific in the Far East. It had its adherents in Egypt, in Roman North Africa, in Spain, Gaul, Italy, and the Balkans, and in the end even in the regions on the South China Coast.[2] Its history covers the period from the beginning of the third century to modern times. Even in our century Manichaeism was still forbidden by law in Vietnam.[3]

THE ORIGINS OF MANI AND MANICHAEISM:
AL-NADIM AND THE CMC

To give an outline of the main points of this Gnostic religion, it seems appropriate to start from the very beginning. Once there lived a certain historical figure named Mani. He was indeed, as he styled himself, a prophet from the land of Babylon. Mani—or, according to his Syriac name, Mani Hajja (that is, the living Mani)—was born in the year 216 C.E. From several sources even the exact day of his birth is known: Sunday, 14 April. For some time past, we have also precise information about the place *where* he was born, namely, near the southern Mesopotamian town of Seleucia-Ctesiphon. This capital city, so famous in late antiquity, was located not far from present-day Baghdad.

In those days, at the beginning of the third century, some ascetic Jewish-Christian sects were found in these regions. From Mohammed Ibn al-Nadim, a Muslim writer who flourished at the end of the tenth century, we have the following important report on the origins of Mani.[4] He relates that once a certain Futtuq, a resident of the Twin Cities (i.e., Seleucia-Ctesiphon), joined a baptizing sect through responding to a call to ascetic living. This Futtuq is said to have been a native of Hamadhan (Ecbatana), and his wife Mays, or Marmaryam, is said to have been related to the then ruling house of the Arsacids. One day, while Futtuq was worshipping in a temple of idols, he heard a loud voice admonishing him not to eat meat, nor to drink wine, nor to have intercourse with women. This happened to him a number of times during the next three days. Futtuq was won over by this voice and joined a sect known as the Mughtasilah—that is, those who wash (or baptize) themselves. His wife Maryam was pregnant when Futtuq decided to join the baptist sect, and in due course she gave birth to their son Mani. His father, so Ibn al-Nadim continues, sent for him so that he could be brought up with him according to the rule of the sect. The passage of his *Fihrist* (Catalog) in which al-Nadim says these things is worth quoting in full:

> Then his father sent and brought him to the place where he was, so that he was reared with him, in accordance with his cult. Even when young, Mani spoke with words of wisdom and then, when he was twelve years old, there came to him a revelation. According to his [Mani's] statement it was from the King of the Gardens of Light [. . .]. The angel bringing the revelation was called the Tawm, which is a Nabataean word meaning "Companion." He said to him, "Leave this cult, for thou art not one of its adherents. Upon thee are laid purity and refraining from bodily lusts, but it is not yet time for thee to appear openly, because of thy tender years." When he had completed his twenty-fourth year, the Tawm came to him saying, "The time is fulfilled for thee to come forth and to give the summons to thy cause."[5]

Al-Nadim then goes on to tell how Mani at this age of twenty-four broke away from the Mughtasilah and formed his own sect together with his father and a handful of fellow Baptists. After that, on the following pages of his *Fihrist,* completed in Baghdad by the year 988 or 989,[6] al-Nadim gives his account of the history and the doctrines of Mani and the Manichaeans.

It must be said that even in modern times al-Nadim's report has aroused great skepticism. To many scholars, the gnosis of Manichaeism seemed to be an offshoot of a kind of dualistic Iranian religion that was closely connected with Zoroastrianism. Evidently, the report of al-Nadim did not support this view. However, this opinion or even dogma of the so-called Religionsgeschichtliche Schule[7] has now turned out to be wrong. In particular, al-Nadim's account has been confirmed magnificently by a new discovery. It is now known for certain that Mani was indeed reared in a baptist community in Southern Mesopotamia. Moreover, we now know that this sect was a Jewish-Christian one and that the origins of Mani's Gnostic-dualistic world religion have to be explained from this background. We know this from the recent discovery of a unique Manichaean document, the so-called Cologne Mani-Codex, the *Codex Manichaicus Coloniensis* or CMC.

Without any exaggeration, it may be said that, in order to understand the origins of Manichaeism, the CMC is of crucial importance. The document was discovered shortly before 1970 in Egypt. It came into the possession of the University of Cologne and hence it received its name. It is the smallest parchment codex yet discovered. Its pages measure only 4,5 by 3,5 cm and the writing on them is 3.5 by 2.5 cm. But, despite its minute format, the Manichaean scribes managed to copy an average of twenty-three lines of Greek majuscules onto each page. The first preliminary report on the CMC was given by Albert Henrichs and Ludwig Koenen in a now famous 1970 issue of the *Zeitschrift für Papyrologie und Epigraphik.*[8] From the following year onward, these scholars gave their editio princeps.[9] A complete critical edition of the CMC appeared in the year 1988 as *Der Kölner Mani Kodex.*[10] But the scholarly discussion on the text and interpretation of the CMC has been going on ever since[11] and a final scholarly edition has not yet appeared.

The CMC is written in Greek and has as its running title *On the Genesis of His Body (Peri tès gennès tou somatos autou).* What does this mean? In the scholarly discussion, two main views prevail. According to one, Mani's physical body is meant and the Greek word *genna* may be translated as "procreation." Indeed, several passages in the codex may support this view.[12] According to the other opinion, the title of the CMC is already an echo of the Pauline elements so evident in the codex. Just as the apostle Paul in his letters described the Church as the body of Christ, so here the Manichaean Church *(ekklèsia)* is described as the body of Mani.[13] In this way, the codex may have constituted the first part of a history of the early Manichaean Church.[14] It is difficult to decide between these two scholarly opinions,[15] although most scholars are now inclined to prefer the first one. In any case, the extant pages of the codex have, as their main theme, the story of young Mani's sojourn among the baptists. But also his earliest missionary journeys after his final break with the sect at the age of twenty-four are related. It is of importance to see that the CMC is not the work of one author, but comprises excerpts from the testimonies of Mani's closest disciples and early followers. Just as the evangelists gave their account of the life and the works of Jesus— or better: their account of Jesus' deeds and words (cf. Acts 1:1)—so here these earliest witnesses give their account of Mani's deeds and words. And just as one Gospel harmony was made from the several Gospels as is, for instance, the case with the *Diatessaron* of Tatian, so here we have a compilation and redaction of the earliest testimonies of Mani's deeds and words. Among the names of the Manichaean witnesses that have been preserved are Salmaios the Ascetic, Baraies the Teacher, a certain Timotheos, Abjesous the Teacher, Innaios the brother of Zabed, a certain Za[cheas?], Koustaios the Son of the Treasure of Life, and Ana the Brother of Zacheas the Disciple. From the number of different authors[16] it must be concluded that Mani spoke frequently and at length about himself and about his supernatural experiences to his closest disciples. In the CMC these earliest disciples function as trustworthy witnesses of Mani's deeds and words.

It is something like a revelation to analyze the contents of the CMC and to detect in this way the essential origins of Mani and his Gnostic world religion. We cannot enter into all details here, but some of the main facts may be mentioned. First, we now see how well founded and in essence reliable Ibn al-Nadim's testimony is, for according to the CMC Mani grew up among "baptists." We learn from the new codex that they performed daily ablutions on themselves and on their food (CMC 80.1– 3, 80.23–83.13, 88.13–15). Besides, their religion is referred to as the Law, *nomos* in Greek, which implies that the sect lived in conformity with the Jewish Law (e.g., CMC 20.9–11, 87.16–18, 89.11–13). Moreover, these baptists appealed to the traditions of the Fathers (CMC 87.2–7, 91.4–9). These all reflect Jewish traditions. Another indication of the Jewish roots of the sect is that their members observed the Rest of the Hands (CMC 102.15). This seems to refer to the observance of the Jewish Sabbath (and probably it is even this custom which can be found in Manichaeism as "the seal of the hands" of the Manichaean Elect). Moreover, in a passage from Baraies, one of the Manichaean authors from which the editor of the CMC compiled his work, no less than five Jewish apocalyptic writings are quoted: an Apocalypse of Adam, an Apocalypse of Sethel, one of Enos, one of Sem, and one of Enoch (CMC 48.16–60.7).

The sectarians of the CMC apparently acknowledged a certain Alchasaios as the founder of their rule. There should be no doubt that, in fact, they were Elchasaites. This again appears to support al-Nadim's remark that the sect of the Mughtasilah was instituted by a certain al-Hasih, an alleged Jewish-Christian prophet said to have lived at the beginning of the second century. Thus it was in a Jewish-Christian[17] community that the young Mani was educated. So we may even suppose that he was circumcised and say with certainty that he lived according to the Mosaic Law.

It was, however, against this Law that Mani protested, and by doing so he became a Gnostic.[18] In the CMC, this break with the religion of his youth is told vividly and even dramatically. Here we read in Mani's words (handed down by his closest disciples) what kind of experience led him to become the founder of a new Gnostic religion. He says that since his youth he had come under special divine protection and instruction. Angels and powers of holiness were entrusted with his safe-keeping. He also received visions and signs (cf. CMC 3ff.). This may perhaps seem somewhat odd from modern viewpoints, but in the apocalyptic Jewish milieu in which Mani was brought up such experiences were quite common.[19] One of these divine messengers turned out to be Mani's special protector. This was his *syzygos*—his Twin, Companion, or guardian angel—the figure that in Manichaean teaching is described as an emanation of the Jesus of Light (who in turn is an emanation of the Nous or Divine Intellect). Between young Mani and his *syzygos* grew an intimate relationship, which in the CMC he praises in poetry:

and he who is the most trusty
him I received piously
and him I acquired as my own property.
Him I believed
and he belongs to me
he is a good and kind[20] guide.
Him I recognized
and I understood that I am he
from whom I was separated. . . .

(CMC 24.2ff.)

The divine revelations and admonitions that Mani received were incompatible with some of the doctrinal tenets and practices of the baptists. The CMC describes how Mani protested, for instance, against their harvesting, against their gathering of firewood, and, moreover, against their ritual ablutions. True purity, according to Mani's claim, can only be achieved through special knowledge *(gnosis)*. This gnosis is not obtained by outward observances, but, on the contrary, by inner revelation. It is only through this gnosis that we know the difference between good and bad, death and life, Light and Darkness (cf. CMC 84.10–17). The baptists, in Mani's eyes, had gone wrong in observing a mere outward purification.

The codex then describes how Mani's severe criticism was accepted by some but in the end rejected by many. A certain Sita and the majority of his fellow elders set up a synod on Mani's account. These leaders of the sect, who constituted its Sanhedrin, certainly would have killed him had not his father Pattig convinced them to desist. After this attempt Mani was left alone and prayed for support. Then, so the codex continues, at that precise moment of despair, his *syzygos* again appeared and encouraged him. In reply to Mani's desperate complaint, the "Splendid One" says:

Not only to this religion
    you have been sent out,
but to every people and school of learning
and to every city and region.
For by you this Hope will be made manifest
and it will be preached in every clime and every zone of
    the world
and in very great numbers men will accept your word.

Therefore,
come forward and travel about.
For I will be with you as your helper and protector in every
place
where you proclaim everything which I have revealed to
you.

(CMC 104–5)

Being comforted and supported by these and similar words from his divine Twin, Mani made the final break with the baptists. In the long passage handed down by Timotheos, Mani's "mission statement," which is remarkably full of biblical references,[21] runs as follows:

Thus,
according to the will of our Lord,
I came forward and left that Law
in order to sow his most beautiful seed,
to light his brightest candles,
to redeem the living souls from their subjection to the
rebels,
to walk in the world after the image of our Lord Jesus,
to throw on to the earth a sword, division and the blade of
the spirit,
to scatter the bread on my people
and to overcome the immeasurable shame which is in the
world.

(CMC 107)

The codex tells that he first went to Ctesiphon, where he was later joined by two fellow baptists, who bear the typical Jewish names of Simeon and Abizachias. Already during Mani's trial before the Sanhedrin, they had considered him to be the true prophet, i.e., the recurrent heavenly figure that according to these and other Jewish-Christians had previously appeared in such figures as Adam, Seth(el), Enoch, Noah, Abraham, and Jesus.[22] Soon his father became an adherent of Mani as well.

This much we know about the origins of Mani's gnosis. Much more might be said about it, and from several original Manichaean sources such as those from Medinet Madi in Egypt or from Turfan in Central Asia. Particularly from the newly discovered Cologne Mani-Codex, however, we gain a fresh perspective. Summarizing its main results we may say:

It is now known for certain that Mani was raised in a Jewish-Christian community of baptists. In this community, he not only heard about baptisms and ablutions (which he rejected) and about the Jewish Law (which he rejected), but among the Elchasaites he also heard that Jesus was the true prophet, a manifestation of God's glory *(kavod)* that was first embodied in Adam, then revealed itself to the Old Testament patriarchs, and finally was incarnated in the Messiah, Jesus.

This may explain the special place of Jesus in Mani's system. It attracts the attention that not only in Western Manichaean sources but even in the sources from Central Asia and China, this Jesus was venerated.[23] From one of the previous important findings, the Coptic manuscripts discovered in Medinet Madi in Egypt about the year 1930, this may be illustrated. In the famous Coptic Psalm-Book, the second part of which was edited by the very promising young British scholar Charles Allberry (an RAF pilot who died when his plane was shot down above the Netherlands just before midnight on 3 April 1943), there are many psalms to Jesus and psalms to Christ.[24] One passage may illustrate the essentially Christocentric character of these psalms:

> Christ, guide me: my Saviour, do not forget me.
> I am the love of the Father, being the robe clothing thee.
> Christ, guide me: my Saviour, do not forget me.
> My brethren are the Aeons and the Aeons of the Aeons.
> Christ, guide me, my Saviour, do not forget me.
> The air and the Land of Light—they travailed with me.
> Christ. . . . [etc.][25]

To say it in a few words, right from its inception the figure of Jesus had an important place in the gnosis of Mani. This Jesus, being in particular the Jesus of Light who in turn is an "emanation" of the Divine Nous (or Intuition or Insight or Gnosis)—this Jesus signified divine redemption of man, divine nourishment of man, divine suffering for man.[26] In essence, these are Gnostic-*Christian* ideas.

THE MANICHAEAN MYTH: AN OUTLINE

Before discussing briefly the question of the possible influences of Manichaeism on western Christianity, let me sketch the main points of the Manichaean myth. Until now, nothing has been said about this myth, for neither in the CMC nor even in the Manichaean Coptic Psalm-Book does the myth come to the fore. Mythical elements are certainly present, but mainly in the background. However, from the many Manichaean writings we can deduce a highly complicated myth, the principal elements of which are as follows:

Mani and his followers taught a cosmogony of a dualistic kind: evil is an eternal cosmic force, not the result of a fall. Two realms or kingdoms, the realm of light and the realm of darkness, good and evil, God and matter, oppose each other implacably.[27] The realm of light is ruled by the Father of Greatness; in his resistance against the attack of the kingdom of darkness he produces Primal Man by emanation or, better, evocation, namely by his Call. When this Man is in danger of perishing in the struggle, there is a new evocation: the Living Spirit is called into being. He directs his Call of salvation to Primal Man and rescues him from matter. However, the soul of the Primal Man remains behind; thus the world is ordered as a mixture of light and darkness, good and evil. A subsequent evocation, the Third Messenger, causes the movement toward the kingdom of light. It is by this Third Messenger that Jesus is sent to Adam and Eve in order to give them gnosis; the revelation by Jesus the Luminous to Adam is the archetype of all future human redemption. Gradually this liberation will be achieved. In order to bring about the redemption of the light, Jesus evokes the Apostle of Light, who becomes incarnate in the great religious leaders throughout the history of mankind such as the Buddha, Zoroaster, and Jesus the Messiah. Finally comes Mani, the promised Paraclete. World history has no other goal than to separate light from darkness so that the primeval state will be restored. This will be the case when all the rescued particles of light have returned to the kingdom of light and the damned will be forever imprisoned in a globe inside a gigantic pit covered with a huge stone. Then the separation of light and darkness will be accomplished for all eternity.

This is a necessarily brief and—inevitably—eclectic account of a very complicated myth. However complex and arcane the various ramifications of the Manichaean myth became in the course of its distribution through many countries and centuries, its essential elements remained the same from the Atlantic to the Pacific. It is Mani's doctrine that there are two principles (or roots or kingdoms or realms or cities) and three "moments": the time before the commingling and the struggle, when the two kingdoms or realms of light and darkness were still separated; the time of the commingling, being the present world time; and future time, in which the two realms will again be (and now definitively) separated. In essence this message of salvation is typically Gnostic: the Nous (the heavenly revelation) rescues the psychè (the divine spark of light in man) from the hylè (the evil matter). Moreover, this myth has to be evaluated as the expression of a "self"-experience. What happens in the macrocosm happens in a similar way in the microcosm that man is; and vice versa. The basis of this myth, its Gnostic feature, seems to be Mani's encounter with his *syzygos*, his heavenly Twin or transcendental Self.

MANICHAEISM AND WESTERN CHRISTIANITY: THE CASE OF AUGUSTINE

Did this gnosis of Manichaeism, once a world religion, exert any influence on western Christianity and in this way on our western civilization? This intriguing question will only be touched upon here. Some references can be made to a number of special studies. Yet, before briefly considering the question, it should be stressed that many of its aspects still have to be explored further.

Our focal point is Augustine. He, the greatest and without doubt most influential Father of the Western Church, once was an adherent of Manichaeism. This period of his life lasted more than ten years. After his Manichaean years Augustine, now being reconverted to Catholic Christianity, wrote many books and tracts against his former coreligionists. Nevertheless, near the end of his life he was again accused of Manichaeism because of his view of sexual concupiscence and original sin. "Even as an Ethiopian, a Moor, can not change his skin nor the leopard his spots, even so it is impossible for you to wipe out your Manichaean past."[28]

There seems to be some truth in this venomous and virulent remark. Three main possibilities may be discerned and about each one a few general observations may be made.

First, there are indeed some striking similarities between Augustine's view of sexual concupiscence and original sin and the Manichaean view of sex and sin. Both views are very negative, in particular with regard to the randomness of the sexual impulse; and, moreover, both stress that this randomness is sin. In its randomness, in its *motus inordinatus*, the sinful nature of sexual desire reveals itself prominently and sin is transmitted through this sexual desire.[29]

Secondly, there are many similarities between Augustine's famous and very influential doctrine of the two cities or kingdoms and the dualistic Manichaean view of the two realms, cities, or kingdoms. Everyone who reads Augustine's famous *City of God*, and book 11 in particular, will be struck by such similarities. These similarities in thought and even terminology seem to give some justification to the perception of direct influences here.[30]

The third and probably most important field of influence seems to be Augustine's spirituality. Nowhere in the early church before 400 does there appear to be such a tender and appealing piety, along with such a prominent place given to the Christ, except for Augustine and the Manichaean writings. When reading Augustine's *Confessions*, for example, one is more than once reminded of the Manichaean psalms.[31] He tells us not accidentally that he also learned from the Manichaeans and it is quite certain that he sang their psalms.[32] In some essential features of Augustine's spirituality we may perceive one of the most important channels through which the Gnostic religion of Manichaeism has exercised a lasting influence on western culture.

NOTES

1. In this general introduction footnotes and references to scholarly discussions are kept to a minimum. The following select bibliography may facilitate further reading. *Primary sources and translations*: A. Adam, *Texte zum Manichäismus* (Berlin, 1969) (still valuable collection of texts); A. Böhlig, *Die Gnosis: Dritter Band, Der Manichäismus* (Zürich and München, 1980) (best short introduction to Manichaeism in German, with excellent choice of Manichaean sources in translation; comprehensive indices); H. J. Klimkeit, *Gnosis on the Silk Road. Gnostic Texts from Central Asia* (San Francisco, 1993) (excellent collection of Iranian and Turkish Manichaean texts in English translation; extensive notes and bibliography); L. Koenen and C. Römer, *Der Kölner Mani-Kodex. Über das Werden seines Leibes. Kritische Edition aufgrund der von A. Henrichs und L. Koenen besorgten Erstedition* (Opladen,

1988) (edition of the CMC in Greek, with introduction, German translation, and short annotations); S. N. C. Lieu, J. van Oort, and A. van Tongerloo, eds., *Corpus Fontium Manichaeorum* (Turnhout, 1996ff.) (edition of all the Manichaean sources in their original languages with translations in English, French, or German; extensive introductions and annotations). *Studies*: F. Decret, *Mani et la religion manichéenne* (Paris, 1974) (fine treatment of Mani and Manichaeism in French; richly illustrated); S. N. C. Lieu, *Manichaeism in the Later Roman Empire and Medieval China* (Tübingen, 1992) (most recent and best historical treatment of Mani and Manichaeism in English; extensive notes and bibliography of primary sources and secondary works); S. N. C. Lieu, *Manichaeism in Mesopotamia and the Roman East* (Leiden, New York, and Köln, 1994) (six selected papers, including the previously unpublished monograph article "From Mesopotamia to the Roman East—The Diffusion of Manichaeism in the Roman Empire"; extensive notes and indices); J. van Oort, *Jerusalem and Babylon: A Study into Augustine's "City of God" and the Sources of his Doctrine of the Two Cities* (Leiden, New York, København, and Köln, 1991) (extensive treatment of Mani, the origins of Manichaeism, and the possible influences of Manichaeism on Augustine); H.-Ch. Puech, *Le manichéisme. Son fondateur, sa doctrine* (Paris, 1949) (still valuable study by an eminent specialist); M. Tardieu, *Le manichéisme* (Paris, 1981) (fine treatment of Mani and Manichaeism in French; with important chronology and diagrams).

2. A Manichaean temple built in the fourteenth century is still standing on Huabiao Hill not far from the modern city of Zhuanzhou. In it one can still see a statue of "Mani, the Buddha of Light."

3. Although this does not necessarily mean that there were or still are Manichaeans in Vietnam. Laws established by foreign (in this case: Chinese) rulers remained in effect. We know for sure, however, that Manichaeans were once present at the court of the Chinese emperors, and that their religion was forbidden in China.

4. The most recent English edition with some elucidations is by Bayard Dodge, *The Fihrist of al-Nadim: A Tenth Century Survey of Muslim Culture* (New York and London, 1970), 2:773ff. Still valuable is the older work of G. Flügel, *Mani, seine Lehre und seine Schriften. Ein Beitrag zur Geschichte des Manichäismus. Aus dem Fihrist des [. . .] an-Nadīm* (1862; reprint, Osnabrück, 1969).

5. Al-Nadim, *Fihrist*, trans. Dodge, 774; cf. Flügel, *Mani*, 84.

6. Cf. Dodge's introduction to al-Nadim, *Fihrist*, xxi.

7. On this important "History of Religion School" and on some scholars still adhering to its main views concerning the origins of Gnosticism, see C. Colpe, *Die Religionsgeschichtliche Schule. Darstellung ihres Bildes vom gnostischen Erlösermythus* (Göttingen, 1961). Cf. also A. F. Verheule, *Wilhelm Bousset. Leben und Werk* (Amsterdam, 1973), 159ff.

8. A. Henrichs and L. Koenen, "Ein griechischer Mani Kodex (P. Colon. inv. nr. 4780," *Zeitschrift für Papyrologie und Epigraphik (= ZPE)* 5 (1970): 97–216 [= "Vorbericht"].

9. Editio princeps of CMC 1-72.7, in *ZPE* 19 (1975): 1–85 (with extensive commentary); of CMC 72.8–99.9, in *ZPE* 32 (1978): 87–199 (with very extensive commentary); of CMC 99.10–120, in *ZPE* 44 (1981): 201–318 (with very extensive

commentary); of CMC 121–92, in *ZPE* 48 (1982): 1–59. An ample commentary on the final section has now been given by C. E. Römer, *Manis frühe Missionsreisen nach der Kölner Manibiographie. Textkritischer Kommentar und Erläuterungen zu p. 121–p. 192 des Kölner Mani-Kodex* (Opladen, 1994).

10. L. Koenen and C. Römer, *Der Kölner Mani-Kodex: Über das Werden seines Leibes: Kritische Edition aufgrund der von A. Henrichs und L. Koenen besorgten Erstedition* (Opladen, 1988). Moreover, a diplomatic text has been edited by L. Koenen and C. Römer, *Der Kölner Mani-Kodex: Abbildungen und diplomatischer Text* (Bonn, 1985).

11. On the extensive and still growing scholarly discussion, see my recent overview, "The Study of the Cologne Mani Codex, 1970–1994," *Manichaean Studies Newsletter* 13 (1996): 21–30.

12. See L. Koenen, "How Dualistic is Mani's Dualism?" in *Codex Manichaicus Coloniensis: Atti del Secondo Simposio Internazionale . . .* , ed. L. Cirillo (Cosenza, 1990), 19ff.

13. Cf. L. Koenen, "Das Datum der Offenbarung und Geburt Manis," *Zeitschrift für Papyrologie und Epigraphik* 8 (1971): 250, and idem, "Augustine and Manichaeism in Light of the Cologne Mani Codex," *Illinois Classical Studies* 3 (1978): 164–66. It should be remarked, however, that in his later publications Koenen did not uphold this view.

14. One of the Coptic Manichaean codices from Medinet Madi, the greatest part of which is now unfortunately lost, appeared to show the same literary structure as the CMC and perhaps was part of the same work. On the contents of this codex, see C. Schmidt and H. J. Polotsky, "Ein Mani-Fund in Ägypten," *Sitzungsberichte der Preussischen Akademie der Wissenschaften, Philos.-Hist. Klasse* 1 (1933): 27–30; on its fate and remains, J. M. Robinson, "The Fate of the Manichaean Codices of Medinet Madi, 1929–1989," in *Studia Manichaica*, ed. G. Wießner and H.-J. Klimkeit (Wiesbaden, 1992), 51–55.

15. Perhaps the best solution is still the one given by K. Rudolph, who with respect to the two viewpoints remarked: "Beides läßt sich natürlich schwer trennen, da die irdische Manifestation Manis über seinen Tod hinaus in seiner Gemeinde fortlebt." See Rudolph, "Die Bedeuting des Kölner Mani-Codex für die Manichäismusforschung: Vorläufige Anmerkungen," in *Mélanges Henri-Charles Puech* (Paris, 1974), 471.

16. It seems plausible that several of the testimonies existed in a written form; see Koenen and Römer, *Mani-Kodex: Kritische Edition* (see note 10), xvi and 17 n. 2.

17. The Christian inspiration of the baptists can be perceived in CMC 91.1–11 (they are told to refer to the commandments of the Savior, i.e., Jesus). Cf. 79.20–21 and 80.11–12.

18. In this respect, one may compare him with the "Gnostic" Marcion, who had a considerable influence upon Mani. According to A. von Harnack, *Marcion: Das Evangelium vom fremden Gott*, 2d ed. (Leipzig, 1924), 22, his reaction against Judaism and its Bible sprang from a resentment that stemmed from his youth.

19. See I. Gruenwald, "Manichaeism and Judaism in Light of the *Cologne Mani Codex*," *ZPE* 50 (1983): 29–45; cf. B. Visotsky, "Rabbinic Randglossen to the Cologne Mani Codex," *ZPE* 52 (1983): 295–300.

20. It is particularly difficult to translate the Greek word *chrèstos*. It can also have the meaning "useful," "good," or "favorable." It seems not accidental, however, that this word is used here. Cf. the testimony of Alexander of Lycopolis (*Critique of the Doctrines of Mani*, XXIV Brinkmann) that Christos (Christ) was called Chrèstos by the Manichaeans. This is found again in a new and unpublished Manichaean text from Kellis (ex P93C), perhaps a fragment from an original letter by Mani: 'Mani, apostle of Jesus Chrestos [. . .]. Peace through God the Father, and our Lord Jesus Chrestos. . . ."

21. Cf. e.g. Mt. 13:37; Gen. 2:7; 1 Cor. 15:45; Mt. 10:34; Lk. 12:51; Eph. 6:17, and Ex. 16:4!

22. It may be noted in passing that this belief in the recurring true prophet is one of the constituent elements in the Islam as well. Here, Muhammad is the true prophet and also the seal of the prophets. Cf. C. Colpe, *Das Siegel der Propheten: Historische Beziehungen zwischen Judentum, Judenchristentum, Heidentum, und frühem Islam* (Berlin, 1989). The more or less common scholarly view that for the Manichaeans Mani was the seal of the prophets can only be evidenced from Islamic sources; see G. G. Stroumsa, "Seal of the Prophets: The Nature of a Manichaean Metaphor," *Jerusalem Studies in Arabic and Islam* 7 (1986): 61–74 (now in French translation in Stroumsa, *Savoir et Salut* [Paris, 1992], 275–88).

23. See E. Waldschmidt and W. Lentz, *Die Stellung Jesu im Manichäismus* (Berlin, 1934) and, in particular, E. Rose, *Die manichäische Christologie* (Wiesbaden, 1979).

24. The same goes for the still unedited first part. A facsimile edition of both parts has been provided by S. Giversen, *Psalm-Book, Parts 1–2*, Cahiers d'Orientalisme, 16-17 (Genève, 1988). An edition of both parts is now being prepared by M. Krause et al. for the new *Corpus Fontium Manichaeorum*.

25. C. R. C. Allberry, ed. and trans., *A Manichaean Psalm-Book, Part II*, Manichaean Manuscripts in the Chester Beatty Collection, 2 (Stuttgart, 1938), 116.

26. Here I deliberately bring to mind a phrase of Francis Crawford Burkitt. See F. C. Burkitt, *The Religion of the Manichees* (Cambridge, 1925), 42. Although his book is now outdated, in the light of the subsequent and newest discoveries (Medinet Madi, the CMC, Kellis!), its underlying view appears to be basically correct.

27. It should be noted that this is not the Hellenistic dualism of spirit and matter, but one of two substances: the divine light is a visible, spatial, and quantifiable element, as is the evil substance of darkness, the active principle of lust, the "thought [or: "counsel," *enthymèsis* in the Coptic and Greek texts] of death."

28. Thus a somewhat free rendering of the saying of the Catholic bishop Julian of Eclanum in Augustine's unfinished work *Contra Iulianum opus imperfectum* 4.42 (*Patrologia Latina* 45.1361): "Si mutabit Aethiops pellam suam aut pardus varietatem; ita et tu a Manichaeorum mysteriis elueris. . . ." Cf. *Opus imp. c. Iul.* 1.66, 1.69, where we find charges made by Julian such as: "Te discipulum fidelem Manichaeorum. . . ." (*Patrologia Latina* 45.1085), and "Caeterum Faustus Manichaeorum episcopus, praeceptor tuus. . . ." (*Patrologia Latina* 45.1092).

29. Cf. my "Augustine and Mani on concupiscentia sexualis," in *Augustiniana Traiectina. Communications présentées au Colloque International d'Utrecht . . .*, ed. J. den

Boeft and J. van Oort (Paris, 1987), 137–52, and "Augustine on sexual concupiscence and original sin," in vol. 22 of *Studia Patristica*, ed. E. Livingstone (Leuven, 1989), 382–86.

30. Cf. J. van Oort, *Jerusalem and Babylon. A Study into Augustine's "City of God" and the Sources of his Doctrine of the Two Cities* (Leiden, 1991), esp. 199–234 and, as regards book 11 in particular, "Manichaeism in Augustine's *De ciuitate Dei*," in: *Il 'De ciuitate Dei': L'opera, le interpretazioni, l'influsso*, ed. E. Cavalcanti (Roma, 1996), 193–214.

31. See my "Augustine's Criticism of Manichaeism: The Case of *Confessions* III,6,10 and its Implications," in *Aspects of Religious Contact and Conflict in the Ancient World*, ed. P. W. van der Horst (Utrecht, 1995), 57–68.

32. Cf. *De utilitate credendi* 36 (*Corpus Scriptorum Ecclesiasticorum Latinorum* 25.47): "Ita quod apud eos [sc., Manichaeos] *uerum* didiceram, teneo. . . ." and *Conf.* 3.7.14 (*Corpus Christianorum, Ser. Latina* 27.34): "Et catabam carmina . . ." resp. For further substantiation, see my "Augustinus als mysticus," in *Mystiek in onze tijd*, ed. G. Quispel (Zeist, 1993), 24–43, and "Augustinus und der Manichäismus," in *The Manichaean NOYS: Proceedings of the International Symposium organized in Louvain . . .* , ed. A. van Tongerloo and J. van Oort (Lovanii, 1995), 289–307.

CHAPTER 4

A CHRISTIAN GNOSTIC TEXT
The *Gospel of Truth*

JAN HELDERMAN

The *Gospel of Truth* is not a gospel in the usual sense but rather a homily of sorts or a eulogy on Christ. It offers an impressive description of the way from the dark world of ignorance, error, anguish, and terror to the blissful realm of light where the real salvation of rest with and within the Father of Truth is enjoyed. The opening lines run as follows: "The gospel of truth is joy for those who have received from the Father of truth the grace of knowing Him through the power of the Word that came forth from the Pleroma."[1] The Greek loanword used for "Gospel" in the Coptic text, *euangelion*, still has its original meaning of "proclamation," as in the New Testament. In later times the word came to be used as *terminus technicus* to indicate the book as such, the four gospels. As we will see, the *Gospel of Truth* (GT) or *Evangelium Veritatis* is a Christian and Gnostic text. With many allusions to the New Testament message, it is based upon the principle of Gnosticism. This can be clarified by the use of the word "way" as a concept. Thus, it is said in GT 18.16ff.: "Jesus the Christ enlightened those who were in darkness through oblivion, He enlightened them, he showed them a way." And then in GT 31.28ff. Jesus the beloved Son of the Father has himself become this way: "He became a way for those who were gone astray and knowledge [*sayne* = Gr. *gnôsis*] for those who were ignorant." At the end of the GT the enlightened people, the pneumatics or Gnostics, are shown as the truth themselves: "But they themselves are the truth and the Father is within them and they are in the Father" (42.25–27). The terminus of the way to Gnosis is the rest in the Father, as is made clear in GT 40.30ff.: "[H]e [the Father] brought him [the Son] forth in order to speak about the place and his resting place from which he had come forth and to glorify the pleroma, the greatness of his name and the sweetness of the Father." To reach that terminus it is necessary for the Gnostics—

53

the living who are inscribed in the book of the living (see below)—to ascend to the Father (GT 21.4–10). As to the gruesome world of darkness and ignorance, represented in GT by the intriguing figure of Error *(planè)*, and the necessity of the ascent, one is reminded of some sentences in the *Corpus Hermeticum* (CH). Thus in CH I.28 *(Poimandres)*, we read: "You who have journeyed with error *(planè)*, who have partnered with ignorance, think again: escape the shadowy light; leave corruption behind and take a share in immortality."² And regarding the ascent, CH 10 *(The Key)*.15 comes to mind: "For God does not ignore mankind; on the contrary, he recognizes him fully and wishes to be recognized. For mankind this is the only deliverance, the knowledge of God. It is ascent to Olympus."³

As we will see, especially with regard to the figure of Planè, there are indications that the GT breathes the spirit of Alexandrian religiosity, the background of the CH as well as of Gnosticism. In GT 22.13ff. we find a true Valentinian/Gnostic basic formula, concerned with leaving behind the world of error and ignorance and gaining the knowledge to salvation: "He who is to have knowledge in this manner knows where he comes from and where he is going." It is essentially the same as the famous formula of the Valentinian Theodotus, transmitted by Clement of Alexandria: "Who were we? What have we become? Where were we? Whither have we been cast? Whither do we hasten? From what have we been set free? What is birth, what rebirth?"⁴

Since the GT as a tractate is part of Codex I and, in a very fragmentary state, of the mutilated Codex XII of the Nag Hammadi Library, let me say a little about the discovery of this library.⁵

The library of papyrus manuscripts, dating from about the middle of the fourth century, consists of twelve codices plus eight leaves from a thirteenth one, and contains fifty-two separate tractates. Due to duplications (as in the case of the GT) there are forty-five separate titles. Because the majority of the library's tractates derive from the Hellenistic sects now called Gnostic, and survive in Coptic translations, it is characterized now as the Coptic Gnostic Library. Although the codices were made and inscribed about the year 350, the origin of the individual documents and their translation into Coptic (the last phase of the old language of the Pharaohs) naturally lie further back, somewhere in the second and third centuries. The discovery was named after Nag Hammadi, the nearest township of any size, about ten kilometers distant. This is the English form of the Arabic name, which is also to be found at the important railway station; it means "highly commendable place." It was in this region that two brothers, Muhammad and Khalifah of the al-Samman clan, digging for *sebach* (a kind of fertilizer) in the talus of the Jabal al Tarif in December 1945, struck upon an earthen jar sealed up with bitumen. Muhammad smashed the jar and found the leather-bound codices. The books must have been buried around 400. The fact that the "library" was hidden in a jar suggests the intention not to eliminate but rather to preserve the writings. With regard to the important question of the language and the cultural background, it is useful to quote a lengthy passage from James Robinson's introduction to the English translation of these texts:

> Although the Nag Hammadi Library is in Coptic, the texts were originally composed in Greek. Hence the fact that they were discovered in Upper-Egypt may be misleading. Some of course have been composed in Egypt, for several contain specific allusions to Egypt: *Asclepius* calls Egypt the "image of heaven"; *On the Origin of the World* appeals to "the water hydri in Egypt" and "the two bulls in Egypt" as witnesses; and *The Discourse on the Eight and the Ninth* instructs the son to "write this book for the temple at Diospolis (Magna near Luxor or Parva near Nag Hammadi) in hieroglyphic characters." Yet the Greek-writing authors may have been located anywhere in the ancient world where Greek was used, such as Greece itself (VI, 5), or Syria (II, 2), or Jordan (V, 5). Much the same is the case with the Bible and other ancient texts written in various parts of the ancient world and preserved in the "dry sands of Egypt." Thus the Nag Hammadi library involves the collecting of what was originally a Greek literary productivity by largely unrelated and anonymous authors spread through the eastern half of the ancient world and covering a period of almost half a millennium (or more, if one takes into consideration a brief section of Plato's *Republic*, VI, 5).[6]

The *Gospel of Truth* has come to be known by its opening phrase or *incipit*, which could have served as a title in antiquity, as did the *incipit* in the Gospel of Mark and the Revelation of John in the New Testament. The work was composed in Greek around 150 and shows features characteristics of the Greek Rhetorica. Interestingly, Jacques E. Ménard made a retroversion in Greek that, its hypothetical character notwithstanding, can be of use while interpreting the text.[7]

Since the *Gospel of Truth* was connected with Valentinus as its possible author as early as in the first publications about the find near Nag Hammadi, a short reminder of facts of his life as communicated by the church fathers is necessary. Valentinus was born in Lower Egypt (presumably in Paralia near the Burullus lagoon at the coast of the Mediterranean)[8], ca. 100 A.D., probably in a Greek-speaking family (in spite of his Latin name, which may have been given later). In Alexandria he received a thorough Hellenistic education, and he must have embraced Christianity there. Later he went to Rome, where he taught quite a long period from 135–65 under the bishops Hyginus, Pius, and Anicetus. He almost became bishop himself, but the congregation preferred the martyr Pius (143). It is important to notice that Valentinus worked in Rome at the same time as Marcion and Justinus Martyr. It is said that after having left Rome, he went to Cyprus.[9]

Initially, Valentinus's authorship of the *Gospel of Truth* was put into doubt by the fact that the latter did not display the well-known characteristics of Valentinianism, such as the emanation of thirty aeons from the Father, the fall and redemption of Sophia, the role of the Demiurge, and the partition of mankind into three classes *(pneumatici, psychici,* and *hylici).* In the debate on the supposed authorship of Valentinus, a famous but quite dark passage from Irenaeus's *Adversus haereses* (namely 3.11.9) always emerges. For the sake of clarity I will quote the passage in full:

> Those who are from Valentinus, setting themselves outside of any fear and producing their own compositions, take pride in the fact that they have more gospels than there really are. For, they even have advanced to such a degree of audacity that they entitle the gospel *written not long ago by themselves* [*ab his non olim conscriptum est*] as the "Gospel of Truth," although it does not at all conform to the gospels of the apostles, so that not even the gospel exists among them without blasphemy. For, if what is produced by them is the "Gospel of Truth", and if it is dissimilar to those which have been transmitted to us by the apostles, those who wish to do so can learn—as is shown by the scriptures themselves—that what has been transmitted by the apostles is not the Gospel of Truth.[10]

It is evident that the italicized line, when taken literally, denies an authorship by one single person, i.e., by Valentinus himself. The passage, which has been debated and denounced for a long period, particularly because of the italicized line, recently came under heavy fire from the German scholar Christoph Markschies. In his book *Valentinus Gnosticus?* he laments about the *ab his* line: "I do not understand how one can overlook the difference here between singular and plural."[11] Granted that he is right on this point, there are other grounds that argue for the authorship of Valentinus. As to the passage concerned however, it has been observed that Irenaeus could possibly have chosen this peculiar formulation for polemical reasons. Standaert's conclusion—"[W]e are dealing here with apologetic clichés"[12]—may be formulated too strongly: the "hi vero qui sunt a Valentino" and their only recently concocted gospel as contrasted with the "nos" of Irenaeus and the old gospels, "quae ab Apostolis nobis tradita sunt" could have brought about Irenaeus's wording.[13] Another possibility is that the *Gospel of Truth* with which Irenaeus may have been more or less acquainted was in some ways different from the Nag Hammadi text.[14]

   As to Mr. Markschies, it is interesting to see how he (attacking the views of scholars in favor of Valentinus's authorship) puts forward his own hypothesis that Valentinus was no Gnostic at all but a talented theologian halfway between Philo and Clement of Alexandria.[15] The main foundation for this quite provocative hypothesis is a thorough degnostification of the so-called *Fragments* transmitted by (among others) Clement of Alexandria, which were certainly written by Valentinus.

   In my opinion, there are sound reasons for assuming Valentinus's authorship of the GT. First of all, there is that important passage in Irenaeus's *Adversus haereses* 1.21.4 and especially the following clause: "Perfect salvation is the cognition itself of the ineffable greatness: *for since through Ignorance came about Defect and Passion, the whole system springing from Ignorance is dissolved by knowledge.*" Irenaeus is discussing the Valentinian views here. This is the fundamental doctrine of Valentinian Christian Gnostic thought.[16] Now, one should link this concept (Gnosis abolishes the precosmic ignorance that led to this execrable world) with the *fourth fragment* of Valentinus, which regarding the immortality of the children of Life says: "For you dissolve the world, you will not be dissolved, be lord over the creation and over the whole ruin."[17] Very important in my view is that the same central verb is used in both texts, namely, *katalyesthai,* "to be dissolved." Markschies gives an interpretation of the verb from John (1 John. 3:8) and Paul's 1 Cor. 7.31 on the one hand, and Plato's *Phaedo* on the other, and is compelled to give a forced, unconvincing explanation of Valentinus's deviation from the apostle John.[18] He then mentions in a footnote EV 24.33–36 and declares: "What seems to link Valentinus' sermon (= Fr. 4) and the *Evangelium Veritatis* can actually be explained as a common reference to John, and should certainly not be used immediately as an clue for solving the question of the authorship of the Nag Hammadi text"[19].

What Markschies fails to see, however, and therefore does not mention, is the close relationship between the Fragment 4 and *Adv. haer.* 1.21.4.[20] And it is precisely this relationship, with which one has to connect GT 24–25, that is the heart of the matter. Hans Jonas already connected *Adv. haer.* 1.21.4 with the GT and concluded his study with these words: "The logic of this message is the one of the Valentinian systematic principle: it, as expressed by the closing figure of the "Formula" (= I, 21, 4), is however the basic idea of the Gospel of Truth."[21] Kurt Rudolph, too, says with regard to the clause in *Adv. haer.* 1.21.4: "This corresponds with what is said in the Gospel of Truth."[22] He then follows with GT 24.28–25.19, where we read:

> Since the deficiency originated because they [the powers] did not know the Father, then when they know the Father the deficiency from this time on will no longer exist. Just as a man's ignorance is dissolved of itself when he comes to know, as darkness dissolves when the light appears, so also the deficiency dissolves in the perfection. From this time on the [external] "form" is no longer visible, but it will be dissolved in the union with the oneness . . . at the time in which unity will perfect the "spaces" [i.e., the aeons]. From the unity each one will [again] receive himself. Through knowledge he will unify himself out of diversity into unity, devouring the matter in himself like a fire, darkness through light, death through life.

The occurrence of ignorance and darkness in GT 24.33 and 24.37 reminds the reader of the beginning of the GT. It is there that Error/Planè appears as a personified entity. This Planè figure is often regarded as a kind of Valentinian demiurge. Before we will take a closer look at this equation, we should read GT 17.10–18.20, where ignorance and darkness belong to the world of Planè:

[I]gnorance of the Father brought about anguish and terror; and the anguish grew solid like a fog, so that no one was able to see. For this reason error became powerful; it worked on its own matter foolishly, not having known the truth. It set about with a creation, preparing with power and beauty the substitute for the truth.

This was not, then, a humiliation for him, the incomprehensible, inconceivable one, for they were nothing, the anguish and the oblivion and the creature of deceit, while the established truth is immutable, imperturbable, perfect in beauty. For this reason, despise error.

Thus it had no root; it fell into a fog regarding the Father, while it was involved in preparing works and oblivions and terrors, in order that by means of these it might entice those of the middle and capture them.

The oblivion of error was not revealed. It is not a [. . .] from the Father. Oblivion did not come into existence from the Father, although it did indeed come into existence because of him. But what comes into existence in him is knowledge, which appeared in order that oblivion might vanish and the Father might be known. Since oblivion came into existence because the Father was not known, then if the Father comes to be known, oblivion will not exist from that moment on.

Through this, the gospel of the one who is searched for, which <was> revealed to those who are perfect through the mercies of the Father, the hidden mystery, Jesus, the Christ, enlightened those who were in darkness through oblivion. He enlightened them; he showed (them) a way; and the way is the truth which he taught them.

In my opinion, Planè is not at all some kind of Valentinian demiurge, but reflects the wandering Isis as described in Plutarch's *De Iside et Osiride* 54:

For the procreation of Apollo by Isis and Osiris, which occurred when the gods were still in the womb of Rhea, intimates that before this world became manifest and was completed by Reason (Logos), *matter*, being shown by its nature to be incapable of itself, *brought forth the first creation*. For this reason they declare that god to have been born maimed in the darkness and they call him the Elder Horus; for he was *not the world, but only a picture and a vision of the world to come*.

In an earlier study on this topic I wrote:

Together with the Hyle-character of Isis, it is thoroughly understandable that *this* Isis-figure could easily be "gnostified" so to say. By her hylic identity she became entangled against her will in the Typhonic sphere of ignorance *(agnoia)*. Once subjected to such a process of degradation, one can easily ascertain the difference with the positive Demiurge of Valentinianism. One could understand that the author of the *Gos. Truth* experienced the famous goddess Isis, celebrated and worshipped in her mysteries in Alexandria in such a way, that he as a Christian Gnostic would have degraded her from the positive goddess of wisdom to the extremely negative Planè. . . . But *why* was it then that this evil character was described especially as *Planè?* In our opinion this was done by the author of the *Gos. Truth* on the basis of the wanderings *(planai)* Isis had to make in her seeking for Osiris. I therefore think it thoroughly feasible that the author of the *Gos. Truth* *devaluated Isis*, goddess of wisdom, harmony and tenacious seeking for truth (the highest god) *towards the opposite: Error embodied*. The Gnostic, disappointed in philosophy, mysteries etc. as a means to reach ultimate certainty concerning the questions of life, sought in *another* direction. Isis underwent an unlimited *Metamorphosis* and became an evil demon, personification of restlessness and instability, whereas the revealed truth is unshakable, leading to the ultimate goal of gnostic salvation: *Rest. So Isis became Planè*. Not her quality as Hyle—how very essential that really was (ch. 54: leading to miscarriage)—but *her wandering* was stressed and *selected, because that would not lead to the truth in gnostic opinion.*[23]

So not "an alternative version of that myth of Sophia (and the Demiurge),"[24] but Planè modeled upon the goddess Isis.

The significance of the Isis-Planè hypothesis is that it makes it probable that the author of GT was acquainted with the Hellenistic-Alexandrian *Bildungsgut*. And was not Valentinus acquainted with that *Bildungsgut*, having been educated in Alexandria? So not only the set of three Valentinian texts (Fr. 4, *Adv. haer.* 1.21.4 and GT 24/25) but also the Isis/Planè hypothesis points to Valentinus as the possible author of the *Gospel of Truth*.

There is one further point that is of great moment for the question of authorship (to put it on a broader base), showing to the modern reader the deeply religious character of the author. I mean the passage in GT 43.1ff. where the author points to his own blissful experience: "that it is not fitting for me, having come to be in the resting place to speak of anything else. But it is in it that I shall come to be and it is fitting to be concerned at all times with the Father of the all and the true brothers."

Here speaks a mystic, a true Gnostic, a Christian Gnostic for that matter, about his own experience of the blessed rest in the Father: in anticipation, being still on earth, but for *ever*, after departing from body and time. And does not this communication of that experience fit with another communication, namely in fragment 7 of Valentinus? There it is said: "Valentinus says that he saw a small newly born child and trying to learn whom he might be, he [the child] answered and said that he was the Logos."[25] Valentinus as a visionary.

To give an impression of the contents and the subdivision of the *Gospel of Truth*, I reproduce here the structure as proposed by Attridge:[26]

A. *Ignorance and Revelation* (17.4–24.9)
I. *The Rule of Error* (17.4–18.11)
Error arises from Ignorance (17.4–17.20)
Qualification: Error is not humiliation for the Father (17.21–17.29)
Error produces a Fog (17.29–17.36)
Qualification: Oblivion is not due to the Father (17.36–18.11)
II. *The Coming of the Revealer* (18.11–19.27)
Revelation comes through Jesus (18.11–18.21)
Revelation produces persecution (18.21–18.31)
Qualification: Though the Father retains perfection, he is not jealous (18.31–19.10)
Jesus as teacher (19.10–19.27)
III. *Revelation as a Book* (19.27–24.9)
Jesus revealed the living Book in the hearts of the little children (19.27–20.14)
The Book as Edict and Testament (20.15–21.2)
The Book as Book of Life (21.2–21.25)
Excursus: Reception of the Book predetermined by calling the name (21.25–22.20)
Excursus: Revelation brings return from error (22.20–22.37)
The Book as Book of Living Letters (22.38–23.18)
Transition: Hymn of the Word (23.18–24.9)

B. *The Effects of Revelation* (24.9–33.32)
IV. *Revelation unifies* (24.9–27.7)
Revelation eliminates deficiencies and restores Unity (24.9–25.18)
Revelation destroys the effect (Jars broken) (25.19–26.27)
Revelation unites with the Father (26.28–27.7)
V. *Revelation brings authentic existence* (27.7–30.16)
Revelation informs, names and matures (27.7–27.34)

Excursus: Ignorance is potential existence (27.34–28.31)
Revelation awakens from a dream-like existence (28.32–30.16)
VI. *Revelation brings a return to the Father* (30.16–33.32)
The Spirit awakens and reveals the Son (30.16–30.32)
The Son's speaking brings return (30.32–31.13)
The Son's speaking destroys error and shows a way (31.13–31.35)
The Son and shepherd (31.35–32.30)
Transition: Paraenesis (32.31–33.32)

C. *The Process of Return* (33.33–43.24)
VII. *Redemption is a gentle attraction* (33.33–36.39)
The Father's children are his fragrance which returns to him (33.33–34.34)
Qualification: Delay in the return is not due to the Father (34.34–35.23)
The breath of incorruptibility produces forgiveness (The Physician) (35.24–36.13)
The Message about Christ is the Father's merciful ointment (36.13–36.39)
VIII. *Return is by the will and through the Name of the Father* (36.39–40.23)
The will and word of the Father (36.39–38.6)
The name of the Father is the Son (38.6–38.24)
The greatness of the Name (38.24–39.28)
Excursus: Objection to the "Name" doctrine (39.28–40.23)
IX. *Goal of return: Rest in the Father* (40.23–43.24)
The Son speaks about the place of rest (40.23–41.14)
The relation of the emanations to the Father (41.14–42.10)
The relation of the blessed to the Father (42.11–42.38)
The place of the Father's worthy children (42.39–43.24)

Having read already some rather disclosing passages from the GT we will, in conclusion, pay attention to a few additional themes and topics. Obviously, it is impossible to discuss all the main subjects of this so significant gospel in one article. Having indicated above the level of education of the author and his familiarity with the Hellenistic-Alexandrian *Bildungsgut*, we will first discuss a passage that was clearly inspired by Homer's *Iliad*, book 22, lines 199–201, where we read: "As in a dream a man is not able to follow one who runs from him; nor can the runner escape nor the other pursue him, so he could not run him down in his speed nor the other get clear."[27] Now we read GT 28.32–30.6:

Thus they were ignorant of the Father, he being the one whom they did not see. Since it was terror and disturbance and instability and doubt and division, there were many illusions at work by means of these, and [they were] empty fictions, as if they were sunk in sleep and found themselves in disturbing dreams. Either [there is] a place to which they are fleeing, or without strength they come [from] having chased after others, or they are involved in striking blows, or they are receiving blows themselves, or they have fallen from high places, or they take off into the air though they do not even have wings. Again, sometimes [it is as] if people were murdering them, though there is no one even pursuing them, or they themselves are killing their neighbors, for they have been stained with their blood. When those who are going through all these things wake up, they see nothing, they who were in the midst of all these disturbances, for they are nothing. Such is the way of those who have cast ignorance aside from them like sleep, not esteeming it as anything, nor do they esteem its works as solid things either, but they leave them behind like a dream in the night. The knowledge of the Father they value as the dawn.

The next passage treats the Gnostics *in statu renascendi* as *living letters* of a living book, each Gnostic being a letter of truth, which the Father has written in order that all of them after having been awakened will reach the knowledge of the Father, to which they were for sure destined, being written by him:[28]

> This is the knowledge of the living book which he revealed to the aeons, at the end, as [his letters], revealing how they are not vowels nor are they consonants, so that one might read them and think of something foolish, but they are letters of the truth which they alone speak who know them. Each letter is a complete <thought> like a complete book, since they are letters written by the Unity, the Father having written them for the aeons in order that by means of his letters they should know the Father. (GT 22.39–23.19)

A very large and revealing passage deals with the Name: the Name of the Father and of the Son. The Name here means the essence or fundamental reality of the Father (which is reminiscent of Jewish speculations on the ineffable name of God, the *Shem hammephorash*). The Son *bears* the Name but also *is* that Name, because he is identical with the

Father, yet is distinct from him, so that he can reveal the Father to his children. The last line of the GT has it in such an appealing way: "And his children are perfect and worthy of his name for He is the Father: it is children of this kind that He loves" (GT 43.20–22). The passage runs from 38.5 to 41.2 and is therefore the largest one in the GT. The Name *(ren)* occurs fifty-four times in the GT and from that total amount forty-two times in this passage on the Name. The Name is often connected with the central theme of the Rest, the repose of the Gnostics in the Father.[29] To get an impression we read these passages:

> In this way, then, the name is a great thing. Who, therefore, will be able to utter a name for him, the great name, except him alone to whom the name belongs and the sons of the name in whom rested the name of the Father, (who) in turn themselves rested in his name? (GT 38.24–34)

> The Son is his name. He did not, therefore, hide it in the thing, but it existed; as for the Son, he alone gave a name. The name, therefore, is that of the Father, as the name of the Father is the Son. (GT 39.20–26)

> For that very reason he brought him forth in order to speak about the place and his resting-place from which he had come forth, and to glorify the pleroma, the greatness of his name and the sweetness of the Father. (GT 40.30–41.2)

The last passage we will discuss is a jubilant one. Here we are eye to eye with the fundamental Gnostic idea of the *consubstantiality* (to use an expression from the theological field) of the Father and his children, the Gnostics. It depicts the eschatological reunion of the Father (who has his root in the Gnostics) with the children (being the truth themselves) having their root in him. For them there will be no Amente (the name of old for hell or Hades in pharaonic and Hellenistic Egypt), no death, but indeed only repose in the Father. We read this passage:

> And they do not go down to Hades nor have they envy nor groaning nor death within them, but they rest in him who is at rest, not striving nor being twisted around the truth. But they themselves are the truth; and the Father is within them and they are in the Father, being perfect, being undivided in the truly good one, being in no way deficient in anything, but they are set at rest, refreshed in the Spirit. And they

will heed their root. They will be concerned with those (things) in which he will find his root. (GT 42.19–36)

It is this reciprocity of the Father and the Gnostics (better: the Pneumatics), partaking of the same pneumatic essence in the Pleroma, that impresses the modern reader too.

As noticed in the beginning of this article, many allusions to New Testament material are found in the EV. Remarkable is the way in which New Testament texts are most of the time reinterpreted, and in so doing receive another focus: a Gnostic one. First of all, Jesus Christ is mentioned in GT 18.16 and 18.24ff. In 18.24ff. it is said that he was nailed to a tree. In sharp contrast with Planè, who was brought to naught (GT 18.24), the crucified Jesus became a fountain of life. The crucifixion was not for the atonement of sins; instead, "he became a fruit of the knowledge of the Father." The cross is reinterpreted, as is the Tree of the Knowledge of Good and Evil (Gen. 2:9). Now the cross is seen as the "tree of the knowledge of the Father." In contradiction to Gen. 2:17, eating of the fruits of the tree is a good, positive act: "[T]o those who ate it it gave [cause] to become glad in the discovery" (GT 18.26–30). In GT 20.24–29 it is said: "Jesus appeared, he put on that book; he was nailed to a tree, he published the edict of the Father on the cross *(stauros)*. O, such great teaching." In Col. 2:14 Paul observes that Jesus blotted out the handwriting of ordinances that was against us, nailing it to his cross. In the GT, on the contrary, no attention is paid to an accusation done away with by Christ's act of atonement on the cross; instead, Jesus is lifted up on the cross and so publishes the "living book," the revelation of the essence of the Father. Therefore, the author exclaims in deep joy: "O, such great [Gnostic] teaching!" The third mention of Christ, in GT 36.14, is not important as to Gnostic reinterpretation, it being a pun on "Christ" in the context of anointing, ointment.

In GT 33.19–21 the devil is mentioned in the following way: "Do not become a dwelling place for the devil *(diabolos)* for you have already brought him to naught." This is probably an allusion to Eph. 4:27 and to the gist of Fragment 2 of Valentinus, where the human heart is depicted as an inn, a residence for foul demons, till the only good Father looks in mercy at the heart, so that it is filled with light.[30]

For the use of other biblical material in EV 1, refer to the studies of Tuckett and Evans *cum suis*.[31]

SUMMARY

The *Gospel of Truth* was, in my opinion, most probably written by Valentinus shortly before he left Rome. In a characteristic Christian-Gnostic way, it teaches that salvation means the knowledge of the Father and the Rest, the *anapausis* in him. This salvation is presented as what is called "realized eschatology." Even in earthly life the pneumatic will enjoy in anticipation the fruits of knowledge destined for her and him.[32] "O such great teaching" indeed!

The *Gospel of Truth* is best viewed as an exoteric work meant for the Christian community (the developing *grande église*). The author takes care to avoid giving offense to the community at large. Rather, he is trying to win people over to his interpretation of the truth of the gospel. Using biblical and (for that matter) especially New Testament motifs, he cannot avoid certain ambiguities and concealments of the implications of the glad tidings in a true Gnostic sense. In the beginning part of his writing he quite succeeds in this approach; later on he cannot restrain himself, as it were. I conclude with an observation by Carsten Colpe: "At the outset of the *Gospel of Truth* one gets the impression that the text is Christian. But by the end the reader knows that impression was wrong. The initial disguise of the essentially non-Christian viewpoint seems to have been intentional."[33] Valentinus Gnosticus.

NOTES

1. For reasons of efficiency we use the English translation in H. W. Attridge, ed., *Nag Hammadi Codex I*, I (*Text*) and II (*Commentary*) Nag Hammadi Studies 22 and 23 (Leiden, 1985), 83. The *Gospel of Truth* was edited, translated, and commented upon by H. W. Attridge and G. W. MacRae. Henceforth, the text is quoted by the page and line numbers of the manuscript only.

2. See A. D. Nock and A. J. Festugière, eds. *Corpus Hermeticum*, vol. 1 (Paris, 1945), 16–17; translation B. P. Copenhaver, *Hermetica* (Cambridge, 1992), 6, 120 (commentary).

3. See Nock and Festugière, *Corpus Hermeticum*, 1:120; translation Copenhaver, *Hermetica*, 33.

4. See F. Sagnard, *Clément d'Alexandrie. Extraits de Théodote* (Paris, 1970) [= *Sources Chrétiennes* 23], 202. Cf. J. Helderman, *Die Anapausis im Evangelium Veritatis* (Leiden, 1984), 26, 92.

5. The facts of the discovery are taken from K. Rudolph, *Gnosis: The Nature*

and History of Gnosticism (Edinburgh, 1983) (English translation of the German original), 42; J. M. Robinson, *The Nag Hammadi Library in English*, 3d ed. (Leiden, 1988), ix (preface), 2, 20, 22–23 (introduction).

6. Robinson, *Nag Hammadi Library*, 12–13.

7. J. E. Ménard, *L'Evangile de Vérité: Retroversion grecque et commentaire* (Paris, 1962).

8. See J. Helderman, "Das Evangelium Veritatis in der neueren Forschung," in *Aufstieg und Niedergang der Römischen Welt* II, 25.5 (Berlin and New York, 1988), 4066–69. Markschies's criticism (see note 11, below), 315–17, is not convincing.

9. The data on Valentinus's life can be found, inter alia, in A. Harnack, *Geschichte der altchristlichen Literatur* (Leipzig, 1893), 1:174–84; H. Jonas, *The Gnostic Religion*, 2d ed. (Boston, 1963), 178; K. Grobel, *The Gospel of Truth* (New York, 1960), 12–13; Rudolph, *Gnosis*, 317–18; and J. Helderman, 'Evangelium Veritatis,' 4064–69.

10. See the text in A. Rousseau and L. Doutreleau, eds., *Irénée de Lyon: Contre les Hérésies*, Livre 3, Sources Chrétiennes 211 (Paris, 1974), 172–74.

11. "Ich verstehe nicht, wie man den Unterschied zwischen Singular und Plural hier übersehen kann." Chr. Markschies, *Valentinus Gnosticus? Untersuchungen zur valentinianischen Gnosis mit einem Kommentar zu den Fragmenten Valentins*, Wissenschaftliche Untersuchungen zum Neuen Testament 65 (Tübingen, 1992), 344.

12. "Il s'agit de clichés apologétiques." B. Standaert, "'Evangelium Veritatis' et 'Veritatis Evangelium'," *Vigiliae Christianae* 30 (1976): 144–45. Attridge, *Text*, 65 n. 6 has a lapse; for "1970," read "1976."

13. See further Grobel, *Gospel of Truth*, 18–19; H. C. Puech, G. Quispel, and W. C. van Unnik, *The Jung Codex: A Newly Recovered Gnostic Papyrus* (London, 1955), 100–101; F. M. M. Sagnard, *La gnose Valentinienne et le témoignage de Saint Irénée* (Paris, 1947), 106–7.

14. Cf. Attridge, *Text*, 66, where it is said "That the two 'gospels of Truth' are identical remains a distinct possibility."

15. Markschies, *Valentinus Gnosticus?*, 404–7.

16. The text is to be found in A. Rousseau and L. Doutreleau, eds., *Irénée de Lyon: Contre les Hérésies*, Livre 1, Sources Chrétiennes 264 (Paris, 1979), 302. See ad hoc H. Jonas, *Gnosis und Spätantiker Geist*, 3d ed., vol. 1, (Göttingen, 1964), 206 n. 2, 375, 418; Sagnard, *Gnose Valentinienne*, 420; Helderman, *Anapausis*, 89–91. Translation from Jonas, *Gnostic Religion*, 176.

17. The text is to be found in W. Völker, *Quellen zur Geschichte der christlichen Gnosis* (Tübingen, 1932), 58.

18. Markschies, *Valentinus Gnosticus?*, 143–44.

19. "Was Valentins Homilie (= Fr. 4) und das *'Evangelium Veritatis'* scheinbar verbindet, kann als gemeinsamer Bezug auf Johannes erklärt werden und darf keinesfalls sofort als Indiz für die Lösung der Verfasserfrage des Nag Hammadi-Textes ausgewertet werden." Ibid., 144.

20. Ibid., 354. Cf. a similar interpretation given by J. Holzhausen, "Gnosis und Martyrium: Zu Valentins viertem Fragment," *Zeitschrift für die Neutestamentliche Wissenschaft* 85 (1994): 116–31, esp. 128–29.

21. "Die Logik dieser Botschaft ist die des valentinianischen Systemprinzips: eben sie, wie die Schlußfigur der 'Formel' (= I, 21, 4) sie ausdrückt, ist aber auch der Grundgedanke des Evangeliums der Wahrheit." Jonas, *Gnosis*, 1:418; cf. his *Gnostic Religion*, 176.

22. Rudolph, *Gnosis*, 116. We prefer Rudolph's translation here; Attridge, *Text*, 93–94 is a bit shallow.

23. J. Helderman, "Isis as Planè in the Gospel of Truth?," in *Gnosis and Gnosticism*, ed. M. Krause, Nag Hammadi Studies 17 (Leiden, 1981), 26–46. We quote here from 34, 39, and 44–45.

24. Attridge, *Commentary*, 44. The equation of Planè and Demiurge is denied also by E. Pagels, in *The Rediscovery of Gnosticism*, ed. B. Layton (Leiden, 1980), 1:345.

25. See for the text Völker, *Quellen*, 59.

26. See Attridge, *Text*, 69-71. For other structures and divisions, see Helderman, "Evangelium Veritatis," 4082–90.

27. In connection with the *Gospel of Truth* this passage was first mentioned by H. Ch. Puech and G. Quispel, *Op zoek naar het Evangelie der Waarheid* (Nijkerk, 1955), 36.

28. See the remarks on the topic in Attridge, *Commentary*, 57, 67–68. See further, for Valentinian alphabet-speculation, F. Dornseiff, *Das Alphabet in Mystik und Magie* (Berlin, 1925; reprint, Leipzig, 1975), 126–33.

29. See Helderman, *Anapausis*, 168-200; and Attridge, *Commentary*, 117–18, 126.

30. See Völker, *Quellen*, 58; cf. the "holy and silent house" in GT 25.21–25.

31. See Chr. Tuckett, *Nag Hammadi and the Gospel Tradition: Synoptic Tradition in the Nag Hammadi Library* (Edinburgh, 1986), 57–68; C. A. Evans, R. L. Webb, R. A. Wiebe, *Nag Hammadi Texts and the Bible: A Synopsis and Index* (Leiden and New York, 1993), 19–41.

32. The question of realized eschatology is a very important one. The German term is *präsentische Eschatologie*. Two significant observations should be made here. In 1932 F. C. Burkitt (*Church and Gnosis: A Study of Christian Thought and Speculation in the Second Century* [Cambridge, 1932]) maintained that "the prime factor in the rise of the Gnostic systems is connected with what is commonly called now Eschatology, that is to say, the problem raised for the Christian Church by the non-arrival of the Last Day and of the confidently expected Second Coming of Christ" (10). And the remark very recently made by K. Koschorke ("Gnosis, Montanismus, Mönchtum: Zur Frage emanzipatorischer Bewegungen im Raum der Alten Kirche," *Evangelische Theologie* 53 [1993]: 216–31): "Meine *These* ist also die, daß die emanzipatorischen Tendenzen der Gnosis in engem Zusammenhang stehen mit der *präsentischen Eschatologie* der Bewegung" (221).

33. See Layton, *Rediscovery* (Leiden, 1981), 2:668.

CHAPTER 5

THE *ASCLEPIUS*
From the Hermetic Lodge in Alexandria to
the Greek Eucharist and the Roman Mass

G. QUISPEL

SURSUM CORDA

Pyotr Ilich Tchaikovsky once said: "The liturgy of Saint John Chrysostom
is one of the greatest of all artistic creations." And he composed music
to accompany it. This liturgy of John Chrysostom is celebrated almost
every Sunday in all Greek, Russian, and other Slavonic churches. It may
not be due to the pen of the church father, who lived about 400 A.D., but
it does come from Antioch, where John lived and worked before he
became patriarch of Constantinople in 398. And it has old roots there.

The Roman Mass is also a beautiful work of art. Until recently it
was celebrated every day in beautiful Latin in all Roman Catholic
churches of the globe. It consists of two parts. First the priests pray and
sing, read lessons from Scripture, and preach if they want to. This part
was simply taken over from the synagogical service, as it must have been
performed at the time everywhere in the Roman Empire. Then follows
the celebration of the sacrament of bread and wine, the reenactment
and representation of Jesus' last meal and sacrifice on the cross. It is
introduced by the so-called Preface.

The priest says: *Dominus vobiscum*, "The Lord *is* with you," thus
affirming that God is present among the faithful through his Spirit. In
antiquity the whole congregation answered: *Et cum spirito tuo*, "And with
thy spirit," alluding to the special charisma of the priest, which was
thought to be enhanced by this acclamation.

Thereupon the priest exclaims: *Sursum corda*, "Lift up your hearts."
The congregation answers: *Habemus ad Dominum*, "We have lifted them
up to the Lord." Thereby the faithful affirm that they have ascended
here and now to heaven, where Christ lives in eternal glory.

69

Then the priest invites all to give thanks to God: *Gratias agamus Domino Deo nostro*, "Let us give thanks to the Lord our God." The congregation answers: *Vere dignum et iustum est*, "It is truly meet and just, right and available to salvation that we always and in all places give thanks to Thee, o Holy Lord." From this thanksgiving (Greek: *eucharistia*) the whole celebration is called the Eucharist.

And the priest goes on to thank God and asks the congregation to join in the song of the angels before God's throne, who do not cease to cry out daily, singing with one voice *(una voce):* "Holy, holy, holy is the Lord God," the so-called *Sanctus*. The angels sing with one voice in heaven above. And the faithful are also there; they harmonize with the angels.

The Greek Eucharist differs considerably from the Roman Mass. It is the enactment of the sacrifice of God for his people, whereas the Missa Romana is a sacrifice of the people to God. The Greeks venerate in their liturgy the Unknown God beyond understanding, they venerate Christ, who in a mysterious way sacrifices and is sacrificed and whose Spirit is invoked upon the faithful and upon the elements of bread and wine in order to divinize the initiates who participate in this mystery, just as it happened before Christ in the mysteries of Eleusis and Orpheus. The Greek Eucharist is Hellenic.

The style of the Roman Mass, on the contrary, is hieratic. It calls to mind the songs of the ancient Roman priests, which addressed an awe-inspiring deity, who had to be placated and propitiated: *Satur fu, fere Mars*, "be satiated, ferocious Mars," sang the *fratres Arvales* in their procession around the fields.[1] The Latin word *hostia* (host), which to pagans meant "a sacrificial animal" and came to mean in the Latin of the Christians "consecrated wafer," shows more than anything else how related Old Roman prayer books and the Roman Mass are. In the Roman Mass God is a tremendous majesty, who is to be atoned by the sacrifice offered to him. The aim and purpose of the Roman Mass is atonement; of the Greek Eucharist, at-one-ment.

And yet, the structure of the Roman Mass is essentially the same as that of the Greek liturgy: mass of the catechumens, mass of the faithful, preceded by the Preface. Both are said to be a thanksgiving *(eucharistia)* and a spiritual sacrifice. In Greek the latter is called *logikè thysia;* in Latin it has a curious name: *oblatio rationabilis*. In the words of the consecration:

Which *oblation* do thou, o God, vouchsafe in all respects to make blessed, approved, ratified, *reasonable* and acceptable, that it may become for us the body and blood of Thy most beloved Son, Jesus Christ our Lord.

In the Greek Eucharist too the faithful lift up their hearts to heaven and sing with the angels there: "Holy, holy, holy."

The idea that the faithful make a heavenly journey during the Eucharist is not just simply a metaphor, but must be taken quite literally. It is alluded to in a passage of the second writing of the Jung Codex, the *Apocryphal Letter of James*. It tells how on Ascension Day, the first Holy Thursday, Jesus manifested himself for the last time to his brother James and the fisherman Peter and ascended on high:

> After He had said this, He departed.
> But we knelt down, I [James] and Peter,
> *we gave thanks* and *sent* up our *hearts* toward the heavens.
> We heard with our ears and saw with our eyes
> the sound of wars and a trumpet-sound and a great
> disturbance.
> And when we had passed beyond that place,
> we sent up our minds still higher
> and we saw with our eyes and heard with our ears
> hymns and praises of the angels and a rejoicing of angels
> and greatnesses of the heavens were singing hymns
> *and we also were rejoicing.*[2]

James and Peter ascend first to the first heaven, of the seven planets, where a war between good and evil spirits is going on, and then to the second heaven of the fixed stars, where angels sing hymns of praise in honor of God above, and they themselves join in with their holy songs. Their ascension is quite real; they become "high." The terminology of this heavenly journey ("gave thanks," "we also") clearly is an allusion to the liturgy, where the hearts are lifted up during the Eucharist and man sings in harmony with the angels.

The *Apocryphal Letter of James* was written in Egypt in the second century. The priority of James rather than Peter hints at Judaic Christianity, which was dominated by James the brother of the Lord. Egyptian Christianity was founded by Palestinian missionaries from Jerusalem.

The concept of the heavenly ascent during the service of the liturgy is very primitive indeed. In any case, this passage proves that the *sursum corda* and *cum omni militia caelestis exercitus* of the Roman Mass can be as old as the second century.

What about *una voce*, the belief that the angels sing with one voice? That expression was also familiar to the Jewish Christians of Alexandria. In a Jewish Christian writing of the first century, composed in Egypt and describing the ascent of the prophet Isaiah through the seven heavens, he hears in the sixth heaven the song of praise of the angels there:

> I sang praise with them. . . . And then they all named the primal Father and his Beloved, Christ, and the Holy Spirit, *all with one voice*.[3]

UNA VOCE

About the beginning of the common era the heavenly journey of the soul was the topic of the day. The greatest writers of Latin literature used this theme as a literary device.

In his *Dream of Scipio* Cicero tells us how a Roman general in his sleep is looking down from the Milky Way upon the rest of this big universe and the earth and receives the message that all souls come from the beyond up there, but that only they who devoted themselves to the glory of their country deserve to walk on the narrow path that leads to the gates of heaven. The visionary general admires the beauty of the cosmos and listens to the harmony of the spheres, which is produced by the seven planets, a beautiful music that common mortals here on earth cannot hear, because they are accustomed to it.

Vergil describes in the sixth book of his *Aeneid* a descent to the underworld, which in reality is an ascent to Elysium on high; there Anchises, the father of the hero Aeneas, reveals to his son the glorious future of Rome.

For many people at that time this was not just literature. Not accidentally, the monograph on the subject by Ioan Couliano is called *Expériences de l'Extase*.[4] It could be an experience. The adepts of Mithras, the Persian God, were initiated into seven grades, which corresponded to the seven planets, a scale or climax with seven gates, through which the initiate had to ascend. The "magical Papyrus" which is called the *Mithras-*

liturgy and describes how one gets "high" and travels through space, is in reality a ritual of initiation that originated in Alexandria and presupposes a mystery religion there that focused on the heavenly journey of the soul.[5]

Not even the Jews were at that time an exception to the rule. The community of the Essenes was linked up with the angels:

> He (God) has joined their assembly
> to the Sons of Heaven.[6]

The hymns contained in the *Angelic Liturgy*, also from Qumran, direct the worshipper to a particular kind of religious experience, a sense of being in the heavenly sanctuary and in the presence of the angels who sing the praise of God. This experience was intended as a communal experience of the worshipping community.[7] There does moreover exist a whole literature of esoteric Judaism in Palestine, which describes how privileged rabbis traveled along the seven planets and through the seven successive palaces of heaven in order to behold the luminous and awe-inspiring Glory of God, the personal manifestation of the hidden Godhead.

The hymns of this so-called Merkabah (Throne) mysticism "describe in a plethora of solemn phrases the spirit of majesty and solemnity that permeates the heavenly realm . . . and express, too, the ideas of the writers about the many different angelic hosts and their part in the celestial liturgy. All these hymns end with the 'Holy, holy, holy,' the song of the angels transmitted by Isaiah in the sixth chapter of his prophecies. The highest angels 'sing songs and hymns, praise and rejoicing and applause, *with one voice*, with one utterance, with one mind and with one melody.'"[8]

The Hebrew words used are: *b⁽e⁾qōl ahad* (in one voice). This corresponds exactly to *una voce* of the Roman Mass. The first scholar to point this out was Gershom Scholem in his book on Jewish Gnosticism. He referred to a note on the Latin Mass by Joseph Kroll, a born Catholic. I do not believe that Scholem ever attended a Roman Catholic Mass or ever consulted a Roman missal. Had he done so, he would have seen immediately that the parallelism is even much stronger. Not only do the angels sing the *Sanctus* with one voice, but also these same hymns are the ones the mystic is instructed to recite during his ecstatic ascent to heaven. He chimes in with the angels during his stay in the heavens, exactly like the faithful do during the celebration of the Roman Mass.

Eminent specialists of the Christian liturgy have failed to pick up Scholem's hint for the simple reason that they did not read him. In general Christian theologians have been hesitant to admit that esoteric Judaism, Gnostic Judaism, as opposed to normative Judaism, is relevant for the study of primitive Christianity, of which the *Missa Romana* is a part. They remain entrenched behind the bulky volumes of Strack-Billerbeck and dismiss this material out of hand, pretending that it is medieval. And even now these Jewish documents are dated to the first three centuries of the Christian era. But their basic ideas must be much older, even pre-Christian.

It is the Hermetic literature that proves this hypothesis.

CUM ANGELIS

Owing to the new Hermetic writings that were discovered near Nag Hammadi in 1945, it has become certain that the Hermetic Gnosis was rooted in a secret society in Alexandria, a sort of Masonic lodge, with certain rites like a kiss of peace, a baptism of rebirth in the Spirit and a sacred meal of the brethren. It started with the astrologic lore contained in works like the Hermetic *Panaretos*, of the second century before the beginning of the common era.[9] Alchemical studies were also integrated into Hermetism at an early date. The seventeen treatises in Greek of the *Corpus Hermeticum* and the Hermetic *Asclepius* in Latin are later, between 1 and 300 A.D., but the ideas they contain can easily be much older.[10] As often as not, they are amplifications of short sayings, like those contained in the *Definitions of Hermes Trismegistus to Asclepius*, a new text recently discovered in Armenia and the Bodleian Library in Oxford. They never contain any train of thoughts but are manuals for meditation, destined to edify the Gnostic and further his progress through the different grades of initiation, which ultimately lead to the ascent beyond the seven planets to a realm beyond. There he beholds God and sees himself.

Greeks, Egyptians, and Jews were members of the Hermetic lodge and unanimously contributed their specific traditions to the common views. Christian influences, however, are completely absent.

During the meetings of the brethren hymns were sung, which have been preserved in part. They were considered to be "spiritual sacrifices": "Accept holy, spiritual *(logikas)* offerings from a heart and soul that reach up to Thee," says the first treatise of the *Corpus Hermeticum*, the *Poimandres*.[11] The same expression, with the same very special meaning of *logikos,* is to be found in the expression "reasonable [= spiritual] and acceptable oblation" *(oblationem rationabilem acceptabilemque)* in the consecration rite of the host in the Roman Mass. But the passage in the *Poimandres* (at latest, first century) is older than the wording of the Mass, which seems to go back to the second century A.D.

Moreover, the Hermetist knew that the angels sang hymns in praise of God and that man joins in with them: "And then, stripped of the effects of the cosmic framework, the Gnostic enters the region of the Ogdoad: he becomes his real Self and with the celestial beings on high he hymns the Father."[12] That happens after death. But it is also possible to ascend to the heaven during one's lifetime: "You heavenly Powers all, sing the hymn with me."[13] The mystic has achieved rebirth and can now sing with the angels.

The Hermetists were even familiar with the *Sanctus (Hagios)* that used to consummate the esoteric hymns of the Jewish Gnostics. This transpires from the hymn at the end of the *Poimandres*, of which every line begins with "Holy":

> Holy is the God and Father of the All;
> Holy is God, whose will is done by His angels;
> Holy is God, who desires to be known and is in fact known
> by his own.

These hymns could focus on the theme of thanksgiving, to such an extent that I am inclined to call the great and beautiful hymn, which ends the *Asclepius*, "The Eucharistic Prayer":

> We give thanks to Thee,
> with our whole soul and our whole heart lifted up unto
> Thee,
> O unutterable Name,
> honored with the appellation: "God"
> and praised with the designation: "Father,"
> because to everyone and to the All

Thou showest Thine fatherly benevolence, affection and
love
and whatever sweet and pure feeling a human being might
experience,
by graciously granting us
> spirit,
> understanding,
> Gnosis,

spirit that we may fathom Thee,
understanding that we may expound Thee,
Gnosis that we may know Thee.

All this leads me to suppose that esoteric traditions of Gnostic Jews
were current in Alexandria long before they are attested for Palestine.
The hymns of the Merkabah must have originated in liberal quarters in
Alexandria long before they were taken over by more orthodox Phari-
saic circles in Palestine. And it must have been early Christians profoundly influenced by Jewish Gnosis who first formulated the Preface
of the Roman Mass. From esoteric Jews these Christians adopted the
wonderful and impressive concept of a harmony between the initiate
above and the angels in heaven, who sing with one voice the Glory of
God: *Sanctus, sanctus, sanctus dominus deus Sabaoth.*

It would lead me too far to discuss the problem of to what extent
these hymns are prefigured in the purely pagan Hermetic hymns with
their Egyptian antecedents, which are said to be an echo of the cosmic
harmony of the spheres.[14] Let me just quote the oldest testimony of the
Roman Mass, the letter that Clement of Rome as secretary of the congregation wrote to the believers in Corinth in 95–96 A.D.:

> Let us subject ourselves to His will; let us consider how the whole
> multitude of His angels (consisting of millions) minister unto His will,
> standing before Him.
>
> For the Scripture says: Ten thousand times ten thousand stood
> before Him and thousand times thousand ministered unto Him, and
> they shouted: "*Holy, holy, holy* is the Lord Sabaoth, full is the whole
> creation of His Glory." Therefore, (noticing this unity in multitude),
> we too, in concord brought together by compliance to the Lord's will,
> let us *from one mouth* cry unto Him with fervor in order that we may
> become sharers in his great and glorious promises.[15]

As early as then they sang the *Sanctus* in Rome with one voice, like the angels.

NOTES

1. On Old Roman rituals and their influence upon the Roman Mass: Eduard Norden, *Aus altrömischen Priesterbüchern* (Lund, 1939); M. P. Ellebracht, "Ancient Orations" (diss., University of Nijmegen, 1963).

2. Nag Hammadi Codex I.15.5–23.

3. *The Ascension of Isaiah* 8.18.

4. Ioan P. Couliano, *Expériences de l'Extase* (Paris, 1984).

5. Reinhold Merkelbach, *Abraxas* (Opladen, 1992).

6. *The Community Rule*, sec. 9.

7. Carol Newsom, *Songs of the Sabbath Sacrifice. A Critical Edition* (Atlanta, 1985).

8. Gershom Scholem, *Jewish Gnosticism* (New York, 1965), 20–30. According to one manuscript of the *Greater Hekkaloth* "they sing songs and hymns, praise and rejoicing with *one voice*, with one utterance, with one mind and with one melody." Joseph Kroll, *Die Lehren des Hermes Trismegistos* (1914; reprint, Münster, 1928).

9. Ioan P. Couliano, "The Counterfeit Spirit in Manichaeism," in *Manichaica Selecta*, ed. A. van Tongerloo and S. Giversen (Louvain, 1991), 53–58; E. Boer, *Heliodori, ut dicitur, in Paulum Alexandrinum commentarium* (Leipzig, 1962).

10. Gilles Quispel, "Hermes Trismegistos and the Origins of Gnosticism," *Vigiliae Christianae* 46 (1992): 1–19. Jean-Pierre Mahé, *Hermès en Haute-Égypte*, vol. 2 (Quebec, 1982), 355–405; idem, "La voie d'Immortalité," *Vigiliae Christianae* 45 (1991): 347–75.

11. *Poimandres*, 31.

12. *Poimandres*, 26.

13. *Corpus Hermeticum* XIII.18.

14. Demetrius, *On Style*, 71, in *A Greek Critic: Demetrius on Style*, trans. G. M. A. Grube (Toronto, 1961), 79: "The priests of Egypt, when singing hymns to their gods, utter the seven vowels in succession and men listen to the singing sound of these vowels instead of to the flute or the lyre, because it is so euphonious." The seven vowels echo the harmony of the seven spheres. The Hermetists took over that device: the *voces magicae* in the Hermetic treatise *Discourse on the Eighth and the Ninth*: a, ō, e, etc. are Egyptian music, variations on the harmony of the spheres. It would be interesting to establish to what extent the idea that angels sing is derived from the Greek (more specifically, Pythagorean) theory of the harmony of the spheres.

15. 1 Clement 34.4–7.

CHAPTER 6

A READING OF THE *DISCOURSE ON THE OGDOAD AND THE ENNEAD* (NAG HAMMADI CODEX VI.6)

JEAN-PIERRE MAHÉ

The so-called *Discourse on the Ogdoad and the Ennead* is a Hermetic dialogue between a teacher and a disciple. The latter calls his teacher "my father" and several times "Hermes"[1] or "Trismegistus" (NH VI.59.15–24). The teacher calls his disciple "my son," or to translate more accurately "my child" *(pashêre/teknon)*, without using any proper name. This anonymous disciple is far from being a novice. Hermes has already explained to him all of his *General Lectures (Genikoi Logoi)* and his *Detailed Lectures (Diexodikoi Logoi)* (NH 6.63.1–2). There is only one thing left to be done: the disciple must pass through the last stage of spiritual perfection, which does not consist merely in learning but demands full personal involvement. In fact he has to undergo an initiation into the divine mysteries of the Ogdoad and the Ennead, so that he may be born again and become a new man, being directly inspired by God's intellect.

This goal cannot be reached through ordinary teaching. The point is not to convey theoretical learning but to share a specific experience, a spiritual attitude, a deep inward frame of mind. The core of this attitude is the hymn of praise *(smou = eulogia)* (NH VI.55.4, 57.10, 60.9.14.18), which lifts up the human soul and disposes it towards silent contemplation. Therefore, from the very beginning, the teaching of Hermes is introduced as a training for prayer.

Let us summarize the dialogue. In a preamble (NH VI.52.1–13) the disciple reminds Hermes that he has promised him to bring his mind first into the Ogdoad and then into the Ennead, according to the order of the tradition. Hermes agrees to making an attempt at doing so, within the limits of human abilities.

This is an abridged version of a text that will appear in French in the volume *Ecrits gnostiques*, vol. 1, *La bibliothèque copte de Nag Hammadi* (Paris).

Then follows a theoretical discussion (NH VI.52.13–55.5) and a mystical liturgy (NH VI.55.6–61.17). The latter begins with a prayer by Hermes and his disciple to the Invisible God, who is one and threefold at once, i.e., Unbegotten, Self-Begotten, and Begotten. Then the two partners, drawing attention to their spiritual nature, ask for the favor of contemplating the Ogdoad and the Ennead.

Once they have said this prayer, they kiss each other. At that very moment, the Power that is light comes down to them. Both of them are lifted up in ecstasy. The teacher explains to the disciple that they have just seen the Ogdoad with the souls that are in it and the angels singing a silent hymn to the Ennead and its Powers.

After their example, the disciple starts praying to Hermes who, from then onward, has become identical with the Self-Begotten Intellect. However, the disciple fails to attain immediately the kind of silent meditation that his teacher exhorts him to.

As soon as he reaches this goal, the disciple can see within Hermes, i.e., through the Self-Begotten Intellect, a second vision, which is far more complete than the former: he can hear how the Ogdoad sings a hymn to the Ennead. He contemplates the One who creates in the Spirit and is superior to all the Powers.

The disciple must still learn how to give thanks for the vision.

In the epilogue (NH VI.61.18–63.32), we hear that the book shall be carved on stelae of turquoise that shall be placed in the temple of Hermes in Diospolis at a specific astrological conjuncture. In addition, Hermes writes a spell directed against whoever would try to misuse the book for a bad purpose.

Both in its form and in its contents, the *Ogdoad and the Ennead* is most similar to *Corpus Hermeticum* XIII: *A secret dialogue of Hermes Trismegistus on the mountain to his son Tat. On being born again, and on the promise to be silent.*[2] The latter text, however, is formally less perfect. The author constantly wavers between visionary enthusiasm and scholastic discussions. By contrast, when in our dialogue the heavenly forces come down (NH VI.57.28–29), the theoretical discussion has been stopped for quite a while, giving way to praise and gratitude which alone can lift up to the supreme vision.

The meaning of this initiatory trip will remain obscure as long as we fail to analyze the underlying mythology of the text. Supposedly the dialogue takes place in Egypt, a matter that is strongly emphasized in the epilogue.

But to what degree does the subject matter of the dialogue—i.e., the revelation of the Ogdoad and the Ennead—derive from ancient Egyptian beliefs? As a matter of fact, the names Ogdoad and Ennead are currently used by Egyptologists as technical terms to indicate groups of primordial deities that were worshipped mainly in Hermopolis and Heliopolis. Thoth, the Egyptian ancestor of Hermes Trismegistus, had been closely associated with these deities for many centuries.

In the second century A.D., when our text was written, the words Ogdoad and Ennead would have evoked astrological ideas, namely the eighth and the ninth heavenly spheres, rather than primeval deities of Egypt. Of course, even the reinterpretation of the Ogdoad in astrological terms might well have been furthered by ancient Egyptian speculations. For example, the theologians of Heliopolis tried to work the Ogdoad into their system by assimilating it to the so-called eight Hehous, the offspring of Shou, that are the pillars that hold up the heavens. The fact remains, however, that the movement of our dialogue depends almost completely on the Hellenistic belief in astral fatality.

Soaring up to the Ogdoad means first of all getting rid of the influence of the seven planets and having access to the superior world, the abode of Divinity. We cannot understand the exact location of the Ogdoad and the Ennead, unless we refer to the vertical section of the universe discussed in the conclusion of our text. Hermes first lists, starting from the bottom, all the entities of the inferior world; then, from the top down to the bottom, all those of the superior world (NH VI.63.16–32). "I adjure whoever reads this holy book by heaven and earth and fire and the Seven Ousiarchs and the demiurgic spirit dwelling in them [thus far for the inferior world, then the superior one] and the Unbegotten God, the Self-Begotten One and him who has been Begotten, that he will guard the things that Hermes has said."

Since the lowest level of the superior world, i.e., the Begotten One, must stay above the Seven Ousiarchs, who like the Seven Governors of CH I.16 are somehow connected with the Hebdomad of the inferior world, we may assume that it is located in the Ogdoad, whereas the Self-Begotten One is in the Ennead, and the Unbegotten One is still higher.

Why does rising again to the Ogdoad and the Ennead necessarily mean being born again, or being granted *re*generation? Let us remember the origin of man and how his coming down to this world has been a *de*generation. In the Hermetic tradition, the most authoritative text in this regard is the celebrated *Poimandrès* (CH I), the first nineteen paragraphs of which should be read as a rewriting of Gen. 1:1–10:1. From this source we learn that God, the Almighty, the Maker of everything, to whom are addressed the eighteen Blessings of the Kedusha, consists in a triad including the following entities: (1) Sovereignty (Authentia), (2) Intellect, and (3) Holy Word, the latter being most likely identical to the Spirit of God, who according to Gen. 1:2 was moving upon the face of the waters. The first two entities may be regarded as unbegotten and self-begotten, whereas the Holy Word is begotten, since it is "the son of God coming from his Intellect" (CH I.6).

As to the origin of humankind, first the Intellect gives birth, after its image, to an androgynous man within the superior world (CH I.12). By being mirrored in the watery nature of the inferior world, this first man produces a form after his own likeness (CH I.14). Thus is begotten a second androgynous man, who is twofold—mortal in his body and immortal in his essential being (CH I.15). The latter in turn begets seven androgynous men, made out of material nature (CH I.16). Then the two sexes are set asunder, time starts its course, along with the revolutions of the heavenly spheres, and human generations like ours are given birth (CH I.19).

Poimandrès teaches that salvation consists in "recognizing oneself as immortal, in knowing that love is the cause of death and in getting acquainted with all that exists" (CH I.18). This goal can be reached by living piously (CH I.22). Then, at the moment of death, when the soul is freed from the material body, "the human being rushes up through the cosmic framework" (CH I.25) and he "enters the sphere of the Ogdoad" (CH I.26). Then he "hears certain Powers that exist above the Ogdoadic sphere and hymn God with sweet voices." God himself dwells on a higher level. All those who have received knowledge are bound to enter into him (CH I.26).

We can easily find in the discourse on the *Ogdoad and the Ennead* equivalents of these same levels. Just as the Ogdoadic nature of CH I.26 is the place where human beings "have their own proper power," the Ogdoad of our text enables "each one to receive what is his" (NH VI.55.18–19). The beings who hymn the Father in CH I are identical with the souls and the angels of the Ogdoad (NH VI.56.1–2, 58.19, 59.29–30). Likewise, the Powers that exist above the Ogdoadic nature in CH I.26 are in fact in the Ennead, which in our text is the abode of the Powers (NH VI.59.32) or the Kingdom of Power (NH VI.55.25–26), i.e., of the Self-Begotten One. Finally, above the Ennead dwells the Unbegotten God "who rules over the Kingdom of Power" (NH VI.55.24–26).

In order to "enter into the way of immortality" (NH VI.63.10–11) under the guidance of Trismegistus, the pupil apparently had to pass through some initiatory mystery, a rite of regeneration. The central experience of this mystery seems to be the vision of oneself—that occurs in both CH XIII and NH VI.6—e.g., "Father I see the All and I see myself in the Intellect" (CH XIII.13) and "I see myself" (NH VI.58.8, 61.1). Not only does this vision bring about the regeneration of the initiate—"for this is rebirth, my child" (CH XIII.13)—but it also enables him to recognize in his initiator Trismegistus himself. This name occurs only twice in our text (NH VI.59.15, 59.24), and precisely between the two visions of the self.

How can we live through such an experience? Theoretical learning is hardly sufficient; we also need spiritual exercise and grace. The main exercise in CH XIII as well as NH VI.6 consists in prayer. Not only does prayer aim at beseeching God's free assistance (NH VI.55.14–15), but it also complements the meditative contemplation of the beauty of the soul started during the previous days. Those who pray become "a reflection of the Pleroma," i.e., of the superior world surrounding God (NH VI.57.8–10). By praising the Divinity the disciple first joins his brothers who live in this world, i.e., the congregation of Hermes' spiritual sons (NH VI.53.27–30). Eventually he also meets the souls and the angels of the Ogdoad, as well as the Powers of the Ennead. True prayer is a "sacrifice of discourse" offered to God (NH VI.57.19). It can be compared—mutatis mutandis—with some kind of seraphic trisagion uniting in one and the same hymn all of the souls and the spirits here below as well as in the highest of heavens. The kiss that follows the first prayers and brings about ecstatic vision is by itself an angelic liturgy.

Since "all which is corporeal cannot possibly express the incorporeal [. . .] what the eye can see, the tongue can also name it [. . .] but what you cannot express is God,"[3] the Hermetic invisible God must be worshipped in silence (NH VI.56.10–11) by means of speechless hymns that can be conceived only by the Intellect, beyond every kind of discourse (NH VI.58.21–22).

By miming the contents of the most blessed vision—i.e., the choir of angels and Powers praising God in the Intellect—we become able to conceive ourselves as pure Intellects, released from our bodies and able to receive from above the "Power that is light" (NH VI.57.29–30). Thus we will change our abstract meditation and our persistent effort to concentrate on the superior world into "a clear and joyful vision" (CH I.4) that is sharper than the ray of the sun and is full of immortality (CH X.4).

No doubt for the Hermetic writer this luminous power is nothing but the Divine Intellect. It consists in divine self-contemplation and manifestation of oneself to oneself. Whoever sees himself by the power of the Intellect tends to become himself and to get assimilated to the Self-Begotten man. Then he can also see the source of the Unbegotten One (NH VI.52.19, 55.22, 58.13).

The unfolding of this initiation raises the question of the existence and nature of Gnostic and Hermetic rites or sacraments. In many respects our text seems to be concerned with the tradition of the pagan mysteries. Moreover, certain details might remind us of the baptism either of the Jewish proselytes or of the Christians. But are these allusions to cultic activities only metaphorical, or do they reflect actual outward practices? Although the existence of Hermetic rites has frequently been doubted before the discovery of our text, I think that a careful analysis of the dialogue allows us to overcome these doubts and conclude that there has really been a Hermetic mystery of regeneration.

Nobody is able to go through the final stage of regeneration without the help of a teacher surrounded by a congregation of brothers (NH VI.53.8–9, 53.29–30). This normally implies the organization of a special ceremony in an appropriate place, which our text does not describe.

We might ask, then, why the dialogue presents itself not as a ritual in the precise sense of this word but as the description of a particular ceremony. The answer is likely to be the following. On the one hand, Hermetic regeneration abides by canonical rules. Thus the first prayer of Hermes (NH VI.55.10–22) sounds somehow like a liturgical preface to the holy communion. On the other hand, Hermetic regeneration is each time lived through like a unique event, a gracious act of Providence in a specific time for a specific person, so that no human promise, no teaching, and no rite may pretend to channel this grace and to convey it to anybody. Most likely it was up to the initiator to organize the preliminary conversation, then the prayers and the responses by using a conventional phraseology. He would take up fragments of hymns previously known, but without devoting himself to absolute accuracy, since much freedom would be allowed within the canonical frame of the ceremony. Thus, the Hermetists would manage to reconcile the sovereign and unique decision of Providence with the tradition of the brotherhood and the personal involvement of the initiate.

Therefore, our text is not properly a ritual, but a typical example, a model, that can be adapted and used by the congregation. This may be the true reason why the name of the disciple is not mentioned. The teacher is always, ex officio, Hermes Trismegistus, but the disciple is not necessarily Tat. The initiation remains open to many brethren.

NOTES

1. Nag Hammadi Codex VI.58.28, 59.11, 63.24. Henceforth referred to in the text as NH.
2. The *Corpus Hermeticum* will henceforth be cited in the text as CH.
3. Stobaeus's Hermetic Fragment I.1–2.

CHAPTER 7

THE CATHARS
Medieval Gnostics?

ROELOF VAN DEN BROEK

The decision to deal with the Cathars in a book on Gnosis and Hermeticism from antiquity to modern times is by no means self-evident.[1] Earlier in this century, there was a strong trend in Cathar scholarship to trace back the distinctive ideas of Catharism through the Byzantine and Slav Bogomils and Paulicians to the Manichees of late antiquity and, finally, even to Zoroaster.[2] If seen from this perspective, Catharism becomes a *corpus alienum* within the western medieval world, a Gnostic offshoot of eastern and non-Christian traditions. In reaction to this view, an increasing number of scholars have argued that Catharism can only be understood within the context of the typically western movements of resistance against the power and wealth of the Church of Rome and the luxury and corruption of its officials. They refuse to label the Cathars as Gnostics and are eager to point out that there are no demonstrable links between Catharism and the various kinds of Gnosticism we know from the late antique world. In this view, the Cathars derived most of their characteristic ideas and practices from their independent, somewhat self-willed reading of the New Testament, just like the Waldenses did. The ecclesiastical, political, and social conditions in northern Italy and southern France formed a fruitful soil for the development and expansion of these movements. The proponents of this view admit that the ritual of the *consolamentum*—the baptism of the Spirit by the laying-on of hands—resembles the Bogomil ritual so closely that it must have been taken over from the Balkans.[3] But not everybody is prepared to take the same stand with respect to Cathar dualism and their doctrine of the soul.[4]

As a result of these recent studies Catharism can no longer be seen as a completely alien element in western society; it has its firm place within the reform movements of the twelfth and thirteenth centuries with their emphasis on poverty and apostolic life. But this stress on the western aspects of Catharism often tends to neglect its eastern affiliations. It is an established fact that the Cathars have always been conscious of their eastern roots: the Cathars who were exposed at Cologne in the Rhineland (1143–44), for example, claimed to have coreligionists "in Greece and certain other lands."[5] In this respect, they distinguished themselves from all other western critics of the Church of Rome, "heretics" and Catholics alike. There cannot be any doubt whatsoever that their dualism has to be traced back to the Bogomils, who not only were consulted repeatedly on this distinctive doctrine but who also thrust their various views on this point upon the Cathars of Italy and Southern France themselves.

Because of their dualism, i.e., their doctrine of two creators and two worlds, the Cathars can, at least phenomenologically, be called "Gnostics." But it is only with some major qualifications that Catharism can be called a medieval form of Gnosticism. There is no Gnostic mythology, there are no elaborate descriptions of the heavenly world that are so characteristic of ancient Gnosticism.[6] The Cathars knew two noncanonical writings—the Bogomil *Interrogatio Johannis* and the early Christian *Ascensio Isaiae*—but that is all. They were much more literate than people thought they were,[7] but there was no production of revelations of divine mysteries: for the Cathars there was only one Book, the Bible. Last but not least, there is in Catharism no emphasis on Gnosis as saving knowledge. Christ is seen as the Divine Messenger who points out the way to salvation; however, it is not by Gnosis but exclusively by the baptism of the Spirit that man can be saved.

Nevertheless, it cannot be denied that the Cathars had some interrelated views that not only had close parallels in ancient Gnosticism but even derived from it. In addition to that, it can be shown that the Cathars did not independently develop their view of the effect of the *consolamentum* but that this view had its origin in Syrian Christianity and must have reached them via the Balkan Bogomils. They came not merely spontaneously, by their close-reading of the Bible, to a form of Christianity that resembled that of the primitive Church; they were also the heirs of eastern Christians who had themselves preserved ideas and practices which had been current in the first centuries. I will underpin my view by focusing on two specific points: the dualism professed by the Cathars and the meaning of the *consolamentum*.

DUALISM

The Cathars were Christian dualists. With respect to the vexed question of the origin of evil they were divided in two factions: the absolute dualists and the moderate dualists. The absolute dualists taught that from the beginning there are two coeternal principles—a good one (God) and an evil one (the devil). We know their views quite well from two Cathar treatises. The first is the so-called *Anonymous Treatise*, written in Southern France in the second decade of the thirteenth century and preserved in the *Liber contra Manicheos* by the Waldensian Durand of Huesca.[8] The second source is the *Book of Two Principles*, which in fact is an abridgment of a much larger treatise, written about 1240–50 by John of Lugio or one of his pupils in the region of Lake Garda in Northern Italy.[9] The moderate dualists held a view that in the last resort can be called monistic. They taught that originally there was only one principle, God, whose son, Satan (called Satanael by the Bogomils and Lucibel [= Lucifer] by the Occitan Cathars), revolted against his Father. The author of the *Book of the Two Principles* combated the views of the moderate dualists, who were centered around the Church of Concorezza in the Milanese region. For the specific views of these groups and also for those of the Cathars in general we have an excellent source in the *Summa de Catharis* written by Rainerius Sacconi, who had been a Cathar perfectus for seventeen years before he converted to Catholicism, entered the Dominican order and even became head of the Milanese Inquisition between 1254 and 1257.[10]

Recent research has shown that this division of the Cathars into moderate and absolute dualists had its origin among the Bogomils. The first Bogomils were moderate dualists, who saw the devil as an fallen angel who had created the material world. This view was generally accepted by the Bogomils and the Cathars until the middle of the twelfth century. Then, however, Byzantine Bogomils began to profess belief in the coeternal principles of good and evil. They were seized by a missionary zeal to convert other Bogomils and the Cathars to their faith. In 1179 Nicetas, the bishop of the Bogomil church of Constantinople, came to the West and arranged a meeting of Cathar bishops from Italy and France at Saint-Félix near Toulouse.[11] From then on, the majority of the Cathars seems to have been absolute dualists, although there have always remained fervent moderates, and not only in the church of

Concorezza. The learned Cathar debate on the question of whether or not there are two coeternal creative principles may have been of importance to the "scholastic" Cathar theologians—it certainly attracted much attention from the Catholic anti-Cathar polemicists—but in practice the two positions hardly led to different opinions about the wickedness of the evil creator and badness of the world he had made.

Their independent reading of the Bible provided the Cathars with a whole arsenal of scriptural weapons to defend their dualistic views. I give a few examples. The *Book of Two Principles* starts its discussion of the two principles as follows:

> Either there is only one First Principle, or there is more than one. If, indeed, there were one and not more, as the unenlightened say, then, of necessity, he would be either good or evil. But surely not evil, since then only evil would proceed from him and not good, as Christ says in the Gospel of the Blessed Matthew: "And the evil tree bringeth forth evil fruit. A good tree cannot bring forth evil fruit, neither can an evil tree bring forth good fruit" (Matthew 7,17–18). And the Blessed James says in his Epistle: "Doth a fountain send forth out of the same hole sweet and bitter water? Can the fig tree, my brethren, bear grapes, or the vine, figs? So neither can the salt water yield sweet" (James 3,11-12)[12]

Logic, confirmed by the Bible, leads to the conviction that there must be two creative powers, a good and a bad one; the good one created all good things, the evil one all bad things. So there is a good creation and a bad creation. The good creation is spiritual, invisible, and eternal; it is the world of God and participates in the divine nature. It is from that spiritual world that the soul has come down. The bad creation is material, visible, and corruptible.

The Cathars found in John 1:3 a scriptural basis for the idea that God had created the good things only. In the first part of this verse the Cathars followed the "Catholic" interpunction that had been in use since the fourth century: "All things were made by him and without him nothing was made. What was made in him was life" (in Latin: *Omnia per ipsum facta sunt et sine ipso factum est nichil. Quod factum est in ipso vita erat*).[13] The Cathars read their idea of the two creations into John 1:3. According to the *Anonymous Treatise*, the words "All things were made by him," referred to the spiritual and good creation, as was shown by the following "What was made in him, was life."[14] The Cathars took the "nothing" of John 1:3 in the sense of "nihility, nothingness." God had created everything that really exists (that is to say, the spiritual, invisible world), but without him, viz., by the Prince of Darkness, nothingness was made (that is to say, the material, visible world). This interpretation of "nothing" in John 1:3 is clearly expressed in the *Anonymous Treatise*: "[W]hat is in the world, that is, of the world, truly should be called 'nothing'." The key text is Paul's exclamation in 1 Cor. 13:2: "If I have prophetic powers, and understand all mysteries, and all knowledge, and if I have all faith so as to remove mountains, and have not charity, I am nothing." From this the following conclusion is drawn: "Whence it appears that if the Apostle were nothing without charity, all that is without charity is nothing." Then a number of other texts in which "nothing" occurs are cited, ending up with John 1:3: "Without him was made nothing." The author then concludes:

> If all the evil spirits and evil men and all things that are visible in this world are nothing because they are without charity, therefore they were made without God. Therefore God did not make them, since without him was made nothing, and as the Apostle testifies: "If I had not charity, I am nothing."[15]

From the perspective of the real world of God our world is nonexistent, but for the soul that has fallen into this world of matter it is a dangerous place to be. The Cathars believed that only they, and not the Catholic Church with its priests and sacraments, offered it a way to escape to the world of light. I will come back to the fate of the soul and its salvation in due course. Now I have first to discuss some other aspects of Cathar dualism.

Both the Cathars of Northern Italy, especially the moderate dualists of Concorezzo and those of Occitania, knew the Bogomil *Interrogatio Johannis*.[16] About 1190, Nazarius, the Cathar bishop of Concorezza, brought it to Italy from Bulgaria where it was in use among the moderate Bogomils. It has survived in two versions in Latin. In this apocryphon, Christ relates to John how Satan originally held the highest position in heaven, near to the throne of the Invisible Father, as the lord and governor of everything. But he desired to be equal to God, revolted, and seduced many angels of the first five heavens to join him. But then the

Father threw him out of the divine realm, divested him of his divine glory, and gave him a human face and seven tails, with which he drew away the third part of the angels of God (cf. Rev. 12:4). He could not find rest and repented, saying: "I have sinned, have patience with me and I will pay thee all" (cf. Matt. 18:26). The Father granted him rest until the seventh day, that is, for seven ages, and then the devil began to create the visible world; but the division of the waters was by command of the Invisible Father. The apocryphon then gives a poetical version of the creation story of Genesis. Satan made man after his own image. He commanded an angel of the second (according to the other version the third) heaven to enter the body of clay he had made, and so Adam came into existence. From a portion of Adam's body he made another body and commanded the angel of the first (according to the other version the second) heaven to enter that body, which became Eve. Through the serpent he had sexual intercourse with Eve and put sexual desire into Adam and Eve; therefore, their children are children of the devil. The spirits that fell from heaven enter female bodies and are joined there to the flesh that derives from sexual desire. That is how propagation works: spirit is born of spirit, flesh is born of flesh. Man is a composite being: his spiritual part comes from heaven, his body from the earth. After the devil had finished his creation and by the institution of animal sacrifices had cut off men from the Kingdom of Heaven, he boasted: "Behold, I am God, and there is no other god beside me."

There are in this story several elements that are also known from the tradition of the *Apocryphon of John*, a basic source of second-century Gnosticism. One is the idea that Satan had sexual intercourse with Eve; another is his boasting that he is the only God. In the *Apocryphon of John*, the evil Demiurge says to his angels after the creation of the cosmos: "I am a jealous God, there is no other god beside me."[17] This exclamation is a combination of two basic texts of the religion of Israel: Exod. 20:5 (part of the Ten Commandments: "For I, the Lord your God, am a jealous God") and Isa. 45:5 (the declaration of absolute monotheism, put into the mouth of God himself: "I am the Lord, there is no other; there is no god beside me"). The same tradition is found in two other Gnostic treatises found in the Nag Hammadi Codices,[18] *On the Origin of the World* (NHC II.103.12–13) and *The Hypostasis of the Archons* (NHC II.86.30). There, the creator exclaims: "I am God and there is no other (God) beside me."[19] Here the word "jealous" has been omitted, but the structural parallel with the *Apocryphon of John* makes it clear that the first part of the exclamation derives from Exod. 20:5. In the *Interrogatio Johannis* we find this same combination of Old Testament texts, again with the omission of the word "jealous": "I am God, there is no other God beside me."[20] We know next to nothing about the direct sources of the *Interrogatio*, but this combination of two Old Testament texts put into the mouth of the evil creator is so typically Gnostic that we have to conclude that at this point the *Interrogatio* transmits a genuine Gnostic tradition that was already in circulation in the second century. It served to express one of the most characteristic views of Gnosticism, i.e., that our bad world had been created by an evil demiurge. The Bogomils, and in their wake the Cathars, recognized in this early Gnostic tradition an excellent expression of their own ideas, and therefore, as far as their dualism is concerned, we are entitled to call the Cathars Gnostics and their religion a medieval form of Gnosticism.

The precise background of Bogomil and Cathar dualism is unknown. In Byzantium and in the West the dualists were labeled "Manichaeans." Both the Catholic and the Waldensian opponents of the Cathars called them by that name because their views at first sight reminded them of the Manichaean doctrines that had been combated so vehemently by Saint Augustine. But soon they discovered with embarrassment that Augustine's arguments did not work against the Cathars. Nevertheless, as said above, even in modern research Bogomilism and Catharism have been seen as a medieval offshoot of ancient Manichaeism. But there is very little in medieval dualism that can be traced back to the Manichees. Manichaeism has a fantastic and very complicated mythology of creation and salvation, which is completely absent in the medieval dualist religions. Moreover, in Manichaeism the creation of the world is not ascribed to the evil principle. It seems more probable that the Bogomils and Cathars derived their dualism from the Paulicians of Asia Minor and Armenia who had been transported to the Balkans. We know that the Byzantine Paulicians were absolute dualists, and it has been suggested that it is due to their influence that among the Bogomils absolute dualism became predominant.[21] But there is no certainty on this point, for the simple reason that there are no sources available.

The dualism of the Cathars determined their view on Christ and salvation as well. The body is the corruptible prison of the soul and was created by the devil. Therefore, Christ cannot have assumed a carnal body nor is the human body to be saved. This view led to a docetic Christology, which means that Christ's body appeared to be carnal but in reality was spiritual and divine.[22] This also led to a docetic Mariology, i.e., the doctrine that Mary was not a woman of flesh and blood but an angel from heaven. The antiheretical writings and the registers of the Inquisition give ample proof of the popularity of this view among the Cathar believers.[23] It is of interest to quote here the testimony of Rainerius Sacconi about the *errores* of the (moderate) Cathar bishop Nazarius, since it clearly demonstrates the connection on this point between the Bogomils and the Cathars:

> Nazarius, a former bishop of theirs and a very old man, said before me and many others that the Blessed Virgin was an angel and that Christ did not assume human nature but an angelic one, or a celestial body. And he said he got this error from the bishop and elder son of the church of Bulgaria almost sixty years ago.[24]

As mentioned, it was Nazarius who about 1190 brought the *Interrogatio Johannis* to the West, and it is precisely in this apocryphon that we find expounded the doctrine of Mary's angelic nature and her heavenly descent. I will pursue this peculiar tradition a little further because it can be traced back to at least the fourth century of our era.[25] The earliest version seems to have been that both Christ and Mary were gods, so that there was a trinity of the Father, the Mother, and the Son, which is strongly reminiscent of Gnostic theology. Epiphanius of Salamis informs us that in the middle of the fourth century there were groups who worshipped Mary as a goddess and taught that her body had come down from heaven. In the fifth and sixth centuries the doctrine that Christ and Mary were gods beside God was ascribed to the Montanists; according to later Syrian and Arabic authors it was also taught by groups who were called the Marianites and the Borborians. The Borborians, "the filthy people," are Gnostics, well known for their sexual rituals, which were abhorred by all decent Catholic believers. They also taught, it is said, that Christ had passed through Mary like water through a reed; he had entered her through her ear and had immediately been brought forth. The doctrine that Christ and Mary were gods beside God became so widespread that it had to be refuted in the Koran. In Sura 5:116, we read:

> And when Allah will say: "O Jesus, son of Mary, didst thou say to men: 'Take me and my mother for two gods beside Allah,'" he will answer: "Holy art thou. I could never say that to which I have no right."[26]

There was also a more moderate form of this doctrine, which did not say that Mary was a goddess beside God and Christ but that she was a heavenly power or an angel. We know about this view from a number of Coptic homilies from the sixth century to the ninth century, which seems to indicate that it enjoyed great popularity in unorthodox circles. In one of them, a homily on the Virgin Mary ascribed to Cyril of Jerusalem, it is said to have been part of the early Jewish-Christian *Gospel of the Hebrews*, but we may be sure that that claim was not justified. According to Pseudo-Cyril, the heretical monk Annarichos said to him:

> It is written in the Gospel according the Hebrews: When Christ wished to come upon the earth to men, the Good Father called a great power in the heavens which was called Michael, and entrusted Christ to it. And it came down into the world and it was called Mary, and Christ was in her womb for seven months.[27]

It was this mitigated form of the doctrine that Mary was a goddess that was adopted (from what source we do not know) by the *Interrogatio Johannis*. There we read, in the short version:

> When my Father sought to send me to this world, he sent before me his angel, called Mary, that she might receive me. And when I descended, I entered through her ear and came forth through her ear.[28]

We saw that this miraculous birth was also taught by the Gnostic Borborians, who also used the very old Gnostic simile of the water and the reed. So it seems possible that these Gnostics contributed to the expression of the peculiar Bogomil and Cathar doctrine of Mary's heavenly nature. In any case, we can be sure that the Bogomils and Cathars did not receive their docetic Mariology from the Paulicians, for these taught without exception that Mary had been a woman of flesh and blood.[29]

The *Consolamentum*

Finally, something must be said of the Cathar doctrine of salvation and the meaning of the *consolamentum*. According to the Cathars, man is an exile on earth; he is locked up in the material body, the prison of the soul.[30] In the immaterial divine world of light man had a body, a spirit, and a soul. His heavenly body and spirit are still in the realm of light. His soul has fallen down into the material world, but it remains of divine nature. But that heavenly soul is not the same as our present soul, which is identical with our blood and will perish together with our body. It is only the third constituent of earthly man, the spirit, that is identical with the soul of his heavenly counterpart. Final salvation means the restoration of that heavenly man, when the fallen soul will be united with its divine body and spirit. This is what in the Bible is called the resurrection of the dead. The reunification with one's original spirit takes place in the sacrament of the *consolamentum*, which, therefore, formed the heart of the Cathar religion.[31]

At this point it should be stressed that Catharism was a thoroughly sacramental religion: only the believer who had received the *consolamentum* was saved. Neither some special kind of gnosis, nor mystical experience, nor belief in a fixed set of doctrines, nor a strictly ascetic life (however important the latter might be), but solely the sacrament of the baptism of the Spirit could save man from this world and the slavery to the devil. In this respect, there is a great difference between Catharism and Gnosticism. There were sacraments in several Gnostic sects—for instance the *apolytrosis* in Valentinianism, which was administered shortly before death—but the Gnostics never declared the reception of such a sacrament to be indispensable for salvation. Catharism was as sacramental as the Catholic Church. The only difference was that the Cathars had only *one* sacrament: the *consolamentum*, the baptism of the Spirit by the imposition of hands, without the use of water.[32]

As is well known, there were two kinds of Cathar adherents: the "believers" *(credentes)* and those who were called the "perfect" *(perfecti/ perfectae)* by their opponents, but *(boni) christiani* and *(bonae) christianae* by the Cathars themselves. From the beginning of the Christian church, baptism has been the initiation rite by which one becomes a Christian. The Cathars, however, rejected the baptism of water as useless for the remission of sins and devoid of the grace of the Holy Spirit. According to them, only the baptism of the Spirit made a man or a woman a "Christian" or a "good Christian." In the catechetical instruction that in the Catharist rituals precedes the ministration of the *consolamentum* proper, many texts of the New Testament are quoted in support of the view that only spiritual baptism is effective. Key texts are, of course, John the Baptist's remark that after him someone would come who would baptize in the Holy Spirit and fire, and also the many stories in the Acts of the Apostles that mention the baptism of the Holy Spirit by the laying-on of hands.[33]

For a clear comprehension of the *consolamentum* we have to look more closely at the Cathars' conception of the Holy Spirit. It is essential to understand that the notion of the Holy Spirit is a collective one. The term "Spirit" can indicate the third person of the Trinity, for instance in the words frequently repeated by the Cathars: "We adore the Father and the Son and the Holy Spirit." According to Moneta of Cremona, this Spirit was called the *Spiritus Principalis*. But at the same time, the spirit that the Father had given to a heavenly soul as a custodian was called the *Spiritus Sanctus*. Moneta informs us, that these spirits were called "steadfast" (*firmus*) because they had not been deceived by the devil. The Holy Spirit that the Cathar received at the *consolamentum* was, according to Moneta, called the *Spiritus Paracliticus*, of which the Father had created a great number.[34] There is no reason to question Moneta's reliability, but it would be wrong to conclude from the distinctions he reports that the Cathars had a refined doctrine of the Spirit. As a matter of fact, we are only concerned here with a play on some biblical names for the Spirit. The name *Spiritus Paracliticus* has, of course, its scriptural base in John 14:15–16, while the name *Spiritus Principalis* is derived from Ps. 50:14 (51:12 in our modern versions). But if we look up this verse in the Book of Psalms it becomes immediately clear that the Cathars must have taken it together with the two preceding verses, with which it forms a unity, and that they must have read the whole passage as an excellent expression of what was to take place in the sacrament of the *consolamentum*:

> 12. Create in me a pure heart, O God,
>   and renew within me the steadfast spirit (*spiritum rectum* or *stabilem*);

13. cast me not away from thy presence
    and take not thy holy spirit *(spiritum sanctum)* from me;
14. restore to me the joy of thy salvation
    and confirm me with the principal spirit *(spiritu principali)*.

Read with Catharist eyes, this psalm shows that there is no real difference between the Holy Spirit and the heavenly spirit of man. The Holy Spirit as the Third Person of the Trinity is at the same time the collective of all heavenly spirits and the individual divine spirit. It is in the *consolamentum* that one receives one's heavenly spirit, the custodian that originally had been united with the soul before the Fall. The baptism of the Spirit is the reunification of the believer's soul—that is to say, his spirit—with its heavenly counterpart; it is the salvation from this world of darkness, the return to the realm of light. It was a spiritual transformation and, therefore, the "Christian" renounced the material world. He was to return good for evil and to accept the inevitable persecution without retaliation. He did not kill, lie, take an oath, or have sex, for that would be committing a mortal sin. As food he only used the fruits of the earth and the sea: bread, fruit, vegetables, and fish. Meat, eggs, and cheese were forbidden, for these were products that came from coition.[35] The Christian who after his baptism by the Spirit was able to maintain this way of life was assured that, at his death, his soul would return to its heavenly origin.

The Cathar notion of the Holy Spirit as the collective of all heavenly spirits was unknown in the western world. Of course, it is conceivable that the Cathars developed this idea on their own, but it seems more reasonable to look for parallels in Byzantine Christianity, especially since the Cathar ritual of the *consolamentum* is nearly identical, not only in structure but also in the formulas used, with the ritual of Spirit baptism of the Bosnian Bogomils. There is no doubt that the Cathars adopted the ritual from the Bogomils, and therefore it is to be expected that they also took over some essential ideas. Unfortunately, the origins of Bogomilism are obscure. The Byzantine heresiologists traced the Bogomil ideas back to Manichaeism, Paulicianism, or Messalianism. The Manichees and the Paulicians were dualists; the Messalians were enthusiasts, for whom the experience of the Holy Spirit was the core of Christianity. It is a well-known law in heresiology that a new religious movement that is held to be heretical is always described by its critics as a revival of some heresy of the past. That mechanism is also to be observed in the heresiological reports about the origins of Bogomilism.[36] There is no independent evidence from the Bogomils or Cathars themselves that could prove that their doctrines derive from those of the Manichees, the Paulicians or the Messalians. This state of affairs has led many modern scholars to neglect completely the information provided by the heresiologists and, therefore, to leave open the whole question of Bogomil and Cathar origins. In my view that is a too critical position. Hypercritical scholarship may be useful to prevent other scholars from jumping to conclusions too quickly, but as a whole it is mostly an impediment to the progress of knowledge. According to Byzantine heresiologists, Bogomilism was a mixture of Paulicianism and Messalianism, and I cannot see any serious reason why there could not be some truth in this suggestion. Of course, Bogomilism and Catharism constituted a religion of its own; typical tenets of the Paulicians and the Messalians are lacking in the Bogomil system. But on the other hand, to limit myself in this context to the Messalians, a number of conspicuous deviations notwithstanding,[37] there are also some typically Bogomil and Cathar views for which distinct parallels can only be found in Messalian sources or writings closely related to it.

The charismatic movement of the Messalians started in the middle of the fourth century and almost immediately met with strong opposition by the ecclesiastical leadership.[38] Their interpretation of Christianity was wholly dominated by the experience of the Holy Spirit: salvation is only possible if one has been baptized of the Spirit. Accordingly, they taught that baptism of water is not effective; only prayer is able to expel the demon who inhabits us from our birth and to make room for the Holy Spirit. Then the believer is transformed into a *pneumatikos*, his soul is deified, and he becomes perfect. Only those who have received the Holy Spirit are to be called "Christians." This terminology was even adopted by Basil of Caesarea, the staunch opponent of these pneumatics, but he applied it to the monks who lived according to his rules. So he says, for instance, that the "Christian" can be recognized by his monk's habit.[39] The Messalians, however, reserved the name "Christian" for those who had been baptized of the Spirit, thus making a difference between the perfect and the ordinary believers who could not yet be called "Christians."

All this is also found in the spiritual homilies and tractates of the Syrian mystic Macarius, who apparently had strong connections with the Messalian movement, if indeed he was not a moderate Messalian himself. It is in his homilies in particular that we find striking parallels to the Cathar ideas about the relationship between the Holy Spirit and the spirit of man. It is only to this aspect that I want to draw attention here, although more could be said about other parallels.[40]

In *Homily* 30.3, Macarius expounds his theory that the soul without the Spirit is dead. It has to be born out of the Spirit and in that way become Spirit itself: "All angels and holy powers rejoice in the soul which has been born out of the Spirit and has become Spirit itself." The soul is the image of the Holy Spirit. Christ, the heavenly painter, paints after his own image "a heavenly man" in the believer who constantly looks at him: "Out of his own Spirit, out of his substance, the ineffable light, he paints a heavenly image and presents that to the soul as its noble and good bridegroom" (*Hom.* 30.4).

This "image of the heavenly Spirit," as it is called, is identified with Christ and with the Holy Spirit. The soul that does not possess "the heavenly image of the divine light, which is the life of the soul," is useless and completely reprehensible: "Just as in this world the soul is the life of the body, so in the eternal, heavenly world it is the Spirit of Divinity which is the life of the soul" (*Hom.* 30.5).

It is absolutely necessary to obtain this life of the soul, the Spirit, in this earthly existence, for otherwise the soul will be unable to enter the Kingdom of Heaven and will end in hell (*Hom.* 30.6). Before the Fall, Adam possessed this heavenly image, which meant that he was in possession of the Holy Spirit; he lost it when he fell (*Hom.* 12.6). Christ, "who had formed body and soul," comes to bring the works of the Evil One to an end: "[H]e renews and gives shape to the heavenly image and makes a new soul, so that Adam [i.e., man] can become king of death and lord of the creatures again" (*Hom.* 11.6). Elsewhere Macarius says:

> The Lord has come to transform and to regenerate our souls, to make them "share in the divine nature," as it is written (2 Peter 1:4), to present our soul with a heavenly soul, that is the Spirit of the Divinity, which leads us to every virtue so that we can live an eternal life. (*Hom.* 44.9)

When the Spirit comes down, "the heavenly man unites with your [earthly] man, resulting in one communion" (*Hom.* 12.18). As a result,

> The Christians are of another world, sons of the heavenly Adam, new-born, children of the Holy Spirit, light-brothers of Christ, like their father, the spiritual and radiant Adam, of that [heavenly] city, of that race, of that power. They are not of this world but are of another world; for He says himself (cf. John 17:16 and 8:23): "You are not of this world, I am not of this world." (*Hom.* 16.8)

Even if it is true, Christians should not say: "We are Christians, we share in the Holy Spirit!" (*Hom.* 17.8).[41]

These ideas can be traced back to the second century. The apologist Tatian (ca. 170) taught that with the transgression of man "the more powerful spirit departed from him," so that man became mortal (*Orat.* 7.3).[42] Before that, man had two different kinds of spirits, the soul and the "image and likeness of God," which is identical with that more powerful spirit (*Orat.* 12.1). Of itself, the soul is mortal, it dies with the flesh (*Orat.* 13.1). Only if the soul obtains knowledge of God is it reunited with the divine Spirit, who is called the soul's companion *(syndiaitos)* (*Orat.* 13.2). This spirit-companion of the soul, who helps it to find the way back to God, is identified with the Holy Spirit. We have to search for what we once lost; we have to link our soul to the Holy Spirit and busy ourselves with the God-willed union *(syzygia)* (*Orat.* 15.1).

The idea of a heavenly counterpart of man, which was considered to be his guardian spirit or angel, has very old roots in the history of Christianity.[43] It would take us too far to discuss here the development of this idea in the first Christian centuries. In this connection I only mention the view of the Syrian writer Aphrahat (ca. 350) that the "angels of the little ones who look continuously on the face of my heavenly Father" (Matt. 18:10) are to be identified with the Holy Spirit.[44]

This whole complex of ideas about a heavenly counterpart of man with whom the soul had been united before the Fall and the identification of this spiritual image with the guardian angel and with the Holy Spirit, which makes this Spirit the collective of all spirits, found acceptance among the Messalians, and from them it must have come to the West. For it is only among the Cathars that we find this same combination of ideas about the Spirit and the soul: the collective notion of the

Holy Spirit as the sum of all individual heavenly spirits, which are also seen as the custodians of the human souls to which they originally belonged, and the idea that only he who has received the baptism of the Spirit—that is to say, he whose soul is reunited with its heavenly spirit—can return to the realm of light. The poor state of our sources does not allow us to discern how these ideas moved from the Messalians to the Cathars, but there can be no doubt that the core of the Cathar religion—the idea that the sacrament of the *consolamentum*, the baptism of the Spirit, meant the reunion of the soul with its heavenly spirit—was not developed by them independently but had its origin in eastern Christianity.

CONCLUSIONS

My conclusions can be summed up in a few words. Because of their dualism, be it moderate or absolute, the Cathars can be called Gnostics. If the idea that the material world is made by an evil creator and that the soul is locked up in the prison of the body, cannot be called Gnostic, then there are no Gnostic ideas at all. In this sense, Catharism is a medieval form of Gnosticism. But as a whole its beliefs and practices cannot be compared with those of the great Gnostic systems of antiquity, among other reasons because it is a sacramental religion in which the notion of gnosis played no greater part than it did in Catholic Christianity. It is probable that its dualism ultimately derived from the Paulicians, but that cannot be proven with certainty. This Gnostic framework of Catharism was combined with ideas about the Spirit and the soul that were not Gnostic at all and that formed the center of Catharist faith. These ideas had originally been at home in eastern, especially Syrian Christianity; most probably they had reached the West through the intermediary of the Messalians or charismatic groups that had picked up some central ideas of Messalianism. The Cathars professed a non-Catholic type of Christianity. They found their dualism and their theology of the Spirit confirmed by the New Testament, which also taught them that the luxury and wealth of the Church of Rome made it a false church, an opinion that was only strengthened by the persecutions launched by that church. That gives Catharism its own place between the reformist poverty movements of the twelfth and thirteenth centuries. The Cathars indeed belonged to medieval Christianity, but within that setting they did not try to reform the western Church. They simply proclaimed a new church, the Church of the Spirit.

NOTES

1. For an extensive survey of scholarship on the Cathars and Catharism, from the sixteenth century to 1976, see M.-H. Vicaire, ed., *Historiographie du catharisme*, Cahiers de Fanjeaux 14 (Toulouse and Fanjeaux, 1979). General works on the Cathars, based on all the sources available, are J. Duvernoy, *Le catharisme*, vol. 1: *La religion des cathares* (1976; reprint, with a few additions, Toulouse, 1979); idem, *Le catharisme*, vol. 2, *L'histoire des cathars* (Toulouse, 1979); and Anne Brenon, *Le vrai visage du catharisme* (1988; reprint, Toulouse, 1993); good introductions in A. Brenon, "Les cathares: Bons chrétiens et hérétiques," in *Christianisme médiévale: Mouvements, dissidents et novateurs* (= *Hérésis. Revue d'hérésiologie médiévale*, 13/14 [1990]), 115–70, and M. Lambert, *Medieval Heresy: Popular Movements from the Gregorian Reform to the Reformation*, 2d ed. (1992; reprint, Oxford, 1994), 105–46. A French translation of the surviving Cathar writings in R. Nelly, *Écritures cathares. Nouvelle édition actualisée et augmentée par Anne Brenon* (Monaco, 1995); English translations of all important Cathar and anti-Cathar writings in W. L. Wakefield and A. P. Evans, *Heresies of the High Middle Ages: Selected Sources Translated and Annotated* (New York and London, 1969).

2. The most extreme representative of this position was H. Söderberg, *La religion des cathares: Etude sur le gnosticisme de la basse antiquité et du Moyen Age* (Uppsala, 1949).

3. For a study of both rites, see Ylva Hagman, "Le rite d'initiation chrétienne chez les cathares et les bogomils," *Hérésis* 20 (1993): 13–31. Nevertheless, Christine Thouzellier, the editor of the Latin Cathar ritual, showed herself somewhat reluctant to accept the eastern origin of that ritual, *Rituel cathar: Introduction, texte critique, traduction et notes*, Sources Chrétiennes 236 (Paris, 1977), 184: "Il y a donc parallélisme entre la liturgie des hérétiques de Dalmatie, Bosnie, et celle des sectes de Lombardie et du Languedoc, sans que l'on puisse, faute de documents, déterminer leur filiation." For the influence of eastern texts among the Cathars, see now B. Hamilton, "Wisdom from the East: The Reception by the Cathars of Eastern Dualist Texts," in *Heresy and Literacy, 1000–1530,* ed. Peter Biller and Anne Hudson (Cambridge, 1994), 38–60.

4. Duvernoy, *Religion*, 361–86, sees at the base of Catharism, in addition to a strong biblical influence, a mixture of Origenistic theology and Basilian monasticism; see his conclusion on p. 387: "Le Catharisme apparaît ainsi relativement teinté de judéo-christianisme, essentiellement origéniste, par ailleurs doté du canon intégral de la Bible, organisé sous une forme monastique manifestement basilienne"; and

the defense of his position against his critics, on the unnumbered pages at the end of the 1979 reprint of his book. Christine Thouzellier sees in the whole ritual of the *consolamentum* a revival of early Christian liturgical traditions that had been in disuse for many centuries; cf., for instance, *Rituel cathare*, 191: "Elle [i.e., la cérémonie cathare] résume, dans ses deux parties, les solennités diverses que, aux IVᵉ et Vᵉ siècles, l'Église pratiquait pour le baptême, la transmission du *Pater*, la réconciliation des pécheurs, la consécration des évêques." The mere fact that so many divergent and long-forgotten traditions would have contributed to the Cathar ritual makes this theory highly unlikely. The studies of Anne Brenon mostly give a well-balanced assessment of the position of the Cathars in the western medieval world, although she, too, shows a tendency to play down the influence of eastern "heretical" traditions. Thus, in "Bons chrétiens et hérétiques," 137, she says that the Cathar doctrine of reincarnation appears "plus comme une conséquence logique de la métaphysique dualiste absolu, que comme un surgeon médiéval de la gnose antique." Lambert, however, seems unimpressed by these efforts to consider Catharism primarily as a medieval type of Christianity; he emphasizes its strongly heretical character and says of its radical dualism that it "can hardly be regarded even as extreme Christian heresy. With its belief in two gods and two creations, it might almost be described as another religion altogether" (*Medieval Heresies*, 124).

5. Everwin of Steinfeld in a letter to Bernard of Clairvaux, included in *Diversorum ad S. Bernardum et alios Epistolae*, Epist. 472, 6 (*Patrologia Latina* 182, 679D: "dixerunt . . . hanc haeresim usque ad haec tempora occultatam fuisse a temporibus martyrum, et permansisse in Graecia et in quibusdam aliis terris"); translation in Wakefield and Evans, *Heresies*, 132.

6. An exception to this rule might be found in the "Gloss on the *Pater*" of the *Ritual of Dublin*, which speaks of a hierarchy of seven "substances" in the divine world. See Th. Venckeleer, "Un recueil cathare: le manuscrit A 6 10 de Dublin, 2. Une glose sur le Pater," *Revue belge de Philologie et d'Histoire* 39 (1961): 759–92, esp. 763f., 774. French translation, with introduction and notes, by Anne Brenon in Nelly, *Ecritures cathares*, 261–322, esp. 290–91; English translation in Wakefield and Evans, *Heresies*, 607–30, esp. 607–9.

7. See P. Biller, "The Cathars of Languedoc and Written Materials," 61–82 and L. Paolini, "Italian Catharism and Written Culture," both in Biller and Hudson, *Heresy and Literacy*, 61–82 and 83–103, resp.

8. Edited by Christine Thouzellier, *Une somme anti-cathare: Le Liber contra Manicheos de Durand de Huesca*, Spicilegium Sacrum Lovaniense 32 (Louvain, 1964); a separate edition of the *Anonymus Treatise*, also by Christine Thouzellier, is *Un traité cathare inédit du début du XIIIᵉ siècle d'après le Liber contra Manicheos de Durand de Huesca*, Bibliothèque de la Revue d'Histoire Ecclésiastique 37 (Louvain, 1961).

9. Edited by Christine Thouzellier, *Livre des deux principes: Introduction, texte critique, traduction, notes et index*, Sources Chrétiennes 198 (Paris, 1975).

10. Edited by A. Dondaine, *Un traité néo-manichéen du XIIIᵉ siècle* (Rome, 1939), and by F. Sanjek, "Rainerius Sacconi Summa de Catharis," *Archivum Fratrum Praedicatorum* 44 (1974): 31–60.

11. For all this see, B. Hamilton, "The Origins of the Dualist Church of Drugunthia," *Eastern Churches Review* 6 (1974): 115–24, and "The Cathar Council of Saint-Felix Reconsidered," *Archivum Fratrum Praedicatorum* 48 (1978): 25–53; both articles reprinted in B. Hamilton, *Monastic Reform, Catharism and the Crusades*, articles 7 and 9, Variorum Reprints (London, 1979). See also L. Denkova, "Les Bogomiles: ontologie du Mal et orthodoxie orientale," in *Christianisme médiévale* (see note 1), 65-87.

12. *Liber de duobus principiis* 1, in Thouzellier, *Livre des deux principes* 162/164; translation by Wakefield and Evans, *Heresies*, 516.

13. There was, however, a conflict about the punctuation of the second part of this verse, the Cathars putting the comma after *in ipso*, the Catholics after *factum est*; see Durand de Huesca, *Liber contra Manicheos* 14, in Thouzellier, *Un somme anti-cathare*, 233–34, and notes. It is interesting to see that the Cathars followed the reading of the Manichaeans that had already been attacked by Augustine, *In Ioannis Evangelium* 1.1.16 (Corpus Christianorum 36.9–10).

14. Durand de Huesca, *Liber contra Manicheos* 12 and 13, in Thouzellier, *Une somme anti-cathare*, 209 (which erroneously follows the Catholic interpunction!) and 227, and her separate edition, *Traité cathare inédit*, 101–2, 104; translation by Wakefield and Evans, *Heresies*, 504, 505): "Quod autem de spiritualibus et bonis hoc dixerit Iohannes, subsequenter adiungit: *Quod factum est in ipso*, vita erat."

15. Durand de Huesca, *Liber contra Manicheos* 13, in Thouzellier, *Une somme anti-cathare*, 217, and her separate edition, *Un traité cathare inédit*, 103; translation by Wakefield and Evans, *Heresies*, 505.

16. Critical edition of the two versions, with French translation and an excellent commentary, by Edina Bozóky, *Le livre secret des Cathare: Interrogatio Iohannis, Apocryphe d'origine bogomile*, Textes Dossier Documents 2 (1980; reprint, Paris, 1990). This edition has replaced that by R. Reitzenstein, *Die Vorgeschichte der christlichen Taufe* (Leipzig and Berlin, 1929), 297–311. English translation in Wakefield and Evans, *Heresies*, 458–65; French translation of both versions in Nelly, *Ecritures cathares*, 39–70.

17. The *Apocryphon of John* exists in two versions, each in two manuscripts. A synoptic edition of the four manuscripts was recently published by M. Waldstein and F. Wisse, *The Apocryphon of John*, Nag Hammadi and Manichaean Studies 33 (Leiden, 1995); the boasting of the Demiurge is on pp. 78–79. See also Irenaeus's abstract from the first part of the *Apocryphon of John*, in his *Adversus Haereses* 1.29.4, in *Irenée de Lyon: Contre les Hérésies*, ed. A. Rouseau and L. Doutreleau (Paris, 1979), 1:364: "Ego sum Deus zelator, et praeter me nemo est."

18. Henceforth abbreviated in the text as NHC.

19. According to Irenaeus, the same tradition was found among the Valentinians and the Ophites of the second century (*Adversus Haereses* 1.5.4, 1.30.6.

20. The Vienna manuscript reads: "Videte quia ego sum Deus et non est alius deus preter me" and the manucripts derived from the lost Carcasonne text: "Videte quia ego sum deus vester et non <est> preter me alius deus" (Bozóky, *Livre secret*, 66). Bozóky, *Livre secret*, 66, 144 n. 180, refers for this expression to Deut. 32:39

("videte quod ego sim solus et non sit alius preter me") and Deut. 4:35 ("Dominus ipse est Deus et non est alius preter unum"). However, the parallel with the Gnostic combination of Exod. 20:5 and Isa. 45:5 is closer than with the texts from Deuteronomy. Bozóky also refers to the parallel Gnostic texts. G. Quispel has repeatedly drawn attention to the use of Isa. 45:5 by the boasting Demiurge in both the *Apocryphon* and the *Interrogatio Johannis* and concluded that there was a direct or indirect dependence of the latter on the former: "Alle origini del Catarismo," *Studi e materiali di storia delle religioni* 52 (1986): 101–12; idem, "Christelijke Gnosis, joodse Gnosis, hermetische Gnosis," in *De Hermetische Gnosis in de loop der eeuwen*, ed. G. Quispel (Baarn, 1992), 616–18, and idem, "The Religion of the Cathars and Gnosis," in *Agathè elpis: Studi storico-religiosi in onore di Ugo Bianchi*, ed. Giulia Sfameni Gasparro (Rome, 1995), 487–91.

21. See Hamilton, *Dualist Church of Drugunthia*, 120.

22. See the documentation in Duvernoy, *Religion*, 77–87.

23. A great number of texts quoted in Duvernoy, *Religion*, 88–89, and Bozóky, *Livre secret*, 151–52.

24. Sanjek, "Rainerius Sacconi Summa de catharis," 58, lines 19–23; translation by Wakefield and Evans, *Heresies*, 344 [25].

25. For a full documentation of the following, see my article "Der Bericht des koptischen Kyrillos von Jerusalem über das Hebräerevangelium," in *Carl-Schmidt-Kolloquium an der Martin-Luther-Universität 1988*, ed. P. Nagel, Martin-Luther-Universität Halle-Wittenberg, Wissenschaftliche Beiträge 1990, 23 (K 9) (Halle [Saale] 1990), 165–79; now also in my *Studies in Gnosticism and Alexandrian Christianity* (Leiden, 1996), 142–56.

26. Quoted after *The Holy Quran with English Translation and Commentary* (Islamabad-Tilford, 1988), 2:666.

27. Pseudo-Cyril of Jerusalem, *On the Virgin Mary*, 28, edited with Italian translation by Antonella Campagnano in *Ps. Cirillo di Gerusalemme: Omelie Copte sulla Passione, sulla Croce e sulla Vergine*, Testi e Documenti per lo studio dell'Antichità, 65 (Milan, 1980), 170–73. Campagnano's edition can only be called semicritical. Therefore, my translation is primarily based on the London MS of this text, which has preserved some better readings, published by E. A. W. Budge, *Miscellaneous Coptic Texts in the Dialect of Upper Egypt* (London, 1915), 59–60 (text) and 637 (trans.).

28. Bozóky, *Livre secret*, 68 (D 141–43): "Cum cogitaret pater meus mittere me in mundum, misit angelum suum ante me nomine Maria ut acciperet me. Ego autem descendens intravi per auditum et exivi per auditum." Translation of the longer version (Bozóky, *Livre secret*, 68 [V 153–56]) in Wakefield and Evans, *Heresies*, 462. For the conception and birth through Mary's ear, see Bozóky's commentary, 153–55; she was not aware of the long history of the idea that Mary was of heavenly descent.

29. This even holds for the radical docetic Paulicians of Byzance; see, for instance, Petrus Siculus, *Historia Manichaeorum*, Patrologia Graeca 104, 1256A.

30. For Cathar anthropology, see Duvernoy, *Religion*, 60–68.

31. A clear exposition of these views is found in Moneta of Cremona, *Adversus*

Catharos et Valdenses libri quinque, ed. Th.A. Ricchini, vol. 1 (1743; reprint, Ridgewood, 1964), 4; translated by Wakefield and Evans, *Heresies*, 309–10.

32. For the *consolamentum* and its ritual, see Duvernoy, *Religion*, 143–70; there is an excellent discussion of the various aspects of this sacrament in Anne Brenon, "Les fonctions sacramentelles du consolament," *Hérésis* 20 (1993): 33–55. Of primary importance are the three ritual texts that have survived: the *Latin Ritual* edited by Christine Thouzellier (see note 3 above), and two Occitan texts, namely, the *Ritual of Lyons*, in *Le Nouveau Testament traduit au XIIIᵉ siècle en langue provençale, suivi d'un rituel cathare*, ed. L. Clédat (1887; reprint, Geneva, 1968), ix–xxvi, 470–79, and the *Ritual of Dublin*, in Venckeleer, "Un recueil cathare" (see note 6 above). French translations of the three rituals are in Nelly, *Ecritures cathares*, 216–322 (the Dublin ritual by Anne Brenon); English translations are in Wakefield and Evans, *Heresies*, 465–94, 592–630 (the Dublin text).

33. See, for instance, the *Latin Ritual*, 9-12, in Thouzellier, *Rituel cathar*, 226–47; English translation in Wakefield and Evans, *Heresies*, 474–79.

34. Moneta of Cremona, *Adversus Catharos* 1 (ed. Ricchini, 4b); also in Thouzellier, *Rituel cathar*, 274 (app. 13), 133, 166, with literature.

35. For the ethics of Catharism, see Duvernoy, *Religion*, 171–201.

36. See A. Rigo, "Messalianismo = Bogomilismo. Un'equazione dell'eresiologia medievale bizantina," *Orientalia christiana periodica* 56 (1980): 53–82.

37. Mentioned by Thouzellier, *Rituel cathare*, 128–29.

38. See M. Kmosko, *Liber Graduum*, in *Patrologia Syriaca* 3.1 (Paris, 1926), cxv–cxlix, and A. Guillaumont, "Messaliens," in *Dictionnaire de Spiritualité* (Paris, 1980), 10:1074–83.

39. Basil of Caesarea, *Longer Rules*, 22.2 (*Patrologia Graeca* 31.980.AB); other texts mentioned by Thouzellier, *Rituel cathare*, 186 n. 100.

40. In the following I confine myself to quotations from his *Fifty Spiritual Homilies*, in *Die 50 Geistlichen Homilien des Makarios,* ed. H. Dörries, E. Klostermann, and M. Kroeger, Patristische Texte und Studien 4 (Berlin, 1964). A useful German translation was made by D. Stiefenhofer, *Des heiligen Makarius des Ägypters fünfzig Geistliche Homilien,* Bibliothek der Kirchenväter 10 (Kempten and München, 1913).

41. For Macarius's definition of a "true Christian," which comes very close to that of the Messalians, see the note to *Hom.* 5.1, in Dörries, Klostermann, and Kroeger, eds., *Geistl. Hom.*, 45–47.

42. Tatian's *Oratio ad Graecos* is quoted here from *Tatian: Oratio ad Graecos and Fragments*, ed. and trans. Molly Whittaker (Oxford, 1982). For Tatian's anthropology, see M. Elze, *Tatian und seine Theologie* (Göttingen, 1960), 88–100. The influence of Tatian's doctrine of the soul on later Syrian Christianity, and on Manichaeism as well, was first pointed out by E. Peterson, "Einige Bemerkungen zum Hamburger Papyrusfragment der Acta Pauli," in *Frühkirche, Judentum und Gnosis: Studien und Untersuchungen* (Rome, Freiburg, and Vienna, 1959), 202–8.

43. See G. Quispel, "Das ewige Ebenbild des Menschen: Zur Begegnung mit dem Selbst in der Gnosis," *Eranos-Jahrbuch* 36 (1967): 9–30, reprinted in G. Quispel, *Gnostic Studies* (Istanbul, 1974), 1:140–57; idem, "Genius and Spirit," in *Essays on the*

Nag Hammadi texts in Honour of Pahor Labib, ed. M. Krause, Nag Hammadi Studies 6 (Leiden, 1975), 155–69. It should be noted that the idea of the heavenly counterpart of man, his Self, was of great importance in Manichaeism too. This was pointed out by Quispel and also by C. Colpe, "Daena, Lichtjungfrau, Zweite Gestalt: Verbindungen und Unterschiede zwischen zarathustrischer und manichäischer Selbst-Anschauung," in *Studies in Gnosticism and Hellenistic Religions presented to Gilles Quispel on the Occasion of his Sixty-Fifth Birthday,* ed. R. van den Broek and M. J. Vermaseren (Leiden, 1981), 58–77.

44. Afrahat, *Demonstrationes,* 6.15, in *Patrologia Orientalis,* vol. 1, ed. I. Parisot (Paris, 1894), 298.

CHAPTER 8

RENAISSANCE HERMETICISM AND THE CONCEPT OF WESTERN ESOTERICISM

ANTOINE FAIVRE

As the title of this contribution indicates, we will be dealing with two different notions, which are interconnected but should not be confused. Let us begin with presenting them both, and reflect upon their interconnectedness.

At the outset, it seems appropriate to devote some explanation to the words "Hermeticism" and "Hermetism," which are coined from the name "Hermes." Now, there are two figures who have gone under that name. On the one hand, Hermes is a Greek god, also known as the Latin Mercurius. On the other hand, there is the semihistorical, semimythical Hermes Trismegistus, who has an anchorage in history because of a number of texts that have been attributed to him.

Let us begin with Hermes Trismegistus, who appeared in the Hellenistic literature of Egypt at the dawn of our era as a kind of avatar of the Egyptian god Thoth. He is called "thrice great," among other things because he possessed the knowledge of the three reigns of nature (mineral, vegetable, animal). To him are attributed a large number of treatises, called the *Hermetica,* which contain reflections on astrology, the creation of the world, the connections between man and spirits, and so on. Among the writings that have come down to us are the texts grouped under the heading *Corpus Hermeticum,* written in the region of Alexandria and dating back to the second and third centuries A.D. The term "Hermetism," in a precise sense, refers to the ensemble of the *Hermetica* as well as to the literature inspired by it during the Middle Ages, the Renaissance, and even thereafter. Since the 1960s a welcome tendency has developed in scholarship to distinguish "Hermetism" in this sense from "Hermeticism"; for the latter term has come to designate other traditions as well.

Roughly stated, it can be said that these traditions are, explicitly or not, placed under the auspices of the *other* Hermes: Hermes-Mercurius. He is the god who stands at the crossroads, who bridges the gaps; he is the interpreter par excellence—the interpreter of signs, of texts—and he is therefore instrumental in enabling Man to pass through various levels of reality. He makes transmutations possible, which is why he frequently appears in alchemical texts under the name Mercurius, to designate one of the three fundamental principles of Nature (the two others being Salt and Sulphur). As a result, "Hermetic science" and "Hermeticism" have come to be used as alternative terms of "alchemy," a usage that is all the more natural since Hermes Trismegistus has often been considered as the founder, or inventor, of alchemy in ancient times.[1] Increasingly, however, the term "Hermeticism" has become used in a wider sense as well, that is, to designate the general attitude of mind underlying a variety of traditions and/or currents beside alchemy, such as Hermetism, Astrology, Kabbalah, Christian Theosophy, and *philosophia occulta* or *magia* (in the sense these two words acquired in the Renaissance, that is, of a magical vision of nature understood as a living being replete with signs and correspondences, which could be deciphered and interpreted). It is in this second sense that we have to understand "Hermeticism" and distinguish it from "Hermetism."

On the following pages, I intend to describe briefly how these various traditions or currents of Hermeticism came to be considered, in the Renaissance period, as different members of one family. Subsequently, through the following centuries, this family was further enlarged and came to be placed under the general rubric "esotericism." I will discuss that latter concept in the second part of my contribution.

THE EMERGENCE OF A RENAISSANCE HERMETICISM

During the Middle Ages, there was hardly a need for a concept covering what was later to be understood by Hermeticism and/or esotericism. The reason is that the specific problems addressed by Hermeticism were still embedded within the prevailing paradigms and were generally regarded as compatible with theology. For the most part, these problems had to do with the connection between metaphysics and cosmology. For example, they had a bearing on the connections that were assumed to exist between Man and intermediate beings or denizens of higher levels of reality, such as angels. The heavens were considered to be replete with entities governing the stars and the planets. Between God, Man, and the universe there were believed to be correspondences of various kinds, worthy of study and reflection. Theology was not yet restricted to the domain of the personal relationship between God and Man.

Beginning in the twelfth century, however, the sciences of nature gradually came to be separated from theology. The latter came to devote itself mostly to metaphysics, whereas the sciences of nature increasingly came to be cultivated for their own sake and were considered as pertaining to profane or secular research. Partly under the influence of Islamic philosophy, this process was accelerated when Aristotelianism began to prevail over the philosophy of Plato, whose major work preserved during the Middle Ages had been the *Timaeus*. In the thirteenth century, the philosophy of the great Arab Aristotelian Averroës had a strong impact on Christian theologians. They preferred his views to those of Avicenna, another Moslem theologian, whose mystical approach to theology was close to Neoplatonism. Although at the time there were some attempts to reinstate a "Platonic" theology, these remained marginal.

Theology having cast off, little by little (during the period from the thirteenth century to the fifteenth century), what had formerly been part of itself, the result was a large abandoned field. The cosmological domain (that of "secondary causes": the realm of nature) came to be badly represented in theology or was no longer articulated at all. Now, at the dawn of the Renaissance (towards the end of the fifteenth century), this domain came to be recuperated by some humanist scholars from a perspective that was neither profane nor theological in a strict sense, although generally Christian. As a response to the appropriation of philosophy by the Scholastic theologians (mostly from an Aristotelian perspective), these humanist scholars appropriated a variety of teachings and traditions that official theology had ignored, namely Hermetism, alchemy, the Jewish Kabbalah, and *magia* (in the sense of a philosophy of Nature). This process developed by easy stages, rather than with a jolt. Purposely or not, a kind of melting pot was created in which various traditions were assimilated.

This process began in Florence by the end of the fifteenth century, in the circles of Cosimo the Medici's Platonic Academy, with humanist scholars such as Marsilio Ficino and Giovanni Pico della Mirandola. The importance of these humanists in the genesis of what is now called Western esotericism cannot be overemphasized. It must be noted that their works were intended as a matter for specialists; they were addressed to an audience of people already "in the know," i.e., of persons who shared the same basic worldview and the same "body of reference" consisting of texts to be scrutinized. Concentrating on the interface between metaphysics and cosmology, they attempted to develop a kind of "extratheological" method for giving an account of the relations between the universal and the particular. In general, their speculations proved to be more cosmological than metaphysical; and they were concerned more with Nature, and with vivid imagery, than with abstract speculation.

Thus, in this period we see the gradual emergence of a kind of collective will to gather together a variety of ancient materials of the type that concerns us here, based on the belief that these materials might constitute a more or less homogeneous ensemble. Most of these materials had already been present as part of the Hellenistic religiosity at the beginning of the common era, particularly in currents such as Hermetism, the Stoa, Gnosticism, Pythagoreanism, and Neopythagoreanism.[2] Renaissance Hermeticism would draw heavily on these schools or currents. Of particular importance in this ensemble of esoteric traditions in the Renaissance period was the discovery, by European scholars and clerics, of the Jewish Kabbalah. This form of theosophy had hitherto remained practically unknown outside Jewish milieus. The expulsion of the Jews from Spain in 1492, however, resulted in a great diaspora that triggered a sudden and widespread interest in Jewish speculative traditions, and in the Kabbalistic tradition particularly. Henceforth, many Christian thinkers for whom (as for the Jewish Kabbalists) every jot and tittle of Scripture had cosmic significance set out reading with the eyes of Christians the basic referential works of the Kabbalah, such as the *Sepher Yetzirah*, the *Bahir*, and the *Zohar*. They attempted to harmonize this tradition with a Christian symbolistic outlook, and the result came to be known as Christian Kabbalah. Thus, for example, the Kabbalistic "tree" of the *sephirot* was "Christianized," as it were, so as to see the Trinity at play within that image; or the Jewish science of numbers and letters, so important to Kabbalistic speculation, was applied by these Christians to a hermeneutics of the New Testament revelation. Clearly, the Christian Kabbalah is an endeavor to harmonize the symbolism of two different religions in a manner that would later be called "esoteric." Pico della Mirandola, in one of his theses of 1486, argued that "nothing proves better the divinity of Christ than Kabbalah and Magic" (understanding "Magic" as a philosophy of Nature, a *philosophia occulta* in the sense alluded to above). The basic differences between Jewish and Christian Kabbalah were, and have remained, great, since each of them is embedded in a different tradition; but their manner of exercising the active imagination in the reading of texts is comparable.[3]

A similar process can be observed with respect to Hermetism. The word, as explained above, refers to the Greek Alexandrian *Hermetica*. Of these texts, only the famous *Asclepius*[4] had been preserved in a Latin version. The most interesting and influential part of the *Hermetica*, known as the *Corpus Hermeticum*, had however been lost throughout the Middle Ages. In 1463, this corpus was rediscovered in Macedonia by a monk, who brought it to the court of Cosimo de Medici in Florence. Soon afterwards it was translated into Latin by Marsilio Ficino. Since Hermes Trismegistus was then believed to have lived at the time of Moses or even before, the texts of which he was the supposed author were considered as extremely ancient—and all the more reliable since, in the Renaissance period, the older a text was, the more trustworthy it was supposed to be. Ficino added copious commentaries to his translation and, from that time on, a whole current of Hermetism (or, rather, neo-Alexandrian Hermetism) developed. This tradition would continue throughout the next two centuries, and it has continued to throw sparks until the present day. Typical of this current is that it endeavored to harmonize various traditions (whereas the Christian Kabbalah had set out harmonizing two of them), such as Christian, Egyptian, and Greek religious speculation.[5]

In the cases both of Hermetism and of Christian Kabbalah, we are dealing with attempts to bring together different traditions with a view to discover, or rediscover, one single spectrum embracing them all. One can say that the various religious traditions were imagined as different strings or keys on one single instrument, arranged in such a way that they could produce multiple, mutually illuminating harmonies. This view was all the more enticing since some scholars engaged in Hermetism were also dealing with Kabbalah, *Magia*, and Plato. These scholars were erudite syncretists who drew on many sources that were more or less related to what they believed to be the core of Hermetic wisdom.

In Ficino's time, expressions were coined for designating what was believed to be this underlying core of all traditions. The term *philosophia perennis* referred to a kind of more or less autonomous "nebula" in the mental universe of the time, detached from theology proper. The historical or mythical representatives of this *philosophia perennis* were thought to constitute so many links in a chain. Among them we find, frequently quoted together, the names of Moses, Zoroaster, Hermes Trismegistus, Orpheus, the Sibyls, Pythagoras, and Plato.[6] At this point, *philosophia perennis* corresponds roughly to what today is often called "Tradition." More importantly, for our understanding of the period it must be noted that, in the late fifteenth century and throughout the sixteenth century, traditions such as Hermetism, Christian Kabbalah, and the *philosophia occulta* emerged as a more or less autonomous body of reference that soon came to be considered as "esoteric" with respect to the "exoteric" religion of the denominational churches.

Let us now try to enumerate the main currents of Renaissance Hermeticism. Two of them were already mentioned: neo-Alexandrian Hermetism and Christian Kabbalah. As regards the former, translations of the *Corpus Hermeticum* were widely disseminated in Europe during the sixteenth and seventeenth centuries. Among the most important representatives of the current that emerged around these texts, let us mention (in the sixteenth century) Marsilio Ficino, Ludovico Lazarelli, Symphorien Champier, Francesco Giorgi of Venice, Henricus Cornelius Agrippa, John Dee, Giordano Bruno, and Francesco Patrizi;[7] and (in the seventeenth century) Robert Fludd, Ralph Cudworth, and Athanasius Kircher. The Christian Kabbalah is represented by figures such as Giovanni Pico della Mirandola, Johannes Reuchlin, Pietro Galatino, Guillaume Postel, again Henricus Cornelius Agrippa, and Francesco Giorgi in the sixteenth century; and Christian Knorr von Rosenroth in the seventeenth.

Other currents of the time were more specifically focused on the observation of nature. It was considered as a text, permeated by "signatures" that can be deciphered by man. In the first place, we should mention Paracelsianism, consisting of the oeuvre of the German Swiss Paracelsus (Theophrastus Bombastus von Hohenheim) and the works influenced by it. Most of Paracelsus's own books were not printed previous to the end of the sixteenth century. Paracelsus developed a chemical—or rather, alchemical—vision of the world that encompassed the theory and practice of medicine and astrology. His influence may be seen operating in several directions, and his contribution has been of paramount importance, not only in the domain of esotericism but more generally in Renaissance philosophy and the history of science. His ideas have been especially congenial to the German mind, on which he has had a powerful hold until the present day.[8]

Another aspect of this esoteric landscape is the *philosophia occulta*, which is actually not precisely a current such as the three mentioned above but rather, and more generally, a "magical" vision of the world. Paracelsianism might be considered as a German manifestation of this "occult philosophy," which means a knowledge and a utilization of the occult forces or virtues that are supposed to be present in nature. *Philosophia occulta* can be considered as an attempt to unify nature and religion, and includes (although not so much in Paracelsianism) so-called white magic or theurgy. This practice makes use of names, rites, and incantations, with a view to establishing a personal relationship with entities such as planetary spirits or angels, i.e., with entities that do not belong to the immediately visible world but to what has been called the *mundus imaginalis*.[9] Among the most celebrated representatives of the *philosophia occulta* are Marsilio Ficino (*De vita coelitus comparanda*, 1486), Henricus Cornelius Agrippa (*De occulta philosophia*, 1533), Jacques Gohory, John Dee, Giordano Bruno, and, in the seventeenth century, Tommaso Campanella. Closely linked to it are various forms of arithmology (the sciences and symbolism of numbers) and speculations on music (as in Francesco Giorgi, Fabio Paolini, and Michael Maier).[10]

Alchemy, considered as a philosophy of nature, is of course one of the esoteric currents of the Renaissance, but like the *philosophia occulta* it was present in Europe as early as the twelfth century. From the end of the sixteenth century, much alchemical literature flourished in the wake of Paracelsianism, and the existence of printed books made its dissemination possible.[11]

Finally, two further esoteric currents must be mentioned that appeared in the late Renaissance, both of them at the beginning of the seventeenth century, namely, Rosicrucianism and Christian theosophy. The two famous Rosicrucian manifestos (*Fama Fraternitatis*, Kassel, 1614; *Confessio Fraternitatis*, Frankfurt, 1615) triggered this current, with their presentation of the mythical figure of Christian Rosenkreutz. According to the *Fama*, Rosenkreutz had founded a fraternity of seekers of Truth—the "Rosicrucians"—whose emblem was a rose drawn in the middle of a cross. The anonymous authors of the manifestos claim to be on the verge of revealing the Adamic language, which will make it possible to understand the hidden meanings of the Bible, and they quote Paracelsus as one of their principal sources of inspiration. The third proto-Rosicrucian writing is a novel, also in German, entitled *The Chemical Wedding of Christian Rosenkreutz* (1616), which describes how the hero Christian Rosenkreutz undertakes an initiatory journey of an alchemical character. We now know that the author of the novel was Johann Valentin Andreae. The antagonism between proponents and opponents of these three works led to a flurry of exchanges and pamphlets throughout the following years.[12] Although it seems that there has never been a real secret society behind the manifestos, many people believed in its existence. By way of consequence, many esoteric societies have been created between the early seventeenth century and the present, claiming to be the regular successors of the original Rosicrucian Fraternity.[13]

The other esoteric current that appeared at the beginning of the seventeenth century was born in Germany as well. It is what might be called "Boehmian theosophy," presented in the works of Jacob Boehme and all the innumerable works inspired by it. Jacob Boehme and most theosophers, like Paracelsus and the Rosicrucians, cannot be considered as humanists or savants. They did not derive their illuminations from the reading of pagan texts (as the representatives of neo-Alexandrian Hermetism did) but directly from their reading of the Bible—and of nature. It is not by accident that both Rosicrucianism and Christian theosophy originated in Protestant Germany, a country where the Bible had come to be the essential and almost unique source of spiritual inspiration. Theosophy is a form of hermeneutics (i.e., of multileveled interpretations) of Scripture, mostly of those passages that are replete with mythical elements (such as Genesis, Ezekiel, the Revelation of John, the Sapiential texts, and so on). The theosopher scrutinizes the mysteries of God or the Godhead (just as the Kabbalah does, which is the Jewish form of theosophy) and of the universe. Suffice it to say here that theosophy, beginning with Jacob Boehme and ever since, represents an all-important esoteric movement that was spread over almost all of Europe. In the seventeenth century it was represented by authors such as Johann Georg Gichtel, Gottfried Arnold, Antoinette Bourguignon, John Pordage, and Jane Lead, and it would continue through the eighteenth and nineteenth centuries.[14]

THE CONCEPT OF ESOTERICISM

I have provided a brief historical sketch of the landscape of Western esotericism, showing how it has emerged over time. Obviously the various currents discussed have commonalities, which is why I have repeatedly used the terms "esotericism" and "esoteric" to designate them individually or collectively. The choice of this particular term needs to be explained, however. Although the noun "esotericism" was coined in the nineteenth century, it is not without its predecessors. During the Renaissance, a need was felt to use general terms (and we have seen why such a need did not yet exist during the Middle Ages). General terms, such as *philosophia perennis* and *philosophia occulta* and later "Hermeticism," were mostly sufficient. Now, if we look for commonalities in all the currents discussed above—the development of which spans more than five centuries and took place in many Western countries—not even a close scrutiny is necessary in order to bring the realization that it is hardly possible to formulate such commonalities in doctrinal terms. To define the field in terms of doctrines is a pitfall that should be avoided, since Western esoteric currents display no doctrinal (let alone dogmatic) unity that can link them all together. For example, some esotericists believe in reincarnation; others do not. Some believe that the world was created ex nihilo; others defend a creation by way of emanation. Similar dissimilarities may even be found in one and the same tradition or current, as can be seen, for example, already in the case of the *Corpus Hermeticum*. But in spite of all this, these currents have always been considered, and with good reason, as a rather homogeneous landscape. Partly, this is due to the fact that many people may belong to several currents simultaneously, but this is not sufficient as an explanation. Another reason consists in the very nature of the commonalities that underlie these various currents. Before presenting a methodological approach to these commonalities, I will first devote some words to a question of vocabulary: the choice of the word "esotericism" itself.

There is no evidence that the noun "esotericism" was used earlier than 1828. It appears in French *(l'ésotérisme)* in a book on Gnosticism published by Jacques Matter.[15] Matter uses the word in a rather vague sense, which corresponds approximately to *philosophia perennis* and to "secret knowledge." From this time on, the term has been used more often. In general, three different meanings can be distinguished, which are still common today. Firstly, it often refers to a "secret knowledge" or "secret science," in the sense of a secrecy that must be preserved by the so-called *disciplina arcani*. Secondly, it refers to what is "hidden" in Nature or Man, which (in contrast with the first meaning) does not necessarily imply that something has to be kept secret. In this second sense, the word is meant to suggest that certain types of knowledge are supposed to emanate from a spiritual center of a divine or semidivine Nature. Here, "esotericism" refers to the paths or techniques enabling man (or only a few rare persons) to have access to this center in order to acquire a genuine gnosis and/or to attain personal transformation. There is now a tendency to refer to this second sense by the word "esoterism" rather than "esotericism" (the term "esoterism" is preferred by the neo-Guénonians and many of Frithjof Schuon's followers). "Esoteric" is something that is hidden, not on purpose but by its very nature; thus, for example, the nineteenth-century German theosopher Franz von Baader speaks of "the esoteric God." Thirdly, "esotericism" is used as a term referring to the diverse group of works and currents mentioned in the first part of this article, in recognition of the fact that they possess some sort of *air de famille*. These currents can be studied as a distinct field by the history of religions, because of the specific forms they have acquired in the West since the Renaissance. Obviously, it is in this third sense that the word is used here.

It is therefore appropriate to dwell now upon this third sense, which corresponds to the "concept of Western esotericism" mentioned in the title of this article. The question that needs to be discussed is: how can we account for this *air de famille?* Although I already had occasion to present and publish my reflections on this point elsewhere,[16] it may be useful to summarize them briefly here. Esotericism can fruitfully be considered, within the context of Western modernity (i.e., the period since the Renaissance), as a form of thought identifiable by the presence of six fundamental characteristics or components. Four of these I call "intrinsic," which means that all four have to be present in order for a body of material to be classified as belonging to esotericism. By nature, these four are more or less inseparable, but it seems methodologically appropriate and relevant to distinguish them from one another. The two remaining components I call "relative" because, although they often appear in combination with the first four, they are not essential (in the sense that they are not indispensable) to the definition of "esotericism" as a form of thought.

Here are the four fundamental elements by which a work, an author, or a current qualify as pertaining to what I propose to call "esotericism":

1. *The idea of correspondences.* Correspondences, symbolic and real, are believed to exist among all parts of the universe, both seen and unseen ("what is below is like what is above, what is above is like what is below"). We find here the ancient idea of the microcosm and the macrocosm, i.e., the principle of universal interdependence. Esotericists weave together the inner and the exterior worlds on the basis of these correspondences. The entire universe is, as it were, a theater of mirrors, an ensemble of hieroglyphs to be deciphered.

2. *Living Nature.* Nature as a whole is a living being, which can be read like a book and is considered to be permeated by an interior light or hidden fire circulating through it. *Magia*, in the sense that the Renaissance philosophers gave to this word, refers to the knowledge of the network of sympathies and antipathies that weave together Nature and Man, as well as to concrete operations informed by that knowledge.

3. *Imagination and mediations.* These two notions are interconnected and complementary. Imagination is considered here as an organ of the soul, permitting access to different levels of reality. It functions in conjunction with mediations of all kinds, such as rituals, symbolic images, numbers, mandalas, intermediate spirits, and the like. It is this type of imagination which makes it possible to use these intermediaries, symbols, and images for the purpose of developing a gnosis capable of penetrating

the hieroglyphs of Nature and understanding the processes of interaction between Man, God, and the universe. In this context, the important thing is considered to be not what one believes, but what one sees (i.e., what and how ones imagines).

4. *The experience of transmutation*. This term refers to the belief that people, and (from an alchemical perspective) parts of nature as well, may undergo a modification of their very being. Lead is transmuted into silver, which in turn becomes gold; and for Man, illuminated knowledge *(gnosis)* is supposed to result in a state of being, conducive to a "second birth" (a notion that, obviously enough, is common in classic mysticism). This notion often has a bearing on the need for man to participate in the process by which the universe is born and moves towards its fulfillment, by undoing the ravages wrought by the Fall of Adam.

The remaining two elements, which I have called "relative," are the following:

5. *The praxis of concordance*. We already encountered this notion in relation to the *philosophia perennis*. It is evidenced by attempts to discover common denominators among two or more different traditions or even among all traditions. This tendency developed strongly during the nineteenth century in influential esoteric environments, under the influence of an increased knowledge about the East and the development of comparative religion. It reached its zenith in the twentieth century, when proponents of "traditionalism," also known as "perennialism," began to postulate and teach the existence of a "primordial tradition" common to all times and places, which is supposed to run through the apparent diversity of the religious traditions of the world.

6. *Transmission*. In the present context, this word means that in order for an esoteric knowledge *(gnosis)* or an initiation to be valid, it must be transmitted in affiliation with unimpeachable authenticity or "regularity." The idea is that a person can not arbitrarily choose to initiate him/herself but must pass through the regular channel of an authorized initiator.

Each of these six components is of course not unique to Western esotericism. It is their simultaneous presence that identifies a work (including books or works of art) or current as esoteric. On the other hand, this analysis does not purport to be applicable to the whole world or all historical eras: the referential corpus of esotericism surveyed here is limited in space (the Western world) and time (modernity). I have made no attempt to discuss a "universal esotericism," because neither the sum of the components described, nor each single one of them, for that matter, are meant here as universal invariants. They also do not emerge from some preconceived idea about what modern Western esotericism *should* be, but from the empirical recognition that certain streams of ideas exhibit themselves in certain ways to the eyes of the observer.

In the field of Western esotericism we commonly encounter the conviction that there exists one great Gnostic tradition running through all the centuries of our era. An example is the great history of heresies (1690–91) by Gottfried Arnold;[17] and the idea of a universal Gnostic tradition is also a cherished idea of modern scholars such as Gilles Quispel. My purpose in this article is neither to deny nor to support such a view, but to point out two things. Firstly, that at the dawn of the Renaissance there emerged a new way of looking at some of the traditions of the past. It is this "displacement," as it were, and the new role these traditions took on in the cultural and spiritual framework of the time, that have made possible the very notion of "esotericism" as applied to modernity. Secondly, it should be noticed that in a scholarly approach to Western esoteric currents, reflection upon what they have in common should be only a preliminary step toward studying their genesis, development, transformations, displacements, migrations, and so on, as well as their historical and cultural (including scientific and ideological) contexts.

Such an empirical approach has the advantage of not being based on axiomatic or ideological prejudices, i.e., it is neither religionist nor reductionist. It is not religionist because it does not aim at fostering a "practice" of esotericism but presents itself as a way of dealing with the study of esotericism as a legitimate part of *Religionswissenschaft* in particular, and of the history of ideas in general. It is not reductionist insofar as empirical scholars do not view religion (of which esotericism is only one sector) "as purely human construction, for definite human needs, which can be fully explained by these needs."[18]

The domain succinctly surveyed here can be fruitfully approached from a multi- and interdisciplinary approach. It intertwines with other domains into which its ideas have always tended to "migrate" and of which it is even often part and parcel, such as the history of science, philosophy, literature, and the arts. And that is not the least interest of the study of esotericism for scholars, however different their respective specialisms may be.

NOTES

1. For a more detailed discussion of the figures of Hermes and Hermes Tris-megistus, cf. Antoine Faivre, *The Eternal Hermes: From Greek God to Alchemical Magus* (Grand Rapids, 1995).

2. See Antoine Faivre, "Ancient and Medieval Sources of Modern Esoteric Movements," in *Modern Esoteric Spirituality*, ed. Antoine Faivre and Jacob Needleman, World Spirituality 21 (New York, 1992).

3. On Christian Kabbalah, see François Secret, *Les Kabbalistes Chrétiens de la Renaissance* (1964; reprint, Paris and Milan, 1985); and the collective work *Kabbalistes Chrétiens*, Cahiers de l'Hermétisme (Paris, 1979).

4. See also G. Quispel's contribution to this volume.

5. See the seminal work by Frances A. Yates, *Giordano Bruno and the Hermetic Tradition* (1964; reprint, Chicago and London 1979); and cf. the bibliography in Faivre, *Eternal Hermes*, 194–201.

6. Apart from the relevant works quoted above, see in particular D. P. Walker, *The Ancient Theology: Studies in Christian Platonism from the Fifteenth to the Eighteenth Century* (Old Working, London, 1972).

7. See the contribution by Cees Leijenhorst, elsewhere in this volume.

8. On Paracelsus, see the classic work by Walter Pagel, *Paracelsus: An Introduction to Philosophical Medicine in the Era of the Renaissance* (1958; reprint, Basel and New York, 1982); and among the most recent studies the two collected works edited by Joachim Telle: *Paraerga Paracelsica: Paracelsus in Vergangenheit und Gegenwart* (Stuttgart, 1992) and *Analecta Paracelsica* (Stuttgart, 1994).

9. This expression was conveniently coined by the French Islamologist Henry Corbin. See his *"Mundus Imaginalis* or the Imaginary and the Imaginal," *Spring*, 1972.

10. On the *philosophia occulta*, see Lynn Thorndike, *A History of Magic and Experimental Science* vols. 5 and 6 (1923–58; reprint, New York, 1984). Among more recent works, see Wayne Schumaker, *The Occult Sciences in the Renaissance: A Study in Intellectual Patterns* (1972; reprint, Berkeley and Los Angeles, 1979). Cf. also, more generally, the bibliography presented in Antoine Faivre, *Access to Western Esotericism* (Albany, 1994), esp. 320–22.

11. A good bibliography is Claudia Kren's *Alchemy in Europe: A Guide to Research* (New York and London, 1990). For a more succinct list, see Faivre, *Access*, 305–11.

12. See the catalog of an exhibition in Wolfenbüttel and Amsterdam, by Carlos Gilly, *Cimelia Rhodostaurotica: Die Rosenkreuzer im Spiegel der zwischen 1610 und 1660 entstandenen Handschriften und Drucke*, 2d rev.ed. (Amsterdam, 1995).

13. The standard work on seventeenth-century Rosicrucianism is Roland Edighoffer's *Rose-Croix et société idéale selon Johann Valentin Andreae*, 2 vols. (Paris, 1982, 1987). A brief introduction by the same author is *Les Rose-Croix* (Paris, 1982); see also his contribution in this volume. For a succinct bibliography, see Faivre, *Access*, 325–26.

14. On the history of the theosophical current, see Antoine Faivre, "Le courant théosophique (XVème–XXème siècles): Essai de périodisation," chap. 1 in vol. 2 of *Accès de l'ésoterisme occidental* (Paris, 1996); and Arthur Versluis, *Theosophia: Hidden Dimensions of Christianity* (New York, 1994). See also his contribution to this volume.

15. Jacques Matter, *Histoire critique du gnosticisme et de son influence* (Paris, 1828), 83. This first usage of the word was noted by Jean-Pierre Laurant in his *L'ésotérisme chrétien en France au XIXè siècle* (Paris, 1992), 19, 42.

16. Studies in English in which I had occasion to present modern western esotericism as a form of thought comprised of four or six components: "Introduction I," in: Faivre and Needleman, *Modern Esoteric Spirituality*, xi–xxx; *Access*, 1–19; Antoine Faivre and Karen-Claire Voss, "Western Esotericism and the Science of Religion," *Numen* 42 (1995): 48–77.

17. Gottfried Arnold, *Unpartheyische Kirchen- und Ketzerhistorie, vom Anfang des Neuen Testaments bis auf das Jahr Christi 1688* (Frankfurt, 1690–91).

18. As formulated in Jan Platvoet, "The Definers Defined: Traditions in the Definition of Religion," *Method & Theory in the Study of Religion* 2, no. 2 (1990): 198. For an encompassing survey of the reductionist, religionist, and empirical approaches in the study of religions in general, as well as for an in-depth discussion of empirical method in the study of esotericism in particular, see the groundbreaking study of Wouter J. Hanegraaff, "Empirical Method in the Study of Esotericism," *Method & Theory in the Study of Religion* 7, no. 2 (1995). Parallel and similar reflections on the study of esotericism are to be found in Faivre and Voss, "Western Esotericism"; and in my "Avant-Propos: L'Ésotérisme et la Recherche Universitaire," in *Accès de l'ésotérisme occidental*, vol. 2 (Paris, 1996).

CHAPTER 9

FRANCESCO PATRIZI'S HERMETIC PHILOSOPHY

CEES LEIJENHORST

In this article we will discuss the attempt by the Croatian-Venetian philosopher Francesco Patrizi (1529–97) to establish a synthesis between Christian faith, Hermetic[1] teachings and Platonist philosophy. After a short biography, we will give a general overview of Patrizi's Hermetic philosophy. We will conclude with an investigation of the use of particular Hermetic tenets in Patrizi's main work, the *Nova de Universis Philosophia*.

BIOGRAPHY

Patrizi was born 25 April 1529 to an Italianized noble Croatian family in Cherso (Cres), Dalmatia, a city that is now part of the republic of Croatia but which in Patrizi's days was ruled by the Venetian Republic.[2] After having studied in Ingolstadt in 1544, he continued his studies of philosophy and medicine at the famous university of Padua, then still one of the most important centers of Renaissance Aristotelianism. There, Patrizi moved in important circles, being associated with men like Niccolò Sfondrati, later Pope Gregory XIV; Ippolito Aldobrandini, later Pope Clement VIII; and Gerolamo della Rovere, Scipione Valiero, and Agostino Valiero, who would all end as cardinals. Each of them was to play an important role in Patrizi's philosophical career. Patrizi soon discovered that the Aristotelianism of his teachers was definitely not his cup of tea. Then, as if by a miracle, he met a Franciscan friar who gave him a copy of the *Theologia Platonica*, the main work of the greatest of all Renaissance Platonists, Marsilio Ficino (1433–94). Patrizi tells us that he immediately fell in love with Platonism, and that this moment "was the beginning of the studies he has pursued ever since."[3] Sometime afterward, he definitively turned his back on what he considered to be the Aristotelian humdrum of Padua. After this disappointing academic experience he wrote his first works, in which the Hermetic-Platonist influence can already be noticed.[4] In the same period he met a young Venetian *nobile*, Giorgio Contarini, future count of Jaffa, and became his teacher. Contarini then employed Patrizi as manager of his estate at Cyprus from 1562 until 1568. Although Patrizi himself afterward considered this period as wasted time, his work seems to have allowed him spare time enough to trace and buy or copy important Greek manuscripts of the *Corpus Hermeticum*, which he was later to use in his new edition of this work. After his stay at Cyprus, Patrizi got himself involved in a number of rather catastrophic business enterprises. Nevertheless, he found the time to publish the first volume of his *Discussiones Peripateticae* (Venetiis, 1571), which contained a biography of Aristotle and a history of the Peripatetic School. In 1575 he went to Spain, where scholars had noticed that his book contained hitherto unpublished material on Aristotle. Through their mediation he managed to sell his manuscripts to King Philip II, who kept them in the library of the Escorial. Most of these precious works were lost after the great fire at the Escorial in 1671, but we still have Patrizi's list of them.[5] Finally, having failed in all his attempts to make a fortune, he found a "safe haven"[6] at Ferrara, still ruled by the splendid court of the Estes, who entertained great artists like Torquato Tasso. Patrizi worked here as professor of Platonist philosophy from 1577 until 1592. During this extremely fruitful period, Patrizi published translations of John Philoponus's *Commentary on Aristotle's Metaphysics*[7] and of Proclus's *Elementa theologica*,[8] wrote a book on Roman military history,[9] and composed his two main philosophical works, the *Discussiones Peripateticae* (Peripatetic discussions)[10] and the *Nova de Universis Philosophia* (New philosophy of everything).[11] In these two works, which will be discussed further on, Patrizi developed a thorough and vehement critique of the then still dominant Aristotelian-Scholastic philosophy and his own alternative Hermetic-Platonist system, which was to replace the former at the curricula of the universities of all Christendom. Patrizi's plea for a new Hermetic-Platonist philosophy fully in accord with Catholic faith at first seemed to find considerable resonance. None other than the pope himself (Clement VIII, as indicated a former fellow student at Padua), called Patrizi to the newly created chair of Platonist philosophy at the Sapienza, the papal university in Rome.[12] At the same time, however, doubts arose within the Curia as to the orthodoxy of the *Nova de Universis Philosophia*. Soon, Patrizi got involved in an intricate trial, conducted by the Index Congregation, which eventually ended with the condemnation of the entire work and the order to submit all copies to the Congregation.[13] Although Patrizi was allowed to continue his teaching activities at the Sapienza, his philosophical career was utterly destroyed, as was his hope for a renewal of Christianity in a Hermetic-Platonist fashion. The only option left open to him was to write on philosophically and theologically harmless matters such as military science.[14] Patrizi died on 6 February 1597.

PATRIZI'S HERMETIC PROJECT

In order to get a closer view of Patrizi's Hermetic philosophy, we will concentrate on his two main works, the *Discussiones Peripateticae*[15] and the *Nova de Universis Philosophia*.[16] The first work takes up one of the favorite themes of Neoplatonist philosophy, especially of its Renaissance variety—namely, that of the *concordia philosophorum*, the idea that there is one basic, common kernel of truth in all philosophical systems, no matter how different they might appear at first sight. This conviction culminated in Giovanni Pico della Mirandola's huge and unfinished project to bring to light the common truth of all philosophical and esoteric traditions, later restricted to the unveiling of the *concordia* between Plato's and Aristotle's philosophies.[17] This idea was closely interrelated with the notion of a "perennial philosophy,"[18] the conviction that there was one, largely secret tradition of esoteric wisdom, dating back to the first beginnings of creation, when man received this wisdom directly out of God's hands. This philosophical-esoteric *sapientia* (wisdom) or "secret doctrine" was passed on from the one "sage" or "magus" to the other, thus constituting a tradition that was thought to include figures like Zoroaster, Moses, Hermes Trismegistus, Orpheus, the Pythagoreans, and Plato. The most important, though not the first, representative of this mode of thought was Marsilio Ficino, who affirmed that long before the Scriptures were revealed to man, there was a tradition of *prisca theologia* (ancient theology) or *prisca philosophia* that foreshadowed Christian truth. According to Ficino, Christian truth was both the culmination of the Mosaic wisdom of the Hebrew prophets and of the Platonist philosophical speculation of the Greeks. Christian revelation was the river in which both the Greek and the Hebrew currents of *prisca sapientia* came together.[19]

By linking Plato with Moses, Ficino made a strong case for his own *Theologia Platonica*, the attempt to develop a Christian philosophy on the basis of Plato. Another important aspect of Ficino's doctrine of *prisca philosophia* is the fact that according to him the Hermetic writings and other important parts of this tradition could be considered the most ancient wisdom on earth. Thus, he lent considerable authority to these writings, because Renaissance philosophers, as opposed to modern scientists, did not seek for the newest of the newest, but for the most ancient, the most venerable and purest knowledge.

Patrizi considerably changed this Ficinian doctrine. First, his genealogy of the *prisca theologia* tradition is somewhat different. According to Patrizi, Ham, the son of Noah, had a son or grandson called Zoroaster,[20] a contemporary (and most probably also a relative) of Abraham, who lived in Chaldea.[21] His teachings were kept by the Persian and Armenian magi. Ham founded colonies in Egypt, and had a son there, King Osiris. Osiris had a counselor with the name Hermes Trismegistus. The grandson of this man was also called Hermes Trismegistus, who was the author of the *Corpus Hermeticum* and lived shortly before Moses.[22] Both seem to have had a son Tat, and both had students named Asclepius.[23] Hermes' wisdom was kept by the Egyptian priests until the time that the Greek Orpheus came to Egypt and imbibed the Hermetic wisdom. He passed his knowledge on to the pre-Socratic *theologi* like Thales and Empedocles and to the Pythagoreans who were the teachers of Plato.

Unlike Ficino, Patrizi places Hermes before Moses. In general, Moses and the Hebrew prophets play a very subordinate role in Patrizi's account. Patrizi does not talk about two distinct traditions, a "philosophical" and a "prophetical" one that were both fulfilled in Christianity, but only about one single continuous tradition of divine wisdom. The most important difference between Patrizi and the other adherents of the *concordia philosophorum* theory, however, is the fact that Patrizi combines this idea with a thorough anti-Aristotelianism.

The *Discussiones* try to show that everything valuable in Aristotle is downright plagiarism, whereas all his original contributions are mere nonsense. Aristotle adopts all important themes of perennial philosophy in general and of Plato in particular. By leaving his source unmentioned, while at the same time explicitly criticizing his master, Aristotle tried to achieve fame at his expense and thus broke the continuous line of the *philosophia perennis*. Patrizi's main criticism of Aristotle in the *Discussiones* and elsewhere is that while "wise men" like Orpheus and Zoroaster taught doctrines that clearly foreshadowed Christian truth, Aristotle's philosophy is utterly heretical. Unlike Hermes and his fellow prophets, he denies a divine creation of the world, affirms the eternity of the world, does not uphold the doctrine of a Triune God, and so on.[24]

We might call the *Discussiones* the *pars destruens* of Patrizi's Hermetic project. His second main work, *Nova de Universis Philosophia*, would accordingly be the *pars construens*. It gives a new, systematic presentation of the *prisca theologia*. This new presentation had become necessary, because the predominance of the Aristotelian philosophy had forced the Hermetic-Platonist philosophy to go more or less underground. In the dedication of the *Nova de Universis Philosophia* to Pope Gregory XIV Patrizi states that he does not understand how the Scholastic philosophy—the synthesis between Christian faith and Aristotelian philosophy paradigmatically developed by Thomas Aquinas—could embrace Aristotle, since Aristotelian philosophy is blatantly heretical: it denies God's omnipotence as well as his providence. According to Patrizi the Platonist tradition would be far better suited to bring about a synthesis between religion and faith. The *Corpus Hermeticum*, for instance, affirms the divine creation of the world and also develops what might be seen as a Trinitarian theology. In the dedication, Patrizi presents his system as an attempt to bring about this new synthesis between Christian faith and rational philosophy on the basis of the Platonist tradition of *prisca sapientia*.

Patrizi claims that this system might help to convert the schismatics (the Protestants) and the infidels (the Muslims) to Catholic faith by rational, peaceful means and asks the pope to instruct the Jesuit order to take up this task. One should not appeal to their faith, because that is exactly what separates them from the Mother Church, but one can appeal to their rational faculties and persuade them to embrace Catholic faith by giving sound, rational arguments. Further, Patrizi advises the pope to put his book on the curriculum of every school and university throughout Christendom as a replacement for the old, basically anti-Christian Scholastic manuals.

Patrizi's request of course represented a serious challenge for contemporary Scholastic philosophy. His book appeared in a period in which the Counter-Reformation forced the university professors to formulate new teaching canons. The most important, and eventually most powerful, response to this need was exactly the one provided by the Jesuit order, founded in the course of the Council of Trent and developed into the standard-bearer of the Counter-Reformation.[25] This new order developed highly efficient new teaching methods, taking Aristotelian philosophy in its Thomistic interpretation as the basis for its philosophy and theology. The order developed a series of new standard textbooks in the form of huge commentaries on the whole of the Aristotelian corpus, which took into account both the new humanistic methods of textual exegesis and all modern commentaries and critiques of Aristotle. The most important were the ones published by the Jesuit *Collegio* at Coimbra (Portugal), which had a tremendous influence throughout the late sixteenth and seventeenth centuries.

Patrizi's alternative textbook[26] was in more than one way a threat for this renewed Scholastic philosophy. Aristotle, who had been declared canonical by the Scholastics, was swept from the daily menu of the philosophy students and replaced with eccentric figures like Zoroaster, Orpheus, and Hermes. But, even more dangerously, Patrizi destroyed the basis of authority of the scholastic *doctores* of theology. In Scholastic theology and philosophy, the main tenets of faith—such as the Trinitarian unity of God, death and resurrection of Christ, and the remission of sins—were declared to be mysteries of faith, which could not be rationally proved but had to be assented to by faith, guided by the Holy Spirit. The correct interpretation of these articles of faith was relegated to the Church, in particular to its doctors of theology. These used their interpretation of central articles of faith as self-evident principles in their rational exposition and explanation of peripheral articles of faith.

Patrizi attacked this theological system right at its roots. According to him man can, by the sole light of reason, arrive at the understanding of the central "mysteries" of faith, such as the doctrine of the Trinity. Patrizi repeatedly says that he does not want to philosophize on the basis of theological *authoritates* of any kind, but only by the aid of rational argumentation.[27] His philosophical system is grounded on "divine oracles, geometrical necessities, philosophical reasons and most evident experience."[28] Thus, in the center of Patrizi's metaphysics we find an exposition of the doctrine of the Trinity that uses Orphic, Zoroastrian, and Hermetic teachings as its point of departure, rationally proving the consubstantiality of the three divine persons in a Neoplatonist vein.[29] The dangerous consequence of this position is that the doctors of theology are no longer invested with the authority to explain the central mysteries of faith: in principle everybody can understand the meaning of the basic articles of faith for himself (with a little help of Patrizi, of course). In this context, Patrizi gives a quite daring interpretation of the term *fides* (faith). Faith is not the principally irrational or prerational acceptance of certain doctrines on the basis of the authority of the Church, but it is the "postrational," final *assensio* to divine truth that is bred by rational cognition *(cognitio).*[30]

That Patrizi's *Nova de Universis Philosophia* was considered a major threat by the ecclesiastical authorities clearly emerges from the documents involved in the condemnation of the work. The objections of the authorities can be divided into three groups:[31]

1. Objections of a theoretical character. The primary problem here was the fact that Patrizi rejected the Aristotelian definition of substance.

2. Objections of a theological kind. The congregation rejected Patrizi's speculation concerning the Trinity and his doctrine that the soul is the central link between the corporeal and incorporeal worlds.

3. Objections against Patrizi's natural philosophy and cosmology. The Church did not agree, for instance, with Patrizi's notion of Empyreum, which in Scholastic theology was considered to be the incorporeal outer heavenly sphere, the abode of the angels and the elect. In Patrizi's conception the Empyreum is an infinite body of pure light that extends through three-dimensional space. Thus Patrizi drops the difference between the corporeal, three-dimensional world and the incorporeal, nondimensional heaven.

Patrizi's doctrine of the Trinity, however, was among the doctrines that aroused most suspicion, as is made clear by Patrizi's (enforced) emendation: "I delete books 9 and 10 [sc., of the *Panarchia:* the books that contain

Patrizi's Trinitarian speculations] in their entirety, because it is impossible for a philosopher to prove that there is a Trinity."[32]

Hitherto we have discussed two parts of Patrizi's Hermetic project: the critical one represented by the *Discussiones Peripateticae*, and the new synthesis elaborated in the *Nova de Universis Philosophia*. There is also a third part of this project: a critical and systematic edition of all the works and fragments of the *prisci theologi*. This subdivision of Patrizi's Hermetic project has clear anti-Aristotelian overtones as well. In his urge for self-affirmation, Aristotle not only heavily criticized the *prisci theologi* but was also responsible for the disappearance of their works. Accordingly, the only material left consists of some scattered fragments, which Patrizi now tries to present in a systematic, scientific order. We can follow the fate of this plan in Patrizi's correspondence. In a letter of 31 May 1571 (addressee unknown), Patrizi speaks about his forthcoming book *Antiquissimorum sapientium, tum Gentilium quam Graecorum, qui ante Platonem atque Aristotelem philosophati sunt, libelli, fragmenta, dogmata a F. P. collecta* (Books, fragments and doctrines of the most ancient wise men, gentiles as well as Greeks, who philosophized before Plato and Aristotle, collected by F. P.). This book was not only intended to contain the fragments of pre-Socratic philosophers like Xenocrates and Parmenides, but also those of Zoroaster, Orpheus and Hermes. In a letter of 22 May 1588[33] to Sigismund Schnitzer, student at Padua, Patrizi speaks about "my Thesaurus of wisdom, to be edited in Greek and Latin" *(Thesauro meo sapientiae, edendo Graece et Latine)*. Again he gives an extensive list of all the fragments to be included. A final catalog of Patrizi's *Thesaurus* is to be found in a letter of 1590 to Johann Hartmann Beyer in Frankfurt.[34] Patrizi did not succeed in his attempt to publish a separate, complete *Thesaurus*,[35] but parts of it were edited in appendices to the *Nova de Universis Philosophia*. The main differences between this edition and the plan he still had in 1590 are: (1) In 1590 Patrizi intends to publish the Kabbalah, which does not appear in the appendices to the *Nova de Universis Philosophia* (in the whole work, Patrizi refers to the Kabbalah only once).[36] (2) The 1590 letter mentions the Orphic Hymns, which do not appear in the appendices but are frequently cited in the *Nova de Universis Philosophia*. (3) The 1590 plan mentions the pre-Socratics and "Socrates, [containing] the entire books of some Socratic disciples."[37]

These fragments are not published in the appendices, but Patrizi often mentions pre-Socratic doctrines in the *Nova de Universis Philosophia*.

We will discuss here only those appendices which are important to the interpretation of the *Nova de Universis Philosophia* against the background of the Hermetic-Platonist tradition. The first appendix is the *Zoroaster et eius CCCXX Oracula Chaldaica*. The *Oracula Chaldaica* was made up of Platonic, neo-Pythagorean, Stoic, Gnostic, and Persian elements, and was compiled by a certain Julianus in the second century A.D.[38] Michael Psellus, the eleventh-century Byzantine scholar, compiled the different fragments and wrote commentaries on the "Chaldean philosophy," to which Patrizi often refers. Georgius Gemisthus Pletho (1355–1452), the great Byzantine scholar who heavily influenced Renaissance Platonism, was the first to infer that Zoroaster and his disciples were the originators of the *Oracula*. Patrizi took over Pletho's edition and his introduction to it and provided additional material collected from Neoplatonists such as Proclus, Synesius, Olympiodorus, Damascius, and others.[39] In his introduction to the *Oracula*, Patrizi affirms that it contains "such admirable, such divine laws concerning the Trinity, the divine orders [sc., the celestial hierarchies] and the excellency of the soul, that you will be baffled by them. Zoroaster can be seen, not without justification, as the one who before all others as it were laid the foundations of Catholic faith, however unpolished they may be." According to Patrizi, Zoroaster not only affirmed the existence of a Triune God, but can also be regarded as the *Urheber* of the (Platonist) doctrine of Ideas.[40]

The next part of Patrizi's *Thesaurus* is his edition of the Hermetic writings: *Hermetis Trismegisti libelli et fragmenta*, the *Asclepius Hermetis Trismegisti dialogus ab Apulei Madaurense platonico in latinum conversus*, and the *Asclepii discipuli tres libelli*. These works present an "amended" and arbitrarily rearranged Greek text and a new Latin translation of the *Corpus Hermeticum*.[41] In the introduction Patrizi himself says that his version contains 1040 corrections of the editions by Ficino (first edition 1471) and Foix de Candalle (1574), but modern scholarship has a rather negative judgment on the philological qualities of his *Hermes*.[42] The introduction repeats Patrizi's plea that Hermes instead of Aristotle should have to be taught at the universities. Most of the Hermetic and Zoroastrian writings were published in a separate edition at Hamburg in 1593.[43]

The third appendix to the *Nova de Universis Philosophia* is the *Mystica*

Aegyptiorum et Chaldaeorum, a Platone voce tradita ab Aristotele excepta et conscripta Philosophia Ingens Divinae sapientiae thesaurus (Mystical philosophy of the Egyptians and Chaldeans, being a great thesaurus of divine wisdom, taught orally by Plato, absorbed and written down by Aristotle), a new version of the well-known pseudo-Aristotelian *Theologia Aristotelis*, a work largely inspired by Plotinus that had a wide circulation in the Middle Ages and the Renaissance.[44] The text is the one edited and translated by Nicolò de Castellani (Rome, 1519).[45] According to Patrizi, the tract finds its origin in the fact that later in life, Aristotle resented having broken with the ancient theology and the teachings of his master Plato. Therefore, he tried to collect the materials from his earlier notes, which he had taken during the teaching courses of Plato, who transmitted the Hermetic-Zoroastrian "secret doctrine" of the Chaldeans and Egyptians orally to his pupils. That is the reason why the ideas of this "mystical Aristotle" differed so much from those expounded in the "official" earlier, anti-Platonist, and heretical works.[46] This interpretation of the *Theologia* differs from that offered in the *Discussiones*, where the tract is considered to be spurious.[47]

"PRISCA THEOLOGIA" IN THE *NOVA DE UNIVERSIS PHILOSOPHIA*

After this general overview of Patrizi's triune Hermetic project, we will now concentrate on how Hermetic teachings were integrated in the *Nova de Universis Philosophia*.

The book consists of four parts: *Panaugia*, which deals with light as the principle of all metaphysical speculation; *Panarchia*, which investigates the Triune God as the principle of all being; *Pampsychia*, which discusses the soul as the principle of life and motion; and *Pancosmia*, which gives an account of the principles of corporeal nature. This methodological partition reflects the ontological structure of being, which Patrizi conceives of in typically Neoplatonist fashion: from the first principle of all being everything else emanates. The first level in this ontological "chain of being" is that of the soul, whereas corporeal nature is the lowest level of being, at the greatest distance from its divine source.

Before describing this descending emanative movement, the *Pan-*

augia presents an ascending movement towards God, starting with a basic natural phenomenon, namely light. Patrizi states that all our knowledge starts with the data provided by the senses. The most noble of our senses is the eye, which cannot operate without light. Light is clearly incorporeal: one cannot touch it, and unlike bodies it is omnipresent and not restricted to one place, since it extends throughout space. The source of this incorporeal, omnipresent light itself can only be a incorporeal, omnipresent entity: God. Patrizi presents this argument as an alternative to Scholastic proofs of the existence of God, which wrongly start with movement instead of light.

The *Panarchia* contemplates God as the absolute One that at the same time comprises all being. God has a triune structure: he gives rise within himself to a second principle, the Son or Logos, in which the All is not present in its absolute, simple form, but in a distinct form. By means of this Logos, the One has become the principle of diversity, i.e., the principle of creation. However, the One and the Son are a perfect unity, since the emanation of the Son out of the Father is completely immanent to the One, or the Paternum Profundum (The Deep of the Father) as Patrizi calls it, using an expression of the *Oracula Chaldaica*. This unity finds expression in the third principle, the Spirit.

In transcending itself, the One originates all being. The first level is that of the world soul, the human soul, and the animal souls that are discussed in the *Pampsychia*. In the *Pancosmia* Patrizi gives an account of the four principles of the corporeal world, namely, space,[48] light, warmth, and *fluor* (fluid), Patrizi's alternative concept of matter. The *Pancosmia* further deals with the different parts of the corporeal world: the stars, sun and moon, earth, and the four elements.

The *Panaugia* contains relatively few references to the *prisca theologia* tradition. The first doctrine taken over by Patrizi is that "the ethereal substance [sc., the region between the moon and the fixed stars] can be nothing else but light. This dogma was upheld by the wise men of the Chaldeans."[49] Patrizi also adheres to the "Chaldean" view that beyond the finite world of earth, planets, and stars there is an infinite body of pure ligh·, which Patrizi calls the Empyreum, after the Chaldean Oracles and Proclus, both said to have also used Zoroastrian teachings in this context.[50] Finally, Patrizi refers to passages of the *Oracula*, the *Corpus Hermeticum*,[51] and the *Mystica Aegyptiorum* in order to show that the origin of this pure light can be nothing else but the Deep of the Father, the triune God.[52]

The most interesting adoption of Hermetic theses can be found in the *Panarchia*.[53] The first important Hermetic doctrine taken over by Patrizi concerns God as the first principle of all being. Patrizi often quotes the passage from the *Corpus Hermeticum* that says that: "The Monad, because it is the beginning and root of all things, is in them all as root and beginning. Without a beginning there is nothing, and a beginning comes from nothing except itself if it is the beginning of other things."[54] In Patrizi's view God, the First Principle, is a perfect unity. He cannot be compared to anything else. As a principle, he is the origin of everything else. Therefore, all being depends on God or, in other words, God pervades all being. God comprises and permeates everything with his being. In this context, Patrizi also quotes another Hermetic text: "For God holds within him the things that are; none are outside of him; and he is outside of none."[55] Following Hermes, Patrizi calls God the "One-All" (Un-Omnia).[56]

However, the fact that God pervades everything does not mean that God is identical to the world. Although the world depends on God, it does have a relatively independent existence, since there is a difference between God and the world as a created being. In God, the Idea of the world is completely united with him, but outside "The Deep of the Father" it is different from God. This difference between what exists as an Idea—or, in other words, as a possibility in God—and what exists as a real thing outside the Paternum Profundum is illustrated by another quotation of the *Corpus Hermeticum*: "He is himself the things that are and those that are not. Those that are he has made visible; those that are not he holds within him."[57]

In the process of the divine creation of the world, change occurs. Something that did not exist at first does exist now, or better: a mere possibility is actualized. However, this change does not affect God himself. Only the world changes from being a mere possibility, a mere idea, to being an actually existing world. That God is immutable is confirmed by the *Corpus Hermeticum*: "[O]nly the one, however, stands still and does not move."[58] God remains the same for all eternity, regardless of whether he creates a world or not.

Patrizi subscribes to the Christian tenet that the world is a created, temporal being. The fact that the world is not eternal does not contradict the eternity of God. One could think that since God is eternal, he should create the world in all eternity. However, this would only be the case if the creation of the world were an action that necessarily flows from God's essence. This would be against the Christian dogma that the creation of the world is a free action on the part of God, a doctrine Patrizi of course subscribes to. As indicated, one of the main reasons why Patrizi rejects Aristotle in favor of Hermes is the fact that Aristotle claimed that the world was eternal and uncreated, whereas Hermes taught that the world is not eternal but created by God's free will.[59]

One of the most important Hermetic doctrines adopted by Patrizi is that the whole Trinity, not only the Father, is involved in the creation of the world. The role of the Son or Logos is attested by Hermes: "[A]nd the Word which came forth from the Light is the Son of God."[60] The participation of the Spirit in the act of creation is affirmed by *Corpus Hermeticum* I.9–11, in which it is said that the Father gives birth to a God of fire and spirit, a "Spirit and Maker" that is of the same nature as the Logos.[61] This maker creates the spirits that direct the world, which Patrizi equates with the (pseudo-)Dionysian celestial hierarchies. These, in turn, are identified with the Zoroastrian hierarchies of "angels."[62]

The reason why God created the world can be found in *Corpus Hermeticum* XI.22: "This is why he made all things: so that through them all you might look on him. This is the goodness of God, this is his excellence: that he is visible through all things."[63] God is Goodness per se. The Good is that what gives everything and never takes away.[64] Therefore, God cannot "exist without making the good."[65] The immense Goodness of his nature forces God to share it with someone else, so he creates a world to which he can reveal himself. However, God is a spiritual being. Therefore, he creates a spirit outside of him, man, whose knowledge and worship of God is the goal of the entire creation.

Like the *Panaugia*, the *Pampsychia* contains few references to Hermetic lore. The "Chaldeans" are said to have already upheld the view that the soul emanates from the Divine Intellect.[66] The opinion that the soul is the medium between the higher incorporeal and the lower corporeal world is also affirmed by means of a quotation from the *Oracula*.[67] Evidence from Zoroaster and Hermes[68] is adduced to confirm the existence of a world soul.[69]

As indicated, in the *Pancosmia* Patrizi discusses the basic principles of corporeal nature. He subscribes to the view expressed by the *Oracula Chaldaica* that God created the corporeal world by means of all-pervading light and concomitant life-creating warmth.[70] The material principle of nature is *fluor* (fluid), which can be found in different degrees of density and rarity: earthly bodies consist of the most dense, the Empyreum of the most rare *fluor*. The fact that God first created fluid or water is not only confirmed by pre-Socratic philosophers, but also by Hermes[71] and of course by Moses himself in the Book of Genesis. In Zoroaster we find the affirmation that the stars are not fixed to material spheres, but are freely moving "fires."[72] Further, Patrizi defends the original Chaldean and Egyptian astrology against the arguments of Ficino and Pico, who grounded their severe judgment upon decadent contemporary pseudo-astrology.[73] Finally, Patrizi takes over the Zoroastrian view that, although the universe is infinite, it does have a fixed center, in which the Divine Creator placed earth.[74]

On the basis of this review of the *Nova de Universis Philosophia*, we can make three concluding remarks. First, Patrizi's Hermetic philosophy is mainly of a speculative, theoretical character. Patrizi is first and foremost interested in Platonist metaphysical doctrines and leaves aside the magical and astrological parts of the Hermetic tradition. However, in the introduction to his *Zoroaster* (appendix to the *Nova de Universis Philosophia*), he qualifies the Persian master as a magus and gives an interesting definition of magic. According to Patrizi, magic is nothing else than knowledge and worship of God. Therefore, the first part of magic is theology and religion, both of which Zoroaster developed in a very high degree. The second part is knowledge of the powers and movements of the celestial bodies, i.e., astrology. Finally, magic consists of the "universal knowledge of the entire nature,"[75] which opens the possibility to interact with nature and to use it for human purposes. Patrizi makes a sharp distinction between this "divine" and Christian magic, on the one hand, and demonical, decadent magic on the other, which he calls *goetia*. Although Patrizi acknowledges a kind of practical magic, it is clear that to him that the theoretical, even theological, aspects are much more interesting than the practical, technical ones. This constitutes a considerable difference between him and his great exemplar Marsilio Ficino, whose *De vita coelitus comparanda* was perhaps the most important and influential work of Renaissance magic.[76] It could be argued that the relative neglect of magic in the *Nova de Universis Philosophia* has to do with the fact that it was meant to be a textbook for university students. Magic would perhaps not really fit in this context. However, in the whole Patrizian corpus we do not find any evidence for a genuine interest in magic, so it seems that its absence in the *Nova de Universis Philosophia* has to be explained in terms of the philosophical orientation of its author rather than from practical, institutional considerations.

The second remark concerns Patrizi's attempt to reunite Christian faith and Hermetic-Platonist philosophy. This project is not entirely convincing. Patrizi does not discuss central issues of Christian faith such as the incarnation, death, and resurrection of Christ, and grace and remission of sins. Instead, he concentrates on the more metaphysical, speculative issues such as the Trinity and the divine creation of the world. In general, the references to Scripture in the *Nova de Universis Philosophia* are far outweighed by those to the principal texts of the *prisca philosophia*. Again, this is a difference between Patrizi and Ficino, who deals with all these thorny issues in his *De Christiana religione*, which similarly tries to establish the conformity of the Hermetic-Platonist tradition and Christian faith. The way in which Ficino deals with an issue such as the Trinity also considerably differs from Patrizi's treatment. Although Ficino recognizes that the *prisci theologi*, mainly Plato himself, had an intuition of the Trinitarian structure of God, he held that they could never have arrived at a complete understanding, since their teachings were developed before Christ, who brought the definitive revelation. Allen has argued that "to have claimed too much for Plato or for Platonism would have been as disastrous for Ficino's goals as an apologist as claiming too little."[77] As an ordained priest, Ficino obviously did not intend to undermine the uniqueness of Christian revelation.

This cautious attitude towards pre-Christian Trinitarian doctrines cannot be found in Patrizi. He continually emphasizes that the writings of the *prisci theologi* contain a nucleus of absolute truth, notably with respect to the Trinitarian structure of the Deity. The dynamic relationship between pre-Christian foreshadowings of the truth and their perfection by the revelation of Christ, as developed by Ficino, is conspicuously absent in Patrizi. The references to the *prisca sapientia* tradition and its Trinitarian ideas completely overshadow the actual Christian elaboration of the doctrine. The relation between the *prisca theologia* and Christian faith as propounded by Patrizi is not so much that of a promising prelude to an exciting drama, but more that of a brilliant story to a brief afterthought or conclusion. This is not to say that we should doubt the sincerity of Patrizi's faith, but it makes clear that Patrizi's interest in the Zoroastrian-Hermetic tradition goes far beyond Ficino's apologetic attitude.[78] Ficino's purpose is to develop a Christian Platonism as the culmination of both the Mosaic prophetical current and the Greek philosophical-theological current. Patrizi elaborates a Hermetic Platonism of which Christian thought seems to be a mere part, rather than the perfection or culmination.

My third remark is that, in this sense, Patrizi's *Nova* (New) *de Universis Philosophia* is a re-naissance, a *re-novatio* of the oldest wisdom on earth. Patrizi stresses that it is not so much the substance of the *Nova de Universis Philosophia* that is new, but rather its methodological, systematic treatment. In this context, Vasoli draws attention to Patrizi's earlier works.[79] In his early *Della Retorica*, and also in his later *Della Poetica*, Patrizi presents a myth about the beginning of time, when man had magical and thaumaturgical powers. Poets could move stones, tame wild animals, cure the ill, and perform other miracles merely by the power of words.[80] These powers were largely destroyed after the Great Flood, which served as a divine punishment for an abundance of hybris on the part of these miracle-performing sages, although Zoroaster, Hermes, and even the Egyptian priests still showed some glimpses of these magical possibilities. Now the poets have to regain by artificial means, i.e. by *ars* (technique), what was inborn to the "sages." The *Nova de Universis Philosophia* seems to present a parallel case. The golden chain of divine knowledge has been broken by Aristotle. The words of the magi have been scattered; their content can no longer be the object of direct intuition, nor can their words work miracles any more. Their sayings now have to be reorganized and systematically grouped. But what is more important, they also have to be rationally explained, i.e., to be translated into the rational vocabulary of Platonist philosophy. Thus, the *Nova de Universis Philosophia* can be considered as a *re-novatio* by "technical," artificial, and rational means of what Patrizi held to be the most divine and the most ancient knowledge on earth.

The Church did not agree that the Hermetic teachings were the most divine knowledge on earth and stopped Patrizi's *reformatio* before it had even begun, just as it would try to stop Bruno's and Galileo's revolutions a few years later. Only twenty-three years after the publication of the *Nova de Universis Philosophia*, Isaac Casaubon would also dispute the claim that the *Corpus Hermeticum* contained the oldest knowledge on earth.

Notes

    1. In this article the term "Hermetic" will be used in a very large sense. It basically refers to the tradition of "ancient wisdom" that, according to Patrizi, included not only Hermes Trismegistus but also Zoroaster, Orpheus, Pythagoras, and many others.

    2. Information on Patrizi's life can be found in an autobiographical letter to Baccio Valori of 1587 (see D. Aguzzi Barbagli, ed., *Francesco Patrizi da Cherso: Lettere ed opuscoli inediti* [Firenze, 1975], 45–51). This letter is paraphrased by Emil Jacobs in his article "Francesco Patricio und seine Sammlung griechischer Handschriften in der Bibliothek des Escorial," *Zentralblatt für Bibliothekwesen* 25 (1908): 19–47. See also C. Vasoli, "La lettera autobiografica di F. Patrizi," *Quaderni di retorica e poetica* 1 (1986): 59–66. For Patrizi's philosophy, see G. Brickman, "An introduction to F. Patrizi's *Nova de Universis Philosophia*" (Ph.D. diss., Columbia University, 1941); P. O. Kristeller, *Eight Philosophers of the Italian Renaissance* (London, 1964), 110–26.

    3. Aguzzi Barbagli, *Lettere*, 47.

    4. *La città felice* (Venetia, 1553); *Della Historia diece dialoghi* (Venetia, 1560); *Della Retorica dieci dialoghi* (Venetia, 1562). On *la città felice*, see M. Mucillo, "Aristotelismo, platonismo ed ermetismo ne 'La città felice' di Francesco Patrizi," in *Utopie per gli anni ottanta*, ed. G. Saccaro del Buffo and A. O. Lewis (Roma, 1986), 553–77; and C. Vasoli, "La città dei sacerdoti-sapienti," in C. Vasoli, *Francesco Patrizi da Cherso* (Roma, 1989), 1–24. On *Della Historia*, see C. Vasoli, "La storia: Una meditazione cinquecentesca su verità, 'occultamento' e linguaggio della memoria umana," in Vasoli, *Francesco Patrizi*, 25–90; F. Lamprecht, *Zur Theorie der humanistischen Geschichtsschreibung: Mensch und Geschichte bei Francesco Patrizi* (Zürich, 1950); E. Keßler, *Theoretiker humanistischer Geschichtsschreibung* (München, 1971), 51–53, 90–105. On *Della Retorica*, see E. Garin, "Note su alcuni aspetti delle retoriche rinascimentali e sulla 'Retorica' del Patrizi," *Archivio della Filosofia*, 1953, 48–56; L. Menapace Brisca, "La retorica di Francesco Patrizi, o del platonismo antiaristotelismo," *Aevum* 26 (1952): 434–61; C. Vasoli, "Linguaggio, retorica e potere," in Vasoli, *Francesco Patrizi*, 91–108.

    5. Published by Jacobs, "Francesco Patritio."

    6. Ibid., 26.

    7. F. Patrizi, *(Pseudo-)Johannis Philoponi Expositiones in omnes XIV Aristotelis libros metaphysicos* (Ferrara, 1583). A modern edition of Patrizi's translation was edited by Ch. Lohr (Stuttgart-Bad Canstatt 1991).

    8. F. Patrizi, *Procli Diadochi Elementa theologica et physica* (Ferrara, 1583).

    9. *La Militia romana* (Ferrara, 1583).

10. *Discussionum Peripateticarum,* Tomi 4 (Basileae, 1581).

11. *Nova de Universis Philosophia* (Ferrariae, 1591).

12. In the trial of Giordano Bruno, a witness reports that the appointment of Patrizi to the chair of Platonist philosophy encouraged Bruno and gave him some hope that the pope might favor him as well. See A. Mercati, *Il Sommario del Processo di Giordano Bruno* (Città del Vaticano, 1942), 56–57: "e quando il Patritio andò a Roma sa Nostro Signore disse Giordano questo Papa è un galant'uomo perchè favorisce i filosofi e posso ancora io sperare d'essere favorito, e so che il Patritio è filosofo, e che non crede niente, et io rispuosi che il Patritio era buono Catholico."

13. For this episode, see L. Firpo, "The Flowering and Withering of Speculative Philosophy—Italian Philosophy and the Counter Reformation: The Condemnation of Francesco Patrizi," in *The Late Italian Renaissance, 1525–1630,* ed. E. Cochrane (London, 1970), 266–84; T. Gregory, "'L'Apologia' e le 'Declarationes' di F. Patrizi," in *Medioevo e Rinascimento: Studi in Onore di B. Nardi* (Firenze, 1955), 385–424; P. O. Kristeller, "Francesco Patrizi da Cherso: Emendatio in Libros Suos Novae Philosophiae," *Rinascimento* 21 (1970): 215–18; A. L. Puliafito Bleuel, *Nova de Universis Philosophia: Materiali per un'edizione emendata* (Firenze, 1993). Benedetto Mammarelli, Patrizi's publisher, succeeded in smuggling some copies out of Rome and had them published in Venice in 1594 (antedated 1593). This 1593 (1594) edition is largely identical to the 1591 Ferrara edition, except of course for the title page. See P. Zambelli, "Anedotti Patriziani," *Rinascimento* 18 (1967): 309–10.

14. *Paralleli Militari* (Roma, 1594–95).

15. On the *Discussiones,* see A. Antonaci, *Ricerche sul neoplatonismo del Rinascimento: Francesco Patrizi da Cherso,* vol. 1: *La redazione delle opere filosofiche. Analisi del primo tomo delle "Discussiones"* (Galatina-Lecce, 1984); M. Mucillo, "La vita e le opere di Aristotele nelle 'Discussiones Peripatetice' di Francesco Patrizi da Cherso," *Rinascimento* 21 (1981): 53–119; C. Vasoli, "Il ritorno alle origini e la difesa della 'libertas philosophandi'. Aristotele e i filosofi 'antiquiores' nelle 'Peripateticae Discussiones' di Francesco Patrizi," in Vasoli, *Francesco Patrizi,* 149–80; M. Wilmott, "Aristoteles Exotericus, Acroamaticus, Mysticus: Two Interpretations of the Typological Classification of the 'Corpus Aristotelicum' by Francesco Patrizi da Cherso," *Nouvelles de la République des Lettres* 1 (1985): 67–91. *Discussiones Peripateticae* will be cited in the notes as *DP,* followed by the book and page numbers in the Basileae 1581 edition.

16. On the *Nova de Universis Philosophia,* see A. L. Puliafito, "Per uno studio della 'Nova de Universis Philosophia' di Francesco Patrizi da Cherso. Note alla 'Panaugia,'" *Atti e Memorie dell'Accademia Toscana di Scienze e Lettere "La Colombaria"* 52 (1987): 161–99; idem, "'Principio primo' e 'principio principati' nella 'Nova de Universis Philosophia' di Francesco Patrizi," *Giornale Critico della Filosofia Italiana* 68 (1988): 154–201. There is one modern edition of the work: Frane Petric, *Nova Sveopca Filozofija* (Zagreb, 1979), a reprint of the 1591 edition plus Croatian translation that now, due to well-known circumstances, is even more rare than the original work. The work will be cited in the notes as *NUPh,* followed by the name of the relevant part and page numbers.

17. For Pico's notion of *concordia philosophorum*, see E. Garin's introduction to *De Hominis dignitate, Heptaplus, de ente et uno, e scritti vari*, by G. Pico della Mirandola (Firenze, 1942), 34ff.

18. The term *philosophia perennis* was introduced by Agostino Steuco, *De perenni philosophia*, 1st ed. (Lyons, 1540). For "perennial philosophy," see Ch. B. Schmitt, "Perennial Philosophy: From Agostino Steuco to Leibniz," *Journal of the History of Ideas* 27 (1966): 505–29 and D. P. Walker, *The Ancient Theology* (London, 1972). Patrizi uses the term "philosophia perennis" in *NUPh*, Panarchia 38v.

19. Michael J. B. Allen, "Marsilio Ficino on Plato, the Neoplatonists, and the Christian Doctrine of the Trinity," *Renaissance Quarterly* 38 (1984): 581.

20. See Patrizi, *Zoroaster et eius CCCXX Oracula Chaldaica* (appendix to *NUPh*), 3; *NUPh*, Panarchia 38v; and *DP* 3.293–94.

21. *DP* 3.292; and *Zoroaster*, 3. This proximity to Abraham is important, because according to the Bible, Abraham had a direct contact with God. See *NUPh*, Panaugia 22r: "What argument can be brought against the possibility that they [sc., Abraham and Zoroaster] had conversations, as is usual between wise men and that thus Zoroaster learned many things concerning God, which God had revealed to Abraham?"

22. Patrizi, *Hermetis Trismegisti Libelli integri xx et Fragmenta* (app. to *NUPh*), 1.

23. Patrizi's duplication of Hermes is needed in order to reconcile the contradictory information on Hermes. See F. Purnell, "Francesco Patrizi and the Critics of Hermes Trismegistus," *Journal of Medieval and Renaissance Studies* 6 (1976): 174–75.

24. Anti-Aristotelianism as such is not a new phenomenon in the Renaissance. It can already be found, for instance, in the works of Patrizi's friend Bernardino Telesio. More important in this connection is Steuco's statement that, although in general Aristotle's thought can be reunited with Christian faith, Aristotle denies the divine creation of the world and affirms its eternity, which not only goes against Scripture, but also steps out of the line of the *prisci theologi* (see M. Mucillo, "Marsilio Ficino e Francesco Patrizi da Cherso," in *Marsilio Ficino e il ritorno di Platone*, ed. G. C. Garfagnini [Firenze, 1986], 651).

25. See Ch. Lohr, "Metaphysics," in *The Cambridge History of Renaissance Philosophy*, ed. Ch. B. Schmitt, Q. Skinner and E. Keßler (Cambridge, 1988), 605ff.

26. Mucillo, "Marsilio Ficino e Francesco Patrizi," 652 states that the *Nova de Universis Philosophia* must be seen against the background of Patrizi's status as university professor of Platonist philosophy. He was forced to provide for a new *Corpus Platonicum* as an alternative to the *Corpus Aristotelicum* that was hitherto used as the standard textbook in academic teaching.

27. See e.g. *NUPh*, Panarchia 10v: "[B]ut we philosophize with the help of authorities more in the sense of an ornament than in the sense of a foundation. Let us therefore deal with rational arguments, if we can find some, in order to prove the matters at hand."

28. *NUPh*, Panaugia 1r.: "divinis oraculis, geometricis necessitatibus, philosophicis rationibus, clarissimisque experimentis."

29. *NUPh*, Panarchia 18rff.

30. *NUPh*, Panarchia 42v. I basically follow C. Vasoli's interpretation of this anti-Scholastic character of Patrizi's philosophy. See C. Vasoli, "Francesco Patrizi e la tradizione ermetica," *Nuova Rivista Storica,* 1980, 25–40; idem, "L'idea della 'Prisca Sapientia' in Francesco Patrizi," in *Roma e l'Antico nell' arte e nella cultura del Cinquecento,* ed. M. Fagiolo (Roma, 1985), 47ff.; and idem, "L'hermétisme à Venise de Giorgio à Patrizi," in *Présence d'Hermès Trismégiste,* ed. A. Faivre (Paris 1988), 142ff. However, Vasoli has the tendency to interpret Patrizi's alternative as a new hierarchy, where "illuminated" "magi" contemplate Hermetic-Platonist divine truth and ordinary folk are the new "believers" who accept the authority of the "wise." His interpretation is mainly based on Patrizi's early work, *La città felice,* which indeed propounds such a structure of society, clearly based on Plato's *Republic.* I think that this model is no longer involved in the *Nova de Universis Philosophia,* which was written nearly forty years later. True, Patrizi does at times distinguish between different levels of understanding, namely, that of ordinary folk and that of the philosophers (see Panarchia 12v and 39r), but I think Patrizi's basic appeal to rationality in the end overcomes this distinction. Since man is intrinsically rational, in principle everybody could arrive at an individual understanding of divine truth. To me, this (implicit) consequence seems to be even more threatening to Scholastic theology than would be a plea for an alternative hierarchy. However, we must avoid elevating Patrizi to the status of a Hermetic, pre-Enlightenment Voltaire, since all these questions are only implicitly hinted at in the *Nova de Universis Philosophia.*

31. A. L. Puliafito Bleuel, *Nova de Universis Philosophia,* xxviii. It should be added that the final verdict on Patrizi's case was laid in the hands of Cardinal Franciscus Toletus, one of the staunchest and most influential Jesuit Scholastics.

32. Kristeller, "Emendatio," 216.

33. Aguzzi Barbagli, *Lettere,* 61–62.

34. See F. Purnell, "An addition to Francesco Patrizi's correspondence," *Rinascimento* 18 (1978): 135–49.

35. In the *DP,* Patrizi refers several times to his forthcoming *Thesaurus.* See *DP* 1.260, 1.292.

36. *NUPh*, Panarchia 23r. The Kabbalah also appears in the 1588 list, but is absent in the 1571 catalog.

37. Purnell, "An addition," 147

38. K. H. Dannenfeldt, "The Pseudo-Zoroastrian Oracles in the Renaissance," *Studies in the Renaissance* 6 (1957): 8. Patrizi refers to the "Greek translation" by "a certain Julian" (Panarchia 19r).

39. Dannenfeldt, "Pseudo-Zoroastrian Oracles," 18.

40. *NUPh*, app. 1, 25v.

41. According to A. L. Puliafito Bleuel, *Nova de Universis Philosophia,* xv, the *Aclepii discipuli libelli* is Patrizi's version of the *Definitiones Asclepii,* translated for the first time by Ludovico Lazzarelli (1st ed., Lyons, 1507).

42. See R. Reitzenstein, *Poimandres: Studien zur griechisch-ägyptischen und frühchristlichen Literatur* (Leipzig, 1904), 321ff; and K. H. Dannenfeldt, "Hermetica Philosophica," in *Catalogus Translationum et Commentariorum: Medieval and Renais-*

sance Translations and Commentaries, ed. P. O. Kristeller (Washington, D.C., 1960), 1:141–42.

43. Complete title: *Magia philosophica, hoc est Francisci Patricii summi philosophi Zoroaster et eius CCCXX Oracula, Asclepi dialogus et Philosophia Magna. Hermetis Trismegistis Poemander, Sermo sacer, Clavis, Sermo ad filium, Sermo ad Asclepium, Minerva mundi et alia miscellanea.*

44. For general information on the *Theologia Aristotelis*, see J. Kraye, "The Pseudo-Aristotelian *Theology* in the Sixteenth and Seventeenth Centuries," in *Pseudo-Aristotle in the Middle Ages*, ed. J. Kraye, W. F. Ryan, and C. B. Schmitt (London, 1986), 265–86.

45. Complete title: *Sapientissimi Philosophi Aristotelis Stagiritae Theologia sive Mystica Philosophia secundum Aegyptios noviter reperta et in latinum castigatissime redacta.* See Puliafito, *Nova de Universis Philosophia*, xv.

46. F. Patrizi, *Plato et Aristoteles mystici atque exoterici* (app. to *NUPh.*), 1rff.

47. According to Wilmott, "Aristoteles exotericus," 87ff. this divergence can be explained by the different contexts of the two works. The *DP* is an erudite, humanistic work in which Patrizi tries to give an account of the Aristotelian corpus by scientific, philological means, whereas the *NUPh* aims at developing Patrizi's own doctrine. See p. 94: "By the time of the *Nova philosophia*, the critical outlook and emphasis upon textual study that led the humanist scholar of the *Discussiones* to dismiss the *Theologia* as apocryphal had clearly been matched or exceeded by the urge of the doctrinal system-maker to concentrate upon what may have seemed the even more crucial task of salvaging that part of Aristotle's supposed output which appeared closest to, because originating from, Platonic-Hermetic doctrine."

48. Patrizi's concept of space lies at the origin of Newton's concept of "absolute space." See J. Henry, "Francesco Patrizi da Cherso's Concept of Space and Its Later Influence," *Annals of Science* 36 (1979): 549–75.

49. *NUPh*, Panarchia 17r.

50. Ibid., 19rff.

51. See A. D. Nock and A.-J. Festugière, eds., *Corpus Hermeticum* (Paris, 1960), 1:4–5.

52. *NUPh*, Panarchia 20rff.

53. Our analysis follows K. Schuhmann, "Francesco Patrizi en de hermetische filosofie," in *De hermetische gnosis in de loop der eeuwen*, ed. G. Quispel (Baarn, 1992), 346–51.

54. *NUPh*, Panarchia 43v. *Corpus Hermeticum* IV.10. We will cite the English translation by B. P. Copenhaver: *Hermetica. The Greek Corpus Hermeticum and the Latin Asclepius in a New English Translation, with Notes and Introduction* (Cambridge, 1992). The *Corpus Hermeticum* will be cited in the notes as *CH*, followed by the number of the tract and the paragraph number.

55. *CH* IX.9.

56. *NUPh*, Panarchia 13v. See A. D. Nock and A.-J. Festugière, eds., *Asclepius* (Paris, 1960), 1: "Omnia unius esse aut unum esse omnia."

57. *CH* V.9. *NUPh*, Panarchia 13v.

58. *CH* X.14. *NUPh*, Panarchia 16r, 21v, 33r.

59. See *CH* I.11, IV.1, V.9.

60. *CH* I.5. *NUPh*, Panarchia 19r, 21v.

61. *NUPh*, Panarchia 18v, 19r. In this context, Patrizi also adduces evidence from the *Oracula Chaldaica*, which according to him proves that Zoroaster also spoke about a triune God.

62. *NUPh*, Panarchia 37v.

63. Ibid., 35v, 43v, 48r.

64. *CH* II.16.

65. *CH* XI.17. *NUPh*, Panarchia 35v, 48r.

66. *NUPh*, Pampsychia 50v.

67. Ibid., 52r.

68. Ibid., 55r. See *CH* XI.4.

69. In fact, Patrizi states that Zoroaster passed the doctrine on to Hermes, who taught it to Orpheus, who in turn spread the word to all Greek philosophers. The only ones to dissent were Leucippus and Democritus, and, of course, Aristotle, who made a *monstrum* out of the world, claiming it to be partly animated, partly inanimated (*NUPh*, Pampsychia 55r).

70. *NUPh*, Panarchia 76v.

71. *NUPh*, Pancosmia 78r. See *CH* I.4.

72. *NUPh*, Pancosmia 88v.

73. *NUPh*, Pancosmia 115r.

74. *NUPh*, Pancosmia 149v.

75. Patrizi, *Zoroaster*, 5.

76. Although it is a matter of debate now whether the Hermetic influence on the *De Vita* 3 was as important as has sometimes been supposed. See B. P. Copenhaver, "Scholastic Philosophy and Renaissance Magic in the 'De Vita' of Marsilio Ficino," *Renaissance Quarterly* 38 (1984): 523–55; idem, "Hermes Trismegistus, Proclus, and the Question of a Philosophy of Magic in the Renaissance," in *Hermeticism and the Renaissance. Intellectual History and the Occult in Early Modern Europe*, ed. I. Merkel and A. G. Debus (Washington, D.C., London, and Toronto, 1988), 79–110.

77. Allen, "Marsilio Ficino on Plato," 583–84.

78. See also M. J. B. Allen, "Marsile Ficin, Hermès et le 'Corpus Hermeticum,'" in *Présence d'Hermès Trismégiste*, ed. A. Faivre (Paris, 1988), 117, who claims that the actual *influence* of the *Corpus Hermeticum* on Ficino's philosophy is relatively small.

79. Vasoli, "Idea della 'prisca Sapientia' in Francesco Patrizi," 47ff.

80. This myth is of course inspired by the Orphic tradition.

CHAPTER 10

SPIRITUAL ALCHEMY
Interpreting Representative Texts and Images

KAREN-CLAIRE VOSS

Alchemy is of interest to the historian of science because of its bearing on the development of modern chemistry, but it is also of special interest to the historian of religions, because it represents a centrally important current within the western esoteric tradition.[1] That tradition was, and still is, as Antoine Faivre expressed it so beautifully, "both a way of life and an exercise of vision."[2] I recall this characterization here to emphasize the fact that the esoteric tradition and the various currents of which it is comprised are not merely historical artifacts but have always been, and continue to be, dynamic, vital actualizations of the human spirit. The texts and the iconography of alchemy are replete with images that attest to that vitality. It is for this reason that I do not attempt to trace the development of what I am calling spiritual alchemy (a distinction that is explained below) in a chronological way. Besides, this has already been done in several easily accessible overviews.[3] My approach will be to treat it as an integral whole, one that escapes what Mircea Eliade (one of the noted commentators on the subject) described as the "terror of history."[4]

In my view the greatest mistake one can make in approaching spiritual alchemy is to come to it with a set of preconceived doctrines concerning the nature of things, which is allowed to function axiomatically. The task then becomes no longer that of trying to understand, but of attempting to valorize or to vilify. While one thing such an approach to spiritual alchemy lacks is subtlety, there is an alternative approach that is potentially very subtle indeed, because it may easily function as a disguised form of the first, albeit unintentionally. This second approach consists in subjecting the materials being examined to the tacit, and hence unexamined, criteria embedded in a mentality, a worldview, which are such that the materials appear as rattling, dry bones, devoid of meaning, perhaps thereby even faintly ridiculous. This often occurs when we utilize an approach found in much late-twentieth-century scholarship, comprised of idiosyncratically (hence, arbitrarily) selected elements from the analytic philosophical tradition, together with the tattered, tired (though still feebly twitching) remnants of ideas of "objectivity" that were developed in the late nineteenth century. Great care must be taken when utilizing such contemporary methodological tools to examine materials like alchemy. Instead, one should try to become intimately familiar with the premodernist worldview that gave rise to spiritual alchemy and to develop a *genuinely* empathetic grasp of both the worldview and its manifestation. Without these two efforts one cannot hope to understand the materials. Such an approach is not to be confused with advocacy or with depreciation; rather, it is related to a third thing: it requires courage. For a scholar, bracketing experience is much easier, and certainly much safer, than to confront it head on. Put very simply, the approach I am using here leaves one open to the possibility of experiencing wonder: of coming to know something we did not know previously, or of deepening our knowledge of something we were already acquainted with. That is my understanding of what being a scholar is essentially all about, and I confess that it is a process that brings me not only pleasure, but joy.

A good example of what I understand by becoming familiar with a particular worldview appears in Robert Darnton's introduction to his *Mesmerism and the End of the Enlightenment in France*. Darnton can hardly be viewed as an apologist with some particular ax to grind, and his refreshingly straightforward approach can only evoke admiration. Darnton writes that his book "attempts to examine the mentality of literate Frenchmen on the eve of the Revolution, to see the world as they saw it. . . ." Although such a "presumptuous undertaking must fail . . . it is worth attempting." His research has lead him to conclude that the "hottest topic" of that period was "science in general, mesmerism in particular", and that "Frenchmen of the 1780s . . . found that mesmerism offered a serious explanation of Nature, of her wonderful, invisible forces, and even, in some cases, of the forces governing society and politics." Darnton adds that it is just too bad for modern readers if they find this fact unpalatable. Accordingly, he writes, his aim is to "restore [Mesmer] to his rightful place, somewhere near Turgot, Franklin, and Cagliostro in the pantheon of that age's most-talked-about men."[5]

It is clear that in the case of spiritual alchemy we have a somewhat analogous situation. It is not only appropriate to discuss an alchemical treatise in terms of the worldview that formed the context within such a treatise was produced; this is even required, lest we distort the very material we seek to understand. The world view which produced the particular corpus of material to which I am referring as "spiritual alchemy" was that of esotericism. Let us therefore begin with examining some of the most important elements of that worldview.

The Worldview of Esotericism

According to the taxonomy devised by Antoine Faivre, the simultaneous presence of four "intrinsic" components or characteristics is the criterion that renders esotericism identifiable. The four are sometimes, though not necessarily, accompanied by two more, which he calls "relative."[6] The fourth component is called "transmutation": a term that is derived directly from alchemy. As explained by Faivre, this term is preferable to "transformation," since the latter "does not necessarily signify the passage from one plane to another, nor the modification of the subject in its very being, i.e., ontologically."[7] Transmutation means metamorphosis and entails a form of gnosis. Together with the idea of transmutation, Faivre's characterization of esotericism as "both a way of life and an exercise of vision" raises important theoretical considerations that have a direct bearing on understanding what I am calling "spiritual alchemy." In an early article to which I am greatly indebted, Faivre has discussed some of the same issues (e.g., the subject/object relation and the alchemical movement from potency to act)[8] that I take up here. However, to my knowledge all of the aforementioned considerations have not been raised, still less developed, nor have their implications been examined in the specific context of the study of esotericism. I will begin developing these ideas in the following sections and continue in the course of examining the texts and images I have selected. My approach to spiritual alchemy (and by extrapolation to esotericism) follows the general approach of authors such as Mircea Eliade.[9]

I said that spiritual alchemy must be approached in terms of the worldview that gave rise to it; and I mentioned the importance of realizing just how different that worldview is from the one prevailing today.

Consider, for example, Leo Stavenhagen's statement in his edition of the dialogues of Morienus and Khalid ibn Yazid:

> Alchemy has suffered the misfortune of being classed as a science from a modern point of view—as a chrysopoietic technology—which has occluded our view of its system. Scientific it certainly was when it first reached the West sometime late in the twelfth century, but in a thoroughly medieval sense, in which nothing, science least of all, could be separated from ethics, morals, and religion. For if science could not substantiate man's claim on immortality, what use was it?[10]

The practitioners of spiritual alchemy based the validity of their worldview on (what they considered to be) the fact that they experienced transmutation, and/or had a vision or revelation that resulted in an experience of transmutation. Their reasoning was that one can only experience things that are real; and experience, for them, was something that has integrity, that can and should be trusted. In sum, experience provided both the criterion and the authority for making the claim that their worldview was valid.

In contemporary usage, the term "worldview" mostly performs a distancing function: it is used to refer to a set of beliefs, doctrines, or philosophical ideas. However, when we say that the alchemists held a particular worldview for which they claimed validity, we cannot mean that they merely held a set of beliefs about the world, or that they merely accepted a set of ideas concerning the world on an intellectual level. Rather, in their context, they claimed that their worldview was immediately derived from an actual experience of the four things that Faivre has called "intrinsic components," which make the esoteric tradition identifiable (to us), and render the esoteric worldview coherent (in terms of our perspective). These four things were experienced as real, i.e., as deriving from the nature of reality itself. To have a worldview both implied and entailed, for the alchemists, a specific *experience* of the world. That experience of the world not only gave rise to beliefs, doctrines, or philosophical ideas, but also supported a praxis that was consistent, congruent, with the worldview. Theory and practice were inextricably woven together. This is why the materials of spiritual alchemy indeed constitute compendia of techniques "of illumination,"[11] written with the intention of making accessible to others a *way of being in the world;* and this is the reason why spiritual alchemy was believed to function as a mode of transmitting gnosis. In short, the spiritual alchemist was an initiate, one "who knows."[12]

A FRAMEWORK FOR UNDERSTANDING

The term "spiritual alchemy" is a precise designation that I chose using the same distinguishing criteria that were used by the alchemists themselves. An alternative form, "material alchemy," was practiced by those who were often referred to as "puffers." Originally, this term simply referred to the efforts with bellows that were needed to keep the fires going. Eventually, however, it came to acquire disparaging connotations; it was used by one group of alchemists to refer to another, i.e., to those who were engaged in a mere pseudoalchemy and whose insight into the nature of the alchemical process never extended beyond the material.[13] Puffers maintained that the Philosopher's Stone was material gold, and only that. They were in the work for the money, or they were in it in order to increase the store of facts that were then available, or both. In contrast to this, "spiritual" alchemy was understood as a form of illumination, a means of transmutation, a method for experiencing levels of reality that are not ordinarily accessible, since they exist beyond the level of everyday reality. "Material alchemy" utilizes substances from the physical world and has for its goal some product or other (e.g., gold or knowledge). "Spiritual alchemy," in contrast, works with physical substances too, but in a very particular way: one that is "spiritual" in that it includes *all* of the characteristics of material alchemy *and* also goes *beyond* them, to an experience of transmutation resulting in an ontological change. Alchemists who practiced "spiritual alchemy" would be the first to insist that, strictly speaking, there is no other kind of alchemy. Whether or not they were correct in this is not for us to decide; but for the sake of brevity, henceforth in this paper I will refer to spiritual alchemy simply as alchemy.

Below, I will provide an overview of the alchemical process. First, however, I want to set forth a partly theoretical, partly descriptive account in order to afford some preliminary help with understanding. In what follows I give an account of the alchemical process that presents, first, a description of three *characteristics* that permit us to distinguish these two types of alchemy (i.e., the experience and concept of the subject/object relation; causality; and time) and, second, a summary of *changes* that took place in an alchemist's conceptual model as the work progressed.[14] For the sake of clarity and brevity each of the three characteristics has been more or less artificially separated from the other two, although in fact of course each is related to the others in exceedingly complex ways.

Here are the three characteristics:

1. *Subject/object relation.* Both types of alchemy exhibit a characteristic experience and concept of the subject/object relation. In material alchemy one conceives reality as an object completely removed from oneself, outside oneself; hence, what we call the self is the subject, what we call the world is the object, and the boundary between subject and object is static, fixed. In spiritual alchemy, however, one finds reality to be a living system in which one participates, to which one contributes, and in which the boundaries between subject and object are fluid.

2. *Causality.* Both types of alchemy exhibit a characteristic experience and concept of causality. Material alchemy is characterized by what one can call *substance* or *mechanistic* causality. This is the kind of causality associated with a "means/ends" approach to reality, one that holds that reality is comprised of only one level and that all of its elements can be manipulated as one manipulates a machine—for example, a lawn mower. Spiritual alchemy, however, is characterized by what one can call *process* causality, the kind that Giordano Bruno had in mind when writing about the "inner artificer."[15] At the level of conceptualization, the operative causality in spiritual alchemy is understood to possess an infinite number of gradations of the movement from potency to act, occurring on an infinite number of levels, which can be modeled (albeit inadequately)[16] as a spectrum marked at one end by absolute potentialization and at the other by absolute actualization.[17]

3. *Time.* The theme of the acceleration of time in alchemy has been discussed at length by Eliade, and I do not intend to do more than mention it here.[18] The basic idea is that telluric processes that took aeons to accomplish within the earth could be radically accelerated in the alchemical laboratory. Here I simply wish to call attention to a contrast

that can be perceived between the conception of time in material alchemy and in spiritual alchemy. In material alchemy one generally finds a conventional conception of time as being comprised of three discrete "parts": past, present, and future. Moreover, time is considered irreversible; it flows in one direction only. In spiritual alchemy one finds a much more subtle conception of time in which these three discrete parts are only *apparently* separated from each other. In spiritual alchemy, time is not experienced as irreversible, but as reversible; not only that, but the "movement" of time is not so much a movement as a *mode* of perception[19] and thus goes far beyond being something that can be conceived of in linear terms, as having a forward or backward motion that could be modeled as occurring on an imaginary line.

I have described these three characteristics for the sake of completion, but in this paper most of the emphasis will be on the first two.

Having outlined these three basic characteristics, I will now give a summary of the changes which took place in the alchemist's conceptual model during the course of the work. The conceptual model with which both material *and* spiritual alchemy began was linear. The goal of the alchemical process was located at the end of a linear series of discrete pairs of causes and effects; the operative causality was conceived of as substance causality. The initial conception of the subject/object relation is evident in the view of the goal as external and unrelated to the alchemist. It can be diagrammed thus:

```
c e c e c e c e c, etc.

Alchemist ------------------ > Philosopher's Stone

                [c = cause; e = effect]
```

The first modification to which this model could be subjected is related for the most part to causality. The conception of the operative causality would change from substance causality to process causality. The task of resolving the elements in the alchemical opposition was considered so formidable that the alchemists were convinced that they could not possibly effect a resolution by themselves. The alchemical Mercurius began to be understood as a kind of divine "other" who would intervene in the work by effecting the resolution of opposites. However, notwithstanding the introduction of Mercurius as an operative factor, the alchemical work would continue to be modeled in a linear way, meaning that the subject/object relation would continue to be conceived of in the same way as before. The second model remained linear, like the first, save for a new understanding of Mercurius as process (along with a burgeoning intuition that the goal was somehow identical with the starting point, symbolically equivalent to the *prima materia* of cosmogonic myth). That model can be diagrammed as follows:

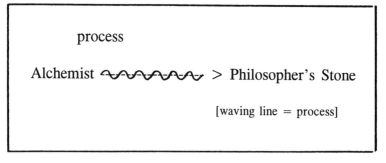

The next modification is very radical because it entails a change in the entire conception of the alchemical work. To begin with, the conception of causality as process would be retained, but now the linear model would be replaced by a circular one reflecting new insight into the nature of the alchemical process.[20] I have described this modification as radical because of its profound implications for the conception and the experience of the subject/object relation, causality, and possibly (although not necessarily) time, and if it were possible to posit a strict demarcation between material and spiritual alchemy one would do it at this juncture. See the diagram on the following page.

Let me try to explain. Many of the alchemists explicitly identified themselves with mythic creators as they struggled with unformed materials and understood their work as being analogous with that of *Terra Mater*. Both identifications can be interpreted as being an imitation, a

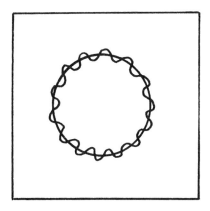

re-creation of sacred processes. I suggest that the extent to which an alchemist subscribed to such an identification and was able to shift away from the normal experience of space, time, and historical process determined the extent to which he or she made a shift *away from* an ordinary mode of conceptualization and experience and its concomitants (that shown in the first diagram) *toward* an extraordinary mode (that shown in the last diagram). In Eliadean terms we might say that profane experience would become increasingly sacralized. The reason I have described this modification as extremely radical is because we are dealing here with no less than the progressive dissolution of normal, dichotomized categories, a shift from the ordinary mode of individual, bounded consciousness to one that was (as I have already said) symbolically equivalent to the *prima materia* of the beginning. To put it in alchemical terms, at a certain point in the alchemical work the alchemists saw that it was necessary for Mercurius to intervene in order to unite the opposites; indeed, by the end of the alchemical work, a whole series of opposites would have to be united by Mercurius. He would transform the two elements within each opposition into one another, until they converged on a central point (e.g., the central axis of the caduceus, or the "sacred center" where heaven and earth meet). The accompanying line of reasoning was that on the most profound level, the alchemist equaled both the alchemical process and the means of the process; alchemical process was tantamount to both self-knowledge and to the knowledge of the divine;[21] and the goal of the alchemical process was somehow equivalent to the starting point, the *prima materia*.

THE ALCHEMICAL PROCESS

I have said that the alchemical texts reflect an understanding of validity based on experience; that they were intended as techniques of illumination, thereby involving theory as well as praxis; and that over the course of the alchemical work, there were radical alterations in the conception and the experience of the subject/object relation, causality, and time, resulting in the transmutation of the alchemist himself. Before turning to the treatises themselves, I will provide an overview of the alchemical process. We must realize, however, that the various divisions to which I will refer (just as the characteristics and the conceptual models that I have already outlined) are useful only as general heuristic tools. Beyond that, they become artificial and forced, and ultimately misleading, since they refer to phenomena and processes that are interrelated in extremely complex ways.

Alchemy can be understood in terms of two aspects, which Carl Gustav Jung has referred to as the "double face of alchemy": the *operatio* (the practical) and the *theoria* (the theoretical). Every alchemist equipped a laboratory, selected and studied texts, and constructed a theoretical framework (which was continuously refined) to reflect the alchemist's conception and experience of the process, as well as his or her relationship to it, both of which changed as the work proceeded. On one level, the alchemists' purpose in the laboratory was the production of gold, the most perfect of all metals; on another level, their goal was to produce the arcane substance known as the Philosopher's Stone.[22] With respect to alchemy's practical aspect, it is virtually impossible to determine the exact order or number of stages in the alchemical work, nor is it always apparent what level is being referred to. For example, we may be told that "mercury" is necessary for a certain procedure, but this might mean a metal, or the qualities of the metal, or the divinity of the same name, or even all three. For a variety of reasons (but primarily because of the esoteric doctrine of correspondences and similitudes, which were linked to the underlying belief in the relation between microcosm and macrocosm) the alchemists were given to making analogies between that which occurred on an "outer," material level and experiences that took place on an "inner," spiritual plane.[23] Thus, an analogy was made between the maturation of the chemical processes in the alchemists' laboratory which would result in the Philosopher's Stone, and the development of their own gnosis. If, on the material level, the alchemists' purpose in the laboratory was the production of gold, the most perfect of all metals, by actualizing all the qualities of gold that were thought to be potentially present in lesser metals, on the spiritual level the purpose was to develop the true Self, to "lead out the gold within," as they said, by actualizing the qualities potentially present in the human being.

The alchemical work has three basic stages: the *nigredo*, the *albedo*, and the *rubedo*. It is true that other stages corresponding to nuances of the alchemical process are mentioned in the texts but, although these would be of utmost importance for an alchemist, they are not so critical for us.[24] The essence of the alchemical movement is contained in the oft-quoted motto: *solve et coagula*, "divide and unite." Like the three stages discussed above, these two movements are essential to the work and comprise cycles that are repeated over and over again, on increasingly subtle levels. Alchemy aimed at the resolution of material and spiritual opposites as conventionally understood. This resolution took place on different levels, corresponding to deepening levels of understanding of the true nature of the alchemical work. At a certain point, a mediating term (often under the form of the alchemical Mercurius) would intervene in the process. The ultimate resolution was characterized by a mode of subtle mutual reciprocity and interpenetration in which each term of an opposition entered fully into the being of the other, transforming and being transformed. This union was frequently imaged as a *hieros gamos*, and its fruit was the Philosopher's Stone.

1. The *nigredo* is the preparatory stage, at which the alchemist must confront unknown, chaotic material. Much has been written (most notably by C. G. Jung and Mircea Eliade) about the analogy between the alchemists and mythic creator divinities, who must grapple with the chaos of the *prima materia* as a prerequisite to creation. In the most general terms, the *nigredo* means a first encounter with darkness, with depth. Symbolically analogous with probing the innermost depths of *Terra Mater* in order to find the Philosopher's Stone and claim it as the prize,[25] the *nigredo* is an encounter with the self, the time of the dark night of the soul, when there is no certainty to be found anywhere. It is at this stage

that the alchemist must plunge into the disorganized, confused welter of material, with no clear instruction. On the level of material process, this stage is associated with blackness; on the level of spiritual process it is associated with melancholy of the extreme Saturnian type.[26] One early-seventeenth-century engraving depicts an alchemist kneeling within an alcove that is set apart from the rest of his laboratory.[27] His kneeling position and his outstretched, supplicating arms give mute testimony to the interrelatedness of the concepts and experience of "spiritual" and "material." This is implicit in the word "laboratory," which is derived from the Latin *laborare*, "to work," but would also remind the alchemist of the verb *orare*, "to pray." For the alchemist, doing the former without the latter would have been unthinkable.[28] At the same time, this image not only testifies to the depression and despair that plagues the alchemist as he seeks to impose form on the chaos that confronts him, but also to the fact that he is still seeking help from outside himself. Thus, it is an indication that the changes related to the subject/object relation and the causality operative in the work have not yet begun.

2. The next stage is the *albedo*. With the aim of imposing norms on chaotic material, the alchemists approached the *massa confusa* of the primal substance by dividing it. Throughout the *albedo* stage they continued to work with the various elements that were derived during the *nigredo*, and by the end of the *albedo* they were left with two elements viewed as though in polar opposition to one another. It is here that the alchemical problem of the *coincidentia oppositorum* arises. Now the task was to effect a successful resolution in order to obtain the Philosopher's Stone. This resolution had to be carried out on many different levels, as indicated by the symbolic representations of pairs of opposites as both material and spiritual—e.g., silver/gold and body/spirit. Once again, these levels correspond to deepening levels of understanding with regard to the true nature of the work. Finally, according to alchemical theory, all the opposing elements would be resolved, all the levels would somehow converge on one another, and the goal would be achieved.

As explained above, the conceptual framework underwent changes at different points in the alchemical work. At the end of the *albedo* stage we can observe the first of them. While the model remains linear, there is a new conception of causality that reflects a new understanding of the significance of the image of Mercurius. While we cannot begin to do justice to the significance of this figure here, it will help to think of

Mercurius as a kind of personification of innumerable paradoxical qualities that would provide the alchemists with the means of the work.[29] As the means of the work—i.e., as the process that effected transmutation—Mercurius functioned as the third term that would bring about a resolution of opposites simultaneously in both the substances and the alchemist. The condensed material, left over from the distillation that took place during the *albedo* stage, corresponded to the spirit, while the substance from which it had been extracted corresponded to matter, the body. Now that the soul had been "led out" from the body, there remained the problem of conflict between them. The substances could not be merely superficially reunited; instead, it was necessary to produce a genuine compound. That compound signified the resolution of opposites, which the alchemists believed could not take place without spiritual help of some sort. Hence, Mercurius would come to resolve the problem by effecting a synthesis. At this stage, the concept of the subject/object relation had not yet changed, but once the understanding of the work as a linear series of single, discrete, and substantial causes and effects was mitigated by the addition of Mercurius, it indicated that the concept of the operative causality was beginning to change from substance to process causality. The model of the work at this point is a linear chain of substantial causes and substantial effects in which Mercurius will intervene so as to effect a synthesis among the various pairs of oppositions. The reason for saying that the concept of the work as a whole remained essentially linear is that the goal was still thought of as being an object to be attained only at the end of the alchemical stages. Mercurius, too, was still viewed as an object relative to the alchemist, i.e., as an external force that would enable the alchemical work to proceed.

3. Thus, at the beginning of the third stage, the *rubedo*, the elements of the *coincidentia oppositorum* had still to be resolved, via Mercurius (the personification of mediating energy, the third term). While the thrust of the first and second stages involved a movement aimed at division, the movement in the third stage emphasizes unity. The aim of the *rubedo* was to join together the two elements left over from the previous stages— one of the processes of this stage being referred to as the *coniunctio*—and the product of the union would be the Philosopher's Stone. As explained above, at the end of the *albedo* the conception of causality began to move from substance to process, but Mercurius continued to be thought of as the *external* cause of the work. Here a linear discussion of the stages,

which involves discussing each of them separately before going on to discuss the Philosopher's Stone, breaks down. One example of the extremely complex issues involved with these changes is that Mercurius (hitherto regarded as the *cause* of the work) begins to become identified with the alchemist himself and with the *goal* of the work. This means that the concept of the subject/object relation changes. The third diagram above is an appropriate model of the alchemical work at this stage, because it reflects the notion of process as well as the circularity that reflects these new insights into the nature of the work.

The successful end to the quest for the Philosopher's Stone, which the alchemists initially regarded as external and "other" to themselves, was spoken of as a return to the *prima materia*. Some years ago, I wrote that the alchemical model appears to have been based on the "myth of the eternal return," the idea that reality consists of an endless, cyclical repetition of events. I argued that, in a certain sense, the idea of a return (modeled by the circle whose circumference is outlined with a waving line) is almost as limiting as the two preceding models. I further argued that if any alchemist had reached the goal of the alchemical work, he or she would not have interpreted the experience in terms of a return to the *prima materia*. I reasoned that since a return is diachronic, it excludes the possibility of a synchronic experience of the totality. That the alchemists nevertheless spoke of their attainment in terms of it being a return clearly indicates that their concept of time had undergone some changes: time had become reversible. The problem is that the idea of a return to the *prima materia* indicates that, even though time is no longer considered irreversible but reversible, we are still dealing with a *linear* concept of time. I argued that not only was this an indication that a new model was needed (I suggested a spiral), but it was an indication that the alchemists in question needed to have gone further.[30] Now I think that what is needed is a much closer look at what was meant by the language about a return to the *prima materia*. If we think of the Stone as the fruit of two elements extracted from out of the chaos of the beginning of the work, which subsequently underwent processes that resulted in their becoming whole again, this is certainly one explanation for the meaning of the "Child of the Work," as it appears under the image of the Hermetic Androgyne and the rubric "Two-in-One." However, the Stone is more than simply the sum of its parts, derived at the end of a series of operations. It is, rather, an emergent property derived from a multileveled union of the two. The Child of the Work necessarily continues to participate in the being of the two, just as the two continue to participate in the one from which they emerge; yet it goes beyond them, and becomes a third thing. For this reason, it is more precise to speak of a "Three-in-One." It is on this basis that one can gain a deeper insight into what it really means to say that the beginning and the end are one.[31] The image of the Child of the Work signifies the second birth in the theosophical sense.[32] The alchemist arrives at his/her goal after a long and arduous journey, involving not only the combination and re-combination of elements that were already extant within, but the integration of new elements as well. On one level, these appear to originate from without but, on another level, they are already potentially extant. Ultimately the alchemist discovers that the Child is his or her true Self. In the context of spiritual alchemy we must grapple with a nuanced aggregate of previously disparate conceptual categories reflecting equally nuanced experience. At this point, our methodological and conceptual tools are pushed to the limits. Here, too, we reach the limits of metaphorical as well as analytic language and, possibly, even the limits of our own experience.

Selected Texts

I have selected four treatises that are representative of spiritual alchemy; two of them have images. The first treatise illustrates the importance accorded to personal experience; the last three illustrate the changes connected with the subject/object relation, causality, and time. I will concentrate on the discursive and pictorial images showing the *coincidentia oppositorum* under the form of the *hieros gamos*, since these are excellent indicators of change in the conceptualization and experience of the subject/object relation.

The Revelations of Morienus to Khalid ibn Yazid

The first alchemical work to appear in the West is a treatise attributed, like many others, to Hermes Trismegistus.[33] According to Leo Stavenhagen this attribution derives from Robertus Castrenis, who translated the text from Arabic into Latin in 1182. It was later published in Paris in 1559, under the title *Booklet of Morienus Romanus, of old the Hermit of Jerusalem, on the Transfiguration of the Metals and the Whole of the Ancient Philosophers' Occult Arts, Never Before Published.*[34]

The story concerns Khalid, a king who had been looking for many years for a man described as "Morienus the Greek, who lived as a recluse in the mountains of Jerusalem," because he wanted to find out from him the secret of the "Great Work." The king has occasion to travel to another town, where a man comes to him and tells him that he has made his home in the mountains of Jerusalem and knows a wise man, a recluse, who possesses the knowledge that the king is looking for. After warning the man about the punishment he can expect if it turns out that he is lying, the king gives him many gifts and arranges for him to lead an expedition in search of the wise man. The narrator Ghalib, who accompanies the expedition, relates how they finally succeed in finding the wise man. "He was tall of stature, though aged," we read, "and although lean, so noble of countenance and visage that he was a marvel to behold. Yet he wore a hair shirt, the marks of which were borne on his skin." At their bidding, he agrees to come to the court for an audience with the king. When the king asks the man his name the answer comes: "I am called Morienus the Greek." The king asks how long he has lived in the mountains and learns that Morienus has been there for over one hundred and fifty years. Well pleased with this stranger, the king gives Morienus his own quarters and begins to visit him twice every day. They speak of many things and grow very close. Finally, one day the king asks Morienus to tell him about the Great Work. Seeing that the king is worthy of this, Morienus tells him that he has achieved initiation and agrees to instruct him, emphasizing that nothing can be achieved if it is counter to divine will. He speaks of how God "chose to select certain ones to seek after the knowledge he had established," and how over time this knowledge has been lost, save for what remains in a very few books, which are difficult to understand since the "ancients" sought to preserve the secrets "in order to confute fools in their evil intentions." Because this knowledge was "disguised," anyone seeking to "learn it must understand their maxims." Morienus begins to emphasize that the Work is but a single thing.

Now in answer to your question as to whether this operation has one root or many, know that it has but one, and but one matter and one substance of which and with which alone it is done, nor is anything added to it or subtracted from it.[35]

Numerous authorities, including Hermes, Moses, Maria, and Zosimos, are cited throughout by Morienus to legitimate what he says, and the lesson concerning oneness is reiterated continually. "There is but one stage and one path necessary for its mastery. Although all the authorities used different names and maxims, they meant to refer to but one thing, one path and one stage." The method to be followed is in imitation of nature; and Morienus's description demonstrates that, like nature, it is characterized by process causality:

> For the conduct of this operation, you must have pairing, production of offspring, pregnancy, birth, and rearing . . . the performance of this composition is likened to the generation of man, whom the great Creator most high made not after the manner in which a house is constructed nor as anything else which is built by the hand of man. For a house is built by setting one object up another, but man is not made of objects.[36]

Morienus then proceeds to instruct the king about the details of the substances to choose, the proportions, how to mix them, and when to heat them and for how long, always repeating that God's help is needed. He insists on the need for personal experience and tells the king that before he will continue with his explanations, he will "bring before [him] the things called by these names": "that you may see them, as well as work with them in your presence. . . . one who has seen this operation performed, is not as one who has sought for it only through books. . . ."[37] Finally, he says once again that "there is no strength nor help except by the will of great God most high," and the narrator writes: "Here ends the book of Morienus, as it is called. Thanks be to God."

This treatise is paradigmatic of the way in which validity and the authority of experience are bound up with each other in the alchemical tradition. Initially, Morienus is able to win the king's trust solely on the basis of the answers he gives to questions concerning his personal experience during his first audience with the king. Later, Morienus tells the king that before he will proceed with instruction, he will perform various steps while the king watches, "so that you may see them," since "one who has seen this operation performed, is not as one who has sought for it only through books."

Rosarium philosophorum

The first printed edition of the *Rosarium philosophorum* appears in a collective work, *Alchimia opuscula complura veterum philosophorum* (. . .), that came out in Frankfurt in 1550.[38] The text is accompanied by twenty images (plus one on the title page). With respect to the idea that experience is the most important criterion for claiming validity, the *Rosarium* states that there is only "one stone, one medicine, one vessel, one regiment, and one disposition, and know this: that it is a most true Art." This is immediately followed by what is intended to be the capstone argument: "Furthermore the Philosophers would never have laboured and studied to express such diversities of colours and the order of them unless they had seen and felt them."[39]

While the text of the *Rosarium* is rich, I find the images even more compelling, since they convey better than the text the most important theme in alchemy: that of the conjunction of opposites. In the *Rosarium*, as in so many other alchemical treatises, this theme appears under the form of the *hieros gamos*. C. G. Jung considers the images of the *Rosarium philosophorum* to be paradigmatic, and says that they constitute the "most complete and simplest illustration" of the importance of the *hieros gamos* in alchemy.[40] In an earlier article about the *hieros gamos* in the context of the history of religions, I discussed some of the implications of its appearance in the images of the *Rosarium*. I argued that many of the alchemists appear to have undergone a complex experience involving mutual reciprocity between the events in the laboratory and within themselves, of a kind that "hearkens back to, and carries forward, the imprint of a religious tradition which combined physical and spiritual levels of transformation"[41] and that texts like that of the *Rosarium* attest to this. Here I wish to emphasize that the alchemical conjunction under the form of the *hieros gamos* is itself illustrative of the changing conception and experience of the subject/object relation, causality, and time.

Plate 1 shows a fountain with three spigots. As the text explains,

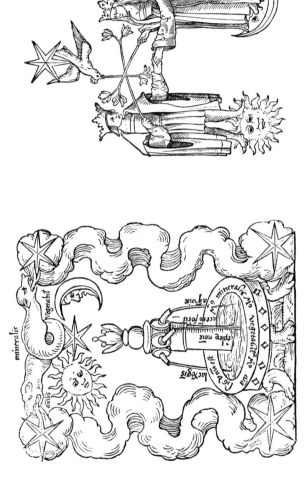

Rosarium plate 2

Wyr sindt der metall anfang vnd erste natur /
Die kunst macht durch vns die höchste tinctur.
Keyn brunn noch wasser ist meyn gleych /
Ich mach gesund arm vnd reych.
Vnd bin doch itzund gysstig vnd dötlich.

Rosarium plate 1. Courtesy of Bibliotheca Philosophica
Hermetica, Amsterdam.

PHILOSOPHORVM.

seipsis secundum æqualitacē inspissentur. Solus enim calor tēperatus est humiditatis inspissatiuus et mixtionis perfectiuus, et non super excedens. Nā generatiōes et procreationes rerū naturaliū habent soli fieri per tēperatisimū calorē et æqua lē, vt est solus fimus equinus humidus et calidus.

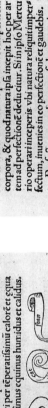

D ij

ROSARIVM

corrūpitur, neq; ex imperfecto penitus secundū artem aliquid fieri potest. Ratio est quia ars primas dispositiones inducere non potest, sed lapis noster est tres media inter perfecta & imperfecta corpora, & quod natura ipsa incepit hoc per artem ad perfectionē deducitur. Si in ipso Mercurio operari inceperis vbi natura reliquit imperfectum, inuenies in eo perfectionē et gaudebis.

Perfectum non alteratur, sed corrumpitur. Sed imperfectum bene alteratur, ergo corruptio vnius est generatio alterius.

Speculum

Rosarium plate 3

Rosarium plate 4

ROSARIVM

CONIVNCTIO SIVE
Coitus.

O Luna durch mein vmbgeben/vnd süsse mynne/
Wirstu schön/starck/vnd gewaltig/als ich byn.
O Sol/du bist vber alle liecht zu erkennen/
So bedarstu doch mein als der hann der hennen.

ARISLEVS IN VISIONE.

Coniunge ergo filium tuum Gabricum dilectiorem tibi in omnibus filijs tuis cum sua sorore
Beya

Rosarium plate 5

PHILOSOPHORVM.

CONCEPTIO SEV PVTRE
factio

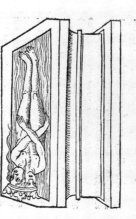

Zye ligen könig vnd köngin dot/
Die sele scheydt sich mit grosser not.

ARISTOTELES REX ET
Philosophus.

Nunquam vidi aliquod animatum crescere sine putrefactione, nisi autem fiat putredo in vanum erit opus alchimicum.

Rosarium plate 6

ROSARIVM
ANIMÆ EXTRACTIO VEL
imprægnatio.

ROSARIVM
MVLTIPLICATIO.

Hye teylen sich die vier element/
Aus dem leyb scheydt sich die sele behendt.

Hye tewt sich das wasser sincken/
Vnd gibt dem erdtrich sein wasser wider zu trincken.

De

CAPIT

Rosarium plate 7

Rosarium plate 8

PHILOSOPHORVM.

ANIMÆ IVBILATIO SEV
Ortus seu Sublimatio.

Hie schwingt sich die seele hernidder/
Und erquickt den gereinigten leychnam wider-

L iij

Rosarium plate 9

PHILOSOPHORVM.

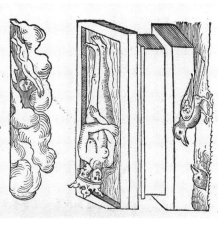

Hie ist geboren die edele Keyserin reich/
Die meister nennen sie ihrer dochter gleich.
Die vermeret sich/gebiert kinder ohn zal/
Sein unndödtlich rein/unnd ohn alles mahl.

Die

Rosarium plate 10

PHILOSOPHORVM.

rea, ergo generabit ſibi ſimile ſpeciū eſt terreū, vt ipſum. Sic & iſtā tincturam & omnē aliam quæ noninueniū in proprietate naturæ deſpicias cū aliis vijs extraneis, quia in ipſis non eſt aliud ſ̄ rerū confumptio, ſeporis perditio et laboris, cū omnia alia apparētia ſunt & nō exiſtētia metalla quæ per minora mineralia vel conſimilia fuerint laborata.

ILLVMINATIO.

Zweiſt Sol widder gar verſuncken/
Vnd in dem Mercurio Philoſophorum erdruncken iſt.

Rosarium plate 12

PHILOSOPHORVM.
FERMENTATIO.

Zye wird Sol aber verſchloſſen
Vnd mit Mercurio philoſophorum ybergoſſen

Rosarium plate 11

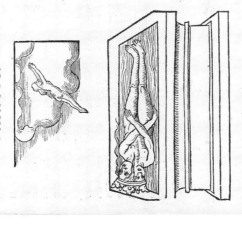

ROSARIVM

Quia dicit Ariſtoteles. Sciant artifices alchi=
miæ, ſpecies rerum transmutari non poſſe ꝗ ve=
rum eſt niſi in primam materiam reducantur vel
conuertantur id eſt in argꝼtum viuũ, & vltra hoc
non conſulit, ſecus fieri eſt impoſſibile. &c.

NVTRIMENTVM

Ʒie iſt Sol worden ſchwarꜩ
Mit dem Mercurio philoſophorum alß ein harꜩ.

SECVN

Rosarium plate 13

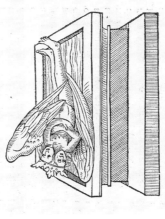

PHILOSOPHORVM
FIXATIO.

Ʒie hat der lune leben gar ein end/
Der geyſt ſteygt in die höhe behend.

R iij

Rosarium plate 14

ROSARIVM
REVIFICATIO.

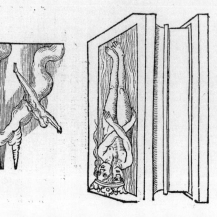

Jeye kompt die Seele vom himmel schon vnd klar.
Vnd macht aufferstehn der philosophi dochter zur
(war.)
Geber

PHILOSOPHORVM
ABLVTIO VEL
Mundificatio.

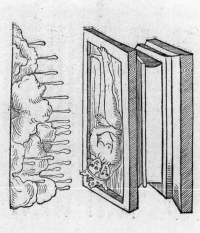

Hie felt der Tauw von himmel herab/
Vnd wascht den schwarzen leyb im grab ab.

K. iiij

Rosarium plate 16

Rosarium plate 15

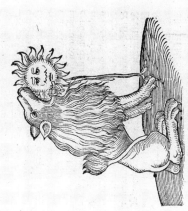

PHILOSOPHORVM.

& ficca foluantur, calcinentur, fiue fublimentur fecundum quod viderit, & melius iudicatur fecundum fanum fenfum operantis.

Ich bin der war grün vnnd guldisch Lewe ohn sorge/
Jnn mir steckt alle heimlickeyt der philosophen verborgen.

Y iij

Rosarium plate 18

ROSARIVM,
PERFECTIONIS
oftenfio.

ÆNIGMA REGIS.
hye ist geboren der keyser aller ehren/

Leyn

Rosarium plate 17

Nach meinem viel vnnd manches leiden vnnd marter
(groß)
Bin ich erstanden/ clarificiert/ vnd aller macel bloß.
& à la/tz

Rosarium plate 20

ROSARIVM.

lisiunctis pariter, quia coniuncta simul magis pro=
funt quam si per se forent separata. Ex iitis con=
fidera necessitatem virorumque mercuriorum,

Rosarium plate 19

although it appears that the waters flowing from each of them are separate, they are really a single water "of which and with which our magistery is effected." One may note the conflation between substance and method that is implicit here. Thus, there are implications for the conventional subject/object relation from the very beginning. Elsewhere I have compared these flowing waters to the image of primordial waters from the *Enuma Elish*, a creation myth dating from c. 1900 B.C.E, which tells how the primordial waters of Tiamat, the female principle, commingle as a single body with those of Apsu, the male principle; in that context, I argued that the theme of the *hieros gamos* is implicitly present already in this first image.[42] Like the primordial hierogamy from which all life sprang, the alchemical fountain is also the source of life.

In plate 2 we see a king and queen dressed in elaborate robes. Each holds out to the other the end of a stalk terminating in two flowers; he stands on the sun, she on the crescent moon. At this stage they are separate, but their union in the "chymical marriage" is symbolically prefigured by their clasped hands. A dove (at once a mediating symbol and a further link with the *hieros gamos*, since it was associated with Eros and with the powerful female divinities of the ancient Near East)[43] is shown hovering just above their heads. It holds its own stalk of flowers, which perfectly intersects the cross formed by those held by the king and queen. This is another symbolic prefiguring that refers to the mediating energy, personified as Mercurius, which would function as the third term that would resolve the elements during the final stage.

Plate 3 shows the royal pair naked; wearing separate crowns they again hold out a stalk to each other. They are becoming closer: here each stalk has but one flower, not two, and each of them has reached out to the other to actually grasp the flower that is being proffered. The banner over the king's head reads: "O Luna, let me be thy husband"; that over the queen's reads: "O Sol, I must submit to thee." Here again the dove appears between them holding a stalk with a single flower in its beak. The dove's banner reads: "It is the Spirit that vivifies."

In plate 4 the king and queen become even closer. They are crowned and naked; the dove is between them; the same configuration of stalks with one flower that appears in plate 3 is repeated here, but now they are shown seated within a single vessel filled with water, thereby evoking the commingling of primordial waters that was already seen in plate 1.

In plate 5 we see the king and queen in sexual embrace. Plates 6–9 form the first of two series (the second being comprised of plates 13–16) that indicate successively deepening levels of conjunction. The king and queen are shown lying in a sepulcher. They appear for the first time in hermaphroditic form. Their bodies are joined, they have two heads, and they wear a single crown.

It is interesting to compare plate 10 with plate 2, because they are like reverse mirror images. In plate 2 the queen stands on the moon; the king on the sun. They are entirely separate. They wear two crowns. In plate 10 we are shown the end of the process that was illustrated in plates 6–9, which is the alchemical two-in-one. The king and queen are joined to form one perfect winged hermaphrodite. They wear one crown; they stand on a single crescent moon. One serpent coils around her outstretched arm; he holds a chalice from which three serpents emerge. Here I would suggest that the serpent and the chalice are close symbolic kin of the *yoni/lingam* symbol as it appears in the context of Hindu tantra. In any case, symbolically speaking, in the context of the western alchemical tradition, serpent and cup are often associated with "masculine" and "feminine" qualities; the fact that here we see the queen with the serpent, and the king holding a chalice from which three serpents emerge, seems to be a further indication of the progressively deepening exchange. The single face that is shown at the top of the plant heralds the complete conjunction, which is now close at hand.

Plate 11 shows the beginning of the last stage of the work. The image is explicitly sexual. The king and queen, both winged, wear two crowns, and are submerged in water. Their limbs are entwined; her hand grasps his phallus; his left hand fondles the nipple of her breast; his right is under her neck supporting her. Plate 12 shows a winged face of the sun arising from a sepulcher; light (i.e., life) comes from out of darkness (i.e., death).

Plate 13 is the first of four images comprising the second series. Here we see the king and queen in hermaphroditic form, winged, with one crown, lying in a sepulcher filled with water. She is on top. Plate 14 is exactly the same, except here they appear without wings. A female figure ascends into a cloud above them on the upper right. Plate 15 is the same again, except here the queen is on the bottom, and the cloud now extends across the entire width of the image at the top. It is full of moisture, which falls down in large drops upon the king and queen. Plate 16 is the last in this series of four. Now we see the female figure again, but this time she is descending from the cloud above them on the upper right. The parallelism that can be seen here shows the exchange between masculine/feminine principles that was symbolically depicted in plates 6–9 continuing, but on a deeper level than previously. Plates 17 is the full flowering of plate 10. It depicts the product of the union between the alchemical opposites. This Child of the Work is not merely the result of a mechanical conjunction of opposites. Plate 18 shows a lion eating the sun. Symbolically this depicts a stage in the development of the alchemist where the illumination that was previously regarded as outside, "other," to himself, is now being assimilated into his or her very being. Plate 19 provides an excellent example of the syncretism we often see between alchemical and Christian symbols. Here Mary is in the center, flanked by the Father and the Son, who are about to crown her. The Holy Spirit, in the form of a dove, hovers above. In the background appear the words *Tria* and *Unum*, Three and One.[44] This image contains a rich variety of hierogamic themes. First, there is the symbolic similarity between the three waters of the alchemical foundation we saw in plate 1 and the Trinity. Second, the incarnation of Christ, the Second Person of the Trinity, was made possible by the hierogamic union between Mary and the Holy Spirit, the Third Person. Third, the Incarnation of the Son entails an ontological condition of simultaneous humanity and divinity—a profound manifestation of hierogamy. Like the marriage between the alchemical opposites, all these unions require mediation. In the alchemical marriage, this function was often performed by Mercurius; in plate 2 we have seen the dove in the role of mediator. Here we see it in that role too, poised above the crown that the Father and Son are about to place on Mary's head, but now it is explicitly associated with the Third Person of the Trinity. That the dove was a symbolic attribute of the female divinities of the ancient near east supports my view that plate 19 is also a hierogamic image, albeit in Christianized form.

Plate 20, the last image in the series, depicts the risen Christ. In his left hand he holds a banner marked with a cross; his right gestures toward the now empty sepulcher. The sepulcher unmistakably indicates that the completed alchemical process has involved the transmutation, not merely the transformation, and certainly not the transcendence, of the body. In the view of the alchemist who wrote the *Rosarium philoso-phorum*, the Christian doctrine of the resurrection of the body signified not the suppression, or even the transcendence, of the physical body, but its glorification and perfection. If the alchemical work necessitated the transcendence of the body, one would not expect to find an empty tomb, but a tomb filled with the putrefying remains of the king and queen. Instead we see the risen Christ, the embodiment of the hierogamic union between human and divine. This last indicates a profound change in the subject/object relation, since the divine is ordinarily viewed as wholly other to the human.

Tractatus aureum

The *Tractatus aureum* (The golden tract) was published in 1566, but is traditionally attributed to Hermes Trismegistus.[45] Appended to the first, theoretical part is a marvelous story "in which the mystery of the whole Matter is Declared." It begins with the universal formula of the fairy tale: "Once upon a time," we read, "when I was walking abroad in a wood, and considering the wretchedness of this life, and deploring that through the lamentable fall of our first parents we had been reduced to this piteous state, I suddenly found myself upon a rough, untrodden, and impracticable path. . . ."[46]

After finding a group of sages in a meadow and impressing them favorably with his quick wit, in a discussion reminiscent of that which took place between Jesus and the elders in the temple, our protagonist is charged with the task of subduing a magical lion. He accomplishes this feat without delay "by gentle, skillful, and subtle means," fortuitously combined with a "knowledge of natural magic." Having finished, he finds himself somehow on top of a wall "which rose more than one hundred yards into the air." With difficulty he proceeds along this wall using a narrow path to the left of a divider that runs along the middle of the wall, and in this way negotiates his path until meeting a person of indeterminate sex, who invites him to try the right side, which is more "convenient." Continuing to the end of the wall, he descends by way of a rather perilous route until he enters a place filled with white and red roses. There he discovers a group of beautiful young women, and some rather distressed young men who find themselves unable to reach the women, on account of the wall that separates them. Undaunted himself, our hero moves on through a series of gates by unlocking them with a "master key" which he has "diligently fashioned" at some unspecified time in the past. At last he comes to the innermost garden, where he meets a wondrous couple, the most beautiful of all he has seen. He asks the young woman how she has managed to scale the wall, and she replies: "This my beloved bridegroom helped me, and now we are leaving this pleasant garden, and hastening to our chamber to satisfy our love."[47]

Going on a little further, the protagonist passes a water mill, exchanges some pleasantries with its miller, and stops in front of a platform where there is gathered a group of old men in deep discussion. It seems the men are engaged in a conversation about "a letter which they had received from the Faculty of the University," and our alchemist knows intuitively that this missive concerns him. He questions the men, who answer that the letter does indeed concern him: "[T]he wife whom you married a long time ago," they tell him, "you must keep forever or else we must tell our chief." Since, as he explains, he and his spouse "were born together, and brought up together as children," he is able to answer truthfully that there is no question of leaving her, and that they will be together even in death.[48]

Next, catching sight again of the gorgeous couple whom he had seen earlier, he notices they are being married properly by the venerable sages, and marvels that the bride, who was also the "mother of the bridegroom," is so youthful in appearance. However, no sooner are the two married than they are accused and convicted of incest, on account of being brother and sister (not mother and son) and are condemned to be "shut up forever in a close prison . . . as pellucid and transparent as glass" (an obvious reference to the alchemical alembic). The door to this chamber is then sealed with the official seal of the faculty, and our friend is given the responsibility of insuring they do not escape and, moreover, of insuring the even temperature of their chamber.

A detailed accounting follows of the mishaps encountered while the alchemist attempts to fulfill this charge. The royal pair have been stripped of their clothes and jewels before being thrust into their prison and readily respond to the earnest (and prayerful) ministrations of their conscientious keeper. We read that, on feeling the warmth, they fall to embracing each other so passionately that the husband's heart is melted with the excessive ardor of love, and he falls down broken in many pieces. When she, who loves him no less than he loves her, sees this, she weeps for him and, as it were, covers him with overflowing tears until he is quite flooded and concealed from view.[49] There is no doubt whatsoever that the reader is here being instructed in the finer points of the alchemical process itself. And so the story of the *coniunctio* continues, until the moment when "the rays of the sun, shining upon the moisture of the chamber, produced a most beautiful rainbow," which gladdens our alchemist immensely. His joy is somewhat dimmed, however, by the sight of the royal pair lying within, apparently lifeless. He does not give up on warning them though, and before long he is rewarded by their resurrection. Thus restored to life, they are more beautiful than ever, and soon a second marriage (the alchemical union) takes place. This ceremony is clearly more significant than anything that has gone before. At this point, the alchemist is shown "all the treasures and riches of the whole world . . . gold and precious carbuncles . . . the renewal and restoration of youth . . . and a never failing panacea for all disease.[50]

Mutus liber

The *Mutus liber* (Silent book) was first published in 1677 by Jacob Saulat, and was later included in Joannes Jacobus Manget's *Bibliotheca Chemica Curiosa*.[51] While many of the images of the *Rosarium philosophorum* are specifically Christian, in the *Mutus liber* we also find references to the Hebrew Bible and to the religious traditions of the ancient Greco-Roman world. Adam McLean points out that the images that are concerned with the specific alchemical processes are enfolded between a first and a last image, which constitute an important reminder about what he calls the "spiritual aspect" of the work.[52] This is quite true, but in my opinion they have another important function as well, which is to provide an unmistakable sign about the beginning and end of the spectrum representing the changes related to the subject/object relation and causality. It is for this reason that my primary focus here will be on the opening and closing images.

The frame within the first plate is oval, a shape that has always been associated with that which gives life, symbolically and literally. This

Mutus liber image 1

Mutus liber image 2

Mutus liber image 3

Mutus liber image 4

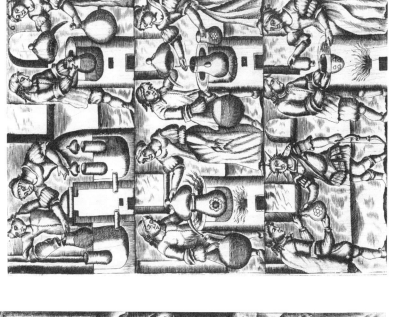

Mutus liber image 6

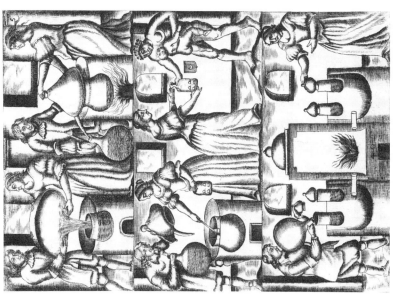

Mutus liber image 5

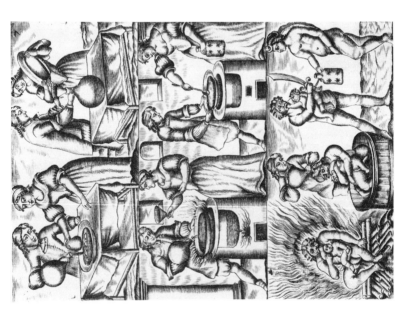

Mutus liber image 8

Mutus liber image 7

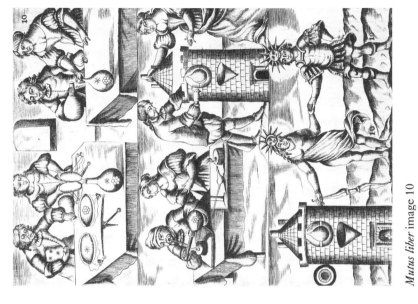

Mutus liber image 10

Mutus liber image 9

Mutus liber image 11

Mutus liber image 12

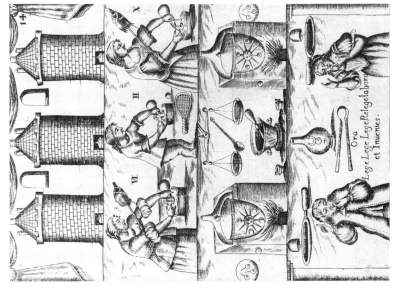

Mutus liber image 14

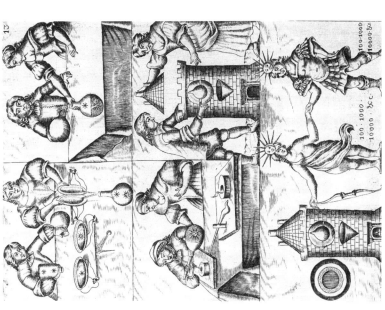

Mutus liber image 13

Mutus liber image 15

life-giving quality is emphasized by the fact that the oval is comprised of two living branches, knotted together. Each of these branches has many leaves, many thorns, and one rose. The combination of roses with thorns emphasizes the complexity of life, as well as the opposites that must be united in the alchemical work. In the frame we see a figure lying on the ground sleeping. On the ladder between heaven and earth are two angels—one descending, the other ascending—who are blowing trumpets by the sleeping figure in order to awaken him. This ladder, a sign of mediation between heaven and earth, connotes Jacob's dream at Bethel (Gen. 28:11–12). Jung has commented that this figure represents a person who is

> profoundly unconscious of himself, one of the "sleepers," the "blind" or "blindfolded," whom we encounter in the illustrations of certain alchemical treatises. They are the unawakened who are still unconscious of themselves, who have not yet integrated their future, more extensive personality, their "wholeness," or, in the language of the mystics, the ones who are not yet "enlightened."[53]

This observation underscores the traditional esoteric meaning of Jacob's ladder. Before Jacob went to sleep, he did not know the sacrality of the place, but when he awakened he did. His subsequent naming of the place (formerly Luz) was thus an intentional (i.e., cognizant) act of cosmicization.[54] Furthermore, again in keeping with the esoteric meaning of Jacob's ladder, such an awakened one becomes responsible for the function previously exercised by the angels; i.e., helping others awaken. Now, Jacob is one who *sees*. With respect to the subject/object relation, we see that here, at the outset, the usual understanding of the subject/object relation prevails. Heaven is above, and separated from the earth; the divine is separated from the human. The ascending and descending angels and the ladder symbolically represent the means of connection between these spheres; it is here a mediated connection. This symbolism, together with the two branches bearing thorns *and* flowers that are *tied* together, refers to the alchemical oppositions that will be resolved; it also tells us something about the initial understanding of causality. When we have two material objects that we want to join, we use glue, or nails, or, as pictured here, we tie them together with a knot. In other words, a mechanical means is used to join two things that are separate. A clear distinction is made between the means or method of performing an action and that which is the object of the action. Mechanistic causality is precisely what is symbolized for us here.

The above and the below are represented in the second image, which is divided into two distinct sections. At the bottom we see the actual condition of the alchemical couple as they are about to begin the work. The ideal or potential condition is imaged in the uppermost frame. The alchemical pair are shown winged, i.e., idealized, holding an alembic within which we see Neptune and a pair of children, one solar, the other lunar.[55] At this stage, the ideal condition that is imaged is regarded as "other" relative to the present. It is the Goal of the Work, which they can hope to reach only after a long and arduous series of tasks.

The third image is an *imago mundi*, showing the macrocosm. In the fourth image we see the couple gathering the morning dew. Adam McLean's interpretation of this image focuses on its significance in terms of the "etheric forces" that are associated with the earth as it goes through seasonal change. I am also reminded of the connection between common dew and the alchemists' repeated insistence on the ordinary nature of the substance that is needed for the work: it is something that is "walked on, children play with it." Images 5 through 14 show successive stages of the work in the laboratory. While comments on each of these would take us too far from the present focus, it should be noted that these images too, just like those in the *Rosarium philosophorum*, are symbolic of a *hieros gamos*. Although never explicitly sexual, as are many of the images in the *Rosarium*, these two show a series of deepening exchanges between the alchemical pair, sometimes with Mercurius appearing as the third enlivening and enabling term. That they are combined here with what could conceivably be construed as directions for actual laboratory work is, in my view, a further indication of the most profound level of hierogamic process. As the *Tabula smaragdina* advises, "The strength of it is complete only if the powers of upper and of lower are combined." That is, heaven and earth must be joined.

In the last image, the ladder is discarded and lies on the ground. The central part of a winged, organic form emerges from what had formerly functioned as a knot tying the two branches together in a mechanical way. Now the joining is organic, not mechanical. The branches no longer have thorns, but berries. They still form an oval, but here it is wide open at the top; in the center of the sky above them is a sun, with a beneficent, smiling face; its rays extend to all around it. The couple who has worked together throughout the work join hands; banners come out of their mouths that say: "[P]rovided with eyes thou departest" *(oculatus abis)*.[56] The figure of Zeus is above them. He stretches a tasseled cord between his hands with the ends hanging down; each of the pair has reached up to grasp one of the tassels. This image reflects an understanding and an experience of the universe as being ontologically whole, which arrives at the end of a long process involving the dissolution of an entire framework that had functioned to support an understanding and experience of separation.

CLOSING REFLECTIONS

The central theme in the *Mutus liber* and the *Rosarium philosophorum* is that of the alchemical conjunction of opposites, imaged under the form of a *hieros gamos*. In the alchemical tradition the *hieros gamos* images represent the process of sacralizing the profane, of cosmicizing chaos, of actualizing that which had previously been potential. In the course of writing this article and thinking about these texts it occurred to me that a fruitful topic for further exploration would be to consider whether the alchemist and his *soror mystica* were intended to be primarily (or exclusively) symbolic representations of a purely interior process. This is particularly important in view of the fact that the alchemists placed so much emphasis on actualizing the potential, on leading out the gold, as they often said.

While commenting on the parts played by the alchemical pair in the *Mutus liber*, Jung states:

> [T]he artificers . . . in the symbolical realm are *Sol* and *Luna*, in the human the adept and his *soror mystica*, and in the psychological realm the masculine consciousness and the feminine unconscious. . . . The two vessels are again *Sol* and *Luna*.[57]

With respect to the exteriorization or actualization of the inner condition, he notes that

Classic pairs are Simon Magus and Helen, Zosimos and Theosebeia, Nicholas Flamel and Peronelle, Mr. South and his daughter (Mrs. Atwood, author of *A Suggestive Enquiry into the Hermetic Mystery*). . . . The *Mutus liber* . . . represents the *Mysterium Solis et Lunae* as an alchemical operation between man and wife.[58]

The nature of the conjunction seems to me to suggest that the tradition of the alchemist and the *soror mystica* was not simply intended as a symbol with no corresponding reality in time and space, but that it was a form of Western tantra. However, to explore such a speculation would go far beyond the scope of the present article. It would require a book to do justice to the different aspects of the symbolism of the alchemical *coniunctio* and the various significations that have been accorded it, and perhaps someday such a book will be written. For the moment we can say that, in general, the attempt to achieve the alchemical conjunction seems to have entailed a relentless striving for perfect congruity between the interior condition of the alchemist and the outer world. As sensible people we know that perfect congruity is impossibly idealistic, and perhaps we might even go so far as to call it impossibly utopian. Yet if one were an alchemist, this would nevertheless be the ideal toward which one would ceaselessly try to move. Here I recall something that Mircea Eliade wrote about his study of tantric texts:

> The Sun and Moon must be made one . . . above all *prajna*, wisdom, must be joined with *upaya*, the means of attaining it. . . . all this amounts to saying that we are dealing with the *coincidentia oppositorum* achieved on every level of Life and Consciousness.[59]

Idealistic or not, it would appear that this actualization of the "*coincidentia oppositorum* on every level of Life and Consciousness," as Eliade put it, was the thing that obsessed the alchemists until their dying breath. Certainly this would have entailed radical changes in both the conception and the experience of the subject/object relation. Does this mean that the tradition should be dismissed because of the presence of what some contemporary psychiatrists might call a manifestation of obsessive compulsive behaviors, mixed with psychological inflation and delusions of grandeur? When viewed from such a perspective, spiritual alchemy certainly could appear to be only that. But then, we could also say that the same thing was manifested by the great spiritual teachers. In my view, in its purest form, spiritual alchemy constitutes a bona fide tradition within the history of religions; one that represented a serious hope that it would be possible to overcome the subject/object dichotomy, that chasm which seems to yawn between the spirit and the body. As such, its praxis was intended as a technique, whose focus was on making the impossible possible.[60] Spiritual alchemy may well have been an obsession, but I submit that it was a truly magnificent obsession.

NOTES

1. Mircea Eliade cautions against conflating the method and raison d'être of alchemy with that of prechemistry in "Alchemy as a Spiritual Technique" in *Yoga: Immortality and Freedom*, 2d ed., Bollingen Series 55 (Princeton, 1969), 290–92. For an excellent contextualization of alchemy within the esoteric tradition, see Antoine Faivre, *Access to Western Esotericism* (Albany, 1994). Cf. idem, "Ancient and Medieval Sources of Modern Esoteric Movements," in *Modern Esoteric Spirituality*, ed. Antoine Faivre, Jacob Needleman, and Karen Voss (New York, 1992), 1–70.

2. Antoine Faivre, "Esotericism," in *Hidden Truths: Magic, Alchemy, and the Occult*, ed. Lawrence E. Sullivan (New York, 1987), 41.

3. The earliest textual evidence of alchemy dates from about the second century B.C.E. See E. J. Holmyard, *Alchemy* (Harmondsworth, 1957), 25; and Rudolf Bernoulli, "Spiritual Development as Reflected in Alchemy and Related Disciplines," in *Spiritual Disciplines: Papers from the Eranos Yearbooks*, Bollingen Series 30, 4 (New York, 1960), 308. An excellent overview of alchemy is F. Sherwood Taylor, *The Alchemists* (1951; reprint, London, 1976). *Al*, meaning "the," comes from the Arabic; *kimia* may derive from the Egyptian *kmt* or *chem*, meaning "black land," or from the Greek *chyma* meaning to "fuse or cast metal." See Holmyard, *Alchemy*, 19.

4. See Eliade, "The Terror of History," chap. 4 in *Cosmos and History: The Myth of the Eternal Return* (New York, 1959), 139–59. The best exposition of the hermeneutical significance of the alchemical tradition is still Mircea Eliade's *The Forge and the Crucible: The Origins and Structures of Alchemy* (Chicago and London, 1978). Also noteworthy is Françoise Bonardel's breathtaking *Philosophie de l'alchimie: Grand oeuvre et modernité* (Paris, 1993).

5. Robert Darnton, *Mesmerism and the End of the Enlightenment in France* (Cambridge, 1968), vii–viii. See also Allen Debus's introduction to the reprint edition of Elias Ashmole's *Theatrum Chemicum Britannicum* (New York and London, 1967), which calls for us to "make the attempt to place ourselves within the intellectual climate" (ix) of the late seventeenth century.

6. See Antoine Faivre, "Renaissance Hermeticism and the Concept of Western Esotericism," in this volume. See also Antoine Faivre and Karen-Claire Voss,

"Western Esotericism and the Science of Religions," *Numen* 42 (1995), for a summary of the components of esotericism.

7. Faivre and Voss, "Western Esotericism," 61. See Eliade, *Forge and the Crucible*, 147, where he states that "Transmutation . . . was the principal aim of Alexandrian alchemy. . . ."

8. See Antoine Faivre, "Pour une approche figurative de l'alchimie," in *Mystiques, Théosophes et Illuminés au siècle des lumières* (Paris, 1971; reprint, Hildesheim and New York, 1976). In my view, this is one of Faivre's most theoretically interesting works.

9. One could also think of scholars such as Rudolf Otto, Gerardus van der Leeuw, or Rudolf Bernoulli. I note that in Faivre's article "Pour une approche," à propos of praising Mircea Eliade he emphasizes that a historical perspective by itself is not adequate for dealing with phenomena like that of alchemical transmutation (202). In the same article, he also states that "il n'est possible de negliger l'hermeneutique spirituelle" while studying alchemy and related topics (212).

10. Leo Stavenhagen, ed., *A Testament of Alchemy: Being the Revelations of Morienus to Khalid ibn Yazid* (Hanover, 1974), 66.

11. Faivre, "Pour une approche," 201.

12. See Mircea Eliade, *The Sacred and the Profane* (New York, 1959), 189, for a description of the initiate as one "who has experienced the mysteries, . . . who knows."

13. See Faivre, "Pour une approche," 201 n. 2; and John Read, *The Alchemist in Life, Literature and Art* (London, 1947), 29. Of course, the separation between "material" and "spiritual" alchemy was not in fact so rigid. An alchemist's conception and experience of the work would change as progress was made, although this change seems to have occurred in only one "direction"; i.e., a material alchemist would become a spiritual alchemist. See also Eliade, *Yoga*, 289–90 for a discussion of the distinction between "esoteric and exoteric alchemy," which has a sense analogous with the distinction made here between material and spiritual alchemy.

14. The present articulation of these three characteristics represents a further theoretical development of work begun in my master's thesis ("Aspects of Medieval Alchemy: Cosmogony, Ontology, and Transformation" [diss., San Jose University, 1984]). A work in progress is devoted to further development of the issues that have been discussed in this article: e.g., taking serious account of the ontological aspect of the experience of transmutation, examining the changing conception of the subject/object relation, causality, and time. In that work I also discuss another change, i.e., in the conception of energy. I argue that material alchemy essentially conceives of energy and power as things that can be possessed, contained, directed; as things that can be used for a purpose, in order to achieve a goal. For example, in material alchemy we think in terms of manipulation, of domination, sometimes even of destruction. In contrast, in spiritual alchemy energy is not approached as a possession, or as something to be used, but as a kind of gift. Energy is therefore experienced and understood as essentially transformative, creative, and enabling. Nothing needs to be done with it, or because of it, or with it; power is noted as a fact. What is required is that one serve the gift.

15. See Giordano Bruno, *Cause, Principle, and Unity,* ed. Jack Lindsay (Westport, 1962), 82.

16. See note 14.

17. See Faivre, "Pour une approche," 202–3, for a discussion that touches on links between physicist Stéphane Lupasco's systematic discussion of the epistemological implications of quantum physics and the alchemical movement from potency to act. Cf. Basarab Nicolescu, *Nous, la particule et le monde* (Paris, 1985), especially the chapter "La genése trialectique de la réalité," for a full explication of Lupasco's work.

18. Eliade, *Forge and the Crucible,* chap. 10, "Alchemy and Temporality."

19. In a personal communication (May 1994) theoretical physicist Basarab Nicolescu expressed the idea that time itself may not be something having ontological status but rather a mode of perception of something else that does have ontological status.

20. Clearly a more developed model is required. The presentation of the underlying theoretical rationale for this and the development of what it entails would take us too far beyond the scope of the present article. With respect to the problem of finding more adequate ways of modeling the alchemical process, it would be worthwhile to explore the potential of computer-imaging technology. See note 30.

21. See the discussion about the dual impetus of gnosis in K.-C. Voss, "Three Exemplars of the Esoteric Tradition in the Renaissance," *Alexandria: The Journal of the Western Cosmological Traditions* 3 (1995): 329–68, esp. 331. Cf. Faivre, "Esotericism," 39.

22. Other names for the Philosopher's Stone were the Hermetic Androgyne and the Rebis. One alchemist writes: "Our matter has as many names as there are things in the world" (from "The Golden Tract," [*Tractatus aureum*], in *The Hermetic Museum Restored and Enlarged,* by A. E. Waite [London, 1893], 1:13). The role of the alchemist was to lead out the gold, to actualize what had existed *in potentia.* In this respect, it is appropriate to speak of the alchemists as "midwives" who, in accord with the cosmic "plan," were enabling the substances in their vessels to be "redeemed" from their actual state of baseness and to attain their potential condition of perfection.

23. There exists an entire literature that is relevant to the phenomenon of analogy making in alchemy and in the esoteric tradition as a whole. See, for example, Michel Foucault, *The Order of Things: An Archaeology of the Human Sciences* (New York, 1970), 17–25, for a discussion of the four similitudes, and 25–30 for a discussion of the doctrine of signatures. See also Ernst Gombrich, "*Icones Symbolicae*: The Visual Image in Neo-Platonic Thought," *Journal of the Warburg and Courtauld Institute* 11 (1948): 163–92, esp. 165. Gombrich seems somewhat discomfited when contemplating the worldview that led to a conflation of the signifier and the signified. This is a very important article, however; it contains a thorough exposition of the most significant issues related to the question of images in the Renaissance Neoplatonic tradition, which is very useful for helping to inform analogy making in alchemy.

24. Every alchemical author gives a different account of the divisions that must be followed; some maintain there must be as many as twelve. Not surprisingly, given

his theories regarding the quaternity, Jung favored a division of four, but notes that an alchemist's choice (and presumably, possibly, the choices of contemporary researchers) of one over another was motivated by what he described as "inner psychological reasons" (*Psychology and Alchemy*, 2d ed., Bollingen Series 20 [Princeton, 1980], 230). Regardless of which choice an alchemist settled on, every schema had its adherents, along with its share of detractors, and there was no dearth of justification for the use of any of them.

25. Mircea Eliade reminds us of Basil Valentine's acrostic made from the word *VITRIOL*: *Visita Interiora Terrae Rectificando Invenies Occultum Lapidem* ("Visit the interior of the Earth, and by purification thou wilt find the stone."), in *Forge and the Crucible*, 162.

26. For a description of the possible initiatory function of depression, see Basarab Nicolescu, "Jung et la science: Histoire et perspectives d'un malentendu," presented at the colloquium "Jung Aujourd'hui," organized by the Groupe d'Etudes C. G. Jung, Paris, 27–28 November 1993.

27. This image is from Khunrath's "Amphitheatrum sapientiae" (1604) and is reproduced as figure 145 in Jung, *Psychology and Alchemy*, 291.

28. It was this that Titus Burckhardt recognized when he wrote that "alchemy is above all the alchemy of prayer" (*Alchemy* [1960; reprint, Dorset 1986], 157).

29. Jung called Mercurius the "paradox par excellence" (*Mysterium Coniunctionis*, Bollingen Series 2 [Princeton, 1968], 43) because numerous apparently disparate qualities are ascribed to him. He is said to be a duality, but at the same time a unity, thereby connoting the function of mediation. Sometimes the figure of Mercurius is assimilated to that of Hermes, who, as messenger of the gods, participates in the ontological realms of human and divine; other times, to the figure of the Christ, who remains divine, even though also becoming human via the Incarnation. Mercurius is thus both material and spiritual. He has an ability to transform the "lower" into the "higher" and the "higher" into the "lower." The caduceus staff, which bears two serpents, one denoting ascending energy, the other descending energy, is associated with Mercurius.

30. See Voss, *Aspects of Medieval Alchemy*, 80–82, 92. While I still think that a spiral may in fact be an excellent basis for a more adequate model, I now envision a model constructed using advanced computer-imaging technology. While the caveat implicit in Alfred Korzybski's observation that "the map is not the territory" (ibid., 36) remains a valid reminder, a computer-generated dynamic holographic image would permit the modeling of the idea of levels of reality in an unprecedented way. This strikes me as a potentially rich alliance between late-twentieth-century technology and esoteric studies. Cf. Korzybski's statement with Adam McLean's remarks concerning virtual reality ("Editorial," *Hermetic Journal*, 1991, 1).

31. On the deep significance of the opposition "beginning/end" as this is related to the term *azoth*, see Bernoulli, "Spiritual Development," 317.

32. Eliade, *Sacred and the Profane*, 200–201.

33. Hermes Trismegistus can be regarded as a kind of patron saint of alchemy, since he is invoked repeatedly, and his mercurial presence, in one guise or another,

is recurrent (see Antoine Faivre, *The Eternal Hermes: From Greek God to Alchemical Magus* [Grand Rapids, 1995]; cf. idem, "Renaissance Hermeticism and the Concept of Western Esotericism," in this volume). For Hermetic images in the alchemical tradition, I already referred to C. G. Jung's memorable characterization of the alchemical Mercurius as the "paradox par excellence" (in *Mysterium Coniunctionis*, 43).

34. *Morieni Romani, Quondam Eremitae Hierosolymitani, de transfiguratione metallorum, & occulta, summaque antiquorum Philosophorum medicina, Libellus, nusquam hactenus in lucem editus* (Paris, 1559). I have used the edition by Leo Stavenhagen, *Testament of Alchemy* (see n. 10, above).

35. Stavenhagen, *Testament of Alchemy*, 13.

36. Ibid., 29.

37. Ibid., 39.

38. Joachim Telle, *Sol und Luna: Literar-und alchemiegeschichtliche Studien zu einem altdeutschen Bildgedicht* (Hürtgenwald, 1980), 7–8, 45, provides complete bibliographic details. Cf. the entry "Rosarium philosophorum" in *Bibliotheca Chemica: A Catalogue of the Alchemical, Chemical and Pharmaceutical Books in the Collection of the late James Young of Kelly and Durris*, by John F. Ferguson, 2 vols. (Glasgow, 1906). See Adam McLean, *The Rosary of the Philosophers* (Edinburg, 1980). This contains a previously unpublished eighteenth-century English translation of the text (Department of Rare Books and Manuscripts, Glasgow University Library, Ferguson MS 210), and McLean's commentary on the images accompanying it.

39. McLean, *Rosary*, 10.

40. See Jung, "The Practice of Psychotherapy: Essays on the Psychology of the Transference and Other Subjects," in vol. 16 of *Collected Works*, 2d ed., Bollingen Series 20 (Princeton, 1983), 200.

41. One of the things that I argued was that the hierogamic images of the alchemical tradition testify to an important thematic continuity between that tradition and certain ancient Near Eastern religious traditions. While there are also of course very important differences (e.g., the latter involved a praxis of ritual public sexual intercourse), there are also important similarities that should not be ignored: "[M]any of the alchemists appear to have undergone a complex experience involving mutual reciprocity between the events in the laboratory and within themselves of a kind that hearkens back to, and carries forward, the imprint of a religious tradition which combined physical and spiritual levels of transformation" (Karen Voss, "The *Hierosgamos* Theme in the Images of the *Rosarium philosophorum*," in *Alchemy Revisited: Proceedings of the International Conference on the History of Alchemy at the University of Groningen, 17–19 April 1989*, ed. Z. R. W. M. von Martels [Leiden, 1990], 148).

42. Ibid., 149.

43. For a brief but illuminating discussion of the symbolism of birds, see Manbu Waida, "Birds," in *The Encyclopedia of Religion*, ed. Mircea Eliade (New York, 1987), 2:224–27, and especially the reference to doves, 2:225. Cf. also the explanation of how the dove in the ancient Near East was associated symbolically with erotic love and with female divinities like Inanna, in Jung, *Collected Works*, 16:238 n. 13. Lastly,

see the discussion concerning the connections between birds in general and the dove in particular and images of the goddess in prehistory up through the classical period in Elinor W. Gadon, *The Once and Future Goddess: A Symbol for Our Time* (San Francisco, 1989), 94.

44. The rubric *tria* and *unum* is interesting. Obviously it relates to the Trinity, but it relates to the Philosopher's Stone as well. Cf. my discussion about "Three-In-One" elsewhere in this article.

45. *Septem tractatus seu capitula Hermetis Trismegisti aurei*, originally in *Ars chemica* (Strasbourg, 1566), 7–31. I have used Arthur Edward Waite, ed., *The Hermetic Museum Restored and Enlarged* (2 vols., London, 1893; reprint, in one vol., York Beach, Me., 1990). The version reedited by Waite was originally published in Latin in Frankfort in 1678. It was an enlarged version of an earlier work that had appeared in 1625. The definitive Latin edition is Karl R. H. Frick, ed., *Musaeum Hermeticum Reformatum et Amplificatum* (Graz, 1970).

46. Waite, *Hermetic Museum*, 1:41.

47. Ibid., 1:45. The peculiar grammar is in the original.

48. Ibid., 1:46; cf. ibid., 2:151: "Hermes, who was one and the same with the mother of sulphur" and 210. Cf. Plutarch, *De Iside et Osiride*, ed. J. Gwyn Griffiths (Cambridge, 1970), in which we find an account of another incestuous union—that of Isis and Osiris, who in their mother's womb were related to each other even before birth. As the result of conception *in utero* they produced a son named Horus.

49. Waite, *Hermetic Museum*, 1:47; cf. the process related here to the description in another alchemical treatise entitled "The Glory of the World," in ibid., 1:207.

50. Waite, *Hermetic Museum*, 1:50.

51. See the commentary in Marc Haven, ed., *Tresor Hermétique comprenant Le Livre d'Images sans paroles (Mutus Liber) et Le Traité symbolique de la Pierre philosophale* (Lyon, 1914).

52. Adam McLean, *A Commentary on the Mutus Liber*, Magnus Opus Hermetic Sourceworks no. 11 (Grand Rapids, 1991), 50.

53. Carl G. Jung, *Alchemical Studies*, Bollingen Series 20 (Princeton, 1983), 195. We cannot do more here than give a sense of the rich symbolism that is connected with the image of a ladder. See also Jung's comment concerning Jacob's ladder (as "symbol for the steps which led to the mystical union with God") in "Exercitia Spiritualia of St. Ignatius of Loyola. Notes on Lectures," *Spring: An Annual of Archetypal Psychology and Analytical Thought*, 1977, 186; and his reminder about the theme of ascent through the spheres in the "late classical syncretism, already saturated with alchemy . . . often represented by a ladder. . . ." ("Dream Symbols of the Individuation Process," in *Spiritual Disciplines: Papers from the Eranos Yearbooks*, Bollingen Series 30, 4, [New York, 1960], 360). Originally published in German in the *Eranos-Jahrbücher* series between 1933 and 1948. Finally, for a discussion of Philo of Alexandria's understanding of Jacob as "seer of God," see Friedrich Heiler, "Contemplation in Christian Mysticism," in *Spiritual Disciplines*.

54. Concerning the significance of "cosmicizing" a territory, see Eliade, *Sacred and the Profane*, 30.

55. In his commentary, McLean merely describes the pair as "two clothed children bearing Sun and Moon symbols" (McLean, *Commentary*, 18), but in my opinion the image is intended to represent the interior reality of the alchemical couple at the end of the Work.

56. See note 53, above.

57. Jung, *Mysterium Coniunctionis*, 153–54.

58. Ibid., 153 n. 8. In his novel *The Chymical Wedding* (New York, 1989), 502–3, Lindsay Clarke writes that he owes much to the inspiration provided by the circumstances surrounding Mary Anne Atwood's book; apparently her father insisted that she withdraw the book, on the grounds that it revealed too much. And, for a characterization of Atwood's work as "the first protest raised against Western philosophy's loss of its philosophical dimension," see Françoise Bonardel, "Alchemical Esotericism and the Hermeneutics of Culture," in Faivre, Needleman, and Voss, *Modern Esoteric Spirituality*, 86.

59. Eliade, *Forge and the Crucible*, 118.

60. Cf. the words that appear on the title page of a slim volume of poems by Gaspard Hons entitled *L'Impossible* (Paris, 1994): "Tout l'intérêt de notre vie est de rendre possible l'impossible. Pour le reste, la vie s'en charge."

CHAPTER 11

MUSIC AND THE HERMETIC TRADITION

JOSCELYN GODWIN

Music has had a long and involved relationship with the Hermetic tradition, whether we understand the latter as alchemy alone, or as the whole complex of the occult arts and sciences in the West. The music in question is of two kinds: *musica speculativa* and *musica practica*. Both are rooted in the Pythagorean tradition, which, like the Hermetic one, is part of the wide spectrum of Western esotericism. The two great insights that emerged from the Pythagorean school are, first, that the cosmos is founded on number, and second, that music has an effect on the body and soul. These insights lie at the heart of speculative and practical music, respectively.

To illustrate these two types of music, we can compare two loci classici of the interaction of music with alchemy. The first is in the third- or fourth-century treatise of Pseudo-Zosimos, *On the making of gold*.[1] The author makes the point that both music and alchemy are based on a set of four and its permutations: in music, the four tones of the tetrachord, which generate all the modes and melodies; in alchemy, the four elements of the primordial egg, which generate all substances. He is therefore using speculative music to support an integrated worldview of the Pythagorean type, in which everything rests on the simple numbers.

The second example is Michael Maier's *Atalanta Fugiens* of 1617.[2] This is a collection of three-part canons or "fugues," hence it belongs to the division of practical music. Maier's intention was that through singing and hearing his fugues, the student would come to a better understanding of alchemy. The fugues themselves are symbolic in form, but that does not make them any the less practical, for they are composed to be heard. *Atalanta Fugiens* is an isolated example of music being used as a handmaid to the Hermetic work.

The Pythagorean insight that the cosmos is founded on number has a corollary, namely, that number has a qualitative element that is perceptible as harmony. Arithmetic considers numbers as pure quantities, whereas music considers them as proportions, comparing them to one another and judging their effect on the ear. Music gives access to number in a particular way, through making it audible. The ear can tell instinctively that some proportions or intervals are harmonious or concordant, others inharmonious or discordant. For example, the proportion of 2 to 3 is harmonious, because two strings of lengths 2 and 3 make the interval of a perfect fifth. But the proportion of 11 to 12 is inharmonious, because it gives an interval that is never used in melody, much less in harmony.

Astrologers from Ptolemy to Johannes Kepler have found in this science of proportions a possible explanation of why certain aspects between signs or planets are effective, and others not.[3] Kepler's method was to imagine the entire zodiacal circle as stretched out in a straight line, like the string of a monochord. In this thought experiment, he stopped the string at the points corresponding to the aspects of opposition, trine, and square, and found that they gave the three "perfect consonances" of octave, fifth, and fourth. Thus, he concluded, both astrology and music rest on the same numerical principles.

Another method of linking music with astrology is to assign the twelve tones or their keys to the twelve signs of the zodiac. There are many different ways of doing this, which I have analyzed elsewhere.[4] One purpose of the process is to judge the aspects or compatibilities of the signs according to whether their tones or keys are harmonious. This is a way of using music to solve a problem that lies at the foundation of astrology, namely, why some aspects are more efficacious than others. Another purpose is to ascertain the astrological qualities of existing pieces of music and thereby to judge their possible effects. For example, if one's theory has determined that the key of E-flat corresponds to Sagittarius and to its ruler, Jupiter, this may account for the character of pieces written in that key.

Kepler's career also illustrates a more lasting effect of the meeting of music with Hermetic ways of thought. His search for the laws of planetary motion was inextricably linked in his mind with finding the harmonies with which God had organized the universe. Forced by Tycho Brahe's observations of the planets to conclude that their orbits were not circular but elliptical, Kepler found a way to justify this seeming imperfection in the divine order by reading musical harmonies into the planetary motions. The discovery of the cosmic harmony was for Kepler the culmination of his life's quest.[5]

Closely parallel to Kepler's planetary harmony was Isaac Newton's discovery and definition of the spectrum of colors. Here again, it was harmony that confirmed an empirical observation. Newton, or his assistant, divided the colors of the spectrum in proportions equal to those of the diatonic scale, thus coming up with the familiar seven colors, whereas there might well have been more or fewer.[6] Newton's satisfaction at his discovery of the seven-colored spectrum was akin to Kepler's joy at the cosmic harmonies: neither man would have felt like that, had he not been convinced of the Hermetic doctrine that the universe is based on the law of correspondences. To a modern scientist, the musical part of their discoveries is so much packaging to be thrown away; to them, it was of the essence.

Music has played only a minor part in the history of magic. In fact, the whole tradition of ceremonial magic is unmusical to a surprising degree. There are two explanations for this. First, the rare talents that make a magician, or for that matter an alchemist, seldom coincide with a talent for music, either as a composer or performer. Secondly, the ceremonial magician usually works either alone or with a single companion. Before the era of recordings there was no way to provide a musical accompaniment for their rituals, such as religion uses to good effect in its own ceremonies.

There is one striking exception to this absence: the Orphic incantations sung by Marsilio Ficino, whose many skills included that of singing to his own accompaniment on the viola da braccio. Ficino's ceremonies consisted in addressing hymns to the planets, while surrounding himself with objects and substances chosen according to the doctrine of correspondences. His music is lost, and was probably improvised.[7] But he regarded it as an essential part of the ceremony, because of music's effects on the *spiritus*, the subtle link between soul and body. Ficino's music, carried by the air, served to impress his *spiritus* with the signature of the appropriate planet, and thence to imbue his soul with the desired qualities.[8]

Ficino's musical magic had no direct progeny, because even within his lifetime the pursuit of such neopagan activities became too hazardous. Cornelius Agrippa wrote of the efficacy of tone on the *spiritus* in the second book of his treatise on magic,[9] but none of his prescriptions make any further use of music. However, a case might be made for the sixteenth-century madrigal as partially an outgrowth of Ficino's experiments. What marked the madrigal, as it emerged shortly after 1500, was its attempt to make the music illustrate the words, hence reinforce their emotional effect. This recalls Ficino's use of music to imprint the poetry of his Orphic hymns on the *spiritus*. And since the texts of the madrigals were with one accord erotic, they could be associated with the cult of love that led an underground existence in the epoch of religious warfare, providing on the one hand an escape from a discredited Christianity, and on the other hand acting, after the example of Plato's *Symposium*, as a gateway to the higher degrees of love.[10]

The watershed event that divides the Renaissance from the Baroque epoch in music was the birth of opera around 1600, and here it is safe to say that it would not have occurred as it did without Hermetic influences. Shortly before, in 1589, the celebrations held in Florence for the marriage of Christina of Lorraine and Ferdinando de Medici had included a sort of proto-opera. It included dramatic presentations of the Harmony of the Spheres, as described in Plato's *Republic*, and of the magical song with which Arion charmed the dolphin,[11] thus representing the twin pillars of the Pythagorean tradition: the harmony of the universe and the marvelous power of music. Not by chance did the first real operas, such as Peri's and Caccini's *Eurydice* and Monteverdi's *Orfeo* of 1607, use the myth of the same Orpheus who had inspired Ficino in his planetary incantations, and who was now represented as charming his way to the Underworld with the irresistible power of his song. Those early operas, written for a select audience familiar with Neoplatonic and Hermetic thought, were magical events, designed to draw down beneficial influences on the couples whose marriage they celebrated, on the listeners, and on the state. The same intention was still alive towards the end of the century in the operas of Jean-Baptiste Lully, which were part of the occult apparatus by which Louis XIV, knowingly or not, established his absolute power.[12]

The relationship of architecture to the Hermetic tradition would be another subject, and a richer one. However, we should glance here at some instances in which the link was established through the mediacy of music. It is a commonplace that all the great schools of architecture—Egyptian, Graeco-Roman, Gothic, Renaissance, and Baroque—have made use of significant numbers in planning their buildings. Some of these numbers have been derived from the numerical equivalents of appropriate words or mottoes, as John James found in the ground plan of Chartres Cathedral.[13] Others reflect musical proportions, as we know from the notebooks of Villard de Honnecourt, an early-thirteenth-century architect.[14] Otto von Simson tested Villard's principles, which had probably come from the Cistercian Order, and found, as he says, that

> the musical ratios occur in some of the most perfect architectural compositions of the thirteenth century. In the southern transept of Lausanne Cathedral (before 1235) the magnificent disposition of the inner wall "conveys an overwhelming experience of harmony" with the 1:2:3 ratio of its horizontal division. The consonance of the fifth is "sounded" in the façades of Paris, Strasbourg, and York.[15]

Hans Kayser, the Swiss writer on harmonics, identified a diagram in the same notebooks of Villard as a canon of proportion drawn from the monochord, which gives a more complex and sophisticated series of proportions than the basic consonances named in the quotation above.[16] This, too, he found reflected in Gothic architecture. One might conclude that some of the secrets of the medieval masons were of a musical, or at least a Pythagorean, nature. The acoustics of medieval buildings, which so enhance the effect of unaccompanied plainsong, are sometimes attributed to the existence of harmonious proportions in their architecture. But as so much of this enhancement is subjective, the result of expectations and of a "sacred" atmosphere, it is unlikely to be proven one way or another.

There is no doubt that the eye is satisfied by many of the same proportions as the ear. However, there is the glaring exception of the golden section (the mathematical ø, approximately the ratio of 1 to 1.618). This has always been a favorite proportion of architects and painters, yet in music it is a very insignificant consonance: a minor sixth, and not even in tune. This is perhaps why the architect-theorists of the Italian Renaissance, who were well aware of the idea of using musical proportions in their buildings, did so in such an inconsistent way.[17] There is no building, as far as one can tell, that is constructed with deliberately musical proportions in its every detail. Certainly the analysis of any Renaissance or Baroque building will yield some musical proportions, but it would be rash to conclude that they were all placed there deliberately. Efforts to prove any theory of the kind through measurement are highly debatable. We have the pseudoscience of pyramidology as a warning of the lengths to which such theories can lead their devotees. The same can be said of Renaissance and Baroque paintings, which are sometimes analyzed with a spider's web of lines joining significant points. The more astounding the conclusions of such analyses, the more likely they are to be nothing but the analyst's fantasy.[18]

The arithmology of poetry seems even more rarely to be musically inspired. The significant numbers that scholars have found in Dante and Spenser, for instance, are all governed by unmusical principles, such as Christian number symbolism or the Kabbalah. On the other hand, we could take the fourteen-line sonnet as an example of harmonic construction of the most perfect kind. The so-called "octave" of the first eight lines, divided into two quatrains, exemplifies the musical interval of an octave (proportion 8:4 or 2:1), while the closing "sestet" of six lines relates to it in the proportion of a perfect fourth (8:6 or 4:3). Moreover, each line is an iambic pentameter of five beats, concluded by a pause or rest of one beat. However much rubato is used in an expressive reading, the underlying meter is triple, like a slow 3/2. This may be somewhat elementary mathematics, but so are the perfect consonances and meters that are the basis of all music. A case such as this illustrates the effectiveness of harmonic proportions when applied to other media.

We turn now to the effects that the Hermetic tradition has had on Western music. Franz Liessem, in his book *Musik und Alchemie*, argues that alchemical symbolism underlies the earliest textbook of polyphony, the *Schola Enchiriadis* of the ninth century.[19] If this were so, then the date of approximately 1150 for the beginning of Latin alchemy would have to be revised. It seems more likely that the Hermetic tradition entered Western music through arithmology, after the invention of mensural notation in the thirteenth century made it possible to incorporate accurate numbers in the rhythms of a piece. No musicologist has yet tried to establish the extent to which this occurred, but isolated and proven instances suggest that it may have been as widespread as the use of arithmology in architecture.

One such instance is Guillaume Dufay's motet, *Nuper rosarum flores*, written for the dedication of Brunelleschi's dome in the Cathedral of Florence (1453). The musical form of the piece is organized according to the proportions of Solomon's Temple, the biblical prototype of all cathedrals.[20] In the same century there are the masses of Jacob Obrecht, *Sub Tuum Presidium* and *Maria Zart*, whose rhythmic structure is based on numbers relating to Marian symbolism.[21] We do not know whether these are just the tip of an iceberg, and whether an analysis of all Obrecht's masses, and those of his contemporaries, would yield similar results. It might well depend on who did the analyzing. As in the example of Carl Jung's famous experiment with astrology, people who believe in something get more confirmation, even from seemingly impartial data, than people who do not.[22]

The music of J. S. Bach is a natural hunting ground for the believers. Bach, without a doubt, used symbolism in his music, some of which was numerical. To give an indisputable example: the "Crucifixus" movement of the *B-minor Mass* is based on thirteen repetitions of a descending chromatic ground bass, combining the falling chromatics that denote sorrow with the baleful number 13. But it takes a peculiar frame of mind to go as far as the Dutch musicologists Kees van Houten and Marinus Kasbergen. After counting up other significant measures in Bach's music, they concluded that the composer had accurately predicted the number of days from his own birth to his death, and encoded the number in his scores.[23] The process of making such a "discovery" may be itself a Hermetic exercise, but like certain claims of the alchemists, it is unlikely to persuade anyone else.

There are many Orphic operas, but there is only one Hermetic one, *The Magic Flute*, which in an appropriately Egyptian setting presents the *separatio* and *conjunctio* of the archetypal principles.[24] Mozart's and Schikaneder's singspiel owes its existence to Freemasonry, which by the late eighteenth century had become the principal shelter of the Hermetic tradition. But there was no successor worthy of the model: nothing to continue a lineage of initiatory operas. How long was it before another musical work appeared that was so clearly within the Hermetic tradition? Richard Wagner's operas can sustain alchemical interpretations, just as they can be made to illustrate Rudolf Steiner's version of cosmic history, or practically any theory one likes to press on them. But Wagner was no Hermeticist. One has to wait for the fin de siècle before one finds works like Erik Satie's Rose-Cross music, or Alexander Scriabin's orchestral poems, inspired respectively by Josephin Peladan's Rosicrucian movement and by H. P. Blavatsky's Theosophical writings. And these, whatever their charms, are no *Magic Flutes.*

Among the composers of modernism, Arnold Schoenberg was the closest to the Hermetic tradition. Arithmology was his native element, especially in the years before World War One when he composed his *Pierrot Lunaire*, that cycle of thrice-seven poems suffused with numerical ingenuities. Schoenberg was a reader of Swedenborg, or at least of Balzac's Swedenborgian novel *Séraphîta*, which not only inspired the composer's song of that name but also played a part in his invention of the "system of twelve tones, related only to one another." To evoke the sensation of freely floating in space, so vividly described at the end of Balzac's novel, was one reason that Schoenberg cut loose from the moorings of tonality, allowing the twelve tones to create their own gravityless, unified musical space.[25] Then again there was the influence of Kabbalah, as the persecution of the Jews forced Schoenberg to reexamine and reaffirm his own roots with the opera *Moses and Aaron* and other works on Jewish themes. In the late *Kol Nidrei* for speaker, chorus, and orchestra, the Kabbalah is actually named, with its legend of the making of worlds and the hiding of the divine sparks in humanity.

The triumvirate of the Second Viennese School—Schoenberg, Alban Berg, and Anton Webern—shared a familiarity with mysticism and Theosophy, and an obsession with hiding significances in their music.[26] The twelve-tone system itself is an example, for it was never intended to be the focus of the listener's attention, but to act as a unifying force replacing tonality. In other words, twelve-tone or serial music is based on imperceptible structures, just as the *Divine Comedy* and the Gothic cathedrals are. The public can enjoy the work of art while unaware of this secret, which the creator perhaps wishes to share only with God.

Secret structures of another kind have been discovered in Claude Debussy's music, and in Béla Bartók's, in both cases based on the golden section as a determinant of form.[27] Neither composer showed any desire to advertise his method, yet they invite comparison with the Renaissance architects, who used that proportion because they were confident that it would imbue their works with beauty and a sense of harmony.

To display one's Hermeticism on the surface was a different matter, and unfashionable, to say the least, between the excesses of Scriabin and the New Age that dawned in the 1960s. A solitary exception is the English composer Gustav Holst.[28] He knew several Theosophists, including the astrologer Alan Leo and Blavatsky's secretary G. R. S. Mead. They introduced him to the ideas that inspired his orchestral suite *The Planets*, *The Hymn of Jesus* (based on Mead's translation from the Gnostic *Acts of John*), and the works on Indian themes such as *Three Hymns from the Rig Veda* and *Savitri*. But they never made a real Theosophist of him. Whereas a Hermetic attitude permeates the whole of Schoenberg's, Berg's, and Webern's works, Holst could compose just as happily in abstract forms or on commonplace texts.

This completes the tally of major composers prior to World War II who can be connected in any definite way with the Hermetic tradition. It needs now to be complemented by those Hermeticists in whose careers practical music has played a part.

Among the Rosicrucians of the early seventeenth century, Simon Studion, Robert Fludd, and Michael Maier were all versed in practical music, as Renaissance gentlemen were supposed to be. Studion was able to compose an effective six-part motet on an alchemical text.[29] Fludd, besides his work on the Harmony of the Spheres that is one of the greatest monuments of speculative music, wrote a large practical textbook on composition and instruments,[30] and composed some light pieces in the style of his time. Maier, the most gifted composer of the three, has already been mentioned, together with his *Atalanta Fugiens*.

Athanasius Kircher was another Christian Hermeticist, whose *Musurgia Universalis* (1650) covers both the speculative and practical sides. The book itself is Hermetic in form, rising up the Great Chain of Being from earthly music to the Harmony of the Spheres, the angelic choirs, and finally to the music of God the Divine Conductor.

After Kircher, such things went very much out of fashion. The eighteenth century was a time in which those who had both Hermetic and musical interests kept them severely apart. A prime example is Thomas Britton, the London small-coal merchant who held concerts in the loft above his store, played host to Handel, and virtually invented the institution of the public concert. Besides his coal business and his concerts, Britton had a third and secret life, centering around a fine occult library and a well-appointed apparatus for the conjuring of spirits: candles, pentacles, an inscribed table, and magic crystals.[31]

The same separation occurs in the case of three violinists of the end of the eighteenth century. First is the Comte de Saint-Germain, who was for a time a professional violinist and composed sonatas and an opera.[32] Second, there is Louis-Claude de Saint-Martin, who was a competent amateur player. The "Unknown Philosopher" does have some important passages in his works on the principles and effects of music, but if he had the means to put them into practice, he never seems to have done so.[33] The third is another professional, François-Hippolyte Barthélémon, who was deeply involved in the Swedenborgian movement. None of these made the slightest difference to the music of their time.

During the heyday of occultism, a century later, there were again a number of doubly gifted figures. Madame Blavatsky herself was a passable musician, according to those who heard her play the piano in her New York apartment. We may or may not believe that she had performed in Paris in a piano recital with Clara Schumann and directed the women's chorus of the king of Serbia.[34] Blavatsky's archrival, the English medium Emma Hardinge Britten, was also a pianist and worked for a time as a demonstrator in Erard's piano studio in Paris.[35] She played music that was dictated to her by spirits, but never wrote it down. Peter Davidson, another rival of Blavatsky who ran the "Hermetic Brotherhood of Luxor," was a violin builder and author of a standard textbook on the instrument. Yet where is music in the teachings of these occultists? It plays virtually no part.

The case is otherwise with Fabre d'Olivet, perhaps the most influential figure of the Hermetic revival around 1800. Before beginning the work for which he is best known—explaining the *Golden Verses of Pythagoras*, unveiling the Hebrew tongue, and writing the secret and sacred history of the world—Fabre d'Olivet tried to make his reputation as a composer.[36] What most distinguished his compositions was his use of a classical Greek mode, with the intention of recreating the marvelous effects claimed for ancient music. Only a want of critical support prevented him from pursuing this Orphic ambition.

Another prominent figure of the French Hermetic tradition was Saint-Yves d'Alveydre, who found in musical proportions a key to the alphabets, astrology, and wisdom of antiquity (expounded in his *Archéomètre*), and a basis for the arts and sciences of the future.[37] Saint-Yves's follower, the architect Charles Gougy, put these into practice, demonstrating how every proportion of a building, and even of its furnishings, could be made to accord with the Archeometric system. Saint-Yves, who was by all accounts a fine pianist and organist, and could compose in a fair imitation of the style of Liszt, also wrote about two hundred short piano pieces to illustrate his system: the *Archéomètre Musical*. This was the most ambitious project of Hermetic composition since *Atalanta Fugiens*, with which it shares a unique atmosphere and an undeniable power over the soul.

These same qualities may well be claimed for the music of another philosopher of universal scope, George Ivanovich Gurdjieff. In his Institute for the Harmonious Development of Man, Gurdjieff taught a Sufi-derived system of movement, accompanied by modal melodies and simple chord-progressions. He played them on the piano or harmonium, then his pupil, the professional musician Thomas de Hartmann, adapted them for the piano and recorded them in the form still used in the Gurdjieff Work. At about the same time, Rudolf Steiner was also teaching a system of body movement aimed at spiritual development, calling it Eurhythmy. This was meant to be a "visible music," to be used on its own or accompanied by music or readings. Steiner's Anthroposophical movement is one place where the Pythagorean vision of music as a molder of body and soul still holds good.

As we conclude this survey, it has become clear that something has been missed. Music has not worked with the Hermetic tradition in any very fruitful or consistent way, as, for example, literature has. Music and Hermeticism resemble two cousins who are not particularly fond of each other, but whose family connections force them occasionally to meet. Each one is sufficient to itself; neither has any real need of the other.

There is a lesson in this. Music is a world of its own, with its own laws founded in number and physical phenomena, which it miraculously transmutes into human feelings. It has an exoteric side, which we know through the everyday experiences of recordings, concerts, and music making. This satisfies most people's needs, just as churches satisfy most religious people. As in religions, there is also an esotericism in music. One aspect of it is the science of speculative music, which searches out the principles and laws underlying both practical music and its reflections in the cosmos. This is comparable to the hermeneutics that seeks for deeper meanings beneath the surface of scripture. It belongs to the path of knowledge, to the philosopher or "lover of wisdom" whose greatest desire is to know and to understand.

The other aspect of musical esotericism is the experiential one, driven by the power of practical music over body and soul. The levels of musical experience extend to degrees of mysticism and crystalline perception that are indescribable in words. Music, in short, contains all the requisites for a path of spiritual development. It offers transformative experiences for the body, the emotions, the intellect, and the soul, as surely as the Hermetic tradition does. The processes are parallel, the ultimate goal probably the same, but the methods are entirely different. That is why music and the Hermetic tradition can happily coexist, but will never become one.

NOTES

1. See Otto Gombosi, "Studien zur Tonartenlehre des frühen Mittelalters III," *Acta Musicologica* 12 (1940): 39; Egon Wellesz, "The Survival of Greek Musical Theory," in *A History of Byzantine Music and Hymnography* (Oxford, 1961), 72–77. On music and alchemy in general, by far the best study is Christoph Meinel, "Alchemie und Musik," in *Die Alchemie in der europäischen Kultur- und Wissenschafts-geschichte*, ed. C. Meinel (Wiesbaden, 1986), 201–27.

2. Edited, with a recording, by J. Godwin in M. Maier, *Atalanta Fugiens* (Grand Rapids, 1989).

3. For a study of interval-aspect systems, see J. Godwin, *Harmonies of Heaven and Earth* (London, 1987), 148–55.

4. Tone-zodiacs are treated in Godwin, *Harmonies*, 153–67.

5. On Kepler's musical astronomy, see Bruce Stephenson, *The Music of the Heavens* (Princeton, 1993).

6. See Isaac Newton, *Opticks* (London, 1730), bk. 1, pt. 2, prop. 6, prob. 2.

7. See Angela Voss, "The Renaissance Musician: Speculations on the Performing Style of Marsilio Ficino," *Temenos* 11 (1990): 31–52.

8. See D. P. Walker, "Ficino's *spiritus* and Music," *Annales Musicologiques* 1 (1953), 131–50; reprinted in D. P. Walker, *Music, Spirit and Language in the Renaissance*, ed. P. Gouk (London, 1985).

9. Henry Cornelius Agrippa, *De Occulta Philosophia Libri Tres* (Antwerp, 1533), bk. 2, chaps. 24–25.

10. On this current, see J. Godwin, "Opera and the Amorous Initiation," *Temenos* 12 (1991): 129–40.

11. See D. P. Walker, ed., *Musique des intermèdes de La Pellegrina* (Paris, 1963).

12. See René Alleau, *Guide de Versailles mystérieux* (Paris, 1966).

13. See John James, *Chartres: The Masons Who Built a Legend* (London, 1982), 108, where the numerical equivalents of Marian mottoes are shown to dictate the dimensions of Chartres Cathedral.

14. See Otto von Simson, *The Gothic Cathedral* (New York, 1962), 199.

15. Ibid., 199–200.

16. See Hans Kayser, *Ein harmonikaler Teilungs-Kanon* (Zürich, 1946).

17. See G. L. Hersey, *Pythagorean Palaces: Magic and Architecture in the Italian Renaissance* (Ithaca, 1976).

18. An example is the use made of Poussin's *Les Bergers d"Arcadie* to prove various theories about Rennes-le-Château. See Henry Lincoln, *The Holy Place* (New York, 1991), 52–64.

19. See F. Liessem, *Musik und Alchemie* (Tutzing, 1969).

20. See Craig Wright, "Dufay's *Nuper rosarum flores*, King Solomon's Temple, and the Veneration of the Virgin," *Journal of the American Musicological Society* 47 (1994): 395–441.

21. See the extensive analyses (in English) by Marius Van Crevel, in his editions of *Missa Sub Tuum Presidium* (Amsterdam, 1959) and *Missa Maria Zart* (Amsterdam, 1964).

22. This experiment is described in C. G. Jung, "Synchronicity: An Acausal Connecting Principle," in *The Collected Works*, vol. 8: *The Structure and Dynamics of the Psyche* (Princeton, 1960).

23. K. van Houten and M. Kasbergen, *Bach en het getal* (Zutphen, 1985), cited in Ruth Tatlow, *Bach and the Riddle of the Number Alphabet* (Cambridge, 1991), 1 n.

24. See J. Godwin, "Layers of Meaning in *The Magic Flute*," *Musical Quarterly* 65 (1979): 471–92.

25. See Dore Ashton, *A Fable of Modern Art* (London, 1980), 99.

26. See Wouter Hanegraaff, "Esoterie en muziek: Aan de hand van Schoenberg en Webern," *Mens en Melodie* 45 (1990): 194–201; idem, "De Gnosis van Arnold Schoenberg," *Vooys* 7 (1988): 28–37.

27. See Roy Howat, *Debussy in Proportion: A Musical Analysis* (Cambridge, 1983); Erno Lendvai, *Bela Bartók: An Analysis of his Music* (London, 1971).

28. See Raymond Head, "Holst—Astrology and Modernism in 'The Planets'," *Tempo* 187 (December 1993): 15–22.

29. *Lilia Nympham colit* (1604). See Adam McLean, "A Piece of 'Rosicrucian' Music Restored," *Hermetic Journal* 42 (1988): 3.

30. Edited by Todd Barton as "Robert Fludd's Temple of Music: A Description and Commentary" (M.A. diss., University of Oregon, 1978).

31. See Ron Heisler, "Introduction to the Hermetic Adepti," *Hermetic Journal* 35 (1987): 34–41.

32. See Manly Palmer Hall, ed., *The Music of the Comte de St. Germain* (Los Angeles, 1981). Unfortunately, this edition gives only the basso continuo line of St.-Germain's trio sonatas.

33. On Saint-Martin and music, see J. Godwin, *Music and the Occult: French Musical Philosophies, 1750–1950* (Rochester, N.Y., 1995), a translation of *L"ésotérisme musical en France, 1750–1950* (Paris, 1991), chapter 1.

34. See the evaluation of these stories in Jean Overton Fuller, *Blavatsky and Her Teachers* (London, 1988), 19.

35. *Autobiography of Emma Hardinge Britten* (Manchester, 1900), 6.

36. On Fabre d'Olivet and music, see Godwin, *Music and the Occult*, chap. 4; also idem, introduction to Fabre d'Olivet, *Music Explained as Science and Art,* trans. J. Godwin (Rochester, Vt., 1989).

37. On Saint-Yves d'Alveydre and music, see Godwin, *Music and the Occult*, chap. 8.

CHAPTER 12

HERMETICISM IN EARLY ROSICRUCIANISM

ROLAND EDIGHOFFER

The very title of this article already sets the limits of my investigation. The expression "Early Rosicrucianism" will not be taken as referring to the mythological origin that some later groups of Rosicrucians believe to have discovered in remote ages. My purpose is not to criticize such a point of view, which chiefly belongs to the category of faith, but to remain within the boundaries of historical inquiry.

It stands for a fact that the name *Orden des Rosenkreutzes* is first mentioned in 1614 in a printed work, and that the three foundational writings of the fictional Rose Cross Order, namely *Fama Fraternitatis*, *Confessio Fraternitatis* and *Chymische Hochzeit Christiani Rosenkreutz*, were published between 1614 and 1616. So-called Early Rosicrucianism represents in several ways an intermediate phase, both in European culture and in the evolution of German Lutheranism. The cultural transition from the Renaissance to the so-called scientific revolution of the seventeenth century has been the object of much research, by Frances A. Yates among others, and therefore only needs to be mentioned here. The religious, ethical, and philosophical climax in the third Protestant generation after the age of the Reformation, which took form and expression in the circle from which the Rosicrucian manifestoes arose, seems however to be of great importance as well. All the work of Johann Valentin Andreae, as a pastor and as an author, was an attempt at awakening the feeling of the divine presence both in Man and in Nature, and to convert the so-called Christians "by mouth" into *renati*—that is to say, into regenerated creatures. In *Christianopolis*, a work Andreae published three years after the *Chemical Wedding*, we find a Confession of Faith which explains that the "new birth" restores the Christian to the dignity that was lost by Adam's fall and, consequently, reconciles Man with Nature.[1] Thus, it abolishes the dualism that original sin had brought about and creates

197

a new relationship between the believer and the natural world of which he is a part.

The Rosicrucian themes of Fall and Reintegration, on the one hand, and of Nature as a book through which God would be known, on the other, are both derived from Alexandrian Hermetism, as will be seen. And the idea that Saint Paul expresses in the Rom. 8:19–21 that the whole earth itself is susceptible to return to its original glorious state is paralleled in Hermetic alchemy. Moreover, those belonging to the circle around Andreae, as well as all other Christians of that time who lived in the expectation of a new Reformation, could discover a modern form of Hermetic tradition in the esoteric ideas of the fifteenth and sixteenth centuries. The manifold translations of the *Corpus Hermeticum*, the increase of Kabbalistic studies, the belief that Hermes Trismegistus might have been a contemporary of Moses—all put forward a new image of Christianity belonging to that form of syncretistic thinking on which Frances Yates has bestowed the term "Hermeticism." In a recent volume devoted to modern esoteric spirituality, as well as in the present volume, Antoine Faivre explains that the word "Hermetism" refers either to the Alexandrian texts called Hermetica, or to later literature directly inspired by such texts, while the term "Hermeticism" covers many other aspects of western esotericism as well, such as alchemy and similar forms of speculation.[2]

The issue addressed in the present study might thus be formulated in two different ways. Early Rosicrucianism must be seen from the double point of view of Hermetism and Hermeticism. My method of investigation will be to take both these aspects into account, and in each case I will start from the texts of Early Rosicrucianism in order to give a true picture of the first Rosicrucian movement.

HERMETISM IN THE FOUNDING WRITINGS
OF THE ROSY CROSS FICTION

The reader of the *Chymische Hochzeit* (Chemical wedding), will notice that the names Hermes and Mercurius appear quite often in this beautiful story. At the beginning of his pilgrimage Christian Rosenkreutz comes to a strange crossroad, which stands explicitly under the sign of

Hermes. It is well known that Hermes was worshipped as the protector of crossroads and that so-called Hermai—that is to say, Hermes stones—were used to mark out ways.

At the crossroad of our story stand three cedars. King Solomon built the temple with this species of tree, and the Song of Solomon (1:17) specifies that cedars are the building material of the house of the King and his sweetheart of Jerusalem. Since the wood of this tree is undecaying, the prophet Hosea compares God to a cedar, thus indicating that cedars are a symbol of eternity. It is therefore no wonder that this tree is also one of the multiple symbols of Mercurius. In the *Chemical Wedding* a marginal note defines the cedar tree as *arbor mercurialis*. Since the Latin word *arbor* is feminine, the cedar represents the feminine aspect of mercury in the *Aurora consurgens* (The break of day) of Pseudo-Thomas Aquinas. The identification of Mercurius with a *virgo* or with Venus is a topos of the alchemical literature, such as *The Book of Crates* and, last but not least, the *Chemical Wedding* itself: in the cellar of the mysterious castle Christian Rosenkreutz discovers the naked love goddess, who will launch the whole alchemical process of death and regeneration.

Furthermore, the three cedar trees are not to be understood as a Christian Trinitarian symbol only, for the number 3 is also connected with the name of Hermes Trismegistus and with the alchemical triad of *sal, sulphur,* and *mercurius*. Heinrich Khunrath therefore says, in his book *Von hylealischen Chaos*, that Mercurius is *triunus* and *ternarius*.[3] Moreover, a marginal note of the *Chemical Wedding* assimilates the *cedri* with *templa* and thus brings the reader back to the sealed letter at the beginning of the narrative, in which three stately temples stand on a mountain. According to the Paracelsist Gerhard Dorn, in his treatise *Congeries Paracelsicae chemiae de transmutationibus metallorum*, Mercurius is a *divinus ternarius* and as such he reveals divine secrets.[4] George Ripley would later say in his *Opera omnia chemica*, which appeared in Kassel in 1649, that Mercurius fecundated the "tree of wisdom" *(arbor sapientiae)*.[5]

On one of the three cedars is affixed a notice that a marginal note characterizes as *Tabula Mercurialis*. The message on it refers to the alchemical doctrine of the four elements, which Andreae, following many Paracelsists, Christianized in the *Chemical Wedding* with particular emphasis. Moreover the way Christian Rosenkreutz will go does not depend on his free choice, but on his response to a symbolic sign given to him by a white dove that flies down from one of the three cedars. This bird symbolizes certainly the Holy Spirit, but also the *avis Hermetis*, which in the alchemical process flies up from the four elements as a symbol of the spirit that is liberated from its confinement in the *physis*. The soaring of the dove is to be interpreted as an invitation to the spiritual journey of regeneration that Christian Rosenkreutz is about to undertake. Therefore, the corresponding marginal note describes the bird as "a white dove sitting on the tree of Mercurius" *(Columba Alba arbori Mercuriali insidens)*. Mercurius, who was often identified with Wisdom *(Sapientia)* or with the Holy Ghost, is also Hermes *Hodègos*, the guide of travelers. Michael Maier explains in his book *Symbola aurea Mensae* that he found during his *peregrinatio* "a statue of Hermes" *(Mercurialem statuam)* that showed the way to Paradise: "With the forefinger of its right hand it showed a straight line that would lead to the same terrestrial Paradise" *(Haec indice manus dextrae rectam quandam lineam demonstravit, qua ad Paradisum terrestrem eundem sit)*.[6] But we must not forget that Mercurius is essentially ambivalent, a seducer as well as a guide: this is why he also appears in the shape of a black crow that attacks the dove. Christian Rosenkreutz saves the white bird and finds the right way without knowing how. But the informed reader understands that Hermes, or in the Lutheran view Hermes as a symbol of the means of grace, has put in his hands the compass that guides him to the philosophical gold of God.

The second mention of Hermes is found in the fourth chapter of the story of the *Chemical Wedding*. A lion, already described in the third chapter as standing upon a fountain, has broken a sword in two, as a sign of the peace of God with mankind and between mind *(mens)* and body *(corpus)* in man. The Paracelsian Gerhard Dorn wrote in a treatise included in the *Theatrum chemicum* of 1602:

O admirable efficacy of the source which . . . makes peace between enemies! The source of love is able to make a mind out of body and soul, but this one makes one man out of mind and body *(O admiranda fontis efficacia, quae . . . pacem inter inimicos facit! Potest amoris fons de spiritu et anima mentem facere, sed hic de mente et corpore virum unum efficit)*.[7]

In the fourth chapter the lion has exchanged the sword for a tablet that "was taken out of the ancient monuments"—that is to say, out of the royal sepulchre glorified by the phoenix as an image of Christ's resurrection.[8] On this tablet stands the following text: "Hermes the Prince. After so many wounds inflicted on humankind, here by God's counsel and the help of Art I flow, a healing medicine." From this inscription it is easy to infer that Hermes is here the *aqua permanens* of the alchemists, that is to say, the "philosophical mercury" *(mercurius philosophicus),* which is also named the "water of life" *(aqua vitae).*[9] That is why the tablet invites to drink from this wonder water: "Drink, brothers, and live" *(Bibite fratres et vivite).*

It does not surprise, then, that Hermes appears as a particularly revered authority, as a "Prince," who leads one to the mysteries of God and the creation. Michael Maier, who obviously was an admirer of the message of the Rosy Cross, designates him as "Philosopher and Priest, greatest King" *(Philosophus et Sacerdos, et Rex maximus).*[10] But Hermes is also *princeps* in the sense of *materia prima,* or Mercurius Primus—that is to say in the alchemical language, "the green Lion, the medium that connects Sun and Moon" *(Leo viridis, medium conjungendi . . . Solem et Lunam).*[11] Johannes Mylius, a contemporary of Johann Valentin Andreae, wrote that Mercurius is the green Lion

> and he is the eternal water and the water of life and death . . . and he is the source of the soul: who drinks from it does not die . . . , and . . . he mortificates, . . . and makes the opposite *(et est aqua permanens et aquae vitae et mortis . . . et est fons animalis: de quo qui bibit non moritur . . . , et . . . mortificat, . . . et facit contraria).*[12]

This quotation shows that the symbolic Lion and fountain have, among alchemists, more levels of meaning than in the *Chemical Wedding.* The text on the tablet in chapter 4 indeed alludes then to the changeable aspect of the many-sided and unstable Mercurius, which several writings in the 1602 volume of the *Theatrum chemicum* describe as *varius* or *versipellis.* But the *Chemical Wedding* shows only the positive evolution of Hermes-Mercurius, who "after so many wounds inflicted upon humankind" has become a "healing medicine." He is in fact *medicina catholica, alexipharmacon* (antidote), and works as "Savior of all imperfect bodies" *(salvator omnium imperfectorum corporum),*[13] insofar as Mercurius is not only *prima materia* but also *ultima materia,* the Philosopher's Stone, *deus terrestris* and *analogia Christi.* The chronogram under the inscription, which consists of code symbols and signifies the year 1378, may also be interpreted in the sense of the divine perfection of Hermes-Mercurius. In this number 1378 the "one" expresses God's unity, which the *Corpus Hermeticum* and the *Asclepius* emphasize by calling the divinity *hen to pan* (the All is one) or *unus et omnia* (one and everything).[14] The "three" alludes to the Trinitarian God as well as to Hermes Trismegistus; the "seven" refers to the book with seven seals in the Apocalypse and also to the seven spheres beneath the ogdoadic nature of the *Corpus Hermeticum*, in which the name Ogdoas (= eight) designates the Almighty. On the other hand, according to the medieval mystical tradition Adam returned to the state before original sin on the eighth day.[15] Since we know from the *Confessio Fraternitatis* that Christian Rosenkreutz was born in this year 1378, we may infer that the author intends to suggest here that his hero, although already an old man at the time of the *Chemical Wedding*, experiences a "rebirth" thanks to the mercurial water, in the sense Christ meant when he said to Nicodemus in John 3:3ff.: "Unless a man be born again, he cannot see the kingdom of God."

HERMETICISM IN THE FOUNDING WRITINGS OF THE ROSY CROSS FICTION

Even when the name Hermes is not quoted, the story of the *Chemical Wedding* alludes frequently to various aspects of Hermeticism. It is not possible in the context of this brief study to discuss all events or indications that point to a Hermeticist background. I will restrict myself to bringing out some particularly significant examples from the *Chemical Wedding*.

The Visit to Venus

After a ritual lustration in the living water Christian Rosenkreutz and his fellows receive a golden fleece, with a medal in which is engraved a quotation from the prophet Isaiah (30:26): "The moonlight will be as the sunlight, and the sunlight will be multiplied by seven." On the one hand, the golden fleece refers to *Hermes Criophorus* (bearing a ram); on the other, the attached medal announces an apocalyptic transformation related to the process of alchemy: sun and moon may be sulphur and mercury or gold and silver. The alchemical process starts in the fifth chapter in the cellar of the castle where Christian Rosenkreutz, under a triangular altar behind a copper door, discovers the naked beauty of Venus, who lies on a bed and sleeps. Later, Cupid appears, who will not "let it pass unrevenged" and pricks his dart into the hand of Christian. His curiosity will entail his banishment at the end of the story, for Cupid is one of the numerous aspects of Mercurius, namely *Mercurius sagittarius* (the archer), whose arrow is called *telum passionis* (the weapon of suffering) in some alchemical writings.[16] The exciting spectacle of the naked Venus in a cellar intends to convey the notion that the way to genuine alchemical transmutation must begin with a descent into Tartarus. Now, it is remarkable that the chemical symbol for *spiritus tartari* is nearly the same as for copper, and that the word "copper" is related to the Greek name *Kypris*, which precisely designates Aphrodite or Venus. It is no wonder that Mercurius is frequently identified with Venus. The symbolic fertility of Venus is closely connected with quicksilver, and thus Christian sees on the mausoleum of Aphrodite an angel holding an unknown tree, from which fruits continually fall into a kettle and then turn into water—that is to say, into philosophical mercury.

An Allegorical Performance

This strange visit to the bowels of the earth follows upon the beheading of the sovereigns, which Christian qualifies as "a bloody Wedding." But he hears also that "the Death shall make many alive." The explanation for such a statement had already been given in the "comedy" that had been performed on the fourth day of the story. A little girl who is found in a chest upon the water is the sole survivor of a royal seed, which the Moor has entirely destroyed. Her uncle, a king, educates the child, who becomes a beautiful young lady. Her cousin will marry her, but the Moor kidnaps her, and although her cousin chivalrously liberates her by fighting the Moor, she goes back and devotes herself to the devil, who makes her a whore. Nevertheless, the young prince still loves her and kills the Moor in a duel. After some further dramatic happenings, the marriage of the young king and the pretty queen is at last joyfully celebrated.

This drama may be interpreted in two ways: on the one hand it is an alchemical allegory in which the Moor represents the stage of *nigredo*, produced by a *conjunctio oppositorum* that takes here the form of a coitus of the devil with the pure girl. Then follows the struggle between the Moor and the young knight, who seems dead for a short time but eventually comes to life again. This leads to the state of *albedo*, and then to that of *rubedo*, when the red king and the white queen celebrate their *nuptiae chemicae*. The second possible interpretation refers to the Christian background of the whole novel. The miraculous discovery of the baby obviously reminds one of the biblical episode of Moses, who founded the first alliance with God and later was to be considered a prototype of Christ. The fickle behavior of the girl symbolizes the disobedience and idolatry of the people of God. The king's son, who seemingly dies and then comes back to life again, seals the new alliance; but at the end the promised wedding, taking place in the seventh act, gives to this symbolic drama its apocalyptic dimension.

These processes, as well as the metamorphosis of Hermes at the mercurial fountain, enable us to grasp the underlying meaning of the *Chemical Wedding*, a novel that presents a particular view of Hermeticism and alchemy. Below, we will return to this important aspect of the Rosicrucian message. But the fact that in the novel the so-called comedy is performed on the fourth day of a drama that covers seven days, as an illustration of a new Genesis, gives to this interlude its significance. Just as in Genesis God separated light from darkness on the fourth day, the "comedy" also leads the reader on the fourth day of the story to the allegory of faith: in this way the author draws the attention of his readers to the predominant religious significance of his fiction. The light of God's love will henceforth bring about the salvific regeneration in the Knights of the Golden Stone, and make the life-giving wedding possible.

Regeneration

In the second part of the story Hermeticism plays an important part. The regeneration process begins with a navigation across a sea, which is one of the multiple forms of Mercurius. During the voyage, the passengers of the seven ships (an image of the seven planets) encounter beautiful nymphs, reminding us of the *serpens mercurialis*. The wonderful love song of these nymphs inspired Goethe, who adapted this poem in a letter to Charlotte von Stein. The navigators with the seven corpses from the "bloody wedding" land on a square island where the so-called

Tower of Olympus stands, the name of which refers to the *ton Olympon anabasis* (the ascent of Olympus) in the tenth treatise of the *Corpus Hermeticum* (X.15). This tower has seven levels but eight rooms, and the last phase of the Great Work, the *rubedo* or resurrection of the King and Queen, takes place in room 8. This number corresponds to the *ogdoatikè physis* in the first treatise of the *Corpus Hermeticum* (1.26), in which the soul is said to possess gnosis and to "enter into God" or be born again in God.

The "birth in God" *(en theoi genesis)* or regeneration is the main theme of the thirteenth book of the *Corpus Hermeticum*. This *palingenesia* means that man must purify himself from his vices (twelve in this treatise, seven in other books of the *Corpus Hermeticum*). Only then can God's gnosis fill him with its ten *dynameis*, which together are Truth, Goodness, Life, and Light, since, as is well known, the decade symbolizes the Pythagorean *tetraktys*. Corresponding to these divine powers, the *Chemical Wedding* describes, on the one hand, the seven weights of the *libra aurea*—that is to say, the golden scale—on which the virtues of the candidates are weighed; and, on the other hand, the so-called *repositio ponderum* on day 3, when the seven virgins carry the seven weights used in the episode of the trial and that represent seven virtues, as they do in the *Psychomachia* of Prudentius.[17]

Festugière has cogently shown that this thirteenth treatise of the *Corpus Hermeticum* nevertheless does not speak of a moral improvement in man: Hermes does not say that the vices are rooted out voluntarily but that it is only by divine grace that man can be purified and born again. Consequently, genuine morality appears only after the regeneration, which God alone can bring about.[18] The Lutheran student and eventual pastor Andreae could only subscribe to such a view, which seemed somewhat similar to the Lutheran formula *sola gratia*.

In the *Chemical Wedding* regeneration is represented by two kinds of symbolic systems, which both derive from the *Corpus Hermeticum*. First, the life-giving bath in and drink from Hermes' fountain correspond to the fourth treatise of the *Corpus Hermeticum*, where initiation is described as a sort of baptism in a crater. The invitation to this rite is partly formulated as in the *Corpus*.[19] As a result of the immersion, men are no longer simply *logikoi* but become *pneumatikoi* who are able to embrace heaven and earth. Secondly, the *Chemical Wedding* describes the mystery of rebirth as an alchemical process that takes place on the different levels of the Tower of Olympus, and thereby suggests a variety of interpretations that are very much in line with the secular traditions derived from Hermeticism. In Zosimos, who probably lived in the third century, alchemy already appears as a process of salvation.[20] In the wonderful little work *Aurora consurgens* (already mentioned above), which abounds with quotations from the Bible, the writer in a series of parables blends alchemical elements with an allusive description of the maturation of the second Adam. In the sixth parable, for example, he writes: "Adam and his sons come from corruptible elements, thus this compound must be corrupted; the second Adam, on the contrary, is called 'philosophical man' since he went out from the pure elements to pass over into eternity." The last chapter of the *Aurora consurgens* unites alchemical wedding and spiritual wedding in the golden dawn and the love melody of a kind of Song of Solomon. In another book, also entitled *Dawn*, namely *Aurora philosophorum* of Gerhard Dorn (a disciple of Paracelsus whose writings were known to Andreae and his friends) we are taught that the philosophical Mercurius is "newly born" as a result of the great mystery of the celestial and supernatural wedding of the soul, which had been purified by the blood of the lamb and also by the purified substance of the body. Gerhard Dorn sees in such a mysterious transmutation the secret of longevity; and in the Philosopher's Stone—that is, in the *Spiritus Mercurius*—he sees the promise of the coming *postremis temporibus* of a Redeemer of matter itself. The mythical figure of Christian Rosenkreutz may be the crystallization of this "most pure man" *(putissimus homo)*. At the end of the *Chemical Wedding*, Christian Rosenkreutz becomes a Knight of the Golden Stone and receives the mission to overcome ignorance, poverty, and illness, to break the limits of matter, and to bring about the reciprocal regeneration of man and nature. This ideal is in accordance with the Hermetic tradition, since the *Asclepius* emphasizes the necessity for man to "prove adequate to both its beginnings, wondering at heavenly beings and worshipping them, tending earthly beings and governing them."[21]

This analysis of the *Chemical Wedding* shows that Hermes or Mercurius is several times invoked in the narrative, and that Hermetism in the garments of alchemy as well as Paracelsian thought constitutes the background of the novel. On day 6, an athanor (an alchemical stove) is described, which bears a cryptic inscription with the initials of

Paracelsus. In the *Fama Fraternitatis* (1614), the first edited Rosicrucian manifesto, the name Paracelsus is mentioned several times and with particular reverence, and the text of this document often refers to his philosophical outlook. As a matter of fact, we find in the *Fama Fraternitatis*, and also in Paracelsian speculation, the analogies and correspondences between macrocosm and microcosm linked to the belief that man unites within himself all the elements of the world, which is the great "Book of Nature." In line with Paracelsus, the *Fama Fraternitatis* emphasizes that the learned, if only they were united, "might out of all those things which in this our age God doth so richly bestow upon us, collect *Librum Naturae*," and rejoices "that finally man might thereby understand his own nobleness and worth, and why he is called Microcosm, and how far his knowledge extendeth into Nature."[22] Similarly the *Confessio Fraternitatis* asserts that "These characters and letters, as God hath here and there incorporated them in the Holy Scriptures, the Bible, so hath he imprinted them most apparently into the wonderful creation of heaven and earth. . . ." (*RE*, 257). Yet not everybody is able to read the book of nature, and that is why the *Confessio* also says: "Although that great book of nature stands open to all men, yet there are but few that can read and understand the same" (*RE*, 257). Who are then the few selected men who are able to decipher God's script in the world? All those who desire the Fraternity "under the seal of secrecy," as the *Confessio* indicates (*RE*, 255); but the *Fama Fraternitatis* gives us to understand that secrecy or silence is only the stage preliminary to the Rosicrucian initiation, as in the thirteenth treatise of the *Corpus Hermeticum*, where silence is a step toward regeneration.[23] The true key is given by the last inscription in the mausoleum of Christian Rosenkreutz: *Ex Deo nascimur, in Jesu morimur, per Spiritum Sanctum reviviscimus* (We are born of God, we die in Jesus, we live again through the Holy Spirit) (*RE*, 248).

KNOWLEDGE OF GOD'S SON

I spoke of a key. Indeed, the theme of the new birth, which is essential in the Hermetica, in alchemy, and also in the *Chemical Wedding*, is the keystone of the manifesto as well. Therefore, it is no wonder that the same formula in the *Fama Fraternitatis* is again quoted in the *Axiomata philosophica* of Christoph Besold, who was at this time a close friend of Andreae.[24] This formula also accounts for the strange and enthusiastic statement, at the beginning of the *Fama*, that by God's mercy ."in these latter days . . . we do attain more and more to the perfect knowledge of his Son and Nature. . . ." (*RE*, 238).[25] Behind this statement we may perceive, among other things, an allusion to the *Corpus Hermeticum*. In the thirteenth treatise, already quoted above, Hermes Trismegistus says (XIII.2) that the reborn person will become a god and God's Son *(theou theos pais)*. Thus the fruit of the regeneration is here a new condition in which man knows God as Father and himself as the Son of God. But this fruit, which has replaced the old ego by the regeneration, is not visible because the real man, *theou theos pais*, is an internal man and an incorporeal being. The regenerated man feels enthusiasm in the literal sense of this word: i.e., he feels God's presence within himself. He masters space and time; he has the feeling that he can be present everywhere—in the sky, in the earth, in the water, in the air.[26] The fourth chapter of the *Confessio Fraternitatis* asks the following question: "Were it not a precious thing, that you could always live so, as if you had lived from the beginning of the world, and, moreover, as you should still live to the end of thereof?" (*RE*, 253). Such a question corresponds to the invitation that we find in the eleventh treatise of the *Corpus Hermeticum*: "Raise yourself above all time, become Eternity; then you will understand God." In the preceding paragraph we read: "Command your soul to be in India, to cross the ocean; in a moment it will be done" (XI.19–20). Similarly the *Confessio Fraternitatis* asks: "Were it not excellent you dwell in one place, that neither the people which dwell beyond the River Ganges in the Indies could hide anything, nor those which life in Peru might be able to keep secret their counsels from thee?" (*RE*, 253).

Although the similarity cannot be complete, Festugière has rightly shown that, according to the thirteenth treatise of the *Corpus Hermeticum*, regenerated man has definitely become a son of God and that consequently he cannot sin any longer.[27] This idea obviously contrasts with traditional Protestant thought and the famous formula of Luther: *simul iustus et peccator* (at the same time righteous and sinner). But we must also underline that the outlook of the *Corpus Hermeticum* is not uniform. For example, the first treatise suggests that even if God has come into man in the process of regeneration, man is nevertheless liable to sin again because he still has the possibility to choose between good and evil.[28]

The enigmatic assertion of the *Fama Fraternitatis* about the son of God must evidently also be interpreted within the context of alchemical ideas. It is a well-known fact that in alchemical works Mercurius is often called *filius macrocosmi*,[29] and sometimes *filius hominis fructus et virginis* (the son, the fruit of Man and Virgin),[30] or *filius unigenitus*.[31] The already quoted *Aurora consurgens* skillfully mixes the biblical and the alchemical representation of the Son of God and concludes, for instance, in the second parable: "My son, enjoy this day, because it is the end of the lamentations and the pains since the old world has passed away."[32] In alchemical literature Mercurius often appears as the second son of God: Christ has redeemed the microcosm, but Mercurius will redeem the macrocosm, and he is therefore the chthonic half of the divinity. However, it would be erroneous to identify him for that reason with evil, since Mercurius is for the alchemists *ambiguus* and *duplex*. Here we should recall the previously quoted episode of the Hermetic Fountain, thanks to which Hermes-Mercurius has become a healing medicine and an *aqua vitae*. In this regard, Hermeticism must be interpreted as a necessary complement of Christian redemption: while the Christian process represents a descent of the celestial realm on earth, the alchemical process leads nature from the lower darkness to the divine light by the mediation of the spiritual and winged *filius macrocosmi* who, as is well known, is also *psychopompus*.[33] This double movement may be compared with the phenomenon of reflection. It is reminiscent of the Hermetic myth of the wedding of man and nature that is depicted in the *Poimandres*, the first treatise of the *Corpus Hermeticum*, and it finds an explanation in the short seventeenth treatise: "[T]he world of the senses reflects itself in the world of the intellect," and vice versa. This image indicates that man needs the mediation of Nature and must take on a body to bring about the encounter with his own perfect shape in God, while nature herself needs the mediation of man to bring about its transmutation and to spiritualize matter.

These indications show that the enthusiastic allusion of the *Fama Fraternitatis* to a better understanding of the Son of God and of Nature goes beyond the field of theology and concerns an aspect of philosophy that may be designated as Hermetic philosophy. The second chapter of the *Confessio Fraternitatis* defines the Rosicrucian philosophy as follows: "No other Philosophy we have, than that . . . which doth manifest and declare sufficiently Man. . . ." (*RE*, 252). This emphasis on the mediate function of man is a typical aspect of Hermetic philosophy. The first section of the *Asclepius* underlines this privileged part of man as a mediator between God and Nature;[34] but Hermes Trismegistus spells out, both here and in some treatises of the *Corpus Hermeticum*, that this ability to mediation is granted only to those who have gnosis, that is to say who have been regenerated, because "not all . . . have attained true knowledge" *(non omnes . . . intelligentiam veram adepti sunt)*.[35] It is therefore no wonder that in the Middle Ages we see cropping up such names as Sanctus Hermes, San Mercurio, and Hermes catholicus christianus, and that the authors of early Rosicrucianism assimilated the "very few who are of a pure mind" *(paucissimi pura mente)* with the members of their brotherhood and their Hermetic philosophy with theology. Thus, we can read in the *Fama Fraternitatis:*

> It shall not be said, this is true according to Philosophy, but false in Theology. And wherein Plato, Aristotle, Pythagoras and others did hit the mark, and wherein Enoch, Abraham, Moses, Solomon did excel, but especially wherewith that wonderful book the Bible agrees. All that same concurreth together, and makes a sphere or Globe, whose total parts are equidistant from the Centre. . . . (*RE*, 250)

All Paracelsian writers, who have inspired the authors of the Rosicrucian manifestoes, refer to the Hermetic or the alchemical philosophy, and in doing so they invoke as referential authorities figures like Moses, Abraham, Solomon, Elijah, and even Adam himself.[36] Similarly, the authors of the *Fama Fraternitatis* declare: "Our Philosophy also is not a new invention, but as Adam after his fall hath received it, and as Moses and Solomon used it" (*RE*, 249).

CONCLUSION

It is not the purpose of this study to give an exhaustive survey of the presence of Hermetism and Hermeticism in Early Rosicrucianism, but only to bring out a few particular elements of the *Chemical Wedding*, the *Fama Fraternitatis*, and the *Confessio Fraternitatis*. These elements are illustrative of a deep interest in a new form of faith and knowledge, which would reconcile the Christian and philosophical tradition with a new understanding of Nature. In addition to that, we should not forget that the Rosicrucian ideas arose in Protestant countries, namely in the third generation of Lutheranism, when lucid and courageous men like Johann Valentin Andreae devoted an important part of their writings to criticizing the general decline in various fields, such as politics, teaching, religion, and morality.[37] Andreae's negative evaluation of the moral situation in Württemberg in his days prompted him to admire the theocratic organization that Calvin had imposed on Geneva. In that same town, Isaac Casaubon demonstrated in 1610 that the *Hermetica* could not have been written by Hermes Trismegistus, and that some of these works were fakes by Christians.[38] At that time, the *Fama fraternitatis* and the *Chemical Wedding* had already been written. However, this discovery would not have had any influence on the authors of the Rosicrucian writings, insofar as Casaubon's concern was to highlight the presence of Christian ideas within the *Corpus Hermeticum*. Moreover, the end of the sixteenth century and the beginning of the seventeenth were in fact the golden age of religious Hermeticism.[39]

Two factors may account for the origin of the Rosicrucian movement: the severe judgment of its first authors on the mistakes made in the individual and social applications of the Lutheran principles of *sola fide* et *sola gratia*; and the development of Hermeticism. In such a context the publication of the "General Reformation" of Traiano Boccalini, which the German Rosicrucians prefixed to their first manifesto, may be considered as something more than a simple joke without further importance. Certainly, Boccalini's *Ragguaglï di Parnasso* was first published in 1612–13 at Venice and, therefore, could not have any influence on the authors of the *Fama Fraternitatis*, which circulated in manuscript form as early as 1610. But the publication of this satire by Boccalini was primarily aimed against the so-called *literati*, who also have been the target of many attacks in other works of Johann Valentin Andreae. Later on, the ridiculous result of the sophisticated deliberations of the Seven Wise Men of Greece[40] and the *literati*, who decided to regulate the price of cabbages, sprats, and pumpkins, sheds an interesting light on the context of the Rosicrucian manifestoes. They intend to persuade us that the religious, moral, and cultural evils of the age could not be rooted out by the conversations of eminent scholars but only by a new Reformation that would combine Hermetic philosophy with Christian theology.

The satirist Boccalini was a great admirer of Henry of Navarre and promulgated a pro-French liberal line of thinking (*GB*, 408). Now, it should be noted that in the sixteenth century religious Hermetism without magic was largely developed in France, where Lefèvre d'Étaples had published in 1505 Ficino's *Pimander* and the *Asclepius* in one volume. In this volume he also included a Christian interpretation of these texts by Ludovico Lazarelli, whose mentor Joannes Mercurius da Corregio "walked through the streets of Rome in 1484 wearing a crown of thorns with the inscription 'This is my child Pimander whom I have elected'" *(Hic est puer meus Pimander quem eligi)* (*GB*, 171 n. 2). Although I have not yet been able to prove that Andreae or his friends were privy to this episode, I think that the concordance of the date of this event with the year of the mythical Christian Rosenkreutz's death is astonishing. However, we stand on more solid ground in referring to the influence of the Protestant Frenchman Philippe Du Plessis Mornay, who at Antwerp in 1581 published a book entitled *De la vérité de la religion chrétienne*. In his dedication to Henry of Navarre he explains that he will study the world as a "shadow of the splendour of God." In chapter 1, Du Plessis Mornay refers to Hermes Trismegistus from the start and says that the whole of Nature is an image of God. Later on, he takes pains to prove that sciences and technology originate in Moses and Hermes Trismegistus, and in chapter 20 he sees in philosophy and theology the two wings that enable us to fly to God.[41] In short, Philippe Du Plessis Mornay, whom Andreae held in great esteem, presented the authors of the Rosicrucian manifestoes with a myth demonstrating how to reconcile nature and grace, philosophy and theology, Lutheran faith and a progressive achievement in experimental sciences.

Andreae points to this interpretation in the *Chemical Wedding* by reproducing the *Monas Hieroglyphica* of John Dee, who "has been lauded for his practical writings on astronomy, navigation and mathematics which seem to give an early indication of the significance and interrelation of technology and science."[42] But Dee was a Hermetic thinker, and Frances Yates has convincingly shown that his true spiritual home is to be found in "religious Hermetism" (*GB*, 188). As Allen Debus writes, his *Monas Hieroglyphica* "is a mystical alchemical text, dedicated to the penetration of divine mysteries through an occult explanation of geometrical figures."[43] The reproduction of this symbol, so replete with significance, on the letter inviting Christian Rosenkreutz to the Chemical Wedding epitomizes the Hermetic purpose of Andreae and the other godfathers of the Rosicrucian movement.

The key to their universal reformation, which aimed at completing the Lutheran Reformation, should therefore be found in religious Hermeticism. It is this same religious Hermeticism which Andreae later on (in his *Civis christianus*, 1619) considered an attribute of all those who, all around the world, are the members of what he called the *Universitas Filiorum Spiritualium Concors*, that is to say, The Harmonious Fellowship of the Spiritual Sons.[44]

NOTES

1. John Warwick Montgomery, *Cross and Crucible: Johann Valentin Andreae (1586-1654), Phoenix of the Theologians* (The Hague, 1973), 1:128.

2. Antoine Faivre, "Ancient and Medieval Sources of Modern Esoteric Movement," in *Modern Esoteric Spirituality*, ed. Antoine Faivre and Jacob Needleman (New York, 1992), 3 n; cf. idem, "Renaissance Hermeticism and the Concept of Western Esotericism" (in this volume).

3. Heinrich Khunrath, *Von hylealischen. Das ist Pri-Materialischen Catholischen, oder algemeinen Natürlichen Chaos* (Magdeburg, 1597), 203.

4. In *Theatrum chemicum* (Strasbourg, 1602), 1:621

5. *Duodecim portarum*, 124ff.

6. Michael Maier, *Symbola aurea Mensae* (Francofurti, 1617), 594.

7. Quoted according to C. G. Jung, *Mysterium conjunctionis*, in vol. 2 of *Gesammelte Werke* (Olten & Freiburg i. Br., 1978), 55 n. 143.

8. Montgomery, *Cross and Crucible*, 2:387.

9. C. G. Jung, *Der Geist Mercurius*, in vol. 2 of *Gesammelte Werke* (Olten & Freiburg i. Br., 1978), 13.

10. Maier, *Symbola aureae Mensae*, 10.

11. Ibid., 464.

12. Johannes Mylius, *Philosophia reformata* (Francofurti, 1622), 303.

13. Siebmacher, *Hydrolithus sophicus, seu Aquarium sapientium*, in *Musaeum Hermeticum* (Frankfurt, 1678), 111.

14. *Corpus Hermeticum* (henceforth abbreviated as CH) XV.3; *Asclepius* 20.

15. Cf. M.-M. Davy, "L'Homme du Huitième Jour," in *Travaux de Villard de Honnecourt* (Paris, 1980), 1:30-38.

16. Jung, *Studien über alchemistische Vorstellungen*, in vol. 13 of *Gesammelte Werke* (Olten, 1978), 278.

17. R. Edighoffer, *Rose-Croix et société idéale selon Johann Valentin Andreae* (Paris, 1982), 1:324.

18. A.-J. Festugière, *La révélation d'Hermès Trismégiste* (Paris, 1954), 4:251ff.

19. CH IV.4; *The Hermetick Romance: or the Chymical Wedding*, trans. E. Foxcroft (Cambridge, 1690), 74, in Montgomery, *Cross and Crucible*, 364.

20. Festugière, *Révélation* (Paris, 1944), 1:261ff.

21. *Asclepius* 8, in Copenhaver, *Hermetica*, 71.

22. F. A. Yates, *The Rosicrucian Enlightenment* (London, 1973), 238. Henceforth abbreviated in the text as *RE*, followed by the page number.

23. Compare the title of CH XIII: *Secret speech on the mountain concerning regeneration and silence.*

24. *Axiomata philosophico-theologica: Vitam vere philosophicam utcunque adumbrantia. In gratiam prophanorum Politicorum Seculi nostri, in hanc collecta formam a Christophoro Besoldo* (Argentorati [= Strasbourg], 1616), 68, Axioma no. 225.

25. The English translation by Thomas Vaughan, edited in 1652 and reproduced by Frances A. Yates in her *Rosicrucian Enlightenment*, specifies "Son Jesus Christ." This precision is not to be found in the original text and modifies the meaning of this passage.

26. See CH XIII.11.

27. Festugière, *Révélation*, 4:256ff.

28. CH I.14, 22–23; XII.3–4. Cf. Festugière, *Révélation*, 4:257.

29. Khunrath, *Von hylealischen . . . Chaos.*

30. *Theatrum chemicum*, 1:681.

31. Khunrath, *Von hylealischen . . . Chaos*, 59.

32. French translation by B. Gorceix, *L'aurore à son lever* (Neuilly-sur-Seine, 1982), 32.

33. Cf. C. G. Jung, *Aion*, in vol. 9, 2 of *Gesammelte Werke* (Olten & Freiburg i. Br., 1978), 25, 222.

34. *Asclepius* 6 (sec. 1e; ed. Copenhaver, 69).

35. *Asclepius* 7 (sec. 1g; ed. Copenhaver, 70).

36. Gerhard Dorn, *Aurora philosophorum* (Basileae, 1577), chap. 3.

37. Cf. Edighoffer, *Rose-Croix et société idéale*, 1:1–147.

38. F.A. Yates, *Giordano Bruno and the Hermetic Tradition* (London, 1964), 170. Henceforth abbreviated in the text as *GB*, followed by the page number.

39. Cf. J. Dagens, "Hermétisme et Kabbale en France de Lefèvre d'Étaples à Bossuet," *Revue de Littérature comparée*, janvier–mars 1961, 6.

40. I.e., the seven philosophers or statesmen who lived in the sixth century before Christ, and described by Plutarch in his *Symposium of the Seven Wise Men.*

41. I refer to the edition that appeared in Leiden in 1651: Philippe Du Plessis Mornay, *De la vérité de la religion chrétienne* (Leiden, 1651), 12, 136ff., 442.

42. Allen G. Debus, *Chemistry, Alchemy and the New Philosophy 1550-1700* (London, 1987), 4:10.

43. Debus, *Chemistry*, 4:11.

44. *Civis christianus* (Argentorati, 1619).

CHAPTER 13

CHRISTIAN THEOSOPHIC LITERATURE OF THE SEVENTEENTH AND EIGHTEENTH CENTURIES

ARTHUR VERSLUIS

While there are numerous studies of Kabbalism and Sufism, precious little has been available in English on the Christian parallel to these forms of esotericism: Christian theosophy (which long predates and has little to do with Blavatsky's Theosophical Society). French scholarship has been far more productive in this field. There is a very helpful survey of the genre by Antoine Faivre, the most important scholar in this field, and another survey by Pierre Deghaye, along with a few other sources that will undoubtedly be useful for those who require either a broad introduction or introductions to specific authors.[1] Here, while offering a general introduction to Christian theosophy, and a survey of primary texts, I will also include a number of works not previously discussed, so that this discussion will be of use both to specialists and to those, undoubtedly a majority, for whom this will be a venture into new terrain.

The word "theosophy" or *theosophia*, as Antoine Faivre has pointed out, has its origins in Greek antiquity, and can be traced in such Neoplatonic authors as Porphyry and Proclus, as well as in seminal early Christian authors like Clement of Alexandria, and Dionysius the Areopagite.[2] The word itself reflects the theosophers' focus on Sophia, Divine Wisdom, and theosophy can be distinguished from theology primarily in its authors' insistence on the primacy of direct Gnostic spiritual experience as opposed to book learning. One can see a lineage that runs from these early Christian Gnostics, through Meister Eckhart and Johannes Tauler, to the modern theosophic movement that began with Jakob Böhme at the inception of the seventeenth century. However, as I have pointed out elsewhere, whereas in Sufism one finds often an emphasis upon a direct initiatory lineage traceable back to the origins of Islam, in Christian theosophy one finds what we may call an "ahistorical continuity" of theosophic authors who identify themselves with this lineage (as when Tauler cites Proclus, for instance).[3]

But our focus is on modern theosophic authors, and the modern theosophic movement began at the turn of the seventeenth century both in Germany and in England. In Germany one finds the most influential or seminal of the theosophic writers, Jakob Böhme (1575–1624), who is certainly also the most well known to many readers, perhaps as the "illuminated cobbler" from Görlitz, a town near the border between Eastern and Western Europe. Böhme's spiritual illumination came after a period of despondency, and it resulted in his first book, *Morgenröte im Aufgang, oder Aurora*, written in 1612, and initially circulated only among friends. Böhme's extraordinary work provoked extreme wrath in a rather hidebound local Lutheran minister named Gregor Richter, and in fact Böhme was forbidden to write anything further. But he eventually developed quite a circle of followers, who asked him for advice, and thus he came to write many more treatises.[4]

Görlitz had become something of a center for heterodox people, or at least people with mystical leanings. And Böhme's own circle eventually included some remarkable people, among whom we should note Balthasar Walter, an extraordinary man who had traveled to the Near East (Arabia, Syria, and Egypt) in search of "Kabbalah, magic, and alchemy" during the late sixteenth century. He came to know Böhme after 1612 and stayed in Böhme's house for several months during 1619 or 1620. Other prominent, sympathetic members of Böhme's circle include Carl von Ender, a nobleman; Johann Huser, editor of an edition of Paracelsus's works; and Dr. Tobias Kober.

Relatively late in his life, Böhme produced a corpus of work that was to inspire virtually the whole of subsequent theosophy, so much so that many later theosophers held that their spiritual lives really began only with their discovery of Böhme's vast body of writings, and even today scientists, philosophers, and literati find inspiration there.[5] In 1618 Böhme began *The Three Principles of the Divine Being*, and between 1619 and his death in 1624, he completed an amazing number of treatises and assorted other manuscripts and letters, including *Forty Questions on the Soul*, *The Signature of All Things*, and the massive *Mysterium Magnum*, a commentary on Genesis, as well as numerous other works, some of which were only published by Werner Buddecke in the mid-twentieth century.[6]

It is not possible to sketch here Böhme's writings, which require each reader to work with them individually over an extended period in order to reveal themselves. Because they are multifaceted and have a specialized Latin-based vocabulary rich in neologisms, each reader will see different aspects of Böhme's insights.[7] But we can say that Böhme's writings are based in a fusion of alchemical, Paracelsian, and Hermetic expressions and concepts with what we may call High German mysticism, so that his works represent a uniquely modern revelation of virtually inexhaustible depth and range. Böhme insists throughout his writings on the necessity that his readers directly experience for themselves the truth of which he writes. This insistence is at the very heart not only of Böhme's books, but of modern theosophy as a whole, which has as its center and fount of inspiration the *Wiedergeburt*, or *metanoia*, the spiritual rebirth.

Böhme's work is intended, above all, to point us toward our own spiritual rebirth, a process or series of births that continues beyond our present lifetime. Indeed, Böhme writes in *Aurora*, there are three births: there is "the outward birth or geniture, which is the house of death," (fleshly life); there is the astral birth, "wherein love and wrath wrestle the one with the other"; and the third birth "the outward man *neither knoweth nor comprehendeth*." While in the flesh, therefore, man must strive with his soul to "press through the firmament of heaven to God, and *live* with God." In this way, then, one must unite all three realms—body, soul, and spirit—in this lifetime, pressing beyond the astral to the transcendent spirit.[8]

Thus Böhme's spiritual path leads through the astral or soul's realm to its spiritual origin. In a sense, Böhme points toward what we might call a Christian shamanism. He writes:

> Some men have many times, according to or in the sidereal or astral spirit, entered in thither, and have been ravished in an ecstasy, as men call it, and have presently known the gates of heaven and of hell, and have told, shown, and declared how that many men dwell in hell. . . . Such indeed have been scorned, derided, or laughed at, but with great ignorance and indiscretion, for it is just so as they declare: which

I will also describe more at large in its due place, and show in what manner and condition it is with them.[9]

"If thy eyes were but open, thou wouldst see *wonderful* things," Böhme chides us. "Heaven is *in* a holy man," and hence everywhere that he stands, sits, or lies, there is heaven also.

Although Böhme marks the beginning of modern theosophy, not least because his works are so overwhelmingly influential in the tradition's entire history, it would be mistaken to think that he was the only theosopher during this time. For not only was Böhme part of an extended group of theosophers, mostly friends in the vicinity of Görlitz, but what is more, there were relatively independent manifestations of similar currents elsewhere, for instance in England. I refer in particular to a hitherto unremarked manuscript in the Ashmolean collection at Oxford University entitled *Aurora Sapientia, or The Daiebreak of Wisdome*, dated 1629, that is by one hand attributed to Dr. John Dee, and by another to one Robert Ayshford, but is signed "P knowen in the Grace of God." This manuscript, which I will shortly publish in a limited edition, includes a number of letters revealing a theosophic circle in England much earlier than previously thought, one without direct allusions to Böhme, but nonetheless showing very similar references to the "three principles" and to "theosophie" "to the service of the sixt Church att Philadelphia."[10]

Aurora Sapientiae is a classic theosophic text in many respects. It is concerned primarily with the revelation of Wisdom, and its author writes with great authority. We are invited, early in the work, to read the three great books: the cosmos, or *physisophia;* Scripture; and Man, in whom is hidden *theosophia.* Our author writes that

> the third Book is Man, who is both the sealed and the open Booke, whereby wee maie learne to understand the theosophia, the secret and hidden wisdome of the Mysterie of God the Father, and of Christ, and of his Church. The beginning and onlie centre of these three Bookes is that onely right and most holie booke that Word, which was in the beginning, of which these three bookes aforesaid doe jointlie beare record, to wit every one in his own Wisdome, in his owne Letters and in his owne Witness, in a verie fine Harmonie, according to which these three are all one and conspire together, and withall the onlie whole and great Librarie of us all wherewith wee who are the Scholars of the true Wisdome ought to be contented.[11]

Although there is in this work no direct reference to Böhme, in its references to "three principles," in its preoccupation with Wisdom's revelation, and in its emphasis upon reading the book of Nature, it is clearly in the classic modern theosophic tradition.

The author's reference to the "sixt Church att Philadelphia" is especially significant, because by the middle of the seventeenth century there was another group of theosophers that had gathered around Dr. John Pordage (1608–81), later to be led by Jane Leade (1623–1704) under the name "the Philadelphians." In this continuity of names is an indication of theosophy's more or less independent parallelism, meaning that theosophers tend to independently corroborate one another's accounts of spiritual experience, so it is not surprising that two English groups might independently draw on the name "Philadelphian" and its symbolism. Theosophy represents a paradigm with certain common elements that reappear even if various groups are wholly unaware of one another, including (1) the focus upon Wisdom or Sophia, (2) an insistence upon direct spiritual experience, (3) reading Nature as a spiritual book, and (4) a spiritual leader who guides his or her spiritual circle through letters and oral advice. These elements all are found in *Aurora Sapientiae*, one of the earliest modern theosophic texts.

Certainly by the 1650s Böhme was well known in England, often under variant names like "Behmen," chiefly through the efforts of translators and biographers including John Sparrow, Humphrey Blunden, John Ellistone, and Charles and Durant Hotham. But it was in the works of John Pordage, who like Böhme was attacked by local clergy, that theosophy had arguably its greatest English exponent. Curiously unavailable in English except for a very few titles, nearly all written late in his life, Pordage's vast works like *Göttliche und Wahre Metaphysica* (1715) are to be found published only in German translation, and represent extremely detailed expositions of his direct visionary experiences in hellish and paradisal realms, as well as his spiritual alchemy and Sophianic mysticism.

Pordage's writing bears the stamp of one who has experienced that of which he writes. Early in his treatise on Sophia—constructed as a diary or series of daily, dated meditations—Pordage explains why he composed this work. In a few lucid words, he details a central turning point of spiritual awakening. The soul seeks, but cannot break through the wall separating it from the heavenly principle. And because it thereupon finds that through *ascending* out it had been constantly misled and had missed its goal, that it is not on the right path ([even] if it were privy to revelations and glimpses of the heavenly countenance). It realizes that the Wisdom of God . . . can be attained [only] through *descending* and sinking into one's own inward ground, and no longer seeking to rise out of oneself.

Whereupon it now thus sinks into itself and before it the gate of Wisdom's depths is opened directly and in the blink of an eye, and it is led into the holy eternal principium of the lightworld in the winecellar of the New Lebanon, in the new magical Earth wherein the Virgin Sophia or the Virgin of God's Wisdom appears and announces her message. This is the content of the other chapters, which [reveal what] is kept in the deep teachings of the passive or enduring stillness or peace of the soul. Because with a praise-song [this] will be resolved: Wisdom will teach her apprentice to sing of this great revelation of the new creation and planting of another paradise.[12]

In *Sophia*, Pordage elaborates on this "great revelation" of the new creation, which bears a striking resemblance to the "celestial earths" of Sufism discussed at length by Henry Corbin.[13]

Of all those who followed in the visionary path of Jacob Böhme, Pordage was without doubt among the most remarkable. Richard Baxter, a contemporary of Pordage's, wrote of him in *Reliquiae Baxterianae* while discussing those in England who followed the inward light: the "Behemenists," he observes, "seem to have attained to greater Meekness and conquest of Passions than any of the rest." "The chiefest of these in England are Dr Pordage and his Family, who live together in Community, and pretend to hold visible and sensible Communion with Angels."[14] Baxter captures well here the essence of Pordage's personal experiences, which did indeed center around visionary trances and communion with angels, resulting in Pordage's expulsion from the Anglican Church and his subsequent retirement as a kind of lay monastic with a small community.

Surrounding Pordage were a number of significant figures, including Thomas Bromley, (1629–91), whose *The Way to the Sabbath of Rest* (1650/1692/1710) represents an enduring, classic elaboration of the stages in the spiritual transmutation of an individual in a theosophic community.[15] Much of this work is published in an appendix to my book *Theosophia: Hidden Dimensions of Christianity* (1994). Bromley's advice is clear and forthright, as when he refers to the culminating union shared with others following the spiritual life:

> And they that are in this near Union, feel a mutual Indwelling in the pure Tincture and Life of each other: And so, the further we come out of the animal Nature, the more universal we are, and nearer both to Heaven, and to one another in the Internal; and the further instrumentally to convey the pure Streams of the heavenly Life to each other, which no external Distance can hinder: For the Divine Tincture (being such a spiritual Virtue, as Christ imprinted into the Heart of the Disciples with whom he talked after his Resurrection, making their *Hearts to burn within them*) is able to pierce through all Distance, and reach those that are far absent; because it is not corporeal, nor subject to the Laws of Place or Time.[16]

Without a doubt, Bromley's writing is among the most accessible of the theosophic authors.

The most well known of Pordage's colleagues is undoubtedly Jane Leade, who after his death went on to lead the theosophic circle, and whose visions were recorded in numerous books published around the turn of the eighteenth century. Her titles include *The Revelation of Revelations* (1683), *The Laws of Paradise* (1695), and *A Fountain of Gardens* (1696–1700). Leade's visions, and her insistence on the doctrine of universal restoration *(apocatastasis)* were not accepted by some other theosophers, including her contemporary Johann Georg Gichtel, an expatriate German known as the "hermit of Amsterdam." Among Leade's companions were Anne Bathurst; the brilliant scholar of Hebrew, Francis Lee (1660/1–1719); Richard Roach (1662–1730), active in establishing the Philadelphians; and Dionysius Andreas Freher (1649–1728), known for his commissioning of various esoteric theosophic illustrations and for his commentaries on Böhmean doctrines, nearly all of which remain unpublished.[17]

Whereas Pordage remained reclusive to the end of his life, and what works were published appeared posthumously, Jane Leade and her companions established a slightly more formal association under the name "The Philadelphian Society," replete with a loose charter and organizational structure. The Philadelphians published a journal called *Theosophic Transactions* and attempted various more public enterprises, including an unsuccessful attempt to establish their association in Germany.[18] Not surprisingly, the Philadelphians' efforts were not rewarded by conventional Christians in England, some of whom accosted the Philadelphians during their public meetings, partly because of their association with French millennialists. But the Philadelphians were also not well received by many theosophers on the Continent, mainly because many agreed with Gichtel's assessment that establishing another sect with a name, however noble one's intent, is just another spiritual dead end, a carapace that prevents one from authentic direct spiritual experience.

Any discussion of seventeenth- and eighteenth-century theosophy, as can already be seen, probably will include reference to Johann Georg Gichtel (1638–1710), the sometimes irascible "hermit of Amsterdam" whose collected letters of spiritual advice under the title *Theosophia Practica* (1722) amount to seven volumes and several thousand pages. Although there is much repetition in his letters, as one would expect, they certainly repay rereading, and even a cursory study will reveal Gichtel's extraordinary authority on a wide range of subjects, including alchemy and what I would call deep prayer. Gichtel and his friend Ueberfeldt also edited the first major edition of Böhme's complete writings, published as *Theosophia Revelata* (1682/1730). A more concise book, often also published under the title *Theosophia Practica*, but actually entitled *Eine kurze Eröffnung und Anweisung der dryen Principien und Welten in Menschen* (A brief opening and demonstration of the Three Principles and Worlds in Man) (1696/1779), is an important guide to Gichtel's spiritual understanding. It includes several illustrations that have been linked to Hindu or Buddhist diagrams of the chakras in the human body, and that certainly show how theosophy had an understanding of the subtle body. Although at first Gichtel's stern rhetoric might well dissuade the casual reader, a closer examination of this treatise reveals that despite the specialized vocabulary Gichtel simply is guiding the reader along the spiritual path that he has himself followed.[19] In essence, he seeks to show us how to go from the "No" of the dark or wrathful world of fallen man to the "Yes" of divinely regenerated man.

A Brief Opening . . . of the Three Principles is among the most detailed of all theosophic texts in revealing spiritual praxis according to this tradition. Gichtel affirms, in the preface to the first chapter, that

> 3. Especially I want to show you the entrance to the first-created image of God before the Fall, which stands hidden in the spirit, which

the author knows by praxis and [also will show] in the figures of the completed man, out of the new birth in Christ, which is to be developed in you.

4. And in the rebirth you will also come to really know in essence, if you earnestly follow the writer.[20]

Gichtel's own struggle was fraught with difficulty from its beginning, for in youth his unorthodox spirituality brought him to the attention of church and city authorities, who

> mocked, insulted, and humiliated me, led me over the streets and wanted to force my head down, but because they could not ultimately agree, they finally took everything away from me and banned me eternally from the city.
>
> 48. So now I lay in a stinking hole, locked up, tempted by the devil and tested by gruesome doubts, so much so that I grasped a knife and would have, in order to save my anxious life from suffering, brought my life with a stab to a quick end.[21]

But instead Gichtel experienced a vision that inspired him to follow a long and difficult path of poverty and spiritual struggle toward Sophianic illumination. In this book, and in Gichtel's letters, he concentrates primarily on this inward life.

Gichtel's outward life began in Ratisbon, Germany, in March 1638, and can be divided into three parts: from 1638 to 1664, when he began to encounter difficulties with the clerical authorities in Ratisbon; from 1665 through 1667, when he moved about, staying for a while with the Protestant author Friedrich Breckling (1629–1711); and from 1668 to his death in 1710, the time during which he lived, wrote, and taught in Amsterdam. Most of our information about Gichtel comes from this last period, during which he established his community of the "Brethren of the Angelic Life"—the *Engelsbrüder*, or the "Angelic Brethren"—and become more generally known as a theosopher.

To read Gichtel's biography is to read Protestant hagiography: not for nothing is his biography entitled *The Wonderful and Holy Life of the Chosen Champion and Blessèd Man of God Johann Georg Gichtel*. Readers are advised to check their disbelief in miracles at this work's portals. For Gichtel's biography includes numerous events that defy our expectations or assumptions about this world and its laws. Gichtel held that he and his Angelic Brethren were supported by prayer and divine mercy—money or food or clothing simply appeared when they were necessary, generally donated by benefactors (although there were rumors that Gichtel was a practicing alchemist). An irascible man, Gichtel quarreled with nearly everyone he knew by the time he died, and it is at times difficult to reconcile this with his spirituality.

Whereas Gichtel is certainly among the most important experiential theosophers—his letters consist often of spiritual advice, and his opinions are generally adamant—Gottfried Arnold (1666–1714) is arguably the most important scholar among the theosophers. Arnold was an acquaintance of Gichtel's, but fell in Gichtel's eyes when he married. Arnold's most important books were published in 1699/1700, and include his *Unparteiische Kirchen- und Ketzer-historie* and *Das Geheimniss der Göttliche Sophia* (1700). Arnold's *Impartial Church and Heretic History* is significant, first of all, for its revolutionary, discerningly undenigrating treatment of authors traditionally deemed heretical, and for this reason it raised some controversy after publication. His *Mystery of the Holy Sophia* is important chiefly for its extensive scholarly treatment of this most central theosophic theme. It is interesting that, although Pordage's work on Sophia was undoubtedly known to Arnold and was almost certainly a source of inspiration for him, he did not allude to it directly.

Arnold is perhaps best characterized as a scholar who, with formidable learning—his book on Sophia ranges throughout the church fathers and elsewhere, including Eastern Orthodox writers—sought to place theosophy within the larger context of the entire Christian tradition, and when one considers that Böhme and many of the other theosophers were dismissed by conventional Christians as heretical, one can see how Arnold's assessment of ancient and more recent heresies was a reaction against this contemporary dismissal. Arnold was also known for his spiritual songs or hymns, some of which were published conjointly with his book on Sophia, and one can find his songs collected in an 1856 edition.[22] His last important theosophic work was *Theologia Experimentalis* (1714). Certainly it is fair to say that Arnold, in his historical method, was influential not only for pietist writers but also for his aim of creating an impartial assessment of Christian mysticism, anticipating much more recent efforts in this direction.

There are numerous other figures who were more or less a part of the circles in which Gichtel and Arnold moved, and we should mention two of the more prominent here: Friedrich Breckling (1629–1711) and Quirinus Kuhlmann (1651–89). Breckling was originally a friend of Gichtel's, but eventually they split and remained on less than friendly terms; Kuhlmann as an enthusiastic young man came into Gichtel's circle in Amsterdam, met Breckling, and traveled also to London, where he came into contact with the English theosophers of that time. Unlike the "hermit" Gichtel, Kuhlmann sought to proselytize his Böhmenist ideas, and traveled not only to Constantinople but to Moscow, where in 1689 he was burnt at the stake as a troublesome heretic on orders of Peter the Great.

One must acknowledge that there are numerous figures who, although not necessarily theosophers in the sense that Böhme and Gichtel were, still represent currents of the theosophic stream. Among these we can include for example Pierre Poiret (1646–1719), who edited numerous works of mystical theology, like Arnold placing theosophy in a larger historical context, and also Angelus Silesius (Johannes Scheffler, 1624–77), whose *Cherubinischer Wandersmann,* undoubtedly his best-known work, consists of short, pithy aphoristic rhymes. In 1657 appeared his *Heilige Seelenlust,* his "spiritually rich rhymes" on "spiritual longing of the soul." This work, like all Scheffler's writing, is pregnant with multiple meanings, as when he writes "I know not what I am; and I am not what I know."[23]

Finally, we might mention William Law (1686–1761), a well-known Anglican author whose close connection to the works of Freher and Böhme is not always mentioned, largely because Law himself submerged their influence on his writing. His best-known work is *A Serious Call* (1729). His *The Spirit of Love* (1752/4) bears the unmistakable influence of theosophy.[24] Law was born in King's Cliffe, Northamptonshire, and was educated at Emmanuel College, Cambridge, of which he became a fellow in 1711. His personal history is interestingly parallel to that of Dr. John Pordage. For like Pordage, Law refused to take an oath of allegiance; in Law's case, it was to King George I in 1714. Thus a Nonjuror, Law was forced to resign his college position and was kept from other public positions as well. Law then lived in Putney, near London, at the home of Edward Gibbon from 1727 to 1737, where he tutored the historian Gibbon's father. In about 1740, Law moved back to King's Cliffe, where he lived a celibate and quiet life in the company of Hester Gibbon, the historian's aunt, and Mrs. Hutcheson, a rich, pious widow. His later years, like Pordage's, were spent studying Böhme; he wrote in relative seclusion until his death in 1761.

In many respects, then, Law followed exactly the model set in the previous century in England by Dr. John Pordage, attracting a kind of Protestant monastic community of laypeople around himself. This community at King's Cliffe was renowned for its generous charity. Law and an anonymous patron established a poorhouse for young girls, teaching them to read, knit, sew, study the Bible, and attend church; they gave clothes, money, and food to the poor through almshouses they established. Mrs. Hutcheson had a substantial income, but she and Law gave away all but a tenth of their income to the poor. They all led an abstemious life, with prayers morning, noon, and night. Law himself would arise at five A.M. and spend much of his day reading in his large library of mystical authors, writing, and praying.

Whereas some theosophers were relatively isolated, it is important to recognize an element of theosophy that has not received sufficient attention as yet: theosophic communities. While Protestantism in general is not monastic, we should recognize that theosophy inspired numerous spiritual communities, ranging from informal circles to actual semimonastic communities complete with modified medieval monastic dress. Probably the closest analogies to theosophic communities are the Friends of God, the Christian medieval lay mystical order, and in Sufism the mystical lay communities known as *tariqah*. Throughout the seventeenth and eighteenth centuries one finds such groups springing up not only in Germany, but also in Northern Europe, England, France, the Netherlands, and America. Around Gichtel in Amsterdam one found the "Angelic Brethren;" in England one found the Philadelphians; and in America one found the mystical communities near the Wissahickon River in Pennsylvania, the best known of which is Ephrata. Each of these communities produced considerable literature, too extensive to catalog here.[25] This central communal aspect of theosophy should not be overlooked, and it is reflected in much of the literature.

Although the Jewish Kabbalah played a role in the whole current of Christian theosophy, arguably its most important eighteenth-century syncretic exponent within theosophy was Friedrich Christoph Oetinger

(1702–82), whose works represent an attempt to synthesize Kabbalistic works—especially those of Isaac Luria—with the theosophical tradition of Böhme. Oetinger's works range from his *Aufmunternde Gründe zur Lesung der Schriften Jacob Böhmens* (1731) to his *Theologia ex idea vitae deducta* (1765) and *Biblisches und Emblematisches Wörterbuch*, (1765), but perhaps best known is his *Die Lehrtafel der Prinzessin Antonia* (1763), in which he offers "an explanation of the most important truths of the holy scriptures according to the knowledge of the Kabbalah."[26] Oetinger also wrote about the visionary Emmanuel Swedenborg's (1688–1772) writings in *Swedenborgs und andere irdische und himmlische Philosophie* (1765). It might be noted in this regard that Swedenborg was not regarded very highly by Böhmean theosophers like Louis-Claude de Saint-Martin, who viewed Swedenborg's visions (and those of Jane Leade) as belonging mainly to the astral realm and not representing complete spiritual experience.

As Antoine Faivre has pointed out, Christian theosophy tends to be divisible into different currents, and although it would be a dubious enterprise to try and categorize authors too strictly, still we can certainly distinguish some of the primary tendencies. If Oetinger represents the Kabbalistic current of theosophy, carried on in the nineteenth century by Franz Josef Molitor (1779–1860), author of *Philosophie der Geschichte, oder über die Tradition* (1854), the magical current within theosophy is represented by Georg von Welling's (1655–1727) *Opus Mago-Cabbalisticum et theosophicum* (1784), and even more clearly by Karl von Eckhartshausen (1752–1803), whose writings range from *Ausschlüße zur Magie* (1788/90) and *Zahlenlehre der Natur* (1794) to the well-known little work *Die Wolke über dem Heiligthum* (The clouds over the sanctuary) (1802), a work closer to theosophy than to the magical-occult tradition that his earlier writings reflect.

Theosophy is a movement whose main stream unquestionably flows through the German tradition, but its literature has been written in numerous languages, including French—and any account of primary literature must consider the remarkable French author Louis-Claude de Saint-Martin (1743–1803), whose early spiritual life was influenced by the occult school of Martinez de Pasqually (1710–74) but who attributed his spiritual rebirth and his profound later writings to his contact with the works of Jakob Böhme. Late in life, he learned German and translated Böhme into French. Saint-Martin, who wrote as "le philosophe inconnu," sought to combat modern rationalist and materialist reductionism with his many books, including *Des Erreurs et de la Verité* (1775), *Tableau Naturel* (1782), *De l'esprit des Choses* (1800), and *Le Ministère de l'Homme-Esprit* (1802), the last two of which translated theosophic thought into terms accessible to his contemporaries. Among the most delightful of Saint-Martin's works is his correspondence with the Swiss Baron Kirchberger during the French Revolution, testimony to the spiritual balance theosophy provided them during the most turbulent of eras.

If Saint-Martin represents the greatest figure of modern French theosophy, its greatest recent German exponent is unquestionably Franz von Baader (1765–1841).[27] Indeed, for a seamless, profound union of science, religion, and literature, and of all three traditions of Christianity (Protestantism [particularly theosophy], Roman Catholicism, and Eastern Orthodoxy)—and for inspiring sheer delight at the range of aphoristic spiritual insights he produced—Baader has no peer. In the sixteen volumes of his collected works one finds discussions that seem uncannily contemporary, for like Saint-Martin, Baader brought a theosophic perspective to the whole range of modern life, from literature and psychology to comparative religion and philosophy to science and esotericism. But the fact that he has not been translated into English bespeaks the often immense difficulty of his language, sometimes hard to parse even for native Germans.

Franz von Baader was born in 1765 in Munich, the son of a physician, and although he was originally trained to take over his father's practice, he went on to study minerology and the other sciences under Alexander von Humboldt. He spent four years in England beginning in 1792, where he came to see at close hand the results of the Industrial Revolution, especially the appearance of a proletariat class. In 1796, he returned to Germany, where in addition to working in a series of ever higher official positions, he was able through various chemical experiments to develop a patented formula for glass fabrication that brought him a substantial income. Thus Baader came to theosophy from an unusually scientific viewpoint.

Having spent years studying Böhme and Louis Claude de Saint-Martin, as well as other mystics, including Meister Eckhart, Baader was termed by August Wilhelm Schlegel "Boehmius redivivus," or "Böhme reborn," a complimentary designation still indissolubly linked to Baader's name. Baader is most famous as a theosopher, but his theosophic writings encompass an extraordinary range of subjects, from religious eros to the political concept of "theodemocracy" to the meeting of Catholicism, Protestantism, and Eastern Orthodoxy.[28] In particular, Baader's emphasis on *erotische philosophie* and on furthering a religious rather than merely materialist science demands much deeper scrutiny than it has yet received.

Having in mind this general sketch of the primary theosophers' works, we may now turn to some more general comments about theosophic literature and its significance, beginning with the question of ecumenicism and esotericism. The twentieth century has seen the development of Christian ecumenicism in unprecedented ways, not only in Roman Catholicism but indeed throughout much of Christianity. No longer is it possible to think of Christianity or its various denominations in isolation from one another or from the other world religions; rather, interreligious dialogue has appeared, and what is undoubtedly more significant in the long run, Christian-Hindu, Christian-Buddhist, Christian-Native American, and other kinds of syncretism also appeared, often bringing meditation praxis into a Christian context.

This religious pluralism has its generally unacknowledged antecedents in theosophic literature, particularly among the English Philadelphians, who wrote late in the seventeenth century that they were certainly not sectarian, but rather were open to wisdom from any tradition.[29] It is true that not all theosophers were quite so open as the Philadelphians to the idea of wisdom manifesting in many traditions. But when one considers theosophic literature as a whole, and especially its golden age in the seventeenth and eighteenth centuries, one cannot escape recognizing that its emphasis upon direct spiritual experience or gnosis and its esoteric disciplines is in fact profoundly resonant, not with conventional "orthodox" Christianity, but with the inward disciplines of Sufism, Kabbalism, and Buddhism. What is more, theosophers like Baader actively sought a reunion of Eastern Orthodoxy, Roman Catholicism, and Protestantism through theosophic spirituality.[30] In theosophy is a deeper foundation for interreligious encounter than just "dialogue."

The center of theosophic literature is undoubtedly Sophia, or Divine Wisdom, and one cannot avoid making some general remarks about Sophia in the larger context we are here considering. I have elsewhere considered at length the parallels between modern theosophy and ancient Gnosticism, so I will not do so now.[31] But it is critical to recognize that theosophic literature appeared precisely during the development of modern rationalist materialism, and represents a hitherto largely unremarked counterbalance to it. Whereas today many people feel the need for a feminine dimension to Christian spirituality, and often seek to interject what is sometimes called feminist "paganism," modern theosophy has produced several centuries of literature founded in Judeo-Christian Sophianic spirituality that directly counters the prevailing notions of Protestantism as excessively masculine and antimystical.

Theosophic literature also reveals an extremely complex iconography that has to be approached within the context of theosophic spirituality as a whole. In the illustrations of Dionysius Andreas Freher, for example, one has a visual manifestation of essential Böhmean concepts, but although Freher's illustrations are especially rich, they are by no means the only such works. Indeed, theosophic literature is replete with examples of illustrations that cannot be fully understood without direct reference to the literature and its tradition.[32] The magnificent images with which the writings of Johann Georg Gichtel and Böhme were adorned are visual manifestations of the works they accompany, and a great deal of transdisciplinary work remains to be done in examining exactly how theosophic illustrations and texts mutually illuminate one another.[33]

Finally, we must point out that in theosophy we find rich sources for understanding science in new ways. It has become evident that the rationalist and materialist premises of what has been called "scientism" are no longer acceptable even among many scientists. In the search to restore science to its place within a more profound cosmology and metaphysics, Christian theosophy may play an important role, for in the encyclopedic cosmological works of Böhme, Pordage, Saint-Martin, and Baader there is an inward science whose amplitude and rich implications might well have an impact in unexpected fields.

Theosophy, far from being an isolated movement limited in its sources and significances to the seventeenth and eighteenth centuries, represents the incorporation into its authors and literature of the main currents in the European esoteric traditions, including St. Clement of Alexandria and Dionysius the Areopagite, the High German mysticism of Tauler and Eckhart and the late medieval alchemy and spagyric of authors like Paracelsus. In fact, theosophy is a synthesis of the main European esoteric traditions under the special genius of Böhme.[34] Although much of the literature we have considered here may well be spoken of as having been historically suppressed, its cultural influence has been immeasurable nonetheless, and, given the reappearance of theosophy in the twentieth century, one has good reason to think that its impact and meanings will be felt far into the future.[35]

But it is critical to keep in mind the transdisciplinary nature of research into esotericism generally and of theosophy in particular. To do justice to these intricate and profound subjects, one must approach them with openness, a willingness to accept them on their own terms rather than to try and judge them based on the latest contemporary fashions in academia; and one will perforce have to range across disciplinary boundaries.[36] Indeed, as we have seen even in this brief survey, the fascination and importance of these works and authors comes precisely from their offering new insights into the coincidences and conjunctions of seemingly disparate fields and subjects, from ecumenicism to science, art, literature, cosmology, philosophy, and metaphysics, not to mention theology. It is a fertile source for further investigation, and one not easily exhausted.

NOTES

1. See Antoine Faivre, "Le courant théosophique (fin xvi–xx siècles): essai de périodisation," *Politica Hermetica* (Paris) 7 (1993): 6–41; see Pierre Deghaye, "Jacob Böhme and His Followers," in *Modern Esoteric Spirituality*, ed. Antoine Faivre and Jacob Needleman (New York, 1992); see also Jean-Paul Corsetti, *Histoire de l'ésotérisme et des sciences occultes* (Paris, 1992); on the Philadelphians, see Nils Thune, *The Behmenists and the Philadelphians* (Uppsala, 1948) and Serge Hutin, *Les Disciples Anglais de Jacob Böhme* (Paris, 1960); for a more general context, see Karl R.H. Frick, *Licht und Finsternis*, 2 vols. (Graz, 1975) and Will-Erich Peuckert, *Pansophie*, 2d ed. (Berlin, 1956).

2. See Antoine Faivre, "Le courant théosophique," 6. Cf. also Jean-Louis Siémons, *Theosophia: Aux sources néo-platoniciennes et chrétiennes (IIe–VIe siècle)* (Paris,

1988); James A. Santucci, "On Theosophia and Related Terms," *Theosophical History* 2, no. 3 (1987): 107–10.

    3. See Versluis, *Theosophia: Hidden Dimensions of Christianity* (Hudson and New York, 1994).

    4. See Böhme, *Sämtliche Schriften*, ed. Will-Erich Peuckert and August Faust, 8 vols. (Stuttgart, 1955–61); see also in English, for example, Jacob Böhme, *Aurora* (London, 1910); *Dialogues on the Supersensual Life*, ed. W. Law (New York, 1957); *Six Theosophic Points* (Ann Arbor, 1958); and *The Way to Christ*, trans. P. Erb (New York, 1978).

    5. See for instance Basarab Nicolescu, *Science, Meaning, and Evolution: The Cosmology of Jacob Böhme* (New York, 1992); and Peter Koslowski, *Die Prüfungen der Neuzeit: Über Postmodernität, Philosophie der Geschichte, Metaphysik, Gnosis* (Wien, 1989); see also my own forthcoming *The Hermetic Book of Nature*, in which I discuss in detail Böhme's influence on Emerson, Alcott, and American transcendentalism in general. See also my "Bronson Alcott and Jacob Böhme," *Studies in the American Renaissance* 16 (1993): 153–59.

    6. See Werner Buddecke, ed., *Jakob Böhme: Die Ur-Schriften* (Stuttgart, 1963); for other editions of Böhme's works, see note 4, above.

    7. On Böhme see Pierre Deghaye, *La Naissance de Dieu* (Paris, 1985); Alexander Koyré, *La Philosophie de Jacob Boehme* (Paris, 1979); Andrew Weeks, *Boehme: An Intellectual Biography of the Seventeenth-Century Philosopher and Mystic* (Albany, 1991); on Böhme's predecessors, see Alexandre Koyré, *Mystiques, spirituels, alchimistes du xvi siècle allemand* (Paris, 1971).

    8. *Aurora* 20.50, 20.51.

    9. *Aurora* 20.87

    10. Robert Ayshford, *Aurora Sapientia, that is to saie, The Daiebreak of Wisdome Of the three Principles and beginning of all in the mysterie of wisdome in which the ground and key of all wisdome is laid open, directing to the true understanding of God, of Man, and of the whole world, in a new and true triune wisdome Physisophie, Theologie, and Theosophie. tending to the Honour of God, Revelation of the true wisdome and to the service of the Sixt Church att Philadelphia By Her Minister called by the Grace of God to beare witness of God and of Jesus Christ* (1629).

    11. Ibid., chap. 1, "Of the threefold Book of Wisdome."

    12. See John Pordage, *Sophia: The Graceful Eternal Virgin of Holy Wisdom, or Wonderful Spiritual Discoveries and Revelations That the Precious Wisdom Has Given to a Holy Soul* (London, 1675), in Versluis, *Wisdom's Book: The Sophia Anthology* (forthcoming), chap. 5. These paragraphs by Pordage also appear in the *Theosophic Correspondence of Louis Claude de Saint-Martin* (Exeter, 1863), 92–93.

    13. See Henry Corbin, *Spiritual Body and Celestial Earth: From Mazdaean Iran to Shi'ite Islam* (Princeton, 1977).

    14. Baxter, *Reliquiae Baxterianae*, 77, quoted in Thune, *Behmenists and Philadelphians*, 14–15.

    15. See also *A catalogue of Mr. T. Bromley's Library* (London, 1691). Bromley's *The Way to the Sabbath of Rest* was a popular work in England and in America, and was

even translated into Swedish and smuggled into Sweden during the eighteenth century. It is worth noting that there was a close connection between theosophy and alchemy, as evidenced for instance in Edmund Brice's translation of Ali Puli, *Centrum Naturae Concentratum* (London, 1696).

16. See Versluis, *Theosophia*, 199.

17. See C. A. Muses, *Illumination on Jacob Böhme: The Work Of Dionysius Andreas Freher* (New York, 1951).

18. For an account of the Philadelphians' abortive missionary effort in Germany, see Thune, *Behmenists and Philadelphians*, 114–35.

19. The first English translation of *Eine kurze Eröffnung* is currently under preparation.

20. Gichtel, *Eine kurze Eröffnung*, preface, 1.3, 1.4.

21. Ibid., 3.47, 3.48.

22. See Arnold, *Sämmtliche geistliche Lieder*, ed. C. Ehmann (Stuttgart, 1856).

23. Angelus Silesius, *Cherubinischer Wandersmann*, 1.5.

24. Much of the Rosicrucian movement also found inspiration in theosophy, and the deep affinities between Rosicrucian works—particularly the tables of correspondences and illustrations—and theosophic works remains an area ripe for further exploration. See Christopher McIntosh, *The Rose Cross and the Age of Reason* (Leiden, 1992).

25. For an overview of theosophic communities in Pennsylvania, see Julius Sachse, *The German Pietists of Provincial Pennsylvania* (Philadelphia, 1895); on Johannes Kelpius, see *The Diarium of Magister Johannes Kelpius*, trans. J. Sachse, *The Pennsylvania-German Society, Proceedings and Addresses* (Lancaster) 25 (1917); on Ephrata, see Peter Erb, *Johann Conrad Beissel and the Ephrata Community: Mystical and Historical Texts* (Lewiston, 1985); on the related doctrines of Zinzendorf, see Pierre Deghaye, *La Doctrine ésotérique de Zinzendorf* (Paris, 1970).

26. See Oetinger, *Lehrtafel der Prinzessin Antonia*, in *Sämmtliche theosophische Schriften*, 2d ed. (Stuttgart, 1858), 1.86.

27. See Peter Koslowski, ed., *Die Philosophie, Theologie und Gnosis Franz von Baaders: Spekulatives Denken zwischen Aufklärung, Restauration und Romantik* (Wien, 1993), esp. Antoine Faivre, "Franz von Baader und die okzidentale Esoterik," 221–42.

28. See Franz von Baader, *Sätze aus der erotischen Philosophie* (Frankfurt, 1966), introduction.

29. See for example the *Acta Philadelphica or Monthly Memoirs of the Philadelphian Society* (London, March 1697), 1–2, where the prefatory remarks refer to the "Extraordinary Appearances of *God* in Nature, and to the Antient *Mystick* Knowledge of the *Eastern Nations*, which we do esteem no contemptible Key, towards a Right and Fundamental Understanding of great Part of the *Sacred Writings*, both of the *Old* and *New Testament*."

30. See Versluis, *Theosophia*, esp. chap. 7, 106ff.

31. See Versluis, *Wisdom's Children: Christian Theosophy* (forthcoming); for a brief overview, by no means complete, of the Sophianic tradition, see Ernst Benz, "Sophia:

Visionen des Westens," in *The Ecumenical World of Orthodox Civilization*, ed. A. Blane (The Hague, 1974), 121–38.

32. See C. A. Muses, *Illumination on Jacob Böhme: The Work of Dionysius Andreas Freher* (New York, 1951).

33. See the short work by Gichtel published under the title *Theosophia Practica* (the title of Gichtel's collected letters) but actually entitled *Eine kurze Eröffnung und Anwesung der drei Prinzipien und Welten im Menschen* (Leipzig, 1696), newly edited version by Agnes Klein (Schwarzenburg, 1979).

34. One has to be especially struck by the "medieval" elements in the letters of Gichtel, on which I comment at length in my forthcoming book, *Wisdom's Children*. Theosophic Protestantism represents a new and condensed application of medieval esotericism and as such is not inherently opposed to Roman Catholicism, only to its institutionalist emphases.

35. See for instance Leopold Ziegler, *Menschwerdung*, 2 vols. (Olten, 1948). See also Koslowski, *Prüfungen der Neuzeit* (Vienna, 1989). Both authors draw extensively on the tradition of Böhme and Baader in a modern and, one may say, using that all too fuzzy word, postmodern context.

36. In this regard the works of Antoine Faivre are exemplary.

CHAPTER 14

ROMANTICISM AND THE ESOTERIC CONNECTION

WOUTER J. HANEGRAAFF

That aspects of the western esoteric tradition have exerted a signifi-cant influence on the leading personalities of romanticism (including German idealism) is not in any doubt. A range of important historical studies, most of them written in French, have investigated the compli-cated avenues by which elements of Hermeticism, Paracelsism, Chris-tian theosophy in the tradition of Jacob Böhme, various traditions of Illuminism, and so on have become of importance to the thinking of such romantics and idealists as Schelling, Goethe, Novalis, Coleridge, Blake, and Hugo, to mention just a few.[1] My intention in this article is not to summarize this detailed historical research or add to it. Instead, I will approach the question of the relation between esotericism and ro-manticism from a systematic angle. Considering the abundant historical evidence for connections between western esoteric traditions and spe-cific romantic thinkers, it is remarkable how few attempts have been made to establish in what sense the phenomenon of romanticism *as such* is indebted to western esotericism. Auguste Viatte's classic study en-titled *Les sources occultes du Romantisme*, to give one example, contains a wealth of highly relevant information but no synthesis. Other than what his title would suggest, no attempt is made to develop a systematic per-spective on the nature of romanticism, or to establish to what extent esotericism has historically contributed to its genesis. Viatte demonstrates in abundant and fascinating detail that many of the romantics were in-terested in esotericism and influenced by it. It remains unclear, how-ever, whether this interest is of merely anecdotal significance or whether

The research for this article was supported by the Foundation for Theology and Religious Studies in the Netherlands (SFT), founded by the Netherlands Or-ganization for Scientific Research (NWO).

it made a fundamental difference to what is specifically *romantic* in their work. This neglected question will be central to my following investigation. Scholars of philosophy and literature have long been reflecting on the nature and definition of romanticism. We will see that in this ongoing systematic debate a modest but undeniable trend has developed towards recognition of western esotericism as not just a contingent but an essential, constitutive factor.[2] I will provide a critical discussion of the main theories that have been put forward and develop my conclusions with reference to them.

Arthur O. Lovejoy

Among students of romanticism, Lovejoy is best known for his article "On the Discrimination of Romanticisms," published in 1924. In order to gain a balanced perspective, however, this early article must be seen in the context of his other publications on the subject, which appeared between 1913 and 1941.[3] In his 1924 article, Lovejoy gives an enormous list of examples of incompatible opinions about the origin, age, historical location, description, offspring, and merits of romanticism. The inescapable conclusion is that romanticism has meant very different things to different people; apparently, it is impossible to reach a consensus even about fundamentals. Lovejoy concludes that scholars should learn to use the word "romanticism" only in the *plural*. There is in fact a variety of so-called romanticisms: a German romanticism starting in the 1790s, an English one starting in the 1740s, a French one since 1801, and a second French one beginning only in the second decade of the century, and so on. Lovejoy's criticism is basically directed against the tendency to "vaguely hypostatize" the term, on the assumption, as he puts it, that "'romanticism' is the heaven-appointed designation of some single real entity, or type of entities, to be found in nature."[4] Against this idea, he defends a consequent nominalism: the simple fact is that "there are various historic episodes or movements to which different historians . . . have, for one reason or another, given the name."[5] With hindsight, it is evident that what particularly offended Lovejoy's sensibilities as an historian was the tradition of defining romanticism as a universal tendency of the human mind, or at least of the European mind, which periodically recurs in all periods of history.[6]

Lovejoy's 1924 article has been quoted again and again, but it is often forgotten that it was not his final word about the subject. In this very article, he conceded that "there may be some common denominator . . . ; but if so, it has never yet been clearly exhibited, and its presence is not to be assumed *a priori*."[7] And indeed, if we follow Lovejoy's intellectual development from 1913 on, when he discussed romantic evolutionism in connection with Henri Bergson, we find him gradually developing a set of common denominators of romanticism, which he finally presented in systematic fashion in 1941. This was not (as has sometimes been assumed)[8] a reversal of his former position: Lovejoy starts with an emphatic reaffirmation of his earlier views. He continues, however, with stating that the last decades of the eighteenth century *did* witness a profound revolution of thought:

> To call these new ideas of the 1780s and 1790s "Romanticism" is confusion-breeding and productive of historical error above all because it suggests that there was only one such idea, or, if many, that they were all implicates of one fundamental "Romantic" idea, or, at the least, that they were harmonious *inter se* and formed a sort of systematic unity. None of these things are true. . . . But though there is no such thing as Romanticism, there emphatically *was* something which . . . may still be called a Romantic period.[9]

Lovejoy then proceeds (albeit with considerable caution)[10] to do what in 1924 he said had never been done properly: to outline a posteriori three different idea complexes that are particularly characteristic of this romantic period. They are associated with three characteristic German words: *das Ganze*, *Streben* and *Eigentümlichkeit*, which may be referred to as *holism* or *organicism*, *voluntarism* or *dynamism*, and *diversitarianism*.

1. The "Idea of the Whole" was defined by Immanuel Kant as an organic unity that is more than the sum of its parts. In such a whole, the various parts can only persist through their interconnection with all the others, and likewise they exist only *for* all the others and for the sake of the Whole.[11] This conception served as a counterpart to seventeenth-/eighteenth-century "mechanistic" conceptions that saw a "whole" as no more than an aggregate of its separate parts.

2. Lovejoy's second idea complex concerns the widespread "assumption of the primacy, in reality and in value, of process, striving, cumulative

becoming, over any static consummation."[12] This idea of romantic evolutionism was closely linked to what he calls "the pathos of struggle,"
especially in the form of *Streben ins Unendliche*: the striving toward the
infinite that was such a well-known theme of the romantics.

3. Finally, Lovejoy emphasized the "assertion of the value of diversity
in human opinions, characters, tastes, arts and cultures."[13] Diversitarianism reversed the Enlightenment assumption of "uniformitarianism," which
means that people are basically the same in all times and places. The
celebration of diversity as a positive value in itself had far-reaching consequences for, as Lovejoy points out, according to Enlightenment assumptions "what is rational is uniform; and what is not uniform is *eo ipso* not
rational; and diversity is therefore the easily recognizable mark of error."[14]

Lovejoy thus defined the "romantic period" as characterized by the
rejection of mechanicism in favor of holistic organicism; of static values
in favor of process and dynamism; and of uniformitarianism in favor of
diversitarianism. In all three cases, the distinctions may be seen as aspects of the general rejection of Enlightenment values in favor of the
new, so-called romantic values. Now, it should be realized that Lovejoy's
analysis of the romantic period is in fact a spin-off from the general story
told in his classic *The Great Chain of Being*. In this book, Lovejoy analyzed the remarkable effects in the history of western thought of a contradiction inherent in the Platonic tradition. The central theme that
occupied Lovejoy is best rendered in his own words:

> The most noteworthy consequence of the persistent influence of
> Platonism was . . . that throughout the greater part of its history West-
> ern religion, in its more philosophic forms, has had two Gods. . . . The
> two were, indeed, identified as one being with two aspects. But the
> ideas corresponding to the "aspects" were ideas of two antithetic kinds
> of being. The one was the Absolute of otherworldliness—self-suffi-
> cient, out of time, alien to the categories of ordinary human thought
> and experience, needing no world of lesser beings to supplement or
> enhance his own eternal self-contained perfection. The other was a
> God who emphatically was not self-sufficient nor, in any philosophi-
> cal sense, "absolute": one whose essential nature required the exist-
> ence of other beings, and not of one kind of these only, but of all
> kinds which could find a place in the descending scale of the possi-

bilities of reality—a God whose prime attribute was generativeness, whose manifestation was to be found in the diversity of creatures and therefore in the temporal order and the manifold spectacle of nature's processes.[15]

If we keep this context in mind, it becomes obvious that when Lovejoy speaks about organicism *and* diversitarianism, what he actually has in mind are aspects of the second strand of Platonic thought. This is indeed borne out by the argument of *The Great of Being*: in the tenth chapter he even goes so far as to describe diversitarianism as the *one* common factor in so-called romanticism.[16] And for the factor of dynamic process we only have to turn to the preceding chapter, where Lovejoy analyzes the eighteenth-century phenomenon of the "temporalizing of the Chain of Being." The Platonic "Great Chain of Being," pictured as the fullness of creation (or emanation) ordered in a graded hierarchy, had always been conceived as the *perfect and complete* unfoldment of divine creativity. It is obvious that this divine perfection excluded the very possibility of change, progress, and the emergence of novelty. This, however, began to change in the eighteenth century. In Lovejoy's words: "The *plenum formarum* came to be conceived by some, not as the *inventory* but as the *program* of nature, which is being carried out gradually and exceedingly slowly in the cosmic history."[17] In this truly momentous development we have the origins of "romantic" evolutionism, as well as of the romantic aspiration towards the "infinite."

Taking this into account, we can conclude that Lovejoy's characterization of the romantic period can actually be reduced to only *two* great idea complexes:

1. *Diversitarian holism.* The belief in an organic cosmos, which represents the triumphant unfolding of God's creative power in a dazzling spectacle displaying infinite diversity. In this cosmos, to quote Pope's famous lines from *An Essay on Man*, "All are but parts of one stupendous whole / whose body Nature is, and God the soul." And if the natural world is thus regarded as God's body, it is evident that God's soul is essentially the power of life and creativity that permeates all.

2. *Romantic evolutionism.* The belief that this cosmos is not static but dynamic, comprised in a process of evolution that is not random but

teleological, oriented toward a goal that is as infinite as divine creativity itself.

In one sense these two characteristics complement each other, because they take account of the universe in space and time respectively. But it is important to realize that, from another perspective, there is a latent tension between them. Diversitarian holism suggests a harmonious universe, which is perfect and complete in itself because it expresses a perfect deity; this is in line with the original Platonic conception. Romantic evolutionism, on the other hand, suggests that the universe is *not* yet perfect because it is ever striving towards higher realizations; this is the characteristically modern, innovative element. The basic dilemma is perhaps best formulated in ethical terms: while "good" originally meant "perfect," according to the new orientation it can only mean "perfectible."[18] The emphasis on God as the infinite creative source of reality implies that neither God nor the universe can be regarded as perfect, for (as formulated in a contemporary romantic source), "A perfect God would end up smothering his own creation. For perfection presupposes that point beyond which development is impossible, and creativity at an end."[19]

René Wellek

Lovejoy's early article on the "discrimination of romanticisms" seems to have been far more influential than his later ones. In 1949, the well-known historian of literature René Wellek launched a frontal attack on what he called Lovejoy's "extreme nominalism."[20] Years afterward, Wellek would explain that he had been "distressed at the general acceptance of Lovejoy's thesis by the American academic community," because it had in practice "encouraged shirking the larger issues of literary history: the concepts of period, movement, development, and the whole question of the unity and diversity of European cultural change. Lovejoy, an eminent historian of ideas, paradoxically contributed to the antihistorical drift of recent American literary scholarship."[21] In reaction to this, Wellek set out to demonstrate that "the major Romantic movements form a *unity* of theories, philosophies, and style, and that these, in turn, form a coherent group of ideas each of which implicates the other" (*CR*, 2). Unfortunately, Wellek's reaction seems to have been based on a misunderstanding of Lovejoy's intentions, as a result of which he attacked a position that Lovejoy himself had never intended to defend.[22] The result was an influential article in which Wellek defined the unity of romanticism in terms of three criteria: "imagination for the view of poetry, nature for the view of the world, and symbol and myth for poetic style" (*CR*, 147).

1. Wellek emphasizes that, for the romantics, the *imagination* was

> not merely the power of visualization, somewhere in between sense and reason, which it had been to Aristotle or Addison ... nor even the inventive power of the poet ... but a creative power by which the mind "gains insight into reality," reads nature as a symbol of something behind or within nature not ordinarily perceived. (*CR*, 159)

In other words, the imagination was "an organ of knowledge which transforms objects, sees through them" (*CR*, 159). This view of the imagination stimulated a conflation of beauty and truth, or as formulated by Keats: "What the Imagination seizes as Beauty must be Truth whether it existed before or not." Wellek quotes Clarence D. Thorpe as giving a perfect summary of the romantic theory of the imagination:

> Such is the power of creative imagination, a seeing, reconciling, combining force that seizes the old, penetrates beneath its surface, disengages the truth slumbering there, and, building afresh, bodies forth anew a reconstructed universe in fair forms of artistic power and beauty. (*CR*, 161)

2. The romantic view of *nature* was a reaction to mechanistic conceptions popular in the eighteenth century. The romantics conceived of nature "as an organic whole, on the analogue of man rather than a concourse of atoms—a nature that is not divided from aesthetic values, which are just as real (or rather more real) than the abstractions of science" (*CR*, 161). To romantics such as Wordsworth, nature was also "a language, a system of symbols" (*CR*, 162). These ideas (living nature, its continuity with man, and its emblematic language) were all closely

related to the romantic concept of an intimate, dialectical cooperation and interaction of subject and object in the act of perception.

3. Finally, the preference for *myth and symbol* is characteristic of the romantic perspective. As Wellek explains, with special reference to Coleridge,

> the artist discourses to us by symbols, and nature is a symbolic language . . . a symbol is characterized by a translucence of the special in the individual, or of the general in the special, or of the universal in the general; above all, a symbol is characterized by the translucence of the eternal through and in the temporal. The faculty of symbols is the imagination. (*CR*, 167)

This last statement is significant, because it demonstrates how closely Wellek's three criteria are actually related. The faculty of symbols (3) is the imagination (1), and it is clear that Wellek's second criterion is actually about nature *as perceived* by the romantic imagination. What Wellek does is describe *one* integral perspective; and its central element seems to be the romantic view of the imagination.

At this point, one is struck by the similarity between romanticism *sensu* Wellek and western esotericism *sensu* Faivre (see his contribution elsewhere in this volume). As it turns out, this similarity is confirmed by Wellek's own comments. At the end of his article, he says that he is perfectly aware that his three elements

> have their historical ancestry before the age of Enlightenment and in undercurrents during the eighteenth century. The view of an organic nature descends from Neoplatonism through Giordano Bruno, Böhme, the Cambridge Platonists, and some passages in Shaftesbury. The view of imagination as creative and of poetry as prophecy has a similar ancestry. A symbolist, and even mythic, conception of poetry is frequent in history, e.g., in the baroque age with its emblematic art, its view of nature as hieroglyphics which man and especially the poet is destined to read. In a sense, Romanticism is the revival of something old, but it is a revival with a difference; these ideas were translated into terms acceptable to men who had undergone the experience of the Enlightenment. It may be difficult to distinguish clearly between a Romantic and a baroque symbol, the Romantic and the Böhmian view of nature and imagination. But for our problem we need only know that there is a difference between the symbol in Pope and in Shelley. (*CR*, 171)

Unfortunately, Wellek himself made no attempt to analyze precisely how these pre-Enlightenment "esoteric" ideas were reinterpreted and retranslated in post-Enlightenment terms. His basic observation, however, is correct and of crucial importance. Romanticism is a revival *with a difference*, and that difference is all-important. It is certainly true that it is difficult to distinguish between, for instance, the romantic and Böhmian view of nature; but I suggest that investigating precisely such distinctions and their backgrounds might well prove to be the key toward understanding the romantic revolution.

Comparing Wellek's and Lovejoy's approaches, most striking is that Wellek completely ignores the evolutionist tendency that is so essential in Lovejoy's analysis. In other words: the spatial universe is accounted for by both, but the factor of time and change is recognized only by Lovejoy. I suggest, however, that this new awareness of change and evolution may well be the most crucial of those "differences" that Wellek referred to but did not investigate. In this respect Lovejoy complements Wellek in a crucial way, but in another respect it is Wellek who complements Lovejoy. Wellek correctly emphasizes that no view of romanticism can be complete that does not take into account the factor of the "imagination." Lovejoy, however, all but ignores it. The explanation for this hiatus should probably be sought partly in his emphasis on philosophical rather than literary traditions, and partly in his general neglect (typical for his generation) of the factor of Hermeticism and related traditions.

MORSE PECKHAM

In an article originally published in 1951 and substantially revised ten years later, Morse Peckham sought to reconcile Lovejoy's and Wellek's approaches and, in the process, presented his own view of the nature of romanticism.[23] I find Peckham's article highly problematic in many respects, but his contribution to the debate must be briefly mentioned. Peckham attempts to prove (very unconvincingly in my view) that Lovejoy's *and* Wellek's characteristics can all be reduced to one single basic or root metaphor, which he refers to as *dynamic organicism*. His conclusion is as follows:

What then is Romanticism? Whether philosophic, theologic, or aesthetic, it is the revolution in the European mind against thinking in terms of static mechanism and the redirection of the mind to thinking in terms of dynamic organicism. Its values are change, imperfection, growth, diversity, the creative imagination, the unconscious. (*TTR*, 240–41)

Remarkably enough, this conclusion is far more convincing than the argument that is supposed to support it. The problem with Peckham's argument is not his definition of romanticism in itself, but his general way of handling definitions (both his own and those of others). Understood as no more than a label that covers a series of complicated and frequently contradictory trends, reduced to a few words for convenience' sake only, his definition of romanticism as "dynamic organicism" has a certain justification. Understood as a statement about "the" real nature of romanticism (in the singular), it has the effect of suggesting uniformity where there is diversity and internal conflict, and finally of "hypostatizing" a concept that actually has no other reality than that of a theoretical abstraction in the mind of scholars. In this sense, Peckham is a perfect example of the kind of approach criticized by Lovejoy.

Peckham's more interesting contribution is his distinction between *positive* and *negative* romanticism. Positive romanticism is simply the worldview based on dynamic organicism, with all the implications it had for romantics. Its "necessary complement," according to Peckham, is negative romanticism: "the expression of the attitudes, the feelings, and the ideas of a man who has left static mechanism but has not yet arrived at a reintegration of his thought and art in terms of dynamic organicism" (*TTR*, 241). Illustrating this distinction with the examples of Wordsworth's *Prelude*, Carlyle's *Sartor Resartus* and Coleridge's *Rhyme of the Ancient Mariner*, he concludes that

all three works are about spiritual death and rebirth, or secular conversion. . . . A man moves from a trust in the universe to a period of doubt and despair of any meaning in the universe, and then to a reaffirmation of faith in the cosmic meaning and goodness, or at least meaning. The transition from the first stage to the second, we may call spiritual death; that from the second to the third, we may call spiritual rebirth. (*TTR*, 242)[24]

Peckham criticizes Wellek, with justification, for ignoring this negative side of the romantic experience. His distinction has the merit of taking seriously the "dark side" of romanticism: the frequent expressions of *Weltschmerz* and metaphysical despair exemplified in the so-called dejection-poems, and the tendency of many romantics to move from one extreme of "joy" into the opposite one of nihilism. Indeed, ignoring this aspect would produce the wrong impression that the romantics subscribed to a worldview of blissful optimism and joyful affirmation of the spectacle of creation; such a view does not account for the fact that most romantics were in fact haunted by, and attempted to come to terms with, the dark and tragic sides of life.[25]

M. H. ABRAMS

Meyer H. Abrams's large study *Natural Supernaturalism* (published in 1971)[26] is a monument of scholarship, too rich in insights to be done justice in a brief discussion. For us Abram's book is essential firstly because, to date, it represents probably the most impressive work of synthesis about romanticism; *and*, secondly, because it is in any case the first major study to give explicit attention to the esoteric connection of romanticism.[27] At the end of his third chapter, Abrams makes "some general observations about the characteristic philosophies of the age." These seven points summarize most of the preceding discussions, and amount to an overview of Abrams perspective on the nature of romanticism.

1. Post-Kantian philosophers described both the universe *and* their own philosophical edifices in terms of a *"self-moving and self-sustaining system"* (*NS*, 172–77). Abrams employs the language of modern systems theory to describe what has elsewhere been referred to by terms like "dynamic organicism." A system is "self-generative, self-determinative, all-inclusive and self-contained," and it is "driven by an internal source of motion to its own completion." The energy that drives it on is the product of a dialectical interaction of opposed forces: polarity is the inner law of life.

2. A system is governed by an *"immanent teleology"* (*NS*, 177–79): it moves toward a built-in goal or end state.

3. The underlying theological design of romantic philosophy is "an extraordinary complex, but nonetheless recognizable, version of *the great circle* of Neoplatonic Christianity, according to which the process of emanation ends in its beginning, and the beginning and ending are the One" (*NS*, 179). The primal fracture has at least two dimensions. In its *cognitive* dimension, a split occurs between mind and outer nature; in its *moral* dimension a similar split occurs in man's original unity with himself. These splits have an ambiguous character: although negative in themselves, they are ultimately justified because they are necessary to release the energy that drives the whole system toward its eventual solution. In this connection, one often speaks of a "fortunate fall."

4. However, the romantic design *differs* from its Neoplatonic original in two chief aspects, and these, Abrams emphasizes, are all-important. Firstly, "the locus and criterion of ultimate value was transferred from the Plotinian other-realm to *this world* of man and nature and human experience" (*NS*, 183). Some romantics considered a final reunion of a reintegrated mind with outer nature to be accessible to humanity; others thought of the goal as "infinitely recessive" so that it could only be approached ever more closely but never reached. In both cases, *history* "became the sole realm in which, in the end, we either find happiness or not at all" (*NS*, 183). Secondly, the recovered unity was no longer "the simple, undifferentiated unity of its origin, but a unity which is *higher*, because it incorporates the intervening differentiations" (*NS*, 183–84). In this way, the Platonic idea of circular return was fused with the idea of linear progress, and the result was "a distinctive figure of Romantic thought and imagination—*the ascending circle, or spiral*" (*NS*, 184). In this "distinctive Romantic innovation . . . the norm of truth, goodness, and beauty is not the *simple* unity of the origin, but the *complex* unity of the terminus of the process of cumulative division and reintegration" (*NS*, 184–85). The final state is higher than the beginning because it preserves diversity and individuality, and also because it has not been simply given but has been *earned* by incessant striving. What we have here is, essentially, Lovejoy's "temporalizing of the great chain."[28] And like Lovejoy, Abrams emphasizes the momentous importance of this event:

> To shift the location of the highest truth and the highest value from
> the simple beginning to the complex end of an extended process is to

transform Plotinus' emanation into evolution, and so to convert Plotinus' derogation of the movement from the One to the many as a descent from perfection to its laudation as an indispensable stage in the ascent toward perfection. (*NS*, 186)

5. In the above context, the history of humanity was reinterpreted in terms of a *Bildungsgeschichte* of human consciousness:

> a process of the self-formation, or self-education, of the mind and moral being of man from the dawn of consciousness to the stage of full maturity. The mind of man, whether generic or individual, is . . . disciplined by the suffering which it experiences as it develops through successive stages of division, conflict, and reconciliation. . . . (*NS*, 187–88)

The emphasis in this educational process lies on the expansion of the *mind*. The most distinctive attribute of the mind is *consciousness*, and its distinctive activity is *knowing*. The process of self-education leads to a progressive evolution of consciousness, culminating in what I suggest may be called a universal *gnosis*, when humanity "by the fullness and perfection of its power of organized knowing ... will utterly repossess everything which it has, in its earlier stages of imperfect and partial knowledge, separated and alienated as object to itself as subject" (*NS*, 189).

6. Thus we get what Abrams calls the essential *plot-structure* of the romantic philosophical, historical and literary imagination:

> the painful education through ever expanding knowledge of the conscious subject as it strives—without distinctly knowing what it is that it wants until it achieves it—to win its way back to a higher mode of the original unity with itself from which, by its primal act of consciousness, it has inescapably divided itself off. (*NS*, 190–91)

7. Abrams emphasizes that "at no other place and time" have technical philosophy and literature been so closely interwoven as in the romantic period, especially in Germany (*NS*, 192). Most congenial to the literary side was the plot structure of the *pilgrimage or quest*, "the journey in search of an unknown or inexpressible something which gradually leads the wanderer back to his point of origin" (*NS*, 193).

By means of his ruling image of the "circuitous journey" or educational spiral, Abrams thus manages to synthesize the various elements that had been emphasized by Lovejoy, Wellek, and Peckham. We already saw that Lovejoy's organicism, diversitarianism, and evolutionism are also central to Abrams. Abrams's "circuitous journey" from unity through alienation to a higher unity obviously incorporates Peckham's movement of spiritual death, crisis, and rebirth, as well as his emphasis on the "myth of the fall" as central to romanticism. Abrams, however, avoids Peckham's tendency to confuse the analysis of romanticism with an apologetics on behalf of it.

Of particular interest is the fact that, on the basis of Abrams's complete study, a connection can be made between Peckham's emphasis on the movement of spiritual death and rebirth and Wellek's emphasis on the role of the imagination. For *what* "unity," we should ask, is lost and regained in the spiral process, and *how* does this happen? At one point, Abrams compares the romantic spiral to "a pagan mystery ritual of death, rebirth, and salvation by means of an initiation into *gnosis*" (*NS*, 128). But the loss and recovery of this particular kind of gnosis is itself dependent on the loss and recovery of a certain faculty or organ; and this faculty, according to Abrams, is the imagination. What Wordsworth does in the *Prelude* is to tell the story of "the birth, growth, disappearance, and resurrection of imagination"; and the spiritual crisis central to this work is basically a crisis of the imagination (NS, *118*). We thus come back (via Peckham and Abrams) to Wellek's identification of the imagination as central to romanticism, but now with the crucial addition of the dimension of *process*. "Spiritual death," to borrow Peckham's formulation, is the loss of the ability to perceive the world through the eyes of the imagination; the result of this loss is a cold, senseless, random, and fragmented world to which human beings can feel no inner connection. Of course, it was especially post-Cartesian philosophy and mechanistic science that the romantics felt "partook of death" in this sense.[29] In the state of "joy" (a popular romantic term for imaginative awareness), however, mind and nature are experienced as interconnected by a common "bond of sympathy." It is only through the imagination that this "holistic" interconnectedness of the diversity of creation is actualized. And "actualized" is indeed the correct term here, for this particular view of the imagination implies a philosophy in which perceiving subject and perceived object *together* constitute reality. The great goal of romanticism is to overcome the alienation between mind and nature; and the means to this unity is the *active* imagination, which creates in the very act of perceiving. When this reunion has become the common experience of humanity, the "new earth" will have become a reality. In Wordsworth's words:

> For the discerning intellect of Man,
> When wedded to this goodly universe
> In love and holy passion, shall find these
> A simple produce of the common day.
> . . . .
> And the creation (by no lower name
> Can it be called) which they with blended might
> Accomplish:—this is our high argument.[30]

The last three lines merit particularly close attention: the mind of man and the universe together (but, significantly, without active participation of a separate God)[31] *accomplish* the creation of the new world; and precisely to this "high argument," Abrams concluded, Wordsworth's great poem *The Recluse* was meant to be devoted.

In explaining the historical genesis of the romantic vision, Abrams emphasizes a number of traditions. One essential component is the Bible and biblical theology; another is the characteristic pattern of what Abrams calls the "crisis-autobiography," of which Augustine's *Confessions* is the classic model. Of particular interest to us is his highlighting of two further traditions: Neoplatonism, on the one hand, and "the esoteric tradition" on the other. The first of these hardly needs further elucidation at this point. We already encountered it as essential to Lovejoy's approach; its importance to Abrams's interpretation has been pointed out above; and in general the importance of Neoplatonism to understanding romanticism has been recognized for a long time.[32] In this sense Abrams hardly diverges from scholarly orthodoxy. Abrams's highlighting of esotericism, however, is innovative. He discusses, at some length, the contribution of the Kabbalah and of Hermeticist traditions, giving particular emphasis to alchemy, Paracelsus, and Jacob Böhme (*NS*, 154–63). These discussions, it must be admitted, are interesting but not particularly profound; and the relevance to romanticism is not demonstrated quite as convincingly as is the case with Neoplatonism.[33] One is left with the impression that Abrams's reading of Frances Yates's *Giordano Bruno and the Hermetic Tradition* and some other classics (Gerschom Scholem, François Secret, Alexandre Koyré) had convinced him that existing scholarship was ignoring an important factor, but that his own knowledge of esotericism was based on a too limited number of sources to permit him to do much more than call attention to that fact. That he did call attention to it remains something to which students of western esotericism should be grateful.[34]

One particular point about Abrams's treatment of Neoplatonism and esotericism requires specific emphasis: the fact that he consistently treats them as if they were two entirely separate traditions. In doing this, Abrams continues a scholarly tradition that I believe to be highly detrimental to developing a balanced view of our subject. Lovejoy, as we saw, emphasized Neoplatonism but was still fully unaware of the Hermeticist strain; with hindsight, one suspects that *The Great Chain of Being* would have been a different book if this had been otherwise. Abrams, on the other hand, is aware of Lovejoy's blind spot but still treats the "esoteric tradition" as entirely separate from the Neoplatonic one. The perspective of both scholars is impaired by a long-standing tendency to emphasize so-called serious and respectable intellectual traditions (Neoplatonism in this case) while neglecting what are regarded as unserious or merely popular ones (i.e., esotericism).[35] In the light of present-day research, neither the distinction between serious and unserious nor the strict distinction between modern Neoplatonism and esotericism can be upheld. As described elsewhere in this volume, Hermetism was revived at the end of the fifteenth century in the Neoplatonic academy of Florence, and the "esoteric tradition" that emerged from that revival has always remained closely interwoven with Neoplatonic elements. What emerged was a characteristic form of religious syncretism that was generally recognized as Platonic-Hermetic in a general sense, regardless of the references it made to the Plato, the Neoplatonists, or to the *Corpus Hermeticum*.[36] Therefore, the distinction assumed by scholars such as Lovejoy and Abrams cannot really be one between esotericism and Neoplatonism. At most, it might be reformulated as a (most questionable) distinction between a "real" and pure Neoplatonism, on the one hand, and a Hermeticized *Vulgarplatonismus*, on the other. However, such a distinction would hardly be helpful to Abrams, for if one applies it to romanticism one finds that much of the romantics' so-called Platonism was derived from sources belonging to the second category (i.e., to western esotericism).

Abrams's final conclusion about the relevance to romanticism of "the esoteric tradition" evidently refers to what should better be called the Hermetic-Platonic esotericism of the Renaissance period and its relation to romanticism:

> Renaissance vitalism had envisioned an integral universe without absolute divisions, in which everything is interrelated by a system of correspondences, and the living is continuous with the inanimate, nature with man, and matter with mind; a universe . . . activated throughout by a dynamism of opposing forces. . . . In this way of thinking some Romantic philosophers detected intimations of a viable counter-metaphysic to contemporary mechanism, elementarism, and dualism; provided that . . . the mythical elements are translated into philosophical concepts, and these are ordered into a "scientific," that is, a coherent conceptual system. (*NS*, 171)

This conclusion demonstrates the importance of the "esoteric connection" in Abrams's interpretation of romanticism. It should be added that, obviously, the criticism formulated above is not intended to discourage the attempt to unravel the Neoplatonic and Hermetic threads within various western esoteric syntheses, including those belonging to the romantic period. On the contrary, such a study is important and long overdue. However, such an *analytic-typological* undertaking should be distinguished from a *historical-empirical* approach. The last author to be discussed here provides a good illustration.

ERNEST LEE TUVESON

The fundamental problem of the relationship between Neoplatonism and Hermeticism within the esoteric tradition dominates Ernest Lee Tuveson's *The Avatars of Thrice Great Hermes* (1982) as well.[37] Tuveson's study merits attention because, to date, it is the most substantial attempt to emphasize the "esoteric connection" as crucial to the understanding of romanticism. Unfortunately, although Tuveson's book contains interesting insights, his central argument is highly problematic.

Tuveson's study is based on his discovery "that much of what we had called, vaguely, 'Neoplatonism' differed in crucial ways from the expressions of philosophers and poets to whom we had attached the label 'Neoplatonic'" (*A*, ix). The so-called Neoplatonism of the romantics turned out to be something else: it constituted a religious philosophy with some resemblances to Neoplatonism, but was basically rooted in a completely different worldview, i.e., Hermeticism. This, as I argued above, is basically correct. Unfortunately, however, this discovery seems to have impressed Tuveson too much. Spurred on by *Entdeckungsfreude*, he attempts completely to *replace* Neoplatonism by Hermeticism as *the* exclusive and all-explaining "key" to romanticism. His procedure is yet another example of the approach that was denounced by Lovejoy in 1924. Throughout his study, Tuveson consistently confuses two very different things: (1) the theoretical distinction, for reasons of analysis, between different structural *types* of speculation; and (2) the description and interpretation of complicated *historical* movements. Tuveson systematically ignores that the so-called Hermeticist tradition since the Renaissance period is, of course, not *exclusively* Hermetic: Neoplatonic, Christian, and various other components are inextricably bound up with it. In historical reality, one does not find those "pure forms" which may (for sound scholarly reasons) be defined by theoretical abstraction. Tuveson, however, focuses entirely on what he considers to be the "true core" of the Hermetic teachings. He sharply separates this quintessential Hermeticism not only from an equally abstract "pure Neoplatonism," but also from what he considers to be merely accidental features of the Hermeticist tradition. These "accidents" (denounced without further ado as "fantasies" [*A*, 116]) include reference to astral beings, gods, demons, aeons, and even to the *anima mundi* as well as to "the whole cosmology of the alchemist" (*A*, 15–16, 34). All this, we are given to understand, is not "truly" Hermetic. Modern attempts to revive such beliefs, by occultists and others, are denounced as "recidivism" (*A*, 34). Now, the mere fact that Tuveson focuses on what he considers the "core" of Hermeticism, and tries to demonstrate that it is also central to romanticism, might in principle be a legitimate procedure; and Tuveson certainly points out some remarkable similarities and continuities. However, his ambition goes much further. He does not merely say that certain elements originally derived from hermetic speculation eventually became important to the romantic worldview. His central thesis is, rather, that the modern romantic worldview has been *implicit in Hermeticism* from the very beginning, and that "the true hermetic teaching" had to gradually free itself over history from "alien" elements (Neoplatonic hierarchies, gods, demons, and various prescientific superstitions) in order to finally become fully conscious of itself in modern times. Therefore it is to the romantics, and to Walt Whitman in particular, that one should turn to learn what the Hermetic teachings *really* meant (*A*, 60).[38] And in doing so, we are initiated into the *truth* about reality that, as Tuveson concludes his book, may be "the way to salvation for modern man" (*A*, 250).

Tuveson is of course entitled to his professed belief in an "evolution of consciousness" culminating in a "cosmic consciousness"; but statements of belief and scholarly research are two different things. Neither do I wish to deny that *The Avatars of Thrice Great Hermes* contains interesting discussions about intellectual developments from Pico della Mirandola through the Cambridge Platonists, Freemasonry, Addison, Shaftesbury, Pope, Thomson, Wordsworth, Goethe, and Humboldt up to Tuveson's ultimate "avatar," Walt Whitman. As a synthetic vision on the nature of romanticism, however, the book is a failure for obvious methodological reasons. Tuveson interprets romanticism in terms of Hermeticism only, but obscures the fact that he has already interpreted "Hermeticism" in terms of romanticism. The result is a huge tautology: while purportedly presenting "Hermeticism" as the key to romanticism, the actual argument of the book implies that romanticism is the key to ("true") Hermeticism.

Nevertheless, it is not superfluous to take a brief look at those elements that Tuveson believes Hermeticism and romanticism have in common. Firstly, he almost completely identifies Hermeticism with *panentheism*, defined by him as the doctrine that "the universe as a whole is the manifestation of God, but that God is a separate Mind" (*A*, 4). Now, that Hermeticism is predominantly panentheistic seems to be correct, but this does not mean that both terms can be used interchangeably. Panentheism is the name of a metaphysical position, while Hermeticism is first and foremost the name of a historical tradition.[39] Tuveson again ignores this crucial distinction. Having highlighted panentheism as the essence of the Hermetic message, *any* expression of panentheism becomes for him, *ex definitione*, an expression of Hermeticism! Whether or not the author in question had any connection to Hermeticist traditions is, from that perspective, of minor importance. If the Hermetic message is panentheism, anyone who brings that message is in fact proclaiming "Hermeticism," whether he or she knows it or not. In this way, Tuveson makes his theory practically immune to historical falsification.

Secondly, Tuveson strongly emphasizes a kind of expansive "*cosmic consciousness*" that consists in internalizing the cosmos in the human mind by means of the imagination. From a panentheistic perspective, Tuveson explains, "to know God's personality is to become godlike; and the only way to know God's being is to *expand* oneself into the comprehensiveness of the divine mind itself" (*A*, 4). As it happens, this aspect had already been stressed forcefully by Abrams as well, who however does not seem to have perceived its full significance in relation to "esotericism." Tuveson, on the other hand, correctly points to the famous "cosmic" passages in, particularly, the eleventh book of the *Corpus Hermeticum*.[40] Indeed, it is here, if anywhere, that we encounter a real similarity between an important aspect of Hermeticism and an equally central theme of romanticism.

CONCLUSIONS

On the basis of the above discussions, three basic categories appear to be central to romanticism. They may be referred to briefly as organicism, imagination, and temporalism. In order to establish to what extent they support the idea of an "esoteric connection" of romanticism, it will be useful to compare them with the four constitutive elements of esotericism as presented by Antoine Faivre.

Organicism

This first element seems the least problematic. All five of our authors agree about the central importance to romanticism of the belief that reality in all its dimensions should be understood not in mechanical but

	ORGANICISM	IMAGINATION	TEMPORALISM
LOVEJOY	Organicism Diversitarianism		Romantic Evolutionism
WELLEK	Nature	Imagination Myth & Symbol	
PECKHAM	Dynamic Organicism?		From negative to positive Romanticism
ABRAMS	System	Imagination	Immanent Teleology/ The Educational Spiral
TUVESON	Panentheism	Cosmic Consciousness?	

FAIVRE

Correspondences Living Nature	Mediations/ Imagination	Transmutation

in organismic terms. The romantics emphasized organismic values in a conscious reaction to the mechanistic models of rationalistic science. While a mechanism is an aggregate of separate parts, an organism is a whole that cannot be broken up into its elements without killing it; and while a mechanism is static and can only be moved by outside forces, an organism is dynamic and has an inner principle of motion. Briefly: organisms are living; mechanisms are dead. In this sense, the romantics saw themselves as asserting the value and autonomy of life, while rejecting the essentially dead universe of Newtonian science and its attendant philosophies (for these too, in Coleridge's words, "partook of DEATH").

With respect to romantic "organicism," the plausibility of the "esoteric connection" lies in the fact that, as we have seen, pre-Enlightenment esotericism and post-Enlightenment romanticism shared a very similar "holistic" and organicistic worldview, *and* that both applied this orientation to nature. Elsewhere in this volume, Antoine Faivre explains the close connection between the "discovery of nature" since the twelfth century and the emergence of western esotericism. Nature was perceived to be in symbolic correspondence with the "higher" world of spiritual reality, and permeated and animated by invisible powers. Hermetic types of *Naturphilosophie*, grounded in a worldview of acausal "correspondences," formed a countertradition opposed to the emerging worldview based on mechanistic causality and a science based on wholly secular principles. That the romantics saw precisely in these traditions "a viable counter-metaphysic to contemporary mechanism, elementarism, and dualism" (Abrams) and were strongly influenced by it[41] is therefore anything but surprising. At least as far as the organismic element is concerned, the "esoteric connection" of romanticism stands on solid ground.

Imagination

This second element is far more complicated. While the "organismic" element concerns the nature of reality, the element of "imagination" in romanticism concerns the cognitive means by which this reality is perceived. It is through the imagination that reality is both perceived *and* constituted as a living whole of mind and nature, in which (in Wordsworth's formulation) "the discerning intellect of man [is] wedded to this goodly universe." In this sense, the imagination is the means to attain gnosis. This high opinion of the imagination evidently stood in sharp contrast with the dominant tendencies of the Enlightenment. The "dead universe" abhorred by the romantics was in fact the kind of universe that resulted from the degradation of the imaginative faculty in favor of rationality only. What particularly worried the romantics was the influence of John Locke: according to his empiricist philosophy, whatever gave to the perceived world its life, beauty, and human interest was degraded to the status of mere "secondary qualities," while only the "primary qualities" such as weight or shape were accepted as real.[42] Such a philosophy left no more than an essentially dead world of "colourless, lifeless, material particles, silently in motion."[43] In such a world, the products of the imagination, such as art and poetry, could only be illusions: pleasant illusions, perhaps, but without a deeper foundation in reality. Now, the romantics did realize that the lifeless universe of the new philosophy is as much a product of the imagination as their own living universe. If one imagines the universe as a dead mechanism then, for all means and purposes, one will "live" in such a universe; but, the romantics would say, actually one will live in an illusionary universe created by a misguided imagination. In the same way, one lives in a living and animated universe if one imagines that it is so. This illustrates why the concept of the "imagination" is so tricky. On one level, the imagination is fundamental to all human thought and perception, including those kinds which were abhorred by the romantics; but on another level it is defined more specifically as only that kind of imagination which is healthy, unifying, animating, and gives meaning to human existence. And this is only the beginning of the problems. For one thing, it wouldn't do, for the romantics, to see these various ways of "imagining the world" as subjective interpretations of one and the same objective reality; this would once more relegate the romantic imagination to the status of illusion or fantasy. The romantic perspective, in contrast, implied a close *participation* of the perceiving subject in the perceived object, which means that the object (the world) is *constituted* in the very act of perception.

Now, if one begins to investigate how this romantic view of the imagination is related to traditional concepts of *imaginatio* that are central to esotericism, one will quickly get the feeling of having opened a can of worms. For the "imagination" may have a variety of connotations in esoteric contexts. A probably incomplete selection includes: (1) The power of visualizing images for magical purposes;[44] (2) the faculty by which images and symbols (for instance, in alchemy) may become vehicles of inner transformation or transmutation;[45] (3) the faculty that gives access to a "mesocosmos" or "mundus imaginalis" that is in between the world of the senses and the world of pure spirit;[46] (4) the process of "internalizing the cosmos," described for example in the eleventh tract of the *Corpus Hermeticum* and of fundamental importance to the celebrated "Art of Memory."[47] I do not know of any major study that clearly distinguishes these various meanings of "imagination" and investigates in depth the ways in which they are related or associated. For, in spite of these distinctions, it is also clear that they all have basic presuppositions in common. In one way or another, the "imagination" always has to do with something "in between" spirit/mind and matter. Its function, in other words, is to transcend dualism. Thus, at a very minimum we may affirm that the centrality of the imagination in esotericism and in romanticism is based on a shared "holistic" perspective. This does not imply that both perspectives are identical, for we have to recognize the difference between a pre- and a post-Enlightenment perspective: the latter is a conscious reaction to something of which the former could not yet have any knowledge.

Obviously, only a very preliminary conclusion about the element of the "imagination" is possible. There is abundant reason to take seriously the hypothesis of a fundamental connection between esoteric and romantic concepts of the imagination; but a major analytic and historical study of the esoteric imagination, in *all* its dimensions, would be needed in order to even begin giving body to this hypothesis. One particularly important aspect of such a study would be the relation between the imagination and *magic*, not only in view of the first meaning of "imagination" mentioned above, but also in view of modern theories in the systematic study of religion that (following the lead of Lévy-Bruhl) have analyzed "magic" as a worldview based on "participation."[48] In the absence of such a study, it is safe to conclude that the connection with romanticism is very plausible indeed but that our understanding of it is as yet rather superficial. Here is another important field for future exploration in the academic study of esotericism.

Temporalism

This third and final element is, perhaps more than any other, likely to breed confusion. Arthur Lovejoy has presented the new evolutionism as the most specifically innovative element in romanticism, and discussed it in close connection with "diversitarianism." This connection is natural, for the new awareness of historical change implied a new awareness of the unicity of historical events, and thus of contingency and diversity.[49] Historical awareness (or temporalistic thinking) obviously involves more than just the commonsense realization that there is a difference between the past, the present, and the future. The truly innovative element was the emphasis on change over continuity; on the diversity of historical periods and events over the idea that history shows us merely variations on the same universal themes; and, finally, on the fact that small contingencies may have the effect of driving events in completely new directions that could not have been foreseen or predicted theoretically. Lovejoy's emphasis on these innovations seems entirely correct and, I would argue, essential to understand the nature of the "esoteric connection" of romanticism. Both "organicism" and (presumably) "imagination" can be regarded as essentially *traditional* ideas that were revived in the romantic period. Temporalism and "historical consciousness," on the other hand, are distinctly *new*. Probably the most important task in studying romanticism's esoteric connection is to elucidate how this momentous innovation influenced the perception of "esoteric" and other traditional elements.[50]

It is of particular importance in this respect to distinguish carefully between the idea of "process," on the one hand, and the modern idea of "evolution" on the other: it seems to me that a failure to make this distinction is responsible for some of the most pervasive misunderstandings about the esoteric connection of romanticism. Faivre's fourth element of esotericism, "the experience of transmutation" essentially refers to dynamic processes of metamorphosis that lead to a higher level of integration. Obvious examples are the alchemical process and the sevenfold cosmogonic process that is fundamental to Jacob Böhme's system. Now, if we try to understand such processes, we almost automatically interpret them in temporalistic terms, i.e., as theories of evolution. A paradigmatic example of this is the tendency of generations of scholars, beginning with the romantics themselves, to interpret Jacob Böhme as a prefiguration of Hegel. This, however, is to impute to Böhme a temporalistic perspective that in effect *reduces* his notion of process to only one of its manifestations, i.e., the temporal. It is true, of course, that a "process" may take place in time (the practitioner of alchemy certainly hoped to gradually purify himself during his life). However, the full archetypal symbology of esoteric "transmutation" is definitely not exhausted by this temporalized manifestation. To take Jacob Böhme as an example: his cosmogony entails something that modern minds find particularly hard to imagine: a dynamic process that *unfolds outside of time*.[51] In order to understand this paradox, it is useful to recall Jacob

Needleman's correct observation that the Hermetic dictum "'As above, so below' by no means entails 'as below, so above'"[52] (i.e., is not to be misunderstood in terms of an *identity* of levels). Böhme's thinking, too, is grounded in a doctrine of symbolic correspondences according to which a "higher" reality is reflected imperfectly by our "lower" world; the former is true and original, while the latter is merely a derivation. A "Feuerbachian" reversal of this doctrine, so that the "higher" is merely a reflection of the "lower" (our everyday world), is alien to Böhme's thinking. Precisely such a confusion of levels, however, underlies the interpretation of Böhme's sevenfold process in evolutionist terms: it implies that the meaning of the process is exhausted by its manifestation in time.

This leads me to the following conclusions. While romantic "organicism" and "imagination" seem to be rooted in traditional esotericism, the phenomenon of temporalism as such (or the "rise of historical consciousness") is a specifically modernist element, probably the most innovative one in romanticism. I see no reason to assume that it owes much to esoteric traditions; it seems to have emerged from other sources, which do not have to concern us here. Once it had established itself, however, it provided a context that seemed to make *new* sense of traditional notions of "process" such as had been expressed mythically and symbolically in mystical, Neoplatonic, alchemical, or theosophical traditions. Some would argue (similar to Tuveson's approach) that the new evolutionist philosophies unveiled the "true meaning" of esoteric mythology and symbology, so that esotericism "comes into its own" in romantic evolutionism. I would argue, on the contrary, that this evolutionistic interpretation of esoteric "transmutation" leads to a reductionist misinterpretation of the original intention. Empirical reality undoubtedly unfolds in time; but Böhme and most other traditional esotericists were convinced that "metaempirical" reality unfolded in eternity.[53]

It is precisely this profoundly paradoxical aspect of traditional esotericism that would become increasingly unfathomable to the romantics and their successors, and has remained alien to most contemporary commentators. The interpretation of esoteric "transmutation" in terms of evolutionism unquestionably opened up entirely new possibilities for speculation. It was by the very success of this interpretation, however, that traditional esotericism was rendered all but unintelligible.

NOTES

1. Auguste Viatte, *Les sources occultes du romantisme: Illuminisme, Théosophie, 1770–1820* (1927; reprint, Paris, 1979); idem, *Victor Hugo et les illuminés de son temps* (1942; reprint, Genève, 1973); Ernst Benz, *Les sources mystiques de la philosophie romantique allemande* (Paris, 1987); idem, "Die Mystik in der Philosophie des Deutschen Idealismus," in *Schelling: Werden und Werken seines Denkens* (Zürich, 1955); Louis Guinet, *Zacharias Werner et l'ésotérisme maconnique* (Paris and The Hague, 1962); Antoine Faivre, *Kirchberger et l'illuminisme du XVIIIe siècle* (The Hague, 1966); idem, *Eckartshausen et la théosophie chrétienne* (Paris, 1969); idem, *Mystiques, théosophes et illuminés au siècle des lumières* (Hildesheim and New York, 1976); Roger Ayrault, *La genèse du romantisme allemand*, vol. 2 (Paris, 1961); Hans Graßl, *Aufbruch zur Romantik: Bayerns Beitrag zur deutschen Geistesgeschichte, 1765–1785* (München, 1968); Rolf Christian Zimmermann, *Das Weltbild des jungen Goethe: Studien zur hermetischen Tradition des deutschen 18th Jahrhunderts*, vol. 1: *Elemente und Fundamente* (München, 1969); Wilhelm Lütgert, *Die Religion des deutschen Idealismus und ihr Ende*, 4 vols. (Gütersloh, 1923, 1925, 1930); A. G. F. Gode-von Aesch, *Natural Science in German Romanticism* (New York, 1941); Mirko Sladek, *Fragmente der hermetischen Philosophie in der Naturphilosophie der Neuzeit: Historisch-kritische Beiträge zur hermetisch-alchemistischen Raum- und Naturphilosophie bei Giordano Bruno, Henry More und Goethe* (Frankfurt a.M., 1984); several contributions to Antoine Faivre and Rolf Christian Zimmermann, eds., *Epochen der Naturmystik: Hermetische Tradition im wissenschaftlichen Fortschritt* (Berlin, 1979).

2. I will restrict myself to the English-speaking domain. Most of the historical research into the "esoteric connection" of romanticism has, however, been published in French or German (see note 1) and has remained largely unknown to English-speaking researchers. The fact that the "esoteric connection" suggested by French and German research is confirmed, as will be seen, by the conclusions arrived at by English and American scholars, *even though* their familiarity with the former is at most superficial, in effect strengthens my argument.

3. "Bergson and Romantic Evolutionism," *University of California Chronicle* 15, no. 4 (1913); "The Meaning of 'Romantic' in Early German Romanticism" (1916), reprinted in *Essays in the History of Ideas* (Baltimore, 1948); "Schiller and the Genesis of German Romanticism" (1920), reprinted in *Essays;* "On the Discrimination of Romanticisms" (1924), reprinted in *Essays;* "Optimism and Romanticism," *PMLA* 42 (1927); *The Great Chain of Being: A Study of the History of an Idea* (1936; reprint, Cambridge and London 1964), chaps. 9–11; "The Meaning of Romanticism for the Historian of Ideas," *Journal of the History of Ideas* 2 (1941).

4. Lovejoy, "Discrimination," 235.

5. Ibid.

6. A classic statement to this effect is by Walter Pater in *Appreciations* (1889), reprinted in Robert F. Gleckner and Gerald E. Enscoe, eds., *Romanticism: Points of View* (Detroit, 1962). H. J. C.Grierson stands in this tradition, in describing "classical"

and "romantic" as "the systole and diastole of the human heart in history" (in *Classical and Romantic* [1923], reprinted in Gleckner and Enscoe, *Romanticism;* the quotation is on page 52).

7. Lovejoy, "Discrimination," 236.

8. See Morse Peckham, "Toward a Theory of Romanticism," reprinted in Gleckner and Enscoe *Romanticism*, 234–35.

9. Lovejoy, "Meaning of Romanticism," 261.

10. Ibid., 272: the three are "by no means the only ones . . . but they are, I incline to think, the most fundamental and most important, though the estimate is certainly debatable."

11. Lovejoy's article was originally delivered, in 1940, as a lecture for political and social historians. In this context, he expands upon the way in which this idea of *das Ganze* underlies the fascist ideology of the national state. These connections between romanticism and fascism were subsequently criticized by Leo Spitzer ("Geistesgeschichte vs. History of Ideas as applied to Hitlerism"; see also Lovejoy, "Reply to Professor Spitzer," both reprinted in Donald R. Kelley, *The History of Ideas: Canon and Variations* [Rochester, 1990]).

12. Lovejoy, "Meaning of Romanticism," 274.

13. Ibid., 275.

14. Ibid., 276.

15. Lovejoy, *Great Chain*, 315.

16. Ibid., 293. As for the holistic character of the "generative" great chain, this is so obvious that it hardly needs to be mentioned explicitly.

17. Ibid., 244.

18. Cf. J. M. R. Lenz, quoted in ibid., 251.

19. Jane Roberts, *The Seth Material: The Eternal Validity of the Soul* (1972; reprint, New York, 1988), 340. This book is a foundational source of the New Age movement, and provides an excellent example of my thesis that New Age religion is crucially indebted to romanticism (in this case, Emersonian transcendentalism in particular). See for this connection my contribution about the New Age movement in the present volume; and cf. my *New Age Religion and Western Culture: Esotericism in the Mirror of Secular Thought* (Leiden, 1996), esp. chap. 15, section 1.

20. René Wellek, "The Concept of 'Romanticism' in Literary History," *Comparative Literature* 1, no. 1 (1949): 1–23, 147–72. Referred to henceforth in the text as *CR*, followed by the page number.

21. René Wellek, "Romanticism Re-examined," in *Romanticism Reconsidered*, ed. Northrop Frye (New York and London, 1963), 107–8.

22. Lovejoy's 1924 thesis is precisely analogous to the empiricist criticism of "religionism" in the study of religions, which assumes that "religion" is a sui generis phenomenon (see my "Empirical Method in the Study of Esotericism," *Method and Theory in the Study of Religion* 7, no. 2 [1995]). Besides the plural "romanticisms," the adjective "romantic" was retained by Lovejoy as applicable to a certain historical movement of thought. His objections concerned only the term "romanticism" in the singular, because this suggested the existence, beyond the contingencies of

space and time, of some real and eternal essence of "romanticism". Lovejoy rejected this for *methodological* reasons, but Wellek attacked his thesis as though it were an *empirical* one. A correct understanding of Lovejoy's point would have presented Wellek with new and serious problems, because he would then have had to compare his own proposals with those made by Lovejoy in 1941 and account for the far-reaching differences between them (on which, see below). Actually, one suspects that Wellek eventually realized that he had misinterpreted Lovejoy but simply did not want to admit it, most probably because he did not wish to deal with the consequences. In "Romanticism Re-examined," 109, he "grants," responding to a critique by Ronald S. Crane, that Lovejoy indeed developed common denominators of "what is usually called romantic." He was, therefore, perfectly aware of the fact. Next, however, he surprisingly ignores Peckham's attempt (see below) to reconcile Lovejoy's views and his own, criticizing Peckham only on other counts. In the rest of the article Wellek discusses a great number of other studies about romanticism, only to conclude at the end that they all confirm his own view of romanticism ("Romanticism Re-examined," 132).

23. Both parts are republished together as "Toward a Theory of Romanticism," in Gleckner and Enscoe, *Romanticism*. The article will be referred to in the text and notes as *TTR*, followed by the page number of the Gleckner and Enscoe volume.

24. Note that both characterizations given in the text are actually incompatible. First, Peckham speaks of a transition from *static mechanism* to doubt to dynamic organicism; later, what actually appears to be meant is a transition from a naïve *trust in the universe* to doubt to a reaffirmation of that trust. The first process (from Peckham's own clearly romantic perspective) is one of gradual spiritual progress; the second one is circular or spiral.

25. Peckham's 1961 reconstruction of his theory is marginal to our concerns. It reflects his personal ideas about how romanticism *should* have developed rather than a historical analysis of how it in fact did develop. It culminates in a celebration of the "self" and its powers to "create its own reality." René Wellek has observed that he cannot find one single writer in the late eighteenth or early nineteenth century who matches Peckham's view of romanticism as "a heroic antimetaphysical subjectivism" (Wellek, "Romanticism Re-examined," 111) that, in Peckham's words, "can do without constitutive metaphysics and can use any metaphysic or world-hypothesis as a supreme fiction" (*TTR*, 256). Indeed, Peckham's vision is close to a postromantic perspective that has sometimes been labeled "self-religion" and is more usually referred to as "New Age" (see my contribution, elsewhere in this volume). As demonstrated by the case of Peckham, assessing theories of romanticism is complicated by the fact that their authors are often themselves latter-day romantics: romantics, that is, *with a difference*, who may easily read their own modern preoccupations back into the historical movement with which they are connected by bonds both of history and of sympathy.

26. M. H. Abrams, *Natural Supernaturalism: Tradition and Revolution in Romantic Literature* (New York and London, 1971). Referred to henceforth in the text and notes as *NS*, followed by the page number.

27. I use this term for convenience' sake, but note that Abrams correctly avoids the essentialistic fallacy attacked by Lovejoy. His basic thesis is that "A number of major poets, who differed markedly from their eighteenth-century predecessors, had in common important themes, modes of expression, and ways of feeling and imagining; the writing of these poets were part of a comprehensive intellectual tendency. . . . These writers shared a concern with certain human problems, and an identifiable way of considering and moving toward the resolution of these problems, which justify Shelley and his contemporaries in distinguishing what they called "the spirit of the age", and what I, for economy of discussion, have chosen to call by the conventional though ambiguous term 'romantic'" (*NS*, 11–12).

28. Note that this is precisely the point where Abrams inserts a critical comment on Lovejoy's approach. This is not surprising, given that Abrams's discussion in fact confirms Lovejoy's stress on "das Ganze, Eigentümlichkeit, Streben." As far as I can see, the difference of opinion that Abrams assumes to exist is based on a misunderstanding. Although Abrams seem to think otherwise, I think that Lovejoy would agree that the romantic ideal did not concern "plenitude as such" or "sheer diversity," but an "organized unity" characterized by "the most inclusive integration" of diversity (*NS*, 185–86).

29. See Coleridge's famous lines about what he learned from the "mystics" (i.e., Böhme in particular): "They contributed to keep alive the *heart* in the *head*; gave me an indistinct, yet stirring and working presentiment, that all the products of the mere *reflective* faculty partook of DEATH, and were as the rattling twigs and sprays in winter, into which a sap was yet to be propelled from some root to which I had not penetrated, if they were to afford my soul either food or shelter" (*Biographia Literaria*, ed. J. Shawcross [Oxford, 1907], 1:98).

30. Quoted by *NS*, 27. Note that, as Abrams remarks, the original MS has "mind" instead of "intellect" (first line).

31. This is emphasized with particular force by *NS*, 88–92.

32. Cf. C. de Deugd, *Het metafysische grondpatroon van het romantische literaire denken: De fenomenologie van een geestesgesteldheid* (Groningen, 1971).

33. Abrams is particularly interested in esoteric speculation about "the myth . . . of primordial man as a cosmic androgyne" (*NS*, 155), and concludes that "the myth of sexual division, opposition, and reconjunction . . . is at the center of occult thought" (*NS*, 169). The relevance to romanticism, however, is suggested rather than demonstrated.

34. Note that, not surprisingly, Abrams feels compelled to explicitly refute the suspicion that "elements derived from the esoteric tradition [are], *ipso facto*, aberrations which discredit the writings in which they occur" (although he hastens to distance himself from the "lunatic fringe of goldmakers, practicing magicians, and spiritual libertines") (*NS*, 170).

35. In Lovejoy's case, this is particularly remarkable, because he used to emphasize that conventional distinctions between "major" and "minor" thinkers are irrelevant to the history of ideas (*Great Chain*, 19–20).

36. Zimmermann, *Weltbild des jungen Goethe*, 1:102. A typical example is Ehregott

Daniel Colberg's polemic against *Das Platonisch-Hermetisches* [sic] *Christenthum* (Frankfurt and Leipzig, 1690/1691).

37. Ernest Lee Tuveson, *The Avatars of Thrice Great Hermes: An Approach to Romanticism* (Lewisburg, London, and Toronto, 1982). Henceforth abbreviated in the text and notes as *A*, followed by the page number.

38. Some more examples: "Only many centuries after they were written did the full meaning of the books of the *Hermetica* become evident" (*A*, 44); "only after the world-view had changed, and society itself had been transformed, could the full reality of the message of Hermes Trismegistus be released" (*A*, 45).

39. It is mostly forgotten, however, that this metaphysical position was developed under the evident influence of esoteric traditions. The term panentheism was introduced by the German idealist philosopher, Freemason, and Swedenborgian K. C. F. Krause (1781–1832). The applicability of the term to western esotericism is confirmed by Karl R. H. Frick, *Die Erleuchteten* (Graz, 1973), 115–16. About Krause's Masonic background, cf. Horst E. Miers, *Lexikon des Geheimwissens* (Augsburg, 1980), 237–38. About Krause's Swedenborgianism, see Robert H.Kirven, "Swedenborg and Kant Revisited: The Long Shadow of Kant's Attack and a New Response," in *Swedenborg and his Influence*, ed. Erland J. Brock et al. (Bryn Athyn, 1988), 106–7.

40. See especially CH XI.20–22.

41. Cf. for example Gode-von Aesch, *Natural Science;* Sladek, *Fragmente;* Faivre and Zimmermann, *Epochen der Naturmystik;* Antoine Faivre, *Philosophie de la nature (physique sacrée et théosophie, XVIIIe–XIXe siècles)* (Paris, 1996).

42. A good discussion is found in T.J.Diffey, "The Roots of Imagination: The Philosophical Context," in *The Romantics*, ed. Stephen Prickett (London, 1981).

43. Diffey, "Roots," 169.

44. See for instance Antoine Faivre, "L'imagination créatrice (fonction magique et fondement mythique de l'image)," *Revue d'Allemagne* (Strasbourg) 3, no. 2 (April–June 1981); Alain Godet, *Nun was ist die Imagination anderst als ein Sonn im Menschen: Studien zu einem Zentralbegriff des magischen Denkens* (Zürich, 1982); I. P. Couliano, *Eros and Magic in the Renaissance* (Chicago and London, 1987).

45. One may think of the works of C. G. Jung about alchemy.

46. The concept of the *mundus imaginalis* was introduced by Henry Corbin and has strongly influenced thinking about the imagination among scholars of esotericism, as shown in Faivre's way of treating "mediations" and "imagination" as closely related. For Corbin's perspective, see for instance his *Creative Imagination in the Sufism of Ibn 'Arabi* (Princeton, 1969), 179–83; idem, "*Mundus Imaginalis* or the Imaginary and the Imaginal," *Spring*, 1972.

47. See Frances Yates, *Giordano Bruno and the Hermetic Tradition* (London and Chicago, 1964); idem, *The Art of Memory* (London, 1966).

48. See Stanley Jeyaraja Tambiah, *Magic, Science, Religion, and the Scope of Rationality* (Cambridge, 1990).

49. Cf. also Isaiah Berlin, "The Counter-Enlightenment," in *Against the Current: Essays in the History of Ideas* (1979; reprint, Harmondsworth, 1982).

50. Cf. the last part of Hanegraaff, *New Age Religion*.

51. See the acute observations on this point in Arthur McCalla, "Illuminism and French Romantic Philosophies of History," in *Western Esotericism and the Science of Religion*, ed. A. Faivre and W. J. Hanegraaff, Gnostica, vol. 2 (Louvain, 1998); and cf. my "In den beginne was de toorn: Het demonische bij Jacob Böhme," in *Kleine encyclopedie van de Toorn*, edited by Ab de Jong and Aleid de Jong, Utrechtse Theologische Reeks 21 (Utrecht, 1993). See also the brilliant analyses by Pierre Deghaye, esp. *La naissance de Dieu, ou la doctrine de Jacob Boehme* (Paris, 1985).

52. Jacob Needleman, "Introduction II," in *Modern Esoteric Spirituality*, ed. Antoine Faivre and Jacob Needleman (New York, 1992), xxviii.

53. Hanegraaff, "In den beginne was de Toorn," 46–47.

CHAPTER 15

WILLIAM BLAKE AND HIS GNOSTIC MYTHS

JOS VAN MEURS

During his life and for a long time after his death the poet-engraver-painter William Blake (1757–1827) remained virtually unknown. Today he is one of the most famous of English poets. His hand-printed texts have gained a unique place in European art for the special effects of his "illuminated printing." The poetic texts, interspersed with illustrations, were engraved on copperplates and the prints were later hand-colored (see plate 1). In this laborious manner he produced limited numbers of his own poems. He never found a regular publisher and his hardworking life was largely spent in great poverty. Only a small volume of youthful poems and his last work, a series of illustrations for the Book of Job, passed through the hands of a printer.

It was not until 1893 that his collected poems were published by the poet W. B. Yeats. In the course of our century Blake has become famous for a small number of short poems in the early *Songs of Innocence and Experience* (engraved 1789–94) and for the playfully satirical, yet deeply serious prose work *The Marriage of Heaven and Hell* (1790–93). His later poetry is much less accessible. It consists of a series of long symbolical poems, the so-called prophetic books. They contain such radical criticism of contemporary beliefs and thinking, and they differ so much from what in his days were considered acceptable forms of art,

---

This is the English version of an article originally published in Dutch in G. Quispel, ed., *De Hermetische Gnosis in de loop der eeuwen* (Baarn, 1992), 539–78. Quotations from the *Corpus Hermeticum*, Jacob Boehme, Paracelsus, and Swedenborg, in the English that Blake himself will have seen, have been taken from the books by Raine and Hirst quoted in the text. The illustrations have been derived from: Kathleen Raine, *William Blake* (London, 1970) (plates 1, 4, 5, 6, 7, 8, 10); D. V. Erdman, *The Illuminated Blake* (London, 1975) (plates 2, 3, 9).

Thus wept the Angel voice & as he wept the terrible blasts
Of trumpets, blew a loud alarm across the Atlantic deep.
No trumpets answer; no reply of clarions or of fifes,
Silent the Colonies remain and refuse the loud alarm.

On those vast shady hills between America & Albions shore;
Now barrd out by the Atlantic sea; calld Atlantean hills;
Because from their bright summits you may pass to the Golden world
An ancient palace, archetype of mighty Emperies,
Rears its immortal pinnacles, built in the forest of God
By Ariston the king of beauty for his stolen bride.

Here on their magic seats the thirteen Angels sat perturbd
For clouds from the Atlantic hover oer the solemn roof.

Plate 1. Orc, spirit of rebellious energy

that they met with no response whatever. His work was not understood even by the few good friends who supported Blake and his wife by buying as many of his paintings and separate prints as they could.

The originality of Blake's art has long stood in the way of its appreciation. In 1809 he organized a private exhibition of his larger tempera paintings in the hope of gaining some recognition. With total lack of sympathy for Blake's symbolic art the reviewer of the leading cultural magazine, *The Examiner*, called him "an unfortunate lunatic," whose work was nothing but "nonsense" and "unintelligibleness" (17 September 1809). The idea that Blake was a very nice man but an "insane genius" has persisted into our own days, although in the meantime a great many scholarly studies and interpretations have clearly shown the profound intelligence of his imaginative symbolical vision of God, man, and society, and the extent to which his idiosyncratic religious mythology was rooted in very influential, if unorthodox, traditions in Western thinking.

Blake was convinced that through materialistic science and philosophy, as represented by Bacon, Newton, and Locke, together with the rationalism of deistic belief, man had lost sight of the reality of the spirit. He placed himself in the tradition of the Old Testament prophets and saw it as his duty to warn his contemporaries. At the beginning of his last great poem *Jerusalem*, Blake addressed his readers, Christians, Jews, and Deists:

> Trembling I sit day and night; my friends are astonished at me.
> Yet they forgive my wanderings. I rest not from my great task!
> To open the Eternal Worlds, to open the immortal Eyes
> Of Man inwards into the Worlds of Thought—into Eternity
> Ever expanding in the Bosom of God, the Human Imagination.
> (K. 623)[1]

Blake was not the only artist-prophet of his time, though he was no doubt the most pronounced visionary. In his well-known study of tradition and revolution in romantic literature, *Natural Supernaturalism* (1971), M. H. Abrams classes Blake with "poet-prophets" and "philosopher-seers" like Wordsworth, Shelley, Coleridge, Schelling, Hegel, Hölderlin, and Novalis.

BLAKE'S SOURCES

Blake was self-taught and received his only formal education in the drawing school of Henry Pars between the ages of ten and fourteen. Yet, judging from the authors he mentions in his work and from what his friends say about him, he must have been a well-read man who taught himself various languages. Frederick Tatham tells us that he owned "books well-thumbed and dirtied by his graving hands in Latin, Greek, Hebrew, French, and Italian, besides a large collection of the mystical writers."[2] His thinking was stamped by four great traditions: the Bible, the great English authors, Neoplatonism, and Gnostic-Hermetic mysticism.

In characteristic, very personal fashion Blake listed his intellectual masters in some verse lines inserted in a letter to his friend the sculptor John Flaxman (12 September 1800):

> Now my lot in the Heavens is this, Milton lov'd me in
> childhood & shew'd me his face.
> Ezra came with Isaiah the Prophet, but Shakespeare in
> riper years gave me his hand;
> Paracelsus & Behmen appear'd to me. . . .

All his writings are in the first place steeped in the Bible. With some exaggeration he says to Crabb Robinson, a literary man who recorded in his diary some conversations with Blake in his old age, that "all he knew is in the Bible." But, the diarist immediately adds, "[H]e understands the Bible in the spiritual sense." That is to say that it is Blake's own, often allegorical, reading, or, as he says to more orthodox readers in the uncompleted poem *The Everlasting Gospel:*

> The Vision of Christ that thou dost see
> Is my Vision's Greatest Enemy:
> Thine has a great hook nose like thine,
> Mine has a snub nose like to mine.
>
> . . . .
> Thy Heaven doors are my Hell Gates.
>
> . . . .
> Both read the Bible day and night,
> But thou read'st black where I read white.
>
> (K. 748)

He derives his names, figures and symbols in particular from the prophetic books of the Old Testament, while his later work centers more and more on an unorthodox Christ figure.

Blake found a variety of further intellectual stimuli in the group of young progressive artists and writers who were his friends in London at the beginning of his own creative period in the 1780s. After 1787, when Blake's close friend Thomas Taylor started his series of translations of Plato and the Neoplatonists, the philosophy of Plato must have become an important influence.

Of equal importance is Blake's acquaintance with a number of writers from the esoteric tradition, which, by the side of the Christian and Greek mainstreams, influenced so many independent thinkers in Europe. Blake derived key ideas in his early work from the eighteenth-century mystic Emmanuel Swedenborg and in particular from the mystical writings of Jacob Boehme (also called Behmen in England), who has been called the first modern Gnostic. Boehme's religious thinking had a large following in Protestant England from as early as the middle of the seventeenth century. Blake read him in the reissue of the English translation of Boehme's writings that appeared in London between 1764 and 1781. Blake also knew other "mystical writers." We saw how he himself mentions the alchemist Paracelsus as one of his masters and we may take it that he read works of the Kabbalists Robert Fludd and Cornelius Agrippa. And no doubt Blake was acquainted with the ultimate sources of alchemy, Kabbala, and esoteric mysticism in the earliest Gnostic and Hermetic writings.

As a reaction against eighteenth-century rationalism and the mechanistic world picture of the new sciences, there arose in Blake's age among romantic thinkers and artists a renewed interest in the Hermetic philosophy that during the Renaissance had been so enthusiastically received in Europe. Blake may have read the translation of the *Corpus Hermeticum* that as early as 1650 was published by John Everard in London.

As for Gnosticism, it is again Crabb Robinson who recorded a conversation with Blake about the Gnostic idea that the creator of this world is not the highest God, but a lower god or demiurge. Blake had asserted that material nature is the work of the devil, to which Robinson had made strong objections:

> On my obtaining from him the declaration that the Bible was the work of God, I referred to the commencement of *Genesis*—"In the

beginning God created the Heaven & Earth." But I gained nothing
by this, for I was triumphantly told that this God was not Jehovah,
but the Elohim, & the doctrine of the Gnostics repeated with sufficient consistency to silence one so unlearned as myself.[3]

In Blake's time good summaries of the Gnostic myths appeared in the
great survey of church history by Joseph Priestley, *A History of Early
Opinions Concerning Jesus Christ* (1786) and earlier in the translation of J.
L. von Mosheim's *An Ecclesiastical History* (1765).

It was an age in which Western man began to realize that important
themes in the myths and religions of people all over the world showed
striking resemblances. We know that Blake read the first English translation of the *Bhagavad Gita*, published in 1785 by Charles Williams, whose
portrait Blake painted. We shall see that for Blake "All Religions are
One," because "all deities reside in the human breast" (K. 153). He
writes about universal man and his mythical figures relate to gods and
symbols from various cultures.

Serious research into the sources of Blake's intellectual background
was only started in the 1950s. For the Hermetic-Gnostic tradition this
was undertaken by two English scholars in particular: Kathleen Raine
studied in detail all the works that we know or may suppose that Blake
had read in the fields of Neoplatonism, mysticism, and alchemy. The
results of her research were gathered in the two volumes of *Blake and
Tradition* (1969),[4] magnificently printed with many illustrations in the
Bollingen series of Princeton University Press. The text is that of her
Mellon lectures delivered in Washington in 1962. The other pioneering
study is the erudite book by Désirée Hirst on the influence of Kabbalah,
Boehme, and Swedenborg: *Hidden Riches: Traditional Symbolism from the
Renaissance to Blake* (1964).[5] Between them Raine and Hirst have con-
vincingly shown that the extent of Blake's reading has been greatly un-
derestimated.

GNOSTIC AND HERMETIC STARTING POINTS

In 1788 Blake engraved the first plates with texts of his own. In these he
tersely formulated in a series of aphorisms his opinions about religion in

general. The two tracts, entitled *There is No Natural Religion* and *All Religions are One* contain among others the following statements:

> The true faculty of knowing must be the faculty which experiences.
> As all men are alike (tho' infinitely various), So all Religions . . . have
> one source. The True Man is the source, he being the Poetic Genius.
> The body or outward form of Man is derived from the Poetic Genius.
> (K. 98)

By "Poetic Genius" or "Spirit of Prophecy" Blake means man's creative genius, his divine core, which he will later call "The Divine Imagination." And "natural" in Blake always means earthly, material, non-spiritual.

Blake's starting point is Gnosis pure and simple: knowledge of reality is based on the personal, inner experience of man, "the faculty which experiences," and not on sense perception or imposed dogma. In essence, the "True Man" or "Universal Man" is a spiritual being, inspired by the biblical "spirit that knoweth all things." Material life in the body and senses, what Blake calls "natural" or "vegetative" life, is only an earthly limitation and covering of the spiritual essence that is "infinite" and "eternal." Man can intuitively perceive and know his essence because "Man's perceptions are not bounded by organs of perception" (K. 98).

Blake is very radical in this. Already as a boy he had trusted his second sight, and later he writes in a matter-of-fact and humorous manner about his "Vision or Imagination of All that Exists." In a verse letter, for instance, he says:

> For double the Vision my Eyes do see,
> And a double vision is always with me.
> With my inward Eye 'tis an old Man grey;
> With my outward, a Thistle across my way.

Or in the famous passage at the end of his elaborate commentary on a large painting of the Last Judgment:

> I assert for My Self that I do not behold the outward Creation & that
> to me it is hindrance & not Action; it is as the Dirt upon my feet, No

part of me. "What," it will be Question'd, "When the Sun rises, do you not see a round disk of fire somewhat 'like a Guinea?'" O no, no, I see an Innumerable company of the Heavenly host crying "Holy, Holy, Holy is the Lord Almighty." I question not my Corporeal or Vegetative Eye any more than I would question a Window concerning a Sight. I look thro' it & not with it. (K. 617)

Blake was in the habit of scribbling approving or critical remarks in the margin of the books he studied. In his copy of Berkeley's philosophical essay *Siris* (1744) about the fire of the sun as the creative source, he writes some significant notes of agreement. Several times Berkeley refers to the ancient Hermetic texts ("the Aegyptians") as a source of statements about the spiritual character of the universe. Berkeley writes:

> Plato and Aristotle considered God as abstracted or distinct from the natural world. But the Aegyptians considered God and nature as making one whole, or all things together as making one universe. (K.774)

Blake comments:

> They also consider'd God as abstracted or distinct from the Imaginative World, but Jesus, as also Abraham & David, consider'd God as Man in the Spiritual or Imaginative Vision. (K. 774)

And an annotation to another passage in Berkeley runs: "Man is All Imagination. God is Man & exists in us & we in him" (K. 775).

"Reason" and "Imagination" are sharply opposed by Blake.

> The Nature of Visionary Fancy, or Imagination, is very little Known, & the Eternal nature & permanence of its ever Existent Images is consider'd less permanent than the things of Vegetative & Generative nature. (K. 605)

What Human Reason does is nothing but ordering and analyzing the transitory material world of sense perceptions by means of abstraction and reduction to general rules. It is the "Human Imagination," however, which discerns the spiritual essence that is eternal and infinite in every living detail—the "minute particulars" of the created world in Blake's well-known phrase: "He who sees the Infinite in all things, sees

God. He who sees the Ratio only, sees himself only." And, Blake immediately adds: "Therefore God becomes as we are, that we may be as he is" (K. 98). This might be taken in terms of orthodox Christian ideas about incarnation and redemption, but what Blake means, in the context of his critique of rationalized religion, is what was formulated in the famous words of the tenth book of the *Corpus Hermeticum*:[6] "For Man is a Divine living thing. . . . Wherefore we must be bold to say: That an Earthly Man is a mortal God, and that the Heavenly God is an immortal Man" (CH X.24, 25).

We shall see that Blake's myth shares other basic features with Gnosticism and Hermeticism:

— the creation, as part of the Fall, is due to a lower god or demiurge, who together with other gods has emanated from the androgynous highest God;

— the original man, the Anthropos, is created in God's spiritual image;

— the separation of the original androgynous unity into male and female elements causes the descent of the spirit into matter as well as the disintegration and fragmentation of earthly existence;

— however, if man becomes aware of his carrying God's spirit within himself, the spiritual unity may be restored on the mystical level, and the soul may be reunited with God.

It is important to note that Blake stresses some principles in which Hermeticism differs from Platonism and Gnosis. Man and his world are a fundamental part of the divine cosmos, since everything is permeated with spirit. Blake affirms the Hermetic rule "as above, so below" in his saying: "God is in the lowest effects as well as in the highest causes" (K. 87). This means, in Hermeticism and for Blake, that earthly existence is valued more positively than in the Platonic and Gnostic vision, since matter and spirit are complementary. The world may not be faultless, but it is "beautifully made," says Hermes (CH X.10). Blake sees our existence in this sublunary vale of tears, like the Gnostics, as a "sleep" or "death," but at the same time he writes lyrical passages about the beauty of the world seen with "the Eye of Imagination." In Blake's later myth the creative god Los and his sons are described as "Creating form and beauty around the dark region of sorrow." And helped by his feminine emanation Enitharmon, Los builds within this chaotic, fallen world "the great city of Golgonooza," the city of human culture, which in its fourfold perfection is symbolic of the manner in which mankind may participate in the divine creativity. Or, to put it differently, this is how the divine spirit expresses itself in man and in matter. "Our Lord is the word of God & every thing on earth is the word of God & in its essence is God" (K. 87). Or as Hermes says: "Whether thou speak of Matter or Body, or Essence, know that all these are Acts of God. . . . And in the whole, there is nothing that is not God" (CH XII.23). When Los begins to build his city, Blake lets him simply say: "God is within and without: he is even in the depths of Hell" (K. 631).

The studies of Raine and Hirst have demonstrated how many ideas, images, and symbols in the work of an unorthodox religious thinker like Blake, who is essentially a Christian, may be traced back to their possible sources in writers of the Western Gnostic-Hermetic tradition or to the original Alexandrian texts on which these are based. Of course, Blake with his critical mind and mythopoeic imagination, may on his own have arrived at age-old archetypal insights and he need not necessarily have derived everything from predecessors. But it is important for a proper understanding of Blake's poetic and artistic works to realize to what extent they are permeated with this fundamental inheritance of Western religious thinking.

In what follows a number of individual poems and etchings will be examined in order to show how Blake embodied basic Gnostic and Hermetic elements in his myths.

INNOCENCE AND EXPERIENCE

The *Songs of Innocence* were the first poems Blake engraved and printed in 1789. The drawings around the poems are still simple decorations that do not yet have the symbolic force of the illustrations in the later texts. Originally meant as a series of idyllic verses for children about feelings of happiness and the joy of living, as in *The Lamb* (plate 2), unavoidably, in the course of writing, intimations of the shadowy sides

Plate 2. From *Songs of Innocence*

of existence crept in: references to child labor in *The Chimney Sweeper*, the treatment of charity children in *Holy Thursday*, slavery in *The Little Black Boy*. And before long Blake was composing contrastive counter-poems, sometimes under the same title, expressing the bitter reality of what people do to each other.

In 1794 he collected more than forty of these short poems in *The Songs of Innocence and Experience, Shewing the Two Contrary States of the Human Soul*. With their concentrated forms and pregnant symbolism some of these later poems, such as *The Tyger* and the two versions of *The Divine Image*, grew into powerful poetic expressions of the great human and divine problems of good and evil. We find the "innocent" images of a humane God and of divine humanity in *The Divine Image* (see, for the text, plate 3), whereas in *A Divine Image* we hear a bitter accusation against man's inhumanity.

> *A Divine Image*
>
> Cruelty has a Human Heart,
> And Jealousy a Human Face—
> Terror, the Human Form Divine,
> And Secrecy, the Human Dress.
>
> The Human Dress is forged Iron,
> The Human Form, a Fiery Forge,
> The Human Face, a Furnace sealed,
> The Human Heart, its hungry Gorge.
>
> (K. 221)

Note that these two poems do not simply express the contrast between paradisal goodness and earthly evil. Paradoxically all qualities, negative and positive, listed in both poems are part of "the Human Form Divine."

INFLUENCE OF SWEDENBORG

Blake's religious background was that of the Protestant Dissenters who, following the tradition of the seventeenth-century Puritan sects, in matters of faith trusted their own "inner light" and sought the "God within."

Plate 3. From *Songs of Innocence*

His father and his brother James became members of the New Jerusalem Church, founded in 1789 by followers of the Swedish mystic Emmanuel Swedenborg. For some time Blake sympathized with them, but he was too independent-minded to join a group. He was, however, permanently influenced by some of Swedenborg's ideas. Central to Blake's thinking are his notions of the "Divine Humanity" and of the spiritual essence of the "True Man." Both were directly derived from Swedenborg's "Divine Man." Blake endorses Swedenborg's statement: "God is a very Man. In all Heavens there is no other idea of God than that of a Man"[7] with his own gloss:

> God is a man, not because he is so perciev'd by man, but because he is the creator of man.
>
> (K. 90)

In *The Everlasting Gospel* Blake puts this very succinctly, when he lets God say to Christ:

> Thou art a Man; God is no more;
> Thy own Humanity learn to adore,
> For that is my Spirit of Life.
>
> (K. 750)

Or elsewhere:

> God is a Man & exists in us & we in him.
>
> (K. 775)

Swedenborg's influence on Blake has been excellently discussed by Kathleen Raine in the introductory chapter to her book *The Human Face of God* (1982), an extensive analysis of Blake's illustrations to the Book of Job.

Hirst points out[8] that Swedenborg probably derived his conception of the "divine man" from Boehme's "Heavenly Adam" and from the Adam Kadmon of the Kabbalists, with whom both Swedenborg and Boehme were familiar. And the lineage may be traced further back to the image of the Anthropos in the Gnostic writings and the Hermetica, and ultimately to Ezekiel's vision of the glory of the Lord in the likeness of a man (Ezek. 1:26). This leads us back to Blake, who made a marvelous watercolor painting of Ezekiel's vision (plate 4).

Plate 4. Ezekiel's vision of the four living creatures in the likeness of man

Other Gnostic notions Blake may initially have met with in Swedenborg and that he afterwards developed through his reading of Boehme,
of other mystics, and of the Hermetica, are the concept of the androgyny
of God; cosmic man seen as a unity of masculine and feminine elements;
and the symbolical analogies between the things above and below.

Yet, however much influenced by Swedenborg, Blake soon reacted
against his conventional views on the absolute division between angels
and devils, and of a God who keeps an easy balance between good and
evil. In his *Treatise Concerning Heaven and Hell* (London, 1778) Swedenborg says: "[H]eaven and hell are to each other as two contraries in mutual
opposition, from the action and reaction of which results that equilib-
rium by which all things subsist."[9]

In his own prose treatise with the ironical title *The Marriage of Heaven
and Hell*, Blake parodies with merciless humor the self-satisfied dialogues
that his master Swedenborg carries on with angels and devils. And at
the same time Blake asks radical questions about the nature of evil and
about God's necessarily ambivalent attitude toward evil. Blake develops herein very personal religious views that no doubt spring from his
own experience and thinking, but that are also related to the ambivalent conception of God found in Boehme's Gnostic mysticism and in
the ancient Gnostic texts.

THE MARRIAGE OF HEAVEN AND HELL

In the title page of his *Marriage of Heaven and Hell*, Blake has drawn
numerous couples embracing each other lovingly (plate 5). Of the first
pair at the bottom, one seems to issue from the flames of hell and the
other from a bank of clouds. From an earthly underworld, souls that
seem to meet in pairs float upward to an earthly upperworld with waving trees and loving couples, while above this level birds strive to climb
still higher. This gives in visual form Blake's symbolic expression of the
spiritual theme of the twenty-seven plates of this inspired piece of writing that in our century has become one of the most famous works in
English literature. In contrast with the duality of body and soul, devil
and god, characteristic of Platonic and Christian thinking, Blake proclaims
the relativity of good and evil, the unity of all things, the "marriage" of

Plate 5. Title page

the oppositions of "heaven" and "hell." And these are not viewed as states contradicting each other ("negations"), but as the antipoles ("contraries") that cause the very energies of life to flow.

Blake takes devilish delight in turning conventional religious notions upside down:

> Without Contraries is no progression. Attraction and Repulsion, Reason and Energy, Love and Hate, are necessary to Human existence. From these contraries spring what the religious call Good and Evil. Good is the passive that obeys Reason. Evil is the active springing from Energy. (K. 149)

All "bibles or sacred codes," says Blake, are mistaken in separating the soul from the body by attributing reason to the soul (= good) and connecting energy with the body (= evil). Blake radically poses the primacy of the spirit or soul and of spiritual energy. This means on the one hand that "Man has no body distinct from his soul" and on the other that "Energy is the only life and is from the body" (K. 149). The human mind, "Reason," is in itself not valued negatively by Blake, but it serves only to keep the spiritual energy within bounds. In Blake's eyes human beings do much harm to their own lives and those of others by imposing on them so-called rational rules and codes of "Moral Virtue," and by thinking that "God will torment man in eternity for following his energies." On the contrary, Blake maintains, "Energy is eternal delight." With sharp psychological insight Blake diagnoses, as the abuse of "reason," what usually happens when man tyrannizes over man.

> Those who restrain desire do so because theirs is weak enough to be restrained; and the restrainer or reason usurps its place and governs the unwilling. (K. 149)

This gives us one of the two main themes of the *Marriage*: people should let themselves be guided more by the "energies of natural desire" than by imposed moral codes. Jesus broke the rules of the Pharisees and was "all virtue," because he acted from impulse, not from "rules." In *Paradise Lost* Milton could not but depict the Old Testament God as the unsympathetic tyrant he really is, while Satan became the true hero of his epic, "because he [Milton] was a true poet, and of the Devil's party without knowing it" (K. 150).

Blake promises to write the "Bible of Hell" and, for a start, gives us a collection of colorful, provocative *Proverbs of Hell* (K. 150–52), the source of most present-day Blake quotations. He is a master of the pithy phrase. His rejection of all forms of social and religious repression is compressed in "Prisons are built with stones of law. Brothels with bricks of Religion." The limitations of the normal fainthearted human perspective on the questions of good and evil are vigorously exposed in:

> The roaring of lions, the howling of wolves, the raging of the stormy sea, and the destructive sword, are portions of eternity, too great for the eye of man.

The vital energy of lion, devil, and serpent is opposed to the stifling "laws" of tyrants, kings, churches, parents, and schoolmasters.

> The tygers of wrath are wiser than the horses of instruction.

The free revolutionary spirit must burst all constricting life-denying bonds. Small wonder that the hippies and the counterculture of the sixties found many of their slogans in these proverbs. Of course, they happily overlooked that, although Blake in essence remained true to these ideas till the end of his life, he considerably modified them after 1790. In the light of what happened in France after the Revolution his early belief "in the necessity for complete moral individualism" naturally could not last, as Stevenson remarks in his commentary in the *Complete Poems*.[10]

The second main idea of the *Marriage* will become the principal theme of Blake's later work. It is summed up in the dictum: "Everything possible to be believed is an image of truth." The "Imagination" is the divine quality in man that allows every individual to grasp the "truth." In former "ages of imagination" people still knew this; in the Age of Enlightenment, the Age of Reason, God and men have grown apart. The "Human Imagination" is the deepest source of Blake's conception of God. In the margin of his copy of Berkeley's *Siris* beside Berkeley's "God knoweth all things, as pure mind or intellect," Blake later writes his own note: "Imagination or the Human Eternal Body in Man" (K. 773), and on the following page: "Imagination or the Divine Body in Every Man." For Blake "the Divine Image or Imagination" is

eternal and infinite. It gives God a "human face" and allows fallen man
to be spiritually reunited with God.

This brings to mind the famous passage in the first book of the *Corpus Hermeticum*, to which Berkeley refers. Poimandres says to his pupil:

> I am that light, the Mind, thy God . . . and that bright and lightful
> Word from the Mind of the Son of God. . . . That which in thee seeth
> and heareth, the Word of the Lord . . . and the Mind of the Father, . . .
> differ not one from the other; and the Union of these is Life. (CH I.6)

Later Blake will identify this spirit of "Divine Humanity" with Christ
in his "Universal Humanity," and together they will simply become
"Jesus the Imagination," when he says:

> All things are comprehended in their Eternal Forms in the divine
> body of the Saviour, the True Vine of Eternity, the Human Imagina-
> tion. (K. 606)

INFLUENCE OF JACOB BOEHME

In chapter 15 of *Blake and Tradition*, Kathleen Raine demonstrates with
many quotations from Boehme and Paracelsus that Blake must have
encountered many of his key terms in the English translations of these
writers. The idea of the marriage between heaven and hell, for instance,
is expressed in this passage from Paracelsus:

> A Concordance of Celestial Virtues may be found with us in the vally
> of darknesse (said Hermes). . . . That which is beneath, is like that
> which is above, and the things beneath are so related to the things
> above as Man and Wife. (Quoted in *BT,* 1:361)

The conception of the world as a unified composite of antithetical forces
originated with the Greek philosophers Heraclitus and Empedocles.
Blake knew of their ideas through the Christian Kabbalists Fludd and
Agrippa and the works of the philosopher Berkeley. But it is probably
the mystic Boehme who, as Blake himself indicates, particularly influenced him in this respect.

Unlike the Greek nature philosophers and the later alchemists, Boehme believed that the unity of the One has it roots, not in the polarities of the material world but in the oppositions within the human mind. Nature is merely a manifestation of the spirit. Boehme distinguished three principles: God as the fire of the eternal spirit, the Son as the light of heaven that issues from the spiritual world, and the transitory material world. The fire of the Father, Boehme says, is the abyss of Hell and the light of the Son is Heaven, but both have one single ground:

> For the God of the holy World, and the God of the dark World, are not two Gods; there is but one only God. He himself is the whole Being; he is Evil and Good, Heaven and Hell; Light and Darkness; Eternity and Time; Beginning and End. Where his Love is in any Thing, there his Anger is manifest.

Both Boehme and Blake see at the same time in God's fire what is usually called "evil" or "hell" *and* the energy that makes all life possible.

> God is also an Angry Zealous or Jealous God, and a consuming Fire; and in that source standeth the Abyss of Hell, the anger and malice of all the Devils, as also the Poison of all Creatures: and it is found that without poison and eagerness there is no Life: and from thence ariseth all contrariety and strife; and it is found, that the strongest and most eager, is the most useful and profitable: for it maketh all things, and is the only cause of all mobility and life. (Quoted in *BT,* 1:363)

It is clear what the authority is behind Blake's provocative (and Gnostic) claim that the Jehovah of the Old Testament is none other than "he who dwells in flaming fire" and that "in the Book of *Job* Milton's Messiah is called Satan" (K. 150). Like Boehme, Blake sees devils as bearers of energy, of divine fire and of "the fury of spiritual existence." That is why he can say that "Energy is the only life and is from the body," for "body" is not used by Blake in the material sense; what really exists is not matter, but the living spirit. In contrast with Platonic dualism, God and nature, soul and body, are not distinct for Blake and Boehme.

> Man has no body distinct from his soul, for that called body is a portion of soul discerned by the five senses, the chief inlets of soul in this age. (K. 149)

The senses merely serve the spirit, they are the eye of the imagination.

> Forms must be apprehended by Sense or the Eye of the Imagination. Man is all Imagination. God is Man & exists in us & we in him. (Marginal note in Berkeley, K. 775)

THE TYGER

Blake never thinks of religion, philosophy, and the history of ideas as abstractions. For him these are human experiences that may be expressed in poetic images. In the prose and poetry of the *Marriage of Heaven and Hell* Blake wrote, from various perspectives, a sort of manifesto of the monism of the Hermetic *Tabula Smaragdina* and of the philosophy of Paracelsus and Boehme: the cosmic "contraries" issue from the One, and they will again resolve in it (BT, 1:100). In Blake's most famous poem, *The Tyger*, he has given us in unforgettable concrete imagery an emotional embodiment of the intellectual paradoxes inherent in the Gnostic-Hermetic vision:

The Tyger

> Tyger! Tyger! burning bright
> In the forests of the night,
> What immortal hand or eye
> Could frame thy fearful symmetry?
> In what distant deeps or skies
> Burnt the fire of thine eyes?
> On what wings dare he aspire?
> What the hand dare sieze the fire?
>
> And what shoulder, & what art,
> Could twist the sinews of thy heart?
> And when thy heart began to beat,
> What dread hand? & what dread feet?
>
> What the hammer? What the chain?
> In what furnace was thy brain?
> What the anvil? what dread grasp
> Dare its deadly terrors clasp?

When the stars threw down their spears,
And watered heaven with their tears,
Did he smile his work to see?
Did he who made the Lamb make thee?

Tyger! Tyger! burning bright
In the forests of the night,
What immortal hand or eye
Dare frame thy fearful symmetry?

(K. 214)

Blake's open questions in the first place evoke the sense of a mysterious, powerful and terrifying creator of destructive forces in a dark world, embodied by the Tyger, always ready to pounce on us. In Blake's poems savage animals, forests, trees, fire, and smoke are parts of the "vegetative" natural world of "Hell or Energy," created by the "God of this World," whom Blake calls "a very cruel Being" (K. 617).

In the counterpoem *The Lamb* (see, for the text, plate 2) the symbols of the child and the lamb suggest a maker who manifests himself as the Son, the Lamb of God, Boehme's second principle of the eternal light of God that also shines in man. The answer to the question "Little Lamb, who made thee?" is not hard to find. But what answer can be given to that most difficult of all religious questions posed by Blake in *The Tyger*: "Did he who made the Lamb make thee?" If we tend to say yes, we are left with the problem of what sort of "cruel being" this high creator must be. If we tend to say no, there must have been more than one creator.

Perhaps Blake suggests the latter possibility by asking "What hand dare sieze the fire?" and by replacing "could" in the first stanza by "dare" in the last. Is there by the side of the highest God a lesser "maker" who like Prometheus steals the creative fire? In Boehme's cosmology, as disclosed in *Aurora*, the seven divine "fountain spirits" are swept along in Lucifer's fall, but they keep their creativity and they shape the corrupt world with all the forms of evil in it, including "that Beast, which had most of the Fire" (quoted in BT, 2:12).

If Blake thought of a lesser creative god, it may, of course, also have been the demiurge of Plato's *Timaeus*, who created the earthly world as an imitation of the eternal world. The Platonist negative view of earthly existence, however, does not tally with Blake's more ambiguous vision.

Kathleen Raine argues that the "maker" of the Tyger rather shows features of the demiurge in Gnostic and Hermetic writings: neither completely good, nor completely evil. Blake may have got his knowledge of Gnosis from Mosheim's history of the church and he would have read there that Jewish Gnostics believed that a demiurge had arisen from the eternal world of the Pleroma. This lesser creator-god would be identical with the God of the Old Testament and is depicted as a mixture of good and bad qualities. For Christian Gnostics the coming of Christ, son of the supreme God, meant that the reign of this lesser god had ended.

But perhaps, in this poem, Blake was inspired in particular by passages from the Hermetica. In his writings he twice refers to Hermes Trismegistus in passing, and rather slightingly. However, as we have seen in the case of Swedenborg, this is not conclusive, for Blake could be very critical of writers who had strongly influenced him. Kathleen Raine makes the attractive suggestion that Blake might have had in mind the following passage from the *Corpus Hermeticum* when he was writing and revising "The Tyger":

> And if thou wilt see and behold this Workman, even by mortal things that are upon earth, and in the deep, consider, O Son, how *Man* is made and framed in the Womb; and examine diligently the skill and cunning of the Workman, and learn who it was that wrought and fashioned the beautiful and Divine shape of *Man*; who circumscribed and marked out his eyes? who bored his nostrils and ears? Who opened his mouth? who stretched out and tied together his sinews? who channelled the veins? who hardened and made strong the bones? who clothed the flesh with skin? who divided the fingers and the joints? who flatted and made broad the soles of the feet? who digged the pores? who stretched out the spleen? who made the heart like a *Pyramis?* (CH V.6)

The creation of Adam by the "Workman," as described in this passage, was depicted by Blake in a masterly painting (plate 6). By one touch the demiurge brings into existence Adam, who is in the coils of the serpent of earthly life and passively stretched out on the rock of the material world, surrounded by "the sea of Time and Space."

Blake's questions about the Tyger have many parallels in the Jewish Bible (the questions God puts to Job, for instance) and in Hellenistic

Plate 6. Jehova Elohim creates Adam. The serpent as symbol of earthly life.

writings. But the correspondences between Blake's poem and this Hermetic text are striking: "What art could twist the sinews of thy heart?." And "the heart like a *Pyramis*" perhaps refers less to a Pyramid than to the *pyr* (fire) and the furnace of the blacksmith Blake evokes. In his later poems the furnaces of the mythical demiurges, Urizen and Los, become Blake's principal metaphors for the creative process.

The Workman, described in the passage quoted from *Corpus Hermeticum* V, not only creates man but also the lower creatures and all of nature. Blake on the one hand envisions the descent of the soul into the body as evil in the Platonic sense. But at the same time the impression given of the demiurge in *The Tyger* is ambivalent. He is closely related to the supreme creator; his "cruel fire" is connected with "distant deeps and skies," the lower and the higher world. In an earlier version of the poem line 7 ran "Could heart descend or wings aspire?.," which leaves open the possibility that the Tyger was created from above. And this may lead to other passages in the Hermetica, also cited by Raine, in which a demiurge is described who partly executes God's plan and who collaborates with the *Logos:*

> For the Mind being God, Male and Female, Life and Light, brought forth by his Word another Mind or Workman; which being God of the Fire, and the Spirit, fashioned and formed seven other Governors, which in their circles contain the Sensible World, whose Government or disposition is called Fate or Destiny. (CH I.9)

In our discussion of Blake's later poems it will appear how much his creation myth makes use of this picture of the androgynous Workman as one of the seven "Governors" who revolve the "Wheels" of the spheres. His poem *The Tyger* evokes the extremely ambiguous image of a "fearful" creator who shapes a "deadly" beast of prey in a fallen world, while at the same time suggesting the beautiful symmetry of the animal and, as the English translation of CH I.10 has it, the skill of a maker who delivers a piece of "clean and pure Workmanship of Nature." To understand fully the effect of this paradoxical "fearful symmetry" we must perhaps try to conceive of a God, or the relationship between a supreme God and a demiurge, for which even Boehme's conception of God seems too simple, when (in the passage already cited) he says:

"[T]he God of the holy World, and the God of the dark World, are not two Gods; there is but one only God . . . the whole Being."

Blake's short lyrical poem is a superb expression of the enigma of the creation and the destruction of life. In the questions it poses and the possible or impossible answers to them, it gives a key to all of Blake's work. Much of what I have said derives from Kathleen Raine's penetrating analysis of the poem. She wonders in the end what sort of answer might be given to Blake's question "Did he who made the Lamb make thee?" And she concludes by saying that Blake leaves his own question unanswered because there is no simple answer,

> because the answer is itself a no and yes of such depth and complexity.
> Nor must we overlook, in analyzing the meaning of the text, all that is conveyed by the powerful exaltation of the meter, by the fiery grandeur of the images. If the discoverable meaning of the poem is that the Tyger is the work of a being ambiguous or evil, the emotive force of meter and image is all affirmation, praising the fiery might, the energy, and the intelligence of the mortal God; and *The Tyger* is in the mood of the *Marriage* (written at about the same time), with its vindication of the fiery energies wrongly condemned as evil.
> Instead of seeking to find a yes or a no, we will be nearest to the truth if we see the poem as an utterance of Blake's delight not in the solution but in the presentation of the problem of evil as he found it in the Hermetic and Gnostic tradition. Instead of the uncompromising, unimaginative, and closed dualism of the conventional picture of heaven and hell, Blake had discovered a world of wider perspectives, a tradition that makes possible the simultaneous contemplation of the perfection of an eternal world and the imperfection of the temporal, as modes of being simultaneously possible within one harmonious whole. (*BT,* 2:30–31)

REVOLUTIONARY MYTHS

After the short lyrical *Songs of Innocence and Experience* and the *Marriage of Heaven and Hell*, Blake begins a series of longer poems which he calls "prophecies." At first he applies in these poems ideas from the *Marriage* to the great revolutionary events of his time. *The French Revolution* (1791) tells enthusiastically of an historical episode in the struggle for freedom in France. Blake adds imaginary details and soon everything takes on mythical dimensions and becomes an allegorical struggle between mythical personages. In the next poem, *America* (1793), the youthful "spirit of freedom," called Orc, "intense, naked, a human fire," rises from the Atlantic Ocean. He helps General Washington and his freedom fighters to defeat the fossilized "Guardian Angel of Albion" with his repressive troops, which are thrown back upon the coasts of England in spite of the divine assistance of the god Urizen.

In *Europe* (1794), Blake's mythical imagination takes over completely. Orc gets certain features of Satan's rebellious serpent and Albion represents the combined repressive aspects of law and religion in British life. Through a kind of earth mother, the nameless "shadowy female," women figures are introduced who seduce the "human race" with "soft delusions" and catch them in the nets of vegetative existence, "the material world." The eternal soul of "caverned man" is imprisoned in his body, "this finite wall of flesh." Urizen, the oppressive god of Reason, often pictured with the stone tables of the Book of Law (plate 7), tries to keep "the spirits of life" in chains. But with the help of Los, the god of the creative spirit, Orc will be delivered from his constricting material bonds, and the spirit of freedom will spread throughout Europe. The two full-page color etchings with which *Europe* opens reveal visually how intensely Blake's mythical imagination has been stimulated. The illustrations have grown into independent symbols that in their own forceful way express the meaning of the text. The frontispiece to *Europe* has over the years become Blake's best-known color etching (plate 8): from his heavenly sphere the demiurge, the lesser creator god, leans down with his compasses to delimit the globe and fix the bounds of our finite physical existence. This picture refers to lines 91–93 of the poem:

> . . . image of infinite
> Shut up in finite revolutions, and man became an Angel,
> Heaven a mighty circle turning, God a tyrant crown'd.

Facing this frontispiece, in sharp symbolical contrast, the title page of the poem is dominated by the spirals of a vitally erect serpent, the rebellious earthbound spirit.

Plate 7. Urizen, the god of reason, with his stone tables and book of law

Plate 8. The demiurge encircles the finite world. *Europe*, pl. 1.

URIZEN AND LOS

In the poems that follow, Blake elaborates his private version of the Gnostic-Hermetic myth of the fall of heavenly man. First in two poems of limited length, called after their protagonists *The First Book of Urizen* (1794) and *The Book of Los* (1795); then extended into a comprehensive myth in a gigantic poem of more than four thousand lines, *Vala or the Four Zoas*. Blake worked on it for ten years, but the text was never engraved and it remained in manuscript. The overwhelming abundance of mythical material in *Vala* was presented in somewhat more structured form in the most accessible of his later prophetic books, *Milton*, written during his stay in Felpham on the south coast of England between 1800 and 1804, and engraved on forty-three plates. This was followed by his last great poem, *Jerusalem*, which Blake started in 1804. Only in 1820 was the enormous labor finished, when he engraved the last of the hundred plates of this poem. He printed five copies, of which only one was fully colored, but it never found a buyer. In the last few years of his life Blake was happily stimulated by a small group of young artists who had gathered around the old "prophet" in his poverty.

It is impossible to summarize these later poems or Blake's mythology. He is a typical romantic artist and man of feeling, who considered the modern world's dependence on logical-systematical thinking as a pitiful limiting of a fully developed spiritual-physical life. A central myth may be distinguished, but it undergoes constant transformation, while Blake inserts new elements and sometimes changes the symbolic functions of its figures. He characterizes his own method in the following well-known lines:

> I must create a System or be enslav'd by another Man's.
> I will not Reason or Compare: my business is to Create.
>
> (K. 629)

Of course, the term "method" hardly applies to the very open and intricately layered myth that Blake's rich imagination finally develops.

The various layers of his myth are defined by Blake as "fourfold vision." "May God us keep from single vision and Newton's sleep." Blake wages mental war with no less than the complete "single vision" of the mechanistic and disintegrative world picture of Western faith and science. In opposition to it Blake works out his cosmic myth of the divine "Human Mind," in which originally four primal powers functioned in harmonious unity.

> Four Mighty Ones are in every Man; a Perfect Unity
> Cannot Exist but from the Universal Brotherhood of Eden
> (K. 264)

He calls these archetypal powers the four Zoas, the four vital principles, inspired by Ezekiel's vision (Ezek. 1:1–25) of the divine appearance of the "four living creatures" in "the likeness of a man." The fall and resurrection of the "Divine Humanity" of this fourfold, spiritual, cosmic Man is the great theme of Blake's prophetic books.

In *The First Book of Urizen* he gives us the first version of his own myth of the creation and fall, in which he moves even further away from traditional Christian views than Boehme had done in some of his Gnostic conceptions. The creation does not precede the fall but is part of it. Just as in the ancient Gnostic text of *The Apocryphon of John*, it is self-reflection within the Eternal Being that causes the androgynous "emanation" of a "selfcontemplating shadow."

To avoid any association with the conventional heaven and the idea of an authoritarian and all-powerful God, Blake seldom mentions the highest God. He places under him in Eternity (Eden) a Council of God, also called the "Republic of the Immortals" or the "Divine Family." In later poems, this Council of God is dramatized in more biblical terms as the "seven Angels of the Presence," or the "seven Eyes of God," viewed by Blake as the seven manifestations of the Most High God. The first of these is Lucifer/Satan ("the Selfhood"), the third is the creator Jehovah Elohim of the Old Testament, and the last one is Jesus, the incarnation of the "Forgiveness of Sins" and the "image of the invisible God" (K. 481).

But in this early prophetic book about Urizen, Blake still uses the personifications of his private myth. The first to separate himself from the Council of God is Urizen, described as "self-closed, abstracted, brooding dark power" (K. 222) who, as the principle of differentiation, creates chaos in the harmonious fullness and unity of Eden. Blake conceives his first mythical personification immediately with the full intensity of moral and social concern that is typical of all his work, but is mostly absent in Boehme and the other mystical and philosophical sources on which Blake draws. Urizen is expelled by the other Eternals, because he is egotistical and wants to lay down the law to others. That is why for Blake he is at the same time Lucifer and Jehovah. In the wonderful symbolic illustrations that accompany the text of *Urizen*, he is pictured as a wrinkled old man whose "prolific life" has shriveled up (plate 7). By means of his "Iron Laws" Urizen weaves the smothering dogmatic "Net of Religion."

To check Urizen's free fall into the "disorganized" chaos of the Abyss, the Eternals appoint one among them as guardian of Urizen. Los, the shaping, creative spirit, tries to mitigate the disaster and by means of time and space he creates boundaries for the fallen world that is issuing from Urizen. But Los himself has been corrupted by Urizen's egotism. His androgynous being splits up, and his feminine side, Enitharmon, breaks away from him. The divided couple still produce the child Orc and, with that, "Cruel Jealousy! Selfish Fear! Selfdestroying!" Self-centeredness and selfish will cause further disintegration of what will become a world divided in itself, which is definitely not the creation of a benevolent God.

Blake identifies the tyrannous God of Reason, Urizen, with the accusing and punishing authoritarian creator and lawgiver of the Old Testament. And in the end he runs them together into "Satan the Selfhood," who is "God of this World," symbol of all the negative, selfish forces in every human being, which can only be overcome by unconditional "forgiveness of sins."

FOURFOLD MAN

Blake's epics recount cosmic conflicts between "Giant Figures" and the sons and daughters that issued from them. The reader must always bear in mind that what Blake describes is meant to suggest "mental wars" enacted between spiritual powers within the human mind. The number 4 is a very significant symbol for Blake. Urizen and Los are later joined by two other figures. Together, these "Four Mighty Ones," the Zoas (from Greek *zoè* = life), are personifications of basic aspects of the human psyche: Urthona (imagination; in his fallen form, Los); Urizen ("your reason"): Luvah (desire; fallen form, Orc); and Tharmas (compassion).

As long as they work in harmony and as long as the masculine and feminine sides of each Zoa are in balance, Universal Man can be "whole." But when after the fall the feminine has split off, and the degeneration of what in themselves are divine qualities has set in, the female emanations try to dominate Man. In this way the seductive Vala breaks away from Luvah, "the Prince of Love," and draws "the body of Man from heaven into the dark Abyss." What remains of fallen Man in this world is only a kind of shadow, his "spectre," always pictured as a sort of threatening bat, hovering above the figure of Man (plate 9).

> I see the Fourfold Man, the Humanity in deadly sleep
> And its fallen Emanation, the Spectre & its cruel Shadow.
>
> (K. 635)

This divided state generates aggression and repression, and Vala becomes the material "veil" (Indian *maya*) that encloses the eternal soul and keeps it imprisoned in the world of time and space. Another image Blake uses to symbolize this "caverning" of the soul is that of the material fabric woven by the goddesses of fate from the intestines of Cosmic Man. They lay him down on the "Rock of Ages," wrapped in the symbolic shroud of earthly existence (plate 9), since, just as in the ancient Gnostic texts, the soul on earth lives in a state of "sleep" or "death."

It is in particular twentieth-century psychology that has given clues to the meaning and relevance of Blake's myth of the "fourfold man." The four Zoas correspond to C. G. Jung's division of the four main psychic functions into intuition, thinking, feeling and sensation, while his concepts of Anima and Shadow have shed light on Blake's "female emanation" and "spectre."

What is enacted "within and without Universal Man" is envisioned by Blake as fourfold in other ways, too. He distinguishes four levels in the spiritual cosmos: Eden – Beulah – Generation – Ulro. They represent: the heavenly harmony of Eden; Beulah, an intermediate level where, just as in dreams and visions, both the gods from "above" and the creatures from "below" may find some rest, and from which human beings may fall back into material existence or their immortal part may rise to the heavenly world that is its real home; the material world of

Plate 9. Albion in his shroud and supported by Christ. *Jerusalem*, pl. 33.

"generating" life; and lastly, at the bottom, there is Ulro (the "abyss"), the state of "non-ens," nonbeing, which, at worst, spiritual man may fall into.

JERUSALEM

In his last prophetic book, *Jerusalem, Emanation of the Giant Albion*, Blake emphasizes more and more the possibilities of "regeneration" for fallen Universal Man. This Man consists of all people, men and women, who are united by their feminine "emanative portion, who is Jerusalem in every individual Man, and her Shadow is Vala, builded by the Reasoning Power in Man" (K. 675). Fallen Man is personified in Albion, the world, concretized in the cities, villages and people of England. And "regeneration" becomes the vision of the "spiritual fourfold city" into which London might be changed. The transformation is envisaged in biblical terms as the common effort of building the spiritual city of Jerusalem, which also lives in "every individual man." In the end regeneration means realizing the "Divine Humanity" of Jesus Christ in ourselves, "he in us and we in him."

Blake had already sounded his passionate appeal to achieve this in the address to his countrymen with which he opens his poem *Milton:*

> Rouze up, O Young Men of the New Age! Set your foreheads against the ignorant Hirelings! For we have Hirelings in the Camp, the Court & the University, who would, if they could, for ever depress Mental & prolong Corporeal War. (K. 480)

And he urges them "to be just and true to our imaginations, those worlds of eternity in which we shall live for ever," and he concludes with the famous visionary poem that became a church hymn:

> And did those feet in ancient times
> Walk upon England's mountains green?
> And was the holy Lamb of God
> On England's pleasant pastures seen?
>
> . . . .
> I will not cease from Mental Fight,
> Nor shall my Sword sleep in my hand

Till we have built Jerusalem
In England's green & pleasant Land.

(K. 480)

The myth that Blake develops in *Jerusalem* pictures this process of re-generation as the work of Los, who represents both the divine and the human creative spirit. He feeds the fires and labors at the anvil of his smithy in the fallen world to build the beautiful city of Golgonooza, mirror image and counterpart of the heavenly Jerusalem. I have not yet come across a convincing explanation of the intriguing name Golgonooza. My guess is that Blake combined the stem of the Greek-Aramaic word *golgotha*, place of skulls, with the Greek noun *nous*, spirit or intellect. The place where the "Human Divine" definitively overcame "selfhood" is in this way related to the God of whom Blake says:

There is no other God, than that God who is the intellectual fountain of humanity. (K. 738)

This is from the preface "To the Christians" which opens the fourth part of *Jerusalem* and in which Blake also says:

I know of no other Christianity and of no other Gospel than the lib-erty both of body & mind to exercise the Divine Arts of Imagination. (K. 716)

In Blake's poetical vision the soul may find its way back to Eden through one of the gates of Golgonooza, the spiritual city that man may help to create, for "to labour in knowledge is to build up Jerusalem." What is needed to achieve this, in the eyes of Blake the Gnostic, is the focusing of our "intellectual vision." To the visionary Blake the eternal is every-where visible in the country of Albion, in the "villages, towns, cities, sea-ports, temples, sublime cathedrals. . . ."

For all are Men in Eternity, Rivers, Mountains, Cities, Villages,
All are Human, & when you enter into their Bosoms you walk
In Heavens & Earths, as in your own Bosom you bear your Heaven
And Earth & all you behold; tho' it appears Without, it is Within,
In your Imagination, of which this World of Mortality is but a Shadow.

(K. 709)

A few lines earlier Blake had for once formulated the same ideas more abstractly, using terms that chime in with the Hermetic "as above, so below":

> What is Above is Within, for Everything in Eternity is translucent.
> (K. 709)

The moral condition for this "eternal vision" is "universal love" and "the forgiveness of sins which is self-annihilation." It should be kept in mind, however, that most of what the "ignorance-loving hypocrite" holds to be sinful "is not so in the sight of our God" (K. 717). In the end a figure, who speaks for Christ as well as for Los and for Blake himself, preaches the fusion of the opposites "wrath" and "love," of multiplicity and oneness, and the identity of the "Humanity Divine" with "Jesus the Imagination":

> Saying, "Albion! Our wars are wars of life, & wounds of love
> With intellectual spears, & long winged arrows of thought.
> Mutual in one another's love and wrath all renewing
> We live as One Man; for contracting our infinite senses
> We behold multitude, or expanding, we behold as one,
> As One Man all the Universal Family, and that One Man
> We call Jesus Christ; and he in us, and we in him
> Live in perfect harmony in Eden, the land of life,
> Giving, recieving, and forgiving each other's trespasses.
> He is the Good shepherd, he is the Lord and master,
> He is the Shepherd of Albion, he is all in all,
> In Eden, in the garden of God, and in heavenly Jerusalem."
> (K. 664)

The condition and model for the spiritual renewal of man is the conquering of the "Selfhood cruel" by the redemptive death of Christ, the "Mysterious Offering of Self for Another," which has made possible "Friendship & Brotherhood in Eternity." The two symbolical pictures of plate 33 of *Jerusalem* visually condense the whole message of Blake's long poem (plate 9). Above "the eternal Saviour" raises Albion, whose soul lies shrouded in earthly existence below.

When finally the sick Albion begins to wake up from his "sleep of death," the transformation of all earthly dividedness into spiritual harmony is poetically expressed in a splendid "multiple fourfold vision," in which all the "visionary forms dramatic" of Blake's myth join together in regeneration. And "at the clangor of the Arrows of Intellect the innumerable Chariots of the Almighty appear'd in Heaven" (K. 745); "intellect," as always in Blake, to be understood as the power of the human imagination.

The four Zoas, "the four senses" of earthly man, now "rejoicing in unity," take on the faces of the "four living creatures" in the vision of Ezekiel and of the Book of Revelation, and they become "four chariots of Humanity Divine incomprehensible." The whole of creation participates in the renewed spirituality:

> Lion, Tyger, Horse, Elephant, Eagle, Dove, Fly, Worm
> And all the wondrous Serpent clothed in gems and rich
>   array,
> Humanize in the Forgiveness of Sins according to thy
> Covenant, Jehovah.
>
> (K. 746)

Blake here views Jehovah as the eternal God, who is not the same as Jehovah Elohim, the "Accuser of Sin" of the Old Testament, or the "God of this World" of rationalistic Christianity.

And once more Blake the artist also gives visual expression to his grand vision of the restoration of heavenly fullness and harmony. Under the words "The End of the Song of Jerusalem" Blake draws his moving full-page picture, at once spiritual and sensual, of the reunion of Albion and Jerusalem (plate 10). The symbolism of this etching perhaps in the first place suggests God who in a tender embrace draws the human soul towards him, but at the same time it is the reunion of the masculine and feminine, "rejoicing in unity" in Universal Man. When Albion, following the example of Jesus, commits his "cruel selfhood" to the fire of the "furnaces of affliction" (from which the two figures in Blake's plate are rising up), the flames change into the "Fountains of Living Waters flowing from the Humanity Divine." In their blending of biblical and Gnostic ideas the last few pages of Blake's *Jerusalem* are a perfect artistic expression of his very personal form of Christian Gnosis.

Plate 10. Reunion of Albion with Jerusalem, the soul with God. *Jerusalem*, pl. 99.

NOTES

1. All Blake quotations from William Blake, *Complete Poems,* ed. G. Keynes (Oxford, 1966); abbreviated in the text as "K."

2. Quoted in Michael Davis, *William Blake: A New Kind of Man* (Berkeley, 1977), 42.

3. Henry Crabb Robinson, *Blake, Coleridge, Wordsworth, Lamb, etc.,* ed. E. J. Morley (Manchester, 1932), 23.

4. Kathleen Raine, *Blake and Tradition,* 2 vols. (Princeton and London, 1969); abbreviated henceforth as *BT.*

5. Désirée Hirst, *Hidden Riches: Traditional Symbolism from the Renaissance to Blake* (London, 1964).

6. *[Corpus Hermeticum:] The Divine Pymander of Hermes Mercurius Trismegistus,* translated from the Arabic by Dr. John Everard (1650; reprint, London 1884); abbreviated CH.

7. Quoted in Hirst, *Hidden Riches,* 206.

8. Ibid., 204.

9. Quoted in ibid., 206.

10. William Blake, *The Complete Poems,* ed. W. H. Stevenson, 2d ed. (1971; reprint, London, 1989), 102.

WESTERN ESOTERIC SCHOOLS IN THE LATE NINETEENTH AND EARLY TWENTIETH CENTURIES

DANIËL VAN EGMOND

In the last quarter of the nineteenth century and the early part of the twentieth, three of the most influential occult movements of western Europe were founded: the Theosophical Society, the Hermetic Order of the Golden Dawn, and the Mysteria Mystica Aeterna. Although many studies on these movements have been published, there still seems to be a lack of clarity about their original motives and aims. Often they are interpreted as exponents of a common "flight from reason" occurring during this period.[1] Yet it is also possible to consider them as organizations that attempted to bring old esoteric traditions within the domain of enlightened reason;[2] this is, for instance, illustrated by their use of Occult Science as one of the names for their particular branch of "occultism." The (in)famous magician Aleister Crowley even tried to develop in some of his works a philosophical foundation for magic in order to show that there need not be a contradiction between science and his own system of "magick."[3] A third approach is to see these movements as part of a many-sided counterculture that opposed the religious and political establishment,[4] or functioned as a source for new creative developments in the arts.[5]

Each of these approaches may help us to understand the many-sided phenomenon of late-nineteenth-/early-twentieth-century occultism. In this article I wish to add another one, in the hope that it will highlight some important aspects that are more or less ignored in most of the other studies. It seems to me that the Esoteric School of the Theosophical Society, the Golden Dawn, and the Mysteria Mystica Aeterna cannot be fully understood if we ignore the fact that these organizations tried to develop a spiritual or "occult" school, intended to enable their students to experience for themselves the other "worlds," considered to be as much a part of reality as the world we discover by means of our sense perceptions. In other words, whereas most other studies focus on the historical, sociological, and psychological aspects of these movements, I will emphasize their experiential dimension. Therefore, I shall mainly deal with the attempts of the founders to establish an esoteric school, rather than with the well-known history of the "exoteric" part of their movements.

I define an esoteric school as any institution that teaches its students particular theories and practices that may enable them to transform themselves into human beings who are aware of, and are guided by, their "souls," "higher selves," or "holy guardian angels." Such schools presuppose that we, as human beings, are not merely biological organisms but, rather, complex beings constituted of physical, psychological, mental and spiritual dimensions, which correspond to the "inner worlds" that are constitutive of our phenomenal universe. According to this perspective, we are "asleep," or "dead" as long as our consciousness is confined to only the physical and psychological aspects of our constitution. Only when our personality and body have become receptive to the influence of the soul are we really transformed into a new human being. We are then able to live in accordance with the universal laws and rhythms of the macrocosm that are reflected in each microcosm, i.e., in each human being. Once this microcosmic structure of our being has been actualized, we may become conscious of, and active in, the "inner worlds" in which we live. However, as long as we remain oblivious to one or more of these worlds we are bound to bring disorder on earth, and even in the cosmos. It is for this reason that the attempt to become an awakened human being is, according to these "occultists," not an individual affair at all. On the contrary, it is the highest possible service one can perform for the welfare of humanity.

THE ESOTERIC SCHOOL OF THE THEOSOPHICAL SOCIETY

During the nineteenth century the West seemed to be the unchallenged global power, although its various nations struggled among themselves for supremacy. Each country was divided into various groups struggling for power and influence. Firstly, the Catholic and Protestant Churches were preaching the absolute truth and trying to convert the heathens of the East. Next, there was an increasing group of intellectuals fighting against religion, because they were convinced that only science was able to discover the truth. Yet other intellectuals, however, joined the many pansophical and occult groups belonging to high-grade Masonry. Many of these groups were involved in political affairs as well, fighting for freedom of thought against the power of the Church, or attempting by all means to defend the status quo against social agitators. As James Webb observed:

> It was not only the efforts of Darwin and a few intellectuals that threatened to take away from man his few illusions of security. Much more potent, because practically observable, were the effects of the Industrial Revolution and social agitation. If the findings of the scientists meant for the thinking classes the destruction of intellectual securities, alterations in the means of production and consumption were establishing a new form of society altogether, one in which the bases of wealth and security were not known from experience and which was therefore threatening.[6]

This was the world in which Helena Petrovna Blavatsky (1831–91), the chief founder of the modern theosophical movement, was born. Although many biographies describe the life of this remarkable woman, there still does not exist a serious scholarly study of her tempestuous career.[7] It is evident, however, that she was involved in some of the most influential secret societies in the West and the East.[8] She claimed to be an envoy of some of these "Lodges" and to be constantly in touch with their adepts or "Masters." It is of great importance to emphasize that these masters were not the invisible "ascended masters" or semidivine beings referred to by the many neotheosophical groups that claimed to be guided by Blavatsky's original teachers. On the contrary, her teachers were quite normal human beings, albeit they were able to produce various kinds of paranormal phenomena and seemed to be in possession of deep wisdom and knowledge. In his recent book, Paul Johnson has tried to establish the historical identities of these masters.[9] Although his conclusions could be contested on some points, his study proves once and for all that Blavatsky's masters were real human beings. Consequently, accusations that they were mere figments of her fantasy, and also all the claims of many of her would-be successors of being the new messenger of these same masters, no longer deserve serious attention.

What was the aim of the Theosophical Society that H. P. Blavatsky, together with some other persons, founded in 1875? I argue that she and her teachers were pursuing several aims at the same time:

— to wake up one of the most influential cultures of the West— Anglo-American culture—from its "dogmatic slumber" in materialism and dogmatic Christianity;
— to prevent the conversion of Hindus and Buddhists to a Christianity that claimed to be the only true religion in the world;
— to emancipate the Indian people, who were still widely considered to be mere barbarians, and to help free them from the colonial system;
— to fight against materialism or scientism by explaining the "unexplained laws in the universe" (which had caught the attention of the Anglo-American public due to the spectacular rise of spiritualism since the 1840s);
— to help some gifted European and American students to follow an authentic esoteric path of initiation.[10]

In 1888, in her introduction to *The Secret Doctrine*, Blavatsky wrote:

> The world of to-day, in its mad career towards the unknown—which it is too ready to confound with the unknowable, whenever the problem eludes the grasp of the physicist—is rapidly progressing on the reverse, material plane of spirituality. It has now become a vast arena— a true valley of discord and of eternal strife—a necropolis, wherein lie buried the highest and the most holy aspirations of our Spirit-Soul. That soul becomes with every new generation more paralyzed and atrophied. . . .
> We have not long to wait, and many of us will witness the Dawn of the New Cycle, at the end of which not a few accounts will be settled and squared between the races.[11]

This "atrophy" of the soul is a reference to the increasing materialism of the West and the oppression of the "barbarian races" by the "civilized" western nations. According to Blavatsky only real *altruism* could alleviate this situation; this virtue, however, could only be developed as a result of spiritual growth. Hence, the Theosophical Society had a *political* agenda as well,[12] which is clearly demonstrated by the many articles

Blavatsky wrote under her nom de plume "unpopular philosopher," in the theosophical journal *Lucifer*. For example:

> Everything under the sun now seems to have become connected with politics, which appear to have become little else but a legal permission to break the ten commandments, a regular government licence to the rich for the commission of all the sins which, when perpetrated by the poor, land the criminal in jail. (CW, 10:82)

This stress on ethics, on the transformation of the person from an egotistic way of life to a life of altruism, is continuously present in most of Blavatsky's writings. Her attacks on Christianity were partly motivated by her conviction that the official churches no longer followed the teachings of Jesus, but had simply become part of the oppressive power of the ruling classes of the West. Where should a person turn if he or she wished to work for the welfare of humanity? Blavatsky's answer was that one should turn to the *theosophia perennis*, the source of all the great religions of the world. Only then would one be able to discover the extent to which the churches had become antispiritual institutions. In her voluminous writings, Blavatsky tried to prove the fundamental unity of all the world religions. All the teachings she could find were interpreted in such a way as to become expressions of the "universal" secret doctrine. Yet, merely studying this secret doctrine would not transform one into an altruistic person. Therefore, an esoteric school was necessary in which this process would be stimulated. For this reason the Theosophical Society soon became a semisecret society divided into three sections consisting of three degrees each. All candidates for membership entered the Society in the third degree of the third section:

> To be admitted into the highest degree, of the first section, the Theosophist must have become freed of every leaning toward any one form of religion in preference to another. He must be free from all exacting obligations to society, politics and family. He must be ready to lay down his life, if necessary, for the good of Humanity, and of a brother Fellow of whatever race, color or ostensible creed. He must renounce wine, and every other description of intoxicating beverages, and adopt a life of strict chastity. Those who have not yet wholly disenthralled themselves from religious prejudice, and other forms of selfishness, but have made a certain progress towards self-mastery and enlightenment, belong to the Second Section. The Third Section

is probationary: its members can leave the Society at will, although the obligation assumed at entrance will continually bind them to absolute secrecy as to what may have been communicated under restrictions. (CW, 1:376)

In sum, the Theosophical Society was clearly meant to be an esoteric school, consisting of nine degrees. A member could only advance if he or she practiced the art of self-mastery. Given the high demands on a member of the first section, we may well ask whether there was any person at all pure enough to reach such a high level. Blavatsky claimed that, indeed, there were in fact a few members who belonged to these highest degrees. They were the real founders of the Theosophical Society, and without their membership the Society could never be a real esoteric school:

It is true that a *wholly esoteric* section exists in our Society; but it is only a section, a very tiny part of the society which would perhaps be best defined if I call it at the outset—not only the trunk of the Theosophical tree or its seed—because it is to that section that our whole Society owes its origin—but the vivifying sap that makes it live and flourish. Without this section, composed solely of Oriental adepts, the Theosophical Society, whose ramifications are beginning to cover the five regions of the globe, would be nothing but a dead and sterile body, a corpse without a soul. And yet the Theosophists who have been admitted therein up to this time [1880] could be reckoned on the fingers of one hand. Admission is not by asking. As for the rest of the Theosophists, with the exception of the passwords and signs that are changed at every expulsion of a bad and false brother—there are no secrets to preserve and nothing to conceal. . . . And before one can be put in touch, direct or indirect, with the adepts of the first section, he must take a most solemn pledge never to reveal what he shall learn or see; or employ his knowledge for personal and selfish motives, or even to refer to it, unless he receives permission to that effect from his Master himself. . . . Day and night, we work in common for the spiritual regeneration of morally blind individuals, as well as for the elevation of the fallen nations. (CW, 3:500f.)

In the same article Blavatsky explicitly states that the esoteric (or second) section consisted only of *five* members, whose names were unknown to the rest of the Society.

It is clear, then, that the Theosophical Society was intended to be a real esoteric school whose aim was to "regenerate morally blind individuals," and to "elevate the fallen nations." The third section was merely an exoteric organization that organized lectures and study groups. Any member who wished to put the theosophical theories into practice could apply for membership in the second section. If admitted, he or she was assigned to a particular Master, or guided by Blavatsky herself. Yet, it appears that most of these Lay Chelas of the second section failed, for in 1883 she wrote:

> One who undertakes to try for Chelaship by that very act rouses and lashes to desperation every sleeping passion in his animal nature. For this is the commencement of a struggle for the mastery in which quarter is neither to be given nor taken. It is, once for all: "To be, or Not to be"; to conquer, means ADEPTSHIP; to fail, an ignoble Martyrdom; for to fall victim to lust, pride, avarice, vanity, selfishness, cowardice, or any other of the lower propensities, is indeed ignoble, if measured by the standard of true manhood. The Chela is not only called to face all the latent evil propensities of his nature, but, in addition, the whole volume of maleficent power accumulated by the community and nation to which he belongs. . . . [T]he strife is in this instance between the Chela's Will and his carnal nature, and Karma forbids that any angel or Guru should interfere until the result is known. . . . It would have been well for some of our Lay Chelas if they had thought twice before defying the tests. *We call to mind several sad failures within a twelvemonth.* One went bad in the head, recanted noble sentiments uttered but a few weeks previously, and became a member of a religion he had just scornfully and unanswerably proven false. A second became a defaulter and absconded with his employer's money—the latter also a Theosophist. A third gave himself up to gross debauchery, and confessed it with ineffectual sobs and tears, to his chosen Guru. A fourth got entangled with a person of the other sex and fell out with his dearest and truest friends. A fifth showed signs of mental aberration and was brought into Court upon charges of discreditable conduct. A sixth shot himself to escape the consequences of criminality, on the verge of detection! And so we might go on and on. . . .
>
> In what precedes we have, of course, dealt but with the failures among Lay Chelas; there have been partial successes too, and these are passing gradually through the first stages of their probation. (CW, 4:606ff.)

This description of the struggle between the "inner man" and the "outer man," on the first stage of the spiritual way, is well-known to anybody who has studied mysticism. It shows that the Theosophical Society was really intended to be an esoteric school. Unfortunately, most of its members were only interested in "phenomena" and in the development of their "occult" powers, so as to strengthen their personalities, instead of working hard to make their personalities more and more receptive to the influence of their "higher Selves."

Although it is possible that all three sections remained in existence as long as Blavatsky lived, most studies of the history of the Theosophical Society are only concerned with the *exoteric* Society, i.e., with the third section. The article quoted was written in 1883, and a year later a group of members of the London Lodge of the Theosophical Society asked for the permission of the Masters to form an "inner group" of this lodge. Some members of the lodge had resigned because they no longer trusted the Masters (of the first section), whereas other members did not like the emphasis on Eastern wisdom and wished to study Hermetic and Christian esoteric doctrines. In reaction to this situation, the "inner group" expressed its confidence in the Masters and their teachings and pledged "unswerving obedience to their wishes in all matters connected with spiritual progress" (CW 6:255). According to Boris de Zirkoff, the compiler of Blavatsky's *Collected Writings*, this "inner group" did not last long, due to internal conflicts (CW, 6:251).[13] It seems to me that this petition shows that, at least in the London Lodge, there were no longer members of the original second section of the Society, for otherwise there would have been no need to establish a new esoteric group in the lodge. To be sure, the purpose of the "inner group" seems to have been more or less similar to that of the original second section. Thus, we may surmise that between 1883 and 1884 (at least in the West) all the Lay Chelas of this section had failed. Only in 1888 was a new attempt made to revive this second section under the name of the Esoteric Section of the Theosophical Society. In the October issue of the English theosophical journal *Lucifer*, its formation was announced as follows:

> Owing to the fact that a large number of Fellows of the Society have felt the necessity for the formation of a body of Esoteric students, to be organized on the ORIGINAL LINES devised by the real founders of the T.S. . . . there is hereby organized a body, to be known as the "Esoteric Section of the Theosophical Society." (CW, 12:481)

The capitalized words "ORIGINAL LINES" stress the fact that here again an attempt was made to realize the original goal of the Theosophical Society, viz., to be a real esoteric school. The purpose of this section was

> to prepare and fit the student for the study of practical occultism or Raj yoga. Therefore, in this [first] degree, the student—save in exceptional cases—will not be taught to produce physical phenomena, nor will any magical powers be allowed to be developed in him; nor, if possessing such powers naturally, will he be permitted to exercise them before he has thoroughly mastered the knowledge of SELF, of the psycho-physiological processes (taking place on the occult plane) in the human body generally, and until he has in abeyance all his lower passions and his PERSONAL SELF. (CW, 12:488)

Blavatsky had certainly learned from the failures of the Lay Chelas. This first degree of the Esoteric Section would now only be devoted to theoretical study. All psychical and magical powers were banned, and in this same "preliminary memorandum" she referred to the "dead failure" of the Theosophical Society, "on all those points which rank foremost among the objects of its original establishment" (CW, 12:489). She referred also to "conspiracies" against the Society that had openly begun in 1884 (CW, 12:490), which explained why there was no esoteric (or second) section in the Society between 1884 and 1888. Again and again she stressed the necessity to "decenter" the personal self and the practice of genuine altruism as the foremost requirement for esoteric training. Student were ordered to train their minds in such a way that they would develop the habit of "careful and constant concentration of mind upon every duty and act in life they may have to do" (CW, 12:493)— a skill that was called *mindfulness* or *awareness* and regarded as necessary for everyone who would like to follow a spiritual training.

Every member had to sign a pledge. Blavatsky told them that, after signing, the masters would test or examine them on the inner planes in order to establish their suitability for this training. One of the students, Alice Leighton Cleather, relates that she was tested as follows:

> So we waited; days, even weeks passed, and nothing occurred. I had almost forgotten what Mrs. Chowne had warned me *might* happen, until, one Tuesday night, (it was Full Moon, I remember) I had the

most wonderful experience, save one, that had ever happened to me. I knew I was myself, lying half awake, half asleep, in my own room at home. Yet I was also in an Egyptian Temple of extraordinary grandeur, and going through things quite unspeakable and most solemn. This experience began soon after 10 P.M., and almost exactly as a neighbouring church clock struck midnight I lost consciousness in an overpowering and almost terrible blaze of light, which seemed completely to envelop me. The next morning I recorded all I could remember in my diary, and on Thursday went up to Lansdowne Road as usual for the Lodge meeting. I was a little early, but H.P.B. at work in the inner room must have known who had arrived, for she called me in, and turning round, said most seriously: "Master told me *last night* that you are accepted." Nothing more; but I at once realised vividly that my experience the previous Tuesday might have indeed been my "testing." Thereupon I related the whole thing to H.P.B., who only nodded several times, but made no remark whatever about it.

Mrs. Chowne told me afterwards that she and her husband had had similar experiences, adding that only a few of the first applicants were so "tested"; that it did not, in fact, apply generally.[14]

If we assume that this "testing" really took place, we may conclude that it was a pity that not all new members were examined in this way, because only one year after the foundation of the Esoteric Section a new crisis broke out within the Theosophical Society and the Esoteric Section.

In 1890 Blavatsky established the third degree of the Esoteric Section, which was called the Inner Group.[15] In this group practical instructions were given, and the meetings were to be held in a special seven-walled room with a glass roof. Each wall would be covered by a particular metal, and "magical mirrors" were present as well.[16] The Inner Group consisted of six women and six men, who became members on invitation. Each had her or his own chair; the men were seated on Blavatsky's right hand and the women on her left, in a semicircular formation.[17] In addition to these twelve members there were two corresponding members who received the minutes of the group meetings. One of them was Dr. William Wynn Westcott, one of the "chiefs" of the Hermetic Order of the Golden Dawn.[18]

It is not easy to gain an impression of the practical nature of the instructions that the members of the Inner Group received. Before the group was well established, Blavatsky died, so the real work had perhaps not yet begun. It seems probable that meditation on the so-called chakras and the awakening of Kundalini power formed part of the curriculum.[19] A simple experiment was as follows:

> Get wool of the seven colours. Wind round the 4th finger of the left hand a piece corresponding to the colour of the day, while meditating, and record the results. This is to discover the day to which the student belongs.[20]

In the two lower degrees of the Esoteric Section specific meditations were practiced, such as the sounding of the sacred letter OM.[21] According to the Rules that every member of the section received,

> Each member is expected to set apart a certain part of the day or night, of no less than half an hour's duration, for meditation upon the Instruction received, for self-examination and self-study. . . . If [self-examination and self-study] were faithfully carried out, we should have less jealousy, less bitterness, less harsh judgement, less disharmony, in the School. . . . Nor can we hope to conquer the subtle forces against which we fight, if we do not clearly know what ingress is given to them by the weaknesses of our own nature. . . . Aspiration towards the Higher Self should form part of the daily meditation, the rising towards those higher planes of our being which cannot be found by us unless they are sought. Earnest and reverent desire for Master's guidance and enlightenment will begin the attainment of the nature to the harmony to which it must one day respond. Concentration on a single point in the teaching is a road to the philosophy: self-examination a road to knowledge of oneself.[22]

In conclusion, the *original* aim of the Theosophical Society was to be an esoteric school in which men and women could be trained in order to become real workers for the elevation of humanity. The Society was divided into three sections. The first one was completely exoteric and provided teachings on Theosophy as the original source of all spiritual traditions. The second section consisted of Lay Chelas who pledged to devote their lives to the greater cause of humanity. Unfortunately, most of them were motivated by selfish motives, lust for psychic power, or a quick personal advancement. This second section proved to be a failure, right up to Blavatsky's death, when even in her Inner Group "hatred, jealousy and ill-feeling" among its members arose more than once.[23]

This would eventually lead to a crisis in which the Theosophical Society split up into various fragments. The highest section consisted of the Masters, advanced human beings who had their own aims and ideals. Blavatsky and her teachers tried to provide the members with a spiritual training outside any orthodox religious tradition. Unfortunately, their efforts ended in an almost complete failure.

THE HERMETIC ORDER OF THE GOLDEN DAWN

Although the exoteric section of the Theosophical Society was devoted to the comparative study of religions, in order to disclose the *theosophia perennis* of which every religion was thought to be a particular revelation, most theosophists preferred to study the eastern traditions. As mentioned, some members of the Society, especially in the London Lodge, were dissatisfied with this strong eastern bias. They wished to study (and practice) the Hermetic Kabbalah and alchemy. In 1883 some members of the London Lodge, among them the president of the Lodge, Dr. Anna B. Kingsford, published a pamphlet, entitled *A letter addressed to the fellows of the London Lodge of the Theosophical Society, by the president and a vice-president of the Lodge.* In this pamphlet they criticized A. P. Sinnett's book *Esoteric Buddhism*, which purported to be a summary of the teachings of Theosophy that Sinnett had received from Blavatsky's masters. Kingsford and Edward Maitland (the vice-president of the lodge), proposed that

> two Sections be created in the London Lodge, one of which shall be formed by those Fellows who desire to pursue exclusively the teachings of the Tibetan Mahatmas, and to recognize them as Masters; and that the Presidency of this Section be conferred on Mr. Sinnett, the only person now in this country competent to fill such a position. The other Section should be composed by Fellows desirous, like myself, to adopt a broader basis, and to extend research into other directions, more especially with the object of encouraging the study of Esoteric Christianity, and of the Occidental theosophy out of which it arose.[24]

The tension between the "western" and the "eastern" factions within the lodge developed into a heated quarrel between Sinnett and Kingsford and their supporters. Blavatsky had to intervene, but in the end it became clear that the only solution was to follow Kingsford's and Maitland's proposal, and thus the Hermetic Lodge was founded.[25] Very soon it became an independent organization, called the Hermetic Society. One of Anna Kingsford's admirers was Samuel Liddell Mathers, who dedicated his book *The Kabbalah Unveiled* (see below) to her and Edward Maitland. Kingsford was a fervent antagonist of vivisection, and even tried to kill Louis Pasteur by means of black magic. According to some rumors, it was Mathers who taught her the necessary rituals.[26] About Mathers's background little is known,[27] but most of his life he was occupied with the occult, as a Mason, as a student of medieval and Renaissance occultism, and as one of the founders of the Golden Dawn. Dr. Wynn Westcott introduced him to the Societas Rosicruciana in Anglia (S.R.I.A.), a society of master Masons devoted to the study of Rosicrucianism.[28] Some of its members, and among them especially Wynn Westcott himself, were interested in a more structured study of the Kabbalah, and they stimulated Mathers to pursue these studies. Westcott provided him with some financial means enabling him to translate three tracts from Knorr von Rosenroth's classical Kabbalistic compendium *Kabbalah Denudata*, which was subsequently published as *The Kabbalah Unveiled* in 1887.[29] Mathers met Anna Kingsford and through her Madame Blavatsky. He joined both the Hermetic Society and the Theosophical Society, and advised Blavatsky about some of the Kabbalistic theories she discussed in the *Secret Doctrine*. He and Westcott lectured for the Hermetic Society on various Kabbalistic and Hermetic subjects. When Kingsford died in the spring of 1888, the Hermetic Society died with her, and this seems to have been the main reason for the establishment of the Isis-Urania Temple of the Golden Dawn, a few days after her death.[30] Mathers and Westcott clearly wished to establish a society organized in the same way as the S.R.I.A., but which would admit both men and women, as was the case with the Theosophical Society and the Hermetic Society:

> As Freemasons they recognized the value of the form of Obligation that bound members to secrecy concerning certain teachings and to promise "never to divulge certain signs and pass-words used by the members of the Society for mutual recognition." As Rosicrucians they recognized the value of superhuman hidden Masters, whose existence—real or imaginary—could be extremely useful to the leaders of

an Order, whether one chose to call them Mahatmas or Secret Chiefs. As men they recognized that the time was ripe for something more splendid than Theosophy.[31]

Actually, the plan for the foundation of a Hermetic order had already been discussed a few years earlier. According to Wynn Westcott, it all started when he received a cipher manuscript from Dr. A. F. A. Woodford, an author of Masonic books:

> About 1886 A.F.A. Woodford gave me Hermetic teaching and old MSS information of G.D. 0 = 0 to 4 = 7. Mathers helped me to write these up—and Woodman as S[upreme] M[agus of the S.R.I.A.] agreed to 1st Principal of the Isis Temple. We 3 co-equal by *my wish*—and this lasted until 1891. Then Mathers brought from Paris the 5 = 6 and said it was a continuation of my G.D. 4 = 7 and I carried 5 = 6 on in England until M[athers] became so eccentric that I resigned in 1897.[32]

The cipher manuscript consisted of fifty-seven sheets of raw notes on five initiation rituals and on some "knowledge lectures." For instance, the notes on the knowledge necessary to progress from the first to the second degree reads as follows:

> 4 Worlds of Qabbalists are Atziluth = Pure Deity; Briah = Creative—Archangelic; Yetzirah = Angels; Assiah = Shells. Man. Demons.
> Tarot Suits. Wands or Batons = Diamonds; Cups = Hearts; Swords = Spades; Pentacles or Coins = Clubs. Of these there are 10.
> For this purpose also Matt = Aquarius, Man, Water; Mark = Leo, Lion, Fire; Luke = Taurus, Earth; John = Scorpio, Air.
> 4 sorts of elementals are Gnomes = Earth; Undines = Water; Sylphs = Air; Salamanders = Fire.[33]

This knowledge is certainly not very profound at all! Folio 25 treats of the ritual of the 2 = 9 degree:

> Officers: H. HS. HG. KX.—*Opening*. Arrange as for 32 Path. H. calls to order—see guarding—who present. Signs given. HG. 2 grade = Luna. HS. 2 grade = Luna. HG. It's Path 32 or Tau. H. Prayer to ShDI AL ChAI. All pass to East. H. makes Pentagrams. H. Let Sylphs adore YHVH and ShDI El ChI. H. Signs Aquarius of Man. Raphael. H. With Cross in names of ORO IBAH AOZPI of Great East Tablet and

Bataivah. All go to places. H. Declares open ''' '''' ''' HS. ''' ''' ''' HG. '''
''' ''' 34

If we compare these notes with the Golden Dawn ritual based on them, as published by Israel Regardie[35] and by R. G. Torrens,[36] it becomes clear how much work Mathers had to do before these rituals were suitable for real ceremonial work.

It is obvious that this new organization was very attractive to members of the Theosophical Society with a more western orientation. According to some historians, it was actually this growing appeal of the Golden Dawn that forced Blavatsky to found her own esoteric school.[37] In view of the first part of this article, however, this can not be quite correct, for it appears that Blavatsky had tried over the years to revive the second section of her Society. Yet the foundation of the Golden Dawn, as well as the fact that many members of the Theosophical Society had also become members of the Hermetic Brotherhood of Luxor, might indeed have inspired her to try again. In October 1888 she published an article entitled "Lodges of Magic" in her London journal *Lucifer*. In it she wrote:

> One of the most esteemed of our friends in occult research,[38] propounds the question of the formation of "working Lodges" of the T.S., for the development of adeptship. If the practical impossibility of forcing this process has been shown once in the course of the theosophical movement, it has scores of times.[39] It is hard to check one's natural impatience to tear aside the veil of the Temple. . . . If the "Lodges of Magic.". . . were founded, without having taken the greatest precautions to admit only the best candidates to membership, we should see. . . . vile exploitations of sacred names and things increase an hundredfold. . . . The plan "A" proposes would be far more likely to end in mediumship than adeptship. . . . The Masters do not have to hunt up recruits in special [York]shire lodges, nor drill them through mystical non-commissioned offices; time and space are no barriers between them and the aspirant; where thought can pass they can come. Why did an old and learned kabbalist like "A" forget this fact? . . . [I]t is quite true that those kabalists who dabble in ceremonial magic as described and taught by Éliphas Lévi, are as full blown *Tantrikas* as those of Bengal.[40]

And in another article, she wrote:

Works [on occultism, magic, and alchemy] for advanced students are many, but these can be placed at the disposal of only sworn or "pledged" chelas, those who have pronounced the ever-binding oath, and who are, therefore, helped and protected. For all other purposes, well-intentioned as such works may be, they can only mislead the unwary and guide them imperceptibly to Black Magic or Sorcery—if to nothing worse.

The mystic characters, alphabets and numerals found in the divisions and sub-divisions of the *Great Kabbalah*, are, perhaps, the most dangerous portions in it, and especially the numerals. We say dangerous, because they are the most prompt to produce effects and results, and this with or without the experimenter's will, even without his knowledge. . . . (CW, 14:59f.)

Stern warnings indeed, but they had little effect; for, as is shown by the lists of members of the various temples, many theosophists were initiated into the Golden Dawn.

In the same issue of *Lucifer* in which Blavatsky's "Lodges of Magic" was published, the formation of the Esoteric Section of the Theosophical Society was announced, presumably in the hope to prevent a defection of theosophists to the Golden Dawn,[41] but this did not have the desired effect. On the other hand, even some of the members of the Golden Dawn now became members of the Esoteric Section as well, such as the Irish poet W. B. Yeats[42] and the Rev. Ayton whose letter had provoked Blavatsky to write her article on magic. When Blavatsky discovered these double memberships, she was furious. In a letter Ayton relates the ensuing developments as follows:

A short time ago, an ukase was issued from the headquarters of the T.S., that members of the Esoteric Section should not belong to any other Occult Order. I at once wrote to say that I belonged to the Rosicrucian Society, but I was ordered to give it up, and I felt bound to do so at once without hesitation, and wrote to some of my Yorkshire chelas, who belonged to it and the T.S., to do the same. They were dismayed, and two of them went, as a Deputation, to H.P.B. to remonstrant against this decision. H.P.B. then began to see she had made a mistake and she wrote to me for advice, which I gave, and the consequence was, she withdrew this ukase as regards this Rosicrucian Society. The result was that Dr. Wynn Westcott, the head of this Rosicrucian Society, joined the Esoteric Section of the T.S. and with him some 20 others, and about 14 from Yorkshire. All is well that ends well![43]

In 1891, Westcott said about this affair:

[S]everal theosophists wished to join the G.D. and difficulties were placed in their ways; to remove these, I was selected as the Hermetist who should endeavour to cast oil on troubled water and to be a bond of union and peace between the two Societies, and the Soc[ietas] Ros[icruciana] in Anglia.[44]

And in 1892 he revealed the details of the agreement he had made with Blavatsky:

By this agreement there was a mutual understanding, by each party— a confession
    A. of a Bona-Fides
    B. of an origin from those who were wiser than those who are actually here teaching.
    C. of an exalted aim,
        1. which tended to the search for the true ideas of the divine
        2. to self sacrifice
        3. to mutual benevolence
        4. to the study of the mysteries of nature
        5. to the hidden workings of the human mind,
and each party, for the sake of a mutual support, in a scoffing and materialistic age, was willing to recognise the fact that although dissimilar in method; using a different mode of tuition; a varying terminology, . . . yet each was making strenuous efforts onward toward the goal of mutual improvement—Self improvement—in order that others might be improved.[45]

Point B of this agreement obviously refers to Blavatsky's masters, but entails that Westcott also believed (or at least pretended to believe) that the real "chiefs" of the Golden Dawn were not he himself and Mathers, but certain "secret chiefs." I have already dealt with the question whether Blavatsky's "hidden masters" really existed. But the same question might be asked about the "secret chiefs" of the Golden Dawn. In 1900, Mathers accused Westcott of having forged the letters written by a German Rosicrucian adept who, according to Westcott, had provided him with a warrant to start the Golden Dawn. Such a warrant is important in Masonic circles, because Masons usually highly value "regular" initiations; but since the Golden Dawn admitted women as well, it is not quite clear why Westcott would have felt the need to invent this German connection. Be this as it may, the investigations of Ellic Howe have uncovered some strong evidence that suggests that Mathers' accusations were correct.[46] Hence, we might be inclined to conclude that Westcott's reference to "hidden masters" was mere pretense. On the other hand, according to Ithell Colquhoun, Mathers himself was quite sure that he really was under the guidance of the "secret chiefs" of the Golden Dawn who resided in Paris,[47] and in her preface to the new edition of *The Kabbalah Unveiled*, published after Mathers's death, his widow wrote about him:

Simultaneously with the publication of the *Qabalah* in 1887, he received instructions from his occult teachers to prepare what was eventually to become his esoteric school. . . . In 1888, after the publication of the *Qabalah Unveiled*, my husband started the working of his esoteric school. To write the consecutive history of an occult Order is a difficult matter, as difficult as to write the life of an Adept, there being so much of an inner and secret nature necessarily involved in both; so much of the symbolical in the historical, so much of the latter in the symbology. The general constitution of the teaching, the skeleton of the work, was handed to him by his occult teachers together with a vast amount of oral instruction. The object of the establishment of this school was similar to that of the foundation in ancient times of centres for the Celebration of the Mysteries. The literature of this school, with a few exceptions, was written by my husband under the direction of these teachers, based upon the ancient mysteries, chiefly those of Egypt, Chaldea and Greece, and brought up to date to suit the needs of our modern mentalities. . . .

As a pioneer movement, for the first ten or twelve years it encountered many of the difficulties that beset work that is given ahead of its time, but we had been told that the beginning would be in the nature of an experiment and that the students would be sifted. Dr. Woodman[48] had died in the year 1890, and in 1897 Dr. Wynn-Westcott resigned, after which my husband entirely reorganized the school under orders, and further teachings were given him. The teaching is principally by Ceremony, Ritual, and Lecture. Purity of aspiration and of life are the first and essential qualities demanded of the student. A simultaneous development of soul, mind and body is insisted upon. . . . The whole aim and object of the teaching is to bring a man to the knowledge of his higher self, to purify himself, to strengthen himself, to develop all qualities and powers of the being, that he may ultimately regain union with the Divine Man latent in himself, that Adam Qadmon, whom God hath made in His Own Image. . . .

Regarding seers and mediums . . . our school lays great stress on the simultaneous development of, crudely speaking, the three planes of being, which development must precede psychic experiment. The methods employed to equilibrate the nature entail considerable study, time and patience. There is no royal road to any science, let alone the science of the occult.[49]

If these words, although they were written in 1926, reflect correctly the aims and principles of the Golden Dawn from its beginnings, we may understand why H. P. Blavatsky no longer objected to a double membership of her Esoteric School and the order. All the practices she had criticized in her "Lodges of Magic" were also rejected by the Golden Dawn. Furthermore, just as this was the case in the Esoteric Section, the members of the Golden Dawn were mainly engaged in a theoretical *study* and only a small part of their activities was of a more practical nature. They did some simple meditation exercises and had to perform the lesser Pentagram Ritual to purify their auras; real magic, however, did not belong to the Golden Dawn curriculum at all. The study of the initiation rituals was emphasized, and the theoretical knowledge of a member was examined before he or she could advance to the next degree. The highest degree was the 4 = 7 degree of Philosophus. After this there was an "administrative degree" of Adeptus Minor 5 = 6, for those members who would function as the Hierophant of a Temple.

In short, although a member of the Golden Dawn was studying the Hermetic Kabbalah, and a member of the Esoteric Section "eastern" theosophy, there was no real difference between these two esoteric schools. Westcott functioned as the "bond of union" between them and followed the discipline of the Esoteric School, but not of the Golden Dawn, because he was already a chief of this order. Gilbert suggests that Westcott did not progress to the Inner Group of the Esoteric Section,[50] but he is mistaken. As we have seen, Westcott received the minutes of all the meetings of the Inner Group. It follows, then, that Blavatsky must have trusted him highly, and perhaps she valued her special relationship with the Golden Dawn.

Be this as it may, Moina Mathers's letter shows that the ultimate aim of the Golden Dawn was to become a *practical* esoteric school. Just as the Esoteric Section of the Theosophical Society had an Inner Group in which the more practical aspects of esotericism were taught, so the Golden Dawn had its own "inner group" that was founded in 1892 as a *separate* order to which only the Philosophi of the Golden Dawn could be invited. This was the Ordo Rosae Rubeae et Aureae Crucis. Central to this Inner Order was the heptagonal "Vault of the Adepts" modeled on the Crypt of Christian Rosenkreutz as described in the *Fama Fraternitatis*. Interestingly enough, there is again a remarkable parallel to Blavatsky's Inner Group, because both made use of a seven-walled room! We may speculate that Mathers received this idea from Westcott, who might have heard about the "occult room" of the Inner Group. Mathers, however, claimed that he had received instructions from his "secret chiefs" to design such a vault. Furthermore, he stated that he had received all the teachings of this second order in a way that in some respects resembles the manner in which Blavatsky claimed to have received the text of the *Secret Doctrine:*

> I make what I can only describe as a sort of vacuum in the air before me, and fix my sight and my will upon it, and soon scene after scene passes before me like the successive pictures of a diorama, or, if I need a reference or information from some book, I fix my mind intently, and the astral counterpart of the book appears, and from it I take what I need. The more perfectly my mind is freed from distractions and mortifications, the more energy and intentness it possesses, the more easily I can do this. . . .[51]

In more or less the same vein, Mathers writes:

> Almost the whole of the Second Order Knowledge has been obtained by me from them[52] in various ways, by clairvoyance—by astral projection on their part and mine— . . . at times copied from books brought before me, I knew not how—and which disappeared from my vision when the transcription was finished. . . .[53]

The degrees of the second order corresponded to the degrees of the first Order. The 0 = 0 Neophyte degree of the Golden Dawn corresponded to the Portal degree of the O.R.R & A.C., for both prepared the candidate for his or her entrance into a Sephirah of the Kabbalistic Tree of Life. The 1 = 10 Zelator degree brought the candidate into the Sephirah Malkuth, whereas the first phase of the 5 = 6 Adeptus Minor degree was called the Zelator Adeptus Minor, which brought the candidate into the Sephirah Tiphereth. Yet, the Adeptus Minor had a lot to do before he or she was able to reach such a state of inner purification and receptivity that he or she could receive the "knowledge and conversation with the Holy Guardian Angel"—an experience that would have been called "an experience of the Higher Self" in Blavatsky's Inner Group. The work that had to be done in the Adeptus Minor degree was divided into five phases: next to the Zelator Adeptus Minor degree came the Theoricus A.M. (corresponding to the 2 = 9 Theoricus degree—the Sephirah Yesod—of the Golden Dawn); the Practicus A.M (corresponding to the 3 = 8 Practicus degree—the Sephirah Hod); the Philosophus A.M. (corresponding to the 4 = 7 Philosophus degree—the Sephirah Netzach); and finally, the Adept Adeptus Minor degree in which the member was at last fully initiated into the Sephirah Tiphereth.[54] The curriculum that led to the subdegree of Zelator Adeptus Minor was quite complex. First of all, the member was taught the real esoteric meanings of the initiation ritual of the Neophyte degree of the Golden Dawn and its practical applications. This ritual could be used for the evocation of a spirit; for the consecration of talismans; for the transformation of the astral body into a Godform; for spiritual development; for divination; and for alchemy.[55] Furthermore, various Pentagram and Hexagram rituals had to be practiced, which were to be used during the consecration of the ritual implements every Adeptus Minor had to construct. One of the most complex parts of the curriculum was the study and practice of John Dee's "Enochian" magic, a system that beautifully synthesized all the knowledge of the Golden Dawn:[56]

> This stupendous amalgam combines Egyptian Tradition, initiated Astrology, Tarot, Geomancy and the Qabalistic Tree of Life with Dee's intense Elemental constructions, to make a single monumentally-impressive whole. No one without the profoundest knowledge of all these symbolic "paths" could thus have built up from them a workable synthesis. . . .
> The system is both macrocosmic and microcosmic, related as much to the human psycho-physical organism as to the depths of space[57]

Such correlations between the macrocosm and the microcosm were also studied in Blavatsky's Esoteric School, so here again we find an interesting parallel between the two schools. By means of this system the Adeptus Minor was able to explore the various dimensions of the astral plane so as to change his or her own inner structure and to enable him or her to mediate divine influences to the world.

The Zelator Adeptus Minor who wished to progress to the Practicus Adeptus Minor subdegree had to study the initiation ritual of the Zelator of the Golden Dawn, in more or less the same way in which he or she had analyzed the esoteric teachings and practices of the Neophyte ritual,[58] and new "Enochian" teachings were received as well.[59] It is not quite clear whether the other subdegrees were already practiced by the time of Mathers' death in 1918.[60] We may speculate that they would also have contained an esoteric and practical analysis of the initiation ritual of the degree of the Golden Dawn to which they corresponded.

The Golden Dawn and its Inner Order has exerted a strong influence on the development of the western magical tradition in West Europe and the United States. Various other orders have been developed on its foundation; some have seriously tried to build up an authentic esoteric school, whereas others degenerated into bogus orders or worse. The same development occurred in the Theosophical Society and its various offshoots, each of which had its own Esoteric School. One of the most interesting offshoots was the school developed by Rudolf Steiner in the early years of this century, in which he attempted to synthesize both the "eastern" and the "western" approach to "occult" development.

The Mysteria Mystica Aeterna

Not only in Great Britain and the United States, but in continental Europe as well, the last quarter of the nineteenth century brought an occult revival. Various high-grade Masonic orders flourished, and the Theosophical Society became rather influential in the artistic and intellectual circles of Vienna, Europe's cultural capital.[61] This Viennese theosophical group, as well as most of the early groups in Germany, was highly influenced by Rosicrucian and mystical Masonic ideas.[62] It was here that Rudolf Steiner (1861–1925) was introduced to theosophy and to other esoteric currents.[63] During this period he was working on his Ph.D. thesis in philosophy (1891) and on his philosophical magnum opus, *The Philosophy of Freedom* (1894). He studied the anarchistic ideas of Stirner, the materialistic monism of Haeckel, Goethe's thought, Fichte's philosophy of the "I," and the revolutionary writings of Nietzsche.[64] Accordingly, Steiner's intellectual background was completely different from that of most of the theosophists he met in Austria and Germany.[65] In 1902 he was appointed general-secretary of the Theosophical Society in Germany, and even in his early lectures he emphasized the importance of Christian mysticism and Rosicrucianism for European Theosophists. He claimed that many of the theosophical ideas could be proved by means of scientific investigation, although it should be added that clairvoyance had to become an important part of that method. Not "mystical contemplation," but scientific and abstract thinking, should be the point of departure. Nevertheless, a comparative study of Steiner's writings with those of Blavatsky and Sinnett shows that, as much as he and his followers may claim that his teaching is based on his own original investigations, their cosmological and anthropological teachings are almost identical.[66] It is very characteristic of Steiner that he consistently denied the strong influence of theosophy on his own ideas, and claimed always to have been critical about H. P. Blavatsky and her "masters." His published writings, however, show us a rather different picture: until his quarrel with the Theosophical Society in 1913 he usually showed a deep respect for them.[67] Similarly, he later denied that Masonry was of any importance to the development of his own ideas[68] although, again, in the first fifteen years of his theosophical work he usually referred to "eastern Freemasonry" as a very important western esoteric school.[69] Both esoteric currents were evidently very important to him, because they together formed the foundation, first for his own "western" esoteric school, and subsequently for the anthroposophical "university" he established in Dornach.

In 1904 Steiner became a member of the Esoteric School of the Theosophical Society in England, and in 1904 he became the "Arch-Warden" of this "eastern" school for Germany and Austria.[70] In July 1904 the first esoteric meeting was held. The notes from the meetings in 1904 show that Steiner followed the system of the Esoteric School in England: he lectured on the significance of the AUM, on the chakras and the *tattva*s (cosmic principles). All these subjects were part of Blavatsky's *Esoteric Instructions No. 1,* which was still an official document of the Esoteric School. Steiner lectured on *Light on the Path,*[71] which, together with Blavatsky's *The Voice of the Silence,* was an obligatory subject for the meditations of the students. He told his students about the necessity to control the breath in order to develop the "light of Kundalini."[72] The principal difference between Steiner's section of the Esoteric School and the British section was that the students in England could choose between four different methods or ways, whereas in Steiner's section only one way was provided (which seems to be more or less a combination of all these four "methods").[73]

A student of this "first section" of the school had to attend Steiner's esoteric lectures, to follow the general rules of the school (e.g., no smoking), and to do the general exercises. Some of the students received personal exercises from Steiner, which they added to their general program of training. Every student had to start the day with an invocation of his or her Higher Self, followed by a meditation on some lines of *Light on the Path.* At the end of the day this invocation had to be repeated, followed by a review of all his or her activities and experiences of the previous day, in order to develop his or her self-knowledge.[74] Steiner's esoteric lectures, however, were claimed not to be *his* lectures but those of the "eastern" Masters:

> First a prayer spoken by Dr. Steiner. Then he indicated that the Masters speak through Dr. Steiner, and that he is only an instrument by means of which the thoughts of the Masters are expressed. Master Morya explained the aim of the development of humanity. He is the one, who guides humanity. . . .[75]

In the light of Steiner's later criticism of Blavatsky's Masters, this statement is very revealing indeed!

Yet, Steiner did not merely follow Besant's interpretation of the esoteric way. From the beginning of his work in the Esoteric School, he also referred to Christian Rosenkreutz and Jesus as the two most important Masters, next to the Masters Morya and Koot Hoomi, who are the real teachers of the school. His school was to be something special because, according to Master Morya speaking through Steiner's mouth, "the German theosophical movement is very important. The German people are the avantgarde of the 6th sub-race."[76]

In October 1905, in Berlin, during the general convention of the German section of the Theosophical Society, Steiner gave a series of thirty-one lectures for his esoteric school on the "principles of esotericism"[77]. His teaching here was still closely related to the theosophical teachings of Annie Besant, although he made use of his own terminology and often referred to Kabbalah, Christianity, and Freemasonry. During this convention he also lectured on "mystical Masonry," and on 2 January 1906 he lectured on "the royal art in a new form."[78] This special esoteric lecture marked the beginning of the second and third section of Steiner's school. According to the editor of Steiner's esoteric papers, it was only from that moment that this school was really established, because it was now complete.[79] Steiner now began to emphasize more and more the importance of the Rosicrucian tradition, both in his public lectures and in his esoteric teachings.[80] Some of the old theosophists in Germany were not very happy with these developments, and they seem to have complained to Annie Besant about the situation. In 1907, Besant granted Steiner's Esoteric School its independence, writing to the members that his occult teaching differed from that of her school. But she emphasized that both schools would continue to work together,[81] although there are no documents known to me which show that this ever really happened. Steiner also told his esoteric students that there was no disharmony between the "Masters of the East" and the "Masters of the West":

> Until now both schools were united in a big circle under the general leadership of the Masters. Now the western School has become independent; hence there are now two equal Schools: one in the East, and the other in the West—two smaller circles instead of a single big one. The eastern School is lead by Mrs. Annie Besant. Every member who in his heart is more attracted to her, can no longer remain in our School. . . . At the top of our western School stand two Masters: the Master Jesus and the Master Christian Rosencreutz.[82]

Consequently, German theosophists who did not like to follow Steiner's "Christian-Rosicrucian" way could now again become a member of the Esoteric School of the Theosophical Society in England, just as this had been the case before Steiner's appointment as "Arch-Warden" of the Esoteric School in Germany.

From this moment Steiner's Esoteric School consisted of three sections, so one might expect that it had the same structure as Blavatsky's Esoteric School, which also had three sections, with the Masters in the third or highest "class." This, however, was not the case. On 3 January 1906, i.e., after the convention, Steiner received from Theodor Reuss[83] a charter that enabled him to start his own (fringe) Masonic organization, called the Mysteria Mystica Aeternis.[84] The different degrees of this organization now constituted the second and third degrees of his school.

The structure of the school was as follows:

The first section was called the *seekers*, and consisted of two degrees. This "class" was nothing else but the former Esoteric School of the German Theosophical Society. In this section Steiner taught his students basic meditation techniques. The members of the second section were engaged in *exercises*, and this section consisted of three "cultic grades" in which the first principles of "mystical Freemasonry," or "Rosicrucianism" were taught, and in which various ritualistic activities took place. Every meeting was opened and closed with a ritual, and one entered the three degrees by means of an initiation. The third section was formed by members who were really following an occult training,[85] and consisted of six grades, to which only a few students were admitted. In these degrees, the students were helped to develop an "intimate knowledge" of all the occult forces they "had symbolically experienced" in the previous three degrees.[86] For instance, in the fourth "cultic" degree (i.e., the first degree of the third section) the student was taught various exercises that involved different physical movements and the "vibration" vowels.[87] These exercises were combined with Masonic signs and "grips," and were taught to be the means by which the "subtle energies" of the body could be harmonized.[88] They show a close affinity with the exercises published by the occultist J. B. Kerning, which had been practiced by the members of the theosophical lodge of Prague (including the famous occult writer Gustav Meyrink) around the turn of the century.[89] Steiner could have met some of these practitioners, because they often attended the same esoteric groups in Vienna as he did.[90]

Now, the question is from what fringe Masonic organization Steiner received his charter and his rituals. According to the editor of Steiner's esoteric papers (and also according to Steiner himself), this organization was the Berlin Grand Lodge of the United Grand Council of Rites of the Ancient and Accepted Scottish Rite & Ancient Primitive Rite of Memphis & Egyptian Rite of Misraim. This was also the opinion of Ellic Howe.[91] Francis King, however, has argued that it must have been the Ordo Templi Orientis, because:

(a) *Mysteria Mystica*[92] normally formed a part of the names of O.T.O. national sections. . . .

(b) Women were admitted into the group led by Steiner; this would be normal in the O.T.O but not in Memphis and Misraim.

(c) By the time he came to write his autobiography Steiner was clearly ashamed of his former ritualistic activities and devoted three pages to an attempt to explain them away. It is difficult to understand why he should have done this if he had been no more than an unorthodox freemason.

(d) Crowley . . . specifically stated that Steiner had been an O.T.O. initiate. It is worth adding that Crowley was usually accurate on matters of fact outside his own personal affairs.

(e) Dr. Felkin, the chief of the Stella Matutina (a magical fraternity derived from the Golden Dawn) and a disciple of Steiner was also a member of the British section of the O.T.O. This, of course, was led by Crowley—regarded by the Stella Matutina as a black magician. It is impossible to explain Felkin's membership of the O.T.O., and consequent association with Crowley, except on the assumption that either Steiner or one of his German lieutenants had suggested it to him.

(f) Descriptions of Steiner's rituals published in the French press before 1914 are reminiscent of the ceremonies of the O.T.O.

(g) There is some evidence that Steiner referred to his group as "Esoteric Rosicrucians"; this was the name given to initiates of the 8th degree of the O.T.O.[93]

It is now possible to confirm Francis King's conclusion. If we compare, for instance, the ritual for the opening of the lodge in the first degree (of the second section)[94] with the same ritual used by the O.T.O.,[95] we will discover that Steiner's ritual is not merely "reminiscent" of the O.T.O. ritual but that many passages are identical. Furthermore, the structure of the O.T.O. is identical with the structure of Steiner's school. The O.T.O. also consisted of three sections or "classes." The first class of "probationers" was formed by "theosophists and martinists"; the second class of "lay-brothers" by Freemasons;[96] and the third class of the "Initiates," who are working in the "proper" O.T.O. degrees, which together are called "Mystic Masonry + Esoteric Rosicrucians + Illuminism." They are called "the real active members of the O.T.O.," and "Hermetic Brothers of Light." Furthermore, the fifth "cultic" degree (i.e., the second degree of the third section) was called by Steiner Knight of the Eagle and Pelican,[97] which corresponds to the fifth degree of the O.T.O.[98] Finally, in 1911, Steiner told his students that they should no longer use the name "Freemasonry" for their occult work, but the name Misraim-Dienst (i.e. Misraim-Service) instead.[99] This order is usually interpreted by anthroposophists as a clear indication that these higher degrees had nothing to do with Freemasonry. Unfortunately, for them, this name was not invented by Steiner but was already used in the original O.T.O. rituals of Reuss!

Why was Steiner so afraid that outsiders would discover his connection with the O.T.O.? What kind of an organization was this order? In order to answer these questions we must turn to the jubilee issue of the *Oriflamme* (the journal of the O.T.O.), July 1914, in which the following statement was published:

> The spiritual Father of the new organized Oriental Order of the Templers was . . . Dr. Carl Kellner. During his many travels in Europe, America, and Asia, Dr. Kellner contacted an organisation which was called "The Hermetic Brotherhood of Light." . . . The Rosicrucian teachings of the "Hermetic Brotherhood of Light" are only available to the few initiates of the occult inner circle. . . .[100]

What were these "Rosicrucian teachings"? The same issue of the *Oriflamme* states:

> Our Order possesses the KEY which opens up all Masonic and Hermetic secrets, namely, the teaching of sexual magic, and this teaching explains, without exception, all the secrets of Freemasonry and all systems of religion.[101]

It is quite possible that Kellner contacted the Hermetic Brotherhood of Luxor, the order to which many theosophists and Golden Dawn adepti also belonged,[102] although he claimed a more remote source for his secrets.

Given this nature of the secrets of the O.T.O., it is quite understandable that Steiner wished to remove all references to this order. There certainly is no evidence that Steiner himself practiced sex magic. On the contrary, Steiner seems to have severed all his contacts with Reuss by 1906,[103] although it is remarkable that one of his closest female associates, Alice Sprengel, very soon became a member of the inner circle of the O.T.O., after she left Steiner's organization following his marriage in 1914 with Marie von Sivers.[104] It is possible that after 1906 some members of Steiner's school still remained in contact with Reuss's order. Furthermore, according to a member of Steiner's school, who is quoted by Francis King, Steiner worked with Reuss until 1914.[105] To be sure, this would explain why Alice Sprengel could so easily become an important member of Reuss's order. We must assume that Steiner knew that sexuality was the "secret key" of this order, but that he interpreted this "secret" in a symbolic way. This assumption is strengthened by the fact that he explained, in his series of lectures on "mystical Freemasonry," the esoteric meaning of the sexes and of the sexual organs.[106] Furthermore, King wrote:

> Steiner did not use the physical sex but only the stored-up Kundalini serpent sex (the white sex magic). So his high degrees saw the symbolism in a different way.[107]

If this is correct, we may conclude that Steiner remained faithful to the teachings about sex and Kundalini that were already taught by Blavatsky in her Inner Group.

The three sections of the Mysteria Mystica Aeterna corresponded to the three levels on which the students had to be trained. In the first section, the "etheric body" was developed; in the second, the "astral body"; and in the third section, the "mental body" and, perhaps, the higher principles as well.[108] It follows, then, that Steiner seems to have had good reasons to combine the Esoteric School of the Theosophical Society with the system of the O.T.O. Most occult traditions teach that we can only work in the "astral world" by means of our "creative imagination" and by means of rituals. Blavatsky's Esoteric School did not provide its members with the instruments to work on that level,[109] so we may assume that Steiner intentionally chose to add the grades of the O.T.O. to his own school but that he wished to work independently from the official O.T.O. and other Masonic orders, without severing all his relations with them. If this assumption is correct, then ritual activities should nowadays still play an essential part in Steiner's school. However, as far as I know, such activities are no longer a part of the training in the modern Anthroposophical Movement.[110]

When the First World War started, Steiner stopped all the activities of the Mysteria Mystica Aeterna. This is quite understandable: since secret societies have always been connected with political aims, during the war the government was opposed to their activities.[111] After the war Steiner attempted to start his Esoteric School again, but in a new form. He called it the Freie Hochschule für Geisteswissenschaft. This name shows that he still wished to emphasize that his method of inner development was a scientific method. There are even some indications that he hoped that this university would be able to grant its students a Ph.D. degree![112] Be this as it may, within the context of this *Hochschule*, Steiner also organized meetings for the first section of a new esoteric "department." Unfortunately, he died before this new Esoteric School was established. In one of his lectures, however, he referred to the importance of ritual work,[113] so we may assume that he intended to revive the ritual degrees as well.[114]

AFTERWORD

In this article I have described three attempts to establish an esoteric school that would train its students in such a way that their "inner aspects" would be enabled to develop. Such schools are an integral part of many religious traditions (e.g., Buddhism), but in the West such schools were often part of a counterculture. This entails that usually they were not embedded in the "exoteric" religious tradition and the official culture. As a result they often tend to become small sectarian organizations with all the negative consequences that this entails. All three schools described in this article disintegrated due to continuous quarrels and other causes. On the other hand, many of their practices seem to be authentic, in the sense that they are similar to the "esoteric" practices of well-established traditions, for instance, with those taught within the various tantric Buddhist traditions. A comprehensive comparative study of the doctrines and practices of these western esoteric schools with those of some of the established traditions might enable us to discover the main causes of their failures, and might help us to understand their importance as a spiritual phenomenon, even within our own culture.

NOTES

1. Cf. James Webb, *The Flight from Reason* (London, 1971); Karl R. H. Frick, *Licht und Finsternis* (Graz, 1975), 1:7.

2. Cf. Jean-Pierre Laurant, "The Primitive Characteristics of Nineteenth-Century Esotericism," in *Modern Esoteric Spirituality*, ed. A. Faivre and J. Needleman (New York, 1992), 277–87.

3. E.g., *What is Magick?* in Aleister Crowley, *Magick without Tears* (St. Paul, 1973), 27–38.

4. E.g., James Webb, *The Occult Establishment* (LaSalle, 1976); Michael Howard, *The Occult Conspiracy* (Rochester, 1989). Howard's book is a very speculative and amusing account of the influence of secret societies; yet he provides some interesting details.

5. Cf. R. Tegtmeier, *Okkultismus und Erotik in der Literatur des Fin de Siècle* (Köningswinter, 1983); Mircea Eliade, *Occultism, Witchcraft, and Cultural Fashions* (Chicago, 1976), 47ff.

6. Webb, *Flight from Reason*, xii.

7. One of the more satisfactory recent works on her life and thought is Sylvia Cranston, *H.P.B.: The Extraordinary Life & Influence of Helena Blavatsky* (New York, 1993). A very useful compilation of eyewitnesses' accounts of her life is provided by Daniel H. Caldwell, *The Occult World of Madame Blavatsky* (Tucson, 1991).

8. Cf. K. Paul Johnson, *The Masters Revealed: Madame Blavatsky and the Myth of the Great White Lodge* (Albany, 1994).

9. Ibid.

10. This is a summary of the topics of the many articles and letters Blavatsky wrote during her theosophical career. Cf. H. P. Blavatsky, *Collected Writings*, vols. 1–15 (Wheaton, London, and Adyar, 1966–91). Henceforth referred to as *CW.*

11. H. P. Blavatsky, *Secret Doctrine* (London, 1888), xxii, xliv.

12. In his book, Paul Johnson also emphasizes this point.

13. However, according to Alice Leighton Cleather, the London Lodge still had in 1885 three sections (*H. P. Blavatsky: A Great Betrayal* [Calcutta, 1922], 84). We must assume that the second section was not the original one, but was identical to the new "inner group" of the London Lodge.

14. A. L. Cleather, *H. P. Blavatsky as I knew her* (Calcutta, 1923), 15f.

15. This Inner Group must not be confused with the inner group of the London Lodge, established in 1884. The second degree of the Esoteric Section consisted of members who received an edited version of the minutes of the Inner Group.

Since they could not attend the meetings in the special room of the Inner Group, we may surmise that the work of this second degree was also mostly of a theoretical nature. Cf. *CW,* 12:655.

16. Cf. H. J. Spierenburg, ed., *The Inner Group Teachings of H. P. Blavatsky* (San Diego, 1985), xvi. According to Jinarâjadâsa, the room may have been eight-sided. But in view of the symbolic meaning of the number seven, and the fact that every wall was to be covered with a different metal, each presumably corresponding to one of the planets, I think we are justified to suppose that the room had seven walls. Interestingly, the "inner Order" of the Golden Dawn made also use of such a heptagonal room!

17. Cleather, *H.P. Blavatsky as I Knew Her,* 24.

18. Ibid., x.

19. Cf. Spierenburg, *Inner Group Teachings,* 2. Mr. Spierenburg recently published a completely new edition of this book (San Diego, 1995) in which he made use of materials that were not available when the first edition was published. This edition also contains a historical introduction written by Mr. Daniel Caldwell. The text on p. 2 of the first edition is incomplete. The new edition, however, clearly shows that Blavatsky is discussing here an exercise for the awakening of kundalini!

20. Ibid., 1st ed., 3.

21. Cf. Dara Eklund, ed., *Echoes of the Orient: The Writings of William Quan Judge* (San Diego, 1987), 3:294–95.

22. Ibid., 3:384–85.

23. Spierenburg, *Inner Group Teachings,* 1st ed., 95.

24. As quoted in George Mills Harper, *Yeats's Golden Dawn* (London, 1974), 5.

25. It was as a reaction to the fact that Kingsford and her supporters did not believe in the existence of Blavatsky's Masters that the "inner group" of the London Lodge (to which I have already referred) was established.

26. Ithell Colquhoun, *Sword of Wisdom* (London, 1975), 76.

27. Colquhoun's book is still one of the better introductions to this interesting man, who, according to Ellic Howe, *The Magicians of the Golden Dawn* (London, 1972), 37, is "a heaven-sent subject for a full-scale biography if there were sufficient material." Unfortunately, there still seems to be a lack of sufficient material.

28. Howe, *Magicians,* 26ff.

29. Colquhoun, *Sword of Wisdom,* 73.

30. Harper, *Yeats's Golden Dawn,* 9

31. R. A. Gilbert, *The Golden Dawn: Twilight of the Magicians* (Wellingborough, 1983), 23.

32. R. A. Gilbert, *The Golden Dawn Companion* (Wellingborough, 1986), 24.

33. *The Cipher MSS of the Golden Dawn* (London, 1974), 8.

34. Ibid., 9.

35. Israel Regardie, *The Golden Dawn,* 5th ed. (St. Paul, 1988), 155f.

36. R. G. Torrens, *The Secret Rituals of the Golden Dawn* (New York, 1972), 118f.

37. R. A. Gilbert, *The Golden Dawn and the Esoteric Section* (London, 1987), 6.

38. This refers to the Rev. W. A. Ayton. Cf. ibid.

39. Cf. the first part of this article.

40. Blavatsky, *Collected Writings*, 11:124ff. "A" refers to the Rev. W. A. Ayton, who was a member of the Theosophical Society, of the Golden Dawn, and of the Hermetic Brotherhood of Luxor (cf. Joscelyn Godwin et al., *The Hermetic Brotherhood of Luxor* [York Beach, 1995], 4). It seems to me that Blavatsky confused the rumors about the Golden Dawn with the rumors about the Hermetic Brotherhood of Luxor, for this last order certainly practiced "black magic" (according to Blavatsky's definition), because some of its members were engaged in sex magic. The Yorkshire group, to which Blavatsky referred, was a group related to the Golden Dawn.

41. Godwin, *Hermetic Brotherhood of Luxor*, 7, argues that Blavatsky was not so much afraid of the competition of the Golden Dawn, but of that of the Brotherhood of Luxor. It seems to me, however, that the Brotherhood of Luxor could not have been a real alternative for Blavatsky's school, because they practiced "black magic," whereas the "white magic" of the Golden Dawn might have been a real alternative to all those students of Blavatsky who accepted her condemnation of sex magic.

42. Harper, *Yeats's Golden Dawn*, 7.

43. Ellic Howe, ed., *The Alchemist of the Golden Dawn*, (Wellingborough, 1985), 29f.

44. As quoted in Gilbert, *Golden Dawn and the Esoteric Section*, 8.

45. Ibid.

46. Howe, *Magicians*, chap. 1.

47. Colquhoun, *Sword of Wisdom*, 35ff. Even such a skeptic as Francis King was eventually convinced of the physical existence of at least one of Mathers's masters. Cf. Francis King, *The Rites of Modern Occult Magic* (New York, 1970), 46.

48. The "Supreme Magus" of the S.R.I.A. and, with Mathers and Westcott, the third chief of the Golden Dawn.

49. S. L. MacGregor Mathers, *The Kabbalah Unveiled* (London, 1970), viiff.

50. Gilbert, *Golden Dawn and the Esoteric Section*, 9.

51. Countess Constance Wachtmeister et al., *Reminiscences of H. P. Blavatsky and The Secret Doctrine* (Wheaton, 1976), 25.

52. I.e., from the "secret chiefs."

53. As quoted by King, *Rites of Modern Occult Magic*, 45.

54. Gilbert, *Golden Dawn Companion*, 101.

55. Regardie, *Golden Dawn*, 376ff. (Z2-document).

56. It is sometimes claimed that Mathers brought the Enochiana into the order, but this is incorrect. In the grade rituals, as they appear in the cipher manuscript, the so-called Enochian Watchtowers are already mentioned and used.

57. Colquhoun, *Sword of Wisdom*, 260f.

58. Cf. Howe, *Magicians*, 288f.

59. Cf. Pat Zalewski, *Golden Dawn Enochian Magic* (St. Paul, 1990), xiif.

60. According to Pat Zalewski, however, in 1900 members of the Inner Order worked on the Zelator and Theoricus A.M. levels. The Practicus A.M. was drafted but never implemented, and the Philosophus and Adept levels were never developed. Cf. Pat Zalewski, *Secret Inner Order Rituals of the Golden Dawn* (Phoenix, 1988), 5.

61. Nicholas Goodrick-Clarke, "The Modern Occult Revival in Vienna, 1880–1910," *Theosophical History* 1 (1986): 97ff.

62. R. H. Frick, *Licht und Finsternis* (Graz, 1978), 2:383.

63. James Webb, *The Occult Establishment* (La Salle, 1976), 62.

64. Richard Geisen, *Anthroposophie und Gnostizismus* (Paderborn, 1992), 207ff.

65. Webb, *Occult Establishment*, 66,

66. Cf. Geisen, *Anthroposophie und Gnostizismus*, 231.

67. Cf. the excellently documented series of papers written by H. J. Spierenburg: "Dr. Steiner on H.P.B.," *Theosophical History* 1 (1986): 159–74; "Dr. Rudolf Steiner on the Mahatmas," *Theosophical History* 1 (1986), 211–23 and *Theosophical History* 2 (1987): 23–31.

68. Geisen, *Anthroposophie und Gnostizismus*, 242.

69. *Orientmaurerei*, cf. Rudolf Steiner, *Die Tempellegende und die goldene Legende*, Gesamtausgabe 93 (Dornach, 1982), 97. As I shall argue in due course, Steiner referred to the "Order of Oriental Templars," the O.T.O.

70. Annie Besant's letter, in which she appointed him, is published in Rudolf Steiner, *Zur Geschichte und Inhalten der ersten Abteilung der Esoterische Schule, 1904–1914*, Gesamtausgabe 264 (Dornach, 1984), 25.

71. An inspired text received in 1885 from the Master Serapis by Mabel Collins, a pupil of Blavatsky's esoteric school.

72. Rudolf Steiner, *Aus den Inhalten der esoterischen Stunden*, vol. 1: *1904–1909*, Gesamtausgabe (Dornach, 1995), 153ff.

73. The four ways were the "general way," the "path of yoga," the "Pythagorean way," and the "Christian-Gnostic way." Cf. GA 264, p. 28. The "general way" followed Blavatsky's original curriculum of the Esoteric School. The other ways were added by Annie Besant when she became the Outer Head of the school, after the death of Blavatsky.

74. Most of Steiner's instructions are published in GA 264 and in Rudolf Steiner, *Anweisungen für eine esoterische Schulung*, Gesamtausgabe 245 (Dornach, 1968).

75. Steiner, *Zur Geschichte und Inhalten*, 206.

76. Ibid., 85.

77. R. Steiner, *Grundelemente der Esoterik*, Gesamtausgabe 93a (Dornach, 1972).

78. Published in GA 93.

79. Steiner, *Zur Geschichte und Inhalten*, 27.

80. Webb, *Occult Establishment*, 69.

81. This letter of Annie Besant is published in Steiner, *Zur Geschichte und Inhalten*, 270.

82. Steiner, *Aus den Inhalten*, 221.

83. Theodor Reuss was a well-known collector of high-grade Masonic initiations. See Helmut Möller and Ellic Howe, *Merlin Peregrinus: Vom Untergrund des Abendlandes* (Würzburg, 1986).

84. Peter-R. König, *Das OTO-Phänomen* (München, 1994), 35.

85. Steiner, *Aus den Inhalten*, 230.

86. Rudolf Steiner, *Zur Geschichte und aus den Inhalten der erkenntniskultischen Abteilung der Esoterischen Schule, 1904–1914,* Gesamtausgabe 265 (Dornach, 1987), 148.

87. Ibid., 214ff.

88. Ibid., 286ff.

89. Karl Weinfurter, *Der brennende Busch* (Bietigheim, n.d.), 46ff.

90. These exercises played also an important role in the O.T.O.; hence it is also possible that Steiner received them from Reuss. They are published by Rudolf von Sebottendorf, *Die geheime Uebungen der türkischen Freimaurer* (Freiburg, 1977); and by Karl Spiesberger, *Magische Einweihung* (Berlin, 1976) (Spiesberger was a member of an offshoot of the O.T.O.). Another version of these exercises was published by Albert Schutz, *Call Adonoi* (Goleta, 1980).

91. Howe, *Magicians,* 263.

92. King writes "Mysteria Maxima," which is clearly a mistake, because that was the name of Aleister Crowley's O.T.O. section in Britain.

93. Francis King, ed., *The Secret Rituals of the O.T.O* (London, 1973), 27.

94. Steiner, *Zur Geschichte und aus den Inhalten,* 153ff.

95. Published by Peter R. König, *Der kleine Theodor-Reuss-Reader* (München, 1993), 40ff.

96. Yes, even of high-grade Masons. According to the O.T.O.: "[T]he mere possession of these various Masonic degrees does not constitute a Member as an 'O.T.O'—properly so called—therefore even a 33-degree Mason is, from the O.T.O. point of view, still considered a 'Lay Brother'." Cf. Peter-R. König, *Materialien zum OTO* (München, 1994), 22–23.

97. Steiner, *Zur Geschichte und aus den Inhalten,* 217.

98. Cf. König, *Materialien,* 22: to the fifth degree belong the Knights of the Rose Croix, Knights of the Pelican, and the Knights of East and West *(Schwarzen Adler).*

99. Steiner, *Zur Geschichte und aus den Inhalten,* 94.

100. König, *Reuss-Reader,* 7–8.

101. Ibid., 10

102. Cf. Francis King, *Sexuality, Magic & Perversion* (London, 1971), 97. Joscelyn Godwin, in *Hermetic Brotherhood of Luxor,* 67, states that the Hermetic Brotherhood of Light, founded in Chicago, might have been the source of the sexual practices of the O.T.O. Yet, it is also possible that Kellner had met some of the French students of the original Hermetic Brotherhood of Luxor.

103. König, *Reuss-Reader,* 28.

104. Ibid., 33.

105. Francis King, *The Rites of Modern Occult Magic* (New York, 1971), 206. This is the American edition of *Ritual Magic in England.*

106. Steiner, *Tempellegende,* 223ff.

107. King, *Rites of Modern Occult Magic,* 206.

108. Steiner, *Tempellegende,* 97.

109. Although we will never know what Blavatsky's plans were. She had only just started to teach her Inner Group when she died.

110. There are, however, some rumors that there exists an "inner circle" in Dornach that is still engaged in ritual activities.

111. Cf. Geisen, *Anthroposophie und Gnostizismus*, 242.

112. In a lecture during a convention of Waldorf teachers on 14 February 1923, he said: "We cannot go further than our current possibilities. Even when the building in Dornach had not been destroyed by fire, it would not have been possible for a long time to get an accreditation for the University at Dornach; they would not permit us to establish a Ph.D.-program." cf. *Chrysostomos* (journal of the Anthroposophical Society Christian Rosenkreutz) (Rotterdam), n.d., 47.

113. *Chrysostomos*, n.d., 125. The lecture was delivered on 2 August 1924.

114. The anonymous author of this article in *Chrysostomos* writes that he is *sure* that Steiner intended to start again with ritual work.

CHAPTER 17

STOCKHAUSEN'S *DONNERSTAG AUS LICHT* AND GNOSTICISM

The German composer Karlheinz Stockhausen, born in 1928, made his reputation as a member of the postwar European avant-garde, along-side Pierre Boulez, Luciano Berio, Luigi Nono, and other composers who have since faded from public view. Stockhausen's place in the history of music was secured by the brilliant series of works he produced in the 1950s and '60s: *Kontra-punkte, Klavierstücke* I–XI; *Zeitmasse* for wood-winds; *Gruppen* for three orchestras; the electronic *Gesang der Jünglinge; Zyklus* for a percussionist; *Carré* for four orchestras and four choruses; *Kontakte* for electronic sounds, piano, and percussion; *Momente* for so-prano, singers, and instruments; *Hymnen* for electronic sounds; *musique concrète* and orchestra; *Stimmung* for six vocalists; and so on. These works created a new world of sound, through electronic music and the use of space, and new concepts of form, both through serial organization and through allowing a role to chance or choice.

Since 1977, Stockhausen has abandoned the composition of single works and devoted himself to one gigantic project: a cycle of seven op-eras collectively called *Licht* (Light), scheduled for completion early in the next century. The separate operas are called after the days of the week. As of 1994, four of them have been performed *(Donnerstag, Samstag, Montag, Dienstag)* and three recorded *(Donnerstag, Samstag, Montag).*[1]

Stockhausen creates not only the music of his operas, but also the words, gestures, and much of the visual design, and controls the electronic side of all the performances. One can scarcely imagine the labor that goes into this, and the obstacles he has to overcome in getting such unconventional works produced in conventional opera houses. Until 1993, when the Tuesday opera, *Dienstag aus Licht*, was premiered in Leipzig, no German opera house would stage his works. *Donnerstag, Samstag*, and *Montag* were all premiered at La Scala, Milan.

Stockhausen puzzles and embarrasses the average critic, impresario, and orchestral musician through being so obviously "spiritual." The other notoriously religious composer of the avant-garde, Olivier Messiaen, is more acceptable because he is easier for them to classify: as a lovable eccentric, whose music commands respect despite the Catholic theology with which it is decked out. But Stockhausen fits into no convenient pigeonhole. He apparently accepts all religions, East and West, North and South, and makes no secret of his belief in reincarnation and astrology. In contrast to Messiaen's humility and self-effacement, Stockhausen leaves one in no doubt of how he sees himself. As soon as he admitted to an interviewer (see below) that he was a being from Sirius who had incarnated on earth to fulfill a special mission through music, his credibility among "intellectuals" vanished. Whereas once he had been in the vanguard, in the epoch of Deconstruction he became as unfashionable as can be: in brief, he appeared to be that despicable thing, a "New Ager." Yet the impulses and convictions that some find embarrassing are the very ones that give him the will and the imagination to carry through his immense project, at a time when the other old avant-gardists are either silent or repeating themselves.

The seven-opera cycle of *Licht*, unlike Wagner's *Ring of the Nibelung*, is truly cyclical, in that it has no beginning or ending. In the cosmologies of the Orient, time is an ever-rolling wheel, not a straight line leading from the Creation to the Last Judgment. Death on Saturn's day (the theme of the opera *Samstag*) is only the prelude to marriage and conception on the Sun's day *(Sonntag)* and rebirth on the Moon's day *(Montag)*. Then comes war on Mars's day *(Dienstag)*, reconciliation on Mercury's or Woden's day *(Mittwoch)*, incarnation on Jupiter's or Thor's day *(Donnerstag)*, and temptation on Venus's or Freia's day *(Freitag)*. Stockhausen says: "[I]t doesn't start anywhere. I composed *Thursday* first, but the week in *Light* is a spiral without end"[2]—a formal concept already present in earlier pieces such as *Zyklus* and *Spiral*.

The musical organization of *Licht* also reflects the composer's cosmology, which in this respect is thoroughly up-to-date. The principle resembles that of fractals: the mathematical patterns in which the part is a replication of the whole. The entire cycle is based on a threefold musical germ or, as Stockhausen calls it, a "triple formula." It comprises Michael's formula of thirteen notes, Eve's formula of twelve, and

Lucifer's formula of eleven. Each formula includes not only pitches but also specific dynamics, rhythms, silences, vocalizations, etc. On the largest scale, the formulas control the entire cycle of operas. On the smallest, they are frequently perceptible as leitmotifs.

Stockhausen's vision of the formula as key to Hermetic correspondences goes beyond the material world. As he says: "[T]he formula is the matrix and plan of micro- and macroform, but also at the same time the psychic gestalt and vibrational image of a supramental manifestation" (TM, 5:667). The roots of this attitude lie far back, in the "total serialism" that Stockhausen and other composers were using in the 1950s, in which every parameter of a piece was integrated through permutations of a single series. Even then, it was with a spiritual intention that Stockhausen (a practicing Catholic at the time) paid tribute to the Creator by making every aspect of his microcosmic universe rational and complete. As his biographer Michael Kurtz says, this early music "was not the expression of human feelings and passions, but rather an attempt at a re-creation, a reconstitution of cosmic order and natural laws in sounds."[3] With the formulaic composition of *Licht*, the correspondence between macrocosm and microcosm comes far closer to that of nature itself. As with a fractal, the same pattern is perceived at every degree of complexity, or, as one might say, at every level of reality.

The three principal characters of *Licht* are Michael, Eve, and Lucifer. In the first act of *Donnerstag* we see Michael as a child with his mother and father, then as an adolescent discovering the feminine, then being examined and approved in his various talents. In the second act, Michael makes a musical journey round the world, culminating in a symbolic crucifixion and ascension. The third act takes place in heaven, as Michael is welcomed home again, to the accompaniment of invisible choirs singing extracts from Hebrew apocryphal literature.

Stockhausen said in an interview of 1981 that

> Michael is the creator-angel who now directs our universe. Creator-angels can create an entire universe in their own image. They go on creating until they see that the process has reached its fullness, and makes sense in every respect. Only then can a second process of inner working and perfection start, when the fullness is no longer increasing. Our universe is still taken up with the process of creating the fullness, and the second process, where the creation settles, fer-

ments, and harmonizes, has not yet quite begun. Everything is still experimental, and creation is still going on.

Michael is the master of our universe. He manifests himself in various forms, just as a person manifests in his works and his children. (TM, 6:203)

Unusually for Stockhausen, these fundamental ideas have a definite and modern source: *The Urantia Book*.[4] Michael Kurtz tells of how the composer was introduced to *Urantia* by a New York hippie in 1971, and of how he urged his students to study it while he was using some of its ideas in *Inori* during 1974.[5] *Urantia* is a text of over two thousand pages, obtained in 1934-35 through the mediumship of Wilfrid C. Kellogg (died 1956), a Chicago businessman and member of the Kellogg's Cornflakes family. He spoke the messages in trance, each of them being "signed" by an angelic source; they were taken down and edited by Dr. William S. Sadler, a psychiatrist and Seventh Day Adventist minister.[6] *Urantia*'s doctrines are consistent with Adventism, a movement that began in 1844 with the revelations of Ellen White. But the Kellogg-Sadler revelations go much further, presenting a panorama of cosmic and human history, then a year-by-year account of Jesus' life.

Stockhausen, always independent-minded, did not slavishly adopt the *Urantia* doctrines, but his admiration for the book led to several of its ideas being incorporated in *Donnerstag*. In act 1 (Michael's Youth) the name "CHRIST MICHAEL" comes twice, highlighted in capital letters in the libretto.[7] The equation of Christ with Michael is one of the main doctrines of *Urantia*, as of the original Adventism. In act 2 of *Donnerstag* (Third Examination), the Jury calls Michael "Michael of Nebadon."[8] *Urantia* uses these terms frequently, stating: "Sometimes we refer to the sovereign of your universe Nebadon as Christ Michael."[9] The name of the earth in *Urantia* is Satania; in *Donnerstag*, act 3, Michael says to Lucifer: "You have seduced all Satania with your false freedom."[10] Shortly afterwards, he refers to Lucifer having reigned over "six hundred and seven inhabited worlds,"[11] while his source states that this earth (whose name is "Urantia") is "the 606th world in this local system on which the long evolutionary life process culminated in the appearance of human beings."[12] Michael's words: "You have been a terror for two hundred thousand years"[13] agree with *Urantia*'s dating of Lucifer's rebellion.[14] As for Michael himself, according to *Urantia* he is one of the

"Creator Sons" who must appear on each of the seven levels of being before he can become the creator of, and ruler over, a universe of his own. Incarnation as a human is the seventh and last in this series of incarnations, after which he returns to the "right hand of the Father,"[15] as we see Michael returning in the third act of *Donnerstag*. Finally, Michael's emblem of three concentric sky-blue circles, prominent in the staging and design of *Donnerstag*, comes directly from *The Urantia Book*, where it appears (as a registered trademark!) on the title page.

Urantia, like most channeled scriptures, has a strong preference for its own religion, giving to the Judeo-Christian tradition an importance far exceeding any other. Stockhausen is not so parochial. The choruses of "Michael's Homecoming" welcome Michael as "Son of God, Guardian Spirit of Mankind, Light, Hermes-Christos, Thor-Donar." In a later interview, Stockhausen says:

> This Michael is soon recognized as emanation of the Michael known from the earliest times, who is called in the Germanic languages Donar or Thor, Toth by the Egyptians, Hermes by the Greeks, Jupiter by the Romans. . . . In the oldest tradition, which goes back to the Indian one, Michael is Mithra, and among the Hebrews he is the guardian spirit of the whole people, just as he is the folk-saint of the Germans.[16]

With these words we leave the influence of *The Urantia Book* and move on to consider Stockhausen's myths in a wider context. To the academic mythologist his syncretism may have its shortcomings. But Stockhausen, like all great creative artists, is a mythographer—a creator of myths in his own right—rather than a mythologist or commentator on them. His Michael figure is first a demiurge or subsidiary creator, responsible for making one universe among myriads of others. Second, he is an avatar or divine incarnation, voluntarily taking human birth in order to give certain gifts to the earth—in this case, music. Third, he is an incomplete being, who needs to discover for himself what human life is like. Incarnation serves a purpose for him as well as for the earth. Michael's speech that ends the opera encompasses all this in a few words:

> . . . I have become man,
> for one world day,
> to live in ignorance,
> only suspecting what an angel is,

a creator-angel,
a deity,
GOD of the universe—
as child to come from a human mother's womb
to grow, learn, strive,
childlike to invent games with sounds,
which even in their human form move the souls of angels:
that is the meaning of THURSDAY from LIGHT.[17]

Fourth, Michael is Everyman (and Everywoman). This is my own interpretation, based on the fact that Stockhausen has used his own childhood as the model for Michael's. The unfriendly critic seizes on this as the composer's self-inflated identification with Christ. But it is more generous to interpret it in the context of the potential divinity of every human being, a doctrine common in esoteric sects. Christian Gnosticism, for example, teaches that we all have the divine spark, the Christ within us, which, if awakened by gnosis, enables us to return home.

The figure of Lucifer is equally complex. In one respect he is the rebel angel of Judeo-Christian mythology. In an interview of 1980, Stockhausen explained the motives of Lucifer's rebellion:

> He wanted independence, self-government for the inhabited planets under him. His direct subordinate is Satan, whom one might call his first minister. So these two caused a rebellion in which most of the inhabited planets joined, and we are still living in this situation.
>
> We experience on this planet every day what this rebellion wants and what its motive is: anti-hierarchy, self-direction, egalitarianism. And through it, the central linkage of our part of the universe is interrupted. No one knows any more how to get connected with other parts of the universe. We are cut off, we find ourselves on an island unconnected to other cosmic regions.
>
> That, in brief, is the theme of *Licht*. (TM, 6:153)

It was statements in this vein that led to Stockhausen's vilification by the left-wing press and to his exclusion by the generally left-leaning artistic and media circles. In the climate of the Federal Republic, it was all too easy to tar this apolitical man with the brush of right-wing elitism.

Stockhausen's Lucifer myth takes further shape with these words from a conversation of 1982:

As the chief administrator of our system Satania, [Lucifer] did not approve of the experiment of creating humanity, for example by mixing beasts with angels (with regard to consciousness) and thus, as he says, making such "sick semi-beings," imperfect bastards, who have to go through a process of becoming conscious in order to develop. Lucifer is simply against such processes because he knows that "the universe is a knowing, a meaning in harmony," and he was simply against the process-idea of "ascent through death." Michael set the process-plan in motion—he is the creator of our universe. Since Lucifer's rebellion, Michael is directly responsible for the fate of our planet. (TM, 6:418)

Stockhausen's Lucifer is a mocker of mankind and a despiser of Michael's efforts on behalf of his creation, especially Michael's own incarnation. Like many villains in drama, Lucifer is the chief source of humor in *Donnerstag*, to the extent that we cannot always take the cosmic war seriously. Michael, played variously by a tenor singer, by a boyish female dancer, and by a virtuoso trumpeter, has an air of the "knight in shining armor" that almost begs to be deflated. Lucifer, on the other hand, appears as a bass singer, a trombonist making grotesque noises, and a tap dancer. He is sleazy, cynical, and knowing. Stockhausen was well aware of the ambiguities of both characters. He writes in an early note for *Licht*: "Lucifer: freedom *from*; Michael: freedom *for* what?" (TM, 5:151)

The opera *Samstag* is a portrait of Lucifer, just as *Donnerstag* is a portrait of Michael and *Montag* of Eve. In the first of its four scenes, Lucifer sits in a chair while a pianist plays a long, phantasmagoric piece that is supposed to be his dream. Occasionally he sings, silencing the piano's music. Stockhausen says that Lucifer "would basically prefer that the whole world could be so dissolved, so compromised, that its form might dissolve, because he is against the creation of banal forms. He would rather have everything raised to a more spiritual, much more lucid form" (TM, 6:417).

The second scene of *Samstag*, "Lucifer's Requiem," is wordless, being a long solo for flute with percussion accompaniment. At the time of composing this scene in 1981, Stockhausen must have become aware of certain teachings of Tibetan Tantrism, especially those of the Dzogchen school that were brought to Europe by Namkhai Norbu, Rinpoche.

Norbu's teachings emphasized the importance of recognizing the moment of "clear light" after death, which, if it can be entered, ensures freedom from involuntary rebirth. Stockhausen conceived "Lucifer's Requiem" as a practical aid for the departed soul. He suggests that it be played after a person's death for forty-nine days, or at least used to prepare oneself for the journey through the *bardo* (the after-death world) and the choices that await the soul there: either reincarnation, or extinction, or entry into the Clear Light" (TM, 6:556).

This has very little to do with the War in Heaven of *Donnerstag*. Indeed, *Samstag* has very little to do with opera, since the remaining scenes comprise "Lucifer's Dance" for large wind band and two dancers on stilts, which ends with the musicians pretending to go on strike; and a setting of Saint Francis's *Hymn to the Virtues* sung by a monkish choir. After embarking on *Licht*, Stockhausen still had to make his living by accepting commissions of many different kinds, and he made them all take their places as parts of one opera or another. Although every piece is thematically locked into the system of formulas that permeates the entire cycle, they could not have formed dramatically unified operas even if Stockhausen had wanted them to. As it is, his conception of opera resembles the tableaux of the Renaissance masque (complete with its Hermetic cosmology) more than the dramatic and climactic structures of the past two hundred years.

The third character, Eva or Eve, appears in two guises in act 1 of *Donnerstag*. First she is Michael's mother, played in triple form by a soprano singer, a basset-horn player, and a dancer. Then she is Mondeva, a bird-woman who provides Michael with his initiation into eroticism. It does not take a professional Freudian to see the sense in this, nor a Jungian to recognize Eve as the archetypal Anima. Eve's own opera is *Montag*, in which she appears as a gigantic sculpture of a woman, from whom a variety of creatures are born. The subject of *Montag*, in Stockhausen's words, is

> new-birth, the new Christmas and the rebirth of humanity from Eve, who is responsible in our universe for the improvement of the human body. There is always the great problem of how a spirit can incarnate itself on various planets or stars. In order to evoke and direct spiritualization, you have to take on a body that can live there. And as body

you are always a child of that particular planet. So you must become a child of a particular planet in order to incarnate there. It is always a big decision to limit oneself so much. . . . You get a monkey skin, and have to transform it through angelic powers. Of course you never quite succeed, because it is so difficult. (TM, 6:199)

The Eve statue of *Montag* gives birth to two separate creations. The first consists of seven animal-headed beings and seven gnomes, who at the end of act 1 are all returned to her womb. The second birthing is of seven human boys (I don't know why they are all male) who correspond to the seven planets, seven days of the week, seven colors, etc. Then they are all led by a Pied Piper to a green heaven where children and birds are singing. This is the place to mention that the whole of *Licht* is permeated by the doctrine of signatures. Eve's color is green, and *Montag* is full of her element as water, steam, and ice. *Donnerstag*, with which we have most to do, is ruled by the planet Jupiter and dominated by Michael's colors: primarily blue, secondarily purple and violet. Stockhausen ensures that all his scores, opera libretti, and compact disks are issued in the appropriate colors.

In Gnostic terms, Stockhausen's Eve is Sophia, the mother and also the enlightener of humanity. Her two birthings recall those of the Valentinian myth, in which Sophia's first birthing is rejected as an abortion. Her story continues in *Freitag*, the opera of her seduction by Lucifer and the separation of the sexes; *Sonntag*, which celebrates her marriage to Michael; and *Mittwoch*, the day of Hermes the mediator, in which the three protagonists work out their relationships in conference.

The "God" whom Stockhausen occasionally mentions in his libretti and published texts is an undefined *deus absconditus*, who may be the focus of meditation or devotion but plays no part in his mythology. It is the impersonal Parabrahman of Vedanta and of certain rare mystics in the Abrahamic traditions. Perhaps it is the same as the Clear Light with which the Tantric initiate hopes to unite after death. In any case, while incarnated on earth we have to deal with deities of an inferior order and with the problems of being ourselves "Michaels" or spiritual beings temporarily inhabiting Eve's physical world.

The Lucifer-Michael pair, once detached from the moralistic *Urantia* cosmology, make a fascinating study in ambiguity. Seen from the viewpoint of Gnosticism, both of them have aspects of the Demiurge. Michael is a creator-god in training. For him the whole difficult process of uniting and disuniting spirit and body, the wheel of birth and rebirth, has an inestimable value, and the experience of being a human being, flawed as he or she is, is worthwhile—even for a god like himself. One hopes that when he comes to create his own universe, he will do a good job of it.

For Lucifer, on the other hand, the whole affair is too messy and inharmonious. He would prefer creation to remain at the spiritual or imaginary level, where it can be summoned and dismissed at will like his own dream in *Samstag*. Because he refuses incarnation, Lucifer's appearances on earth are grotesque and even pitiable. He has not accepted the rules of the game, as Michael has, so he is always a misfit. Yet to the world-rejecting strain common to much of Gnosticism, Lucifer's plan might seem preferable to Michael's. If the dream of this "light-bearer" were realized, humanity would have been spared the bondage to matter and the miseries of physical existence.

Stockhausen certainly has had cause to sympathize with Lucifer's complaints. In 1978, when the project of *Licht* was first underway, he made some of his freest remarks in an interview with Jill Purce. He spoke there of the tremendous difficulty of getting things done on earth, where trivial jobs like carrying loudspeakers and setting up music stands can take five or six hours a day, and where so few of the inhabitants listen to his music. "It's all very primitive here," he says. In contrast, the main characteristic of Sirius is that:

> [E]verything is music there, a living art of coordination and harmony of vibrations. Music in a very much higher sense than on this planet: a highly developed art, in which every composition arises in connection with the rhythms of Nature. An inner revelation has often shown me that I was educated on Sirius and have come here from Sirius. But usually people laugh at it and don't understand it, so there's not much sense in talking about it. (TM, 6:365)

I feel no urge to laugh. On the contrary, I find it admirable that a person as eminent as Stockhausen should hazard his reputation by saying such things, and have no reason to disbelieve him. What musician does not sympathize with his longing for a world freed from the conflicts and density that make earthly music such a laborious and often imperfect affair?

Gnosticism comprises both a myth and a method, the latter being the gnosis or saving knowledge that is supposed to restore us to our spiritual nature. Stockhausen offers with his music nothing less than a Gnostic method, applicable at many levels according to the aspirant's ability. At the lowest level, which he does not at all despise, is the mere exposure to his music. He still speaks of the 1970 German Pavilion at the World's Fair in Osaka, Japan, as one of the high points of his life: his music was broadcast there for hours every day, so that it was heard by about a million visitors. Because of the way it is composed, he says that it has a beneficial effect on people even when their attention is not focused upon it. This reminds me of the Buddhist idea that merely to hear the Noble Truths of Buddhism, whether or not one believes or follows them, plants a seed that will spare one many lifetimes of unnecessary suffering.

At the other end of the hierarchy is the devotee who studies the intellectual construction of Stockhausen's music and then listens repeatedly to it, until it makes the same intuitive sense as most of us get from a piece by Mozart or Bach. To do this one has to cultivate a sensitivity to dynamics, timbres, overtones, and other aspects of sound that are usually taken for granted. In a class apart are the specialist performers, especially Stockhausen's companion Suzanne Stephens, who plays Eva's basset-horn in all the operas, and his son Markus who plays Michael as trumpeter. The difficulty of the roles created for them, and for that matter of nearly all Stockhausen's music, is so immense that to master it is to reach an almost superhuman refinement of the senses of hearing and of time. Without a doubt, such refinement affects the whole of a person's perception and life.

In my other contribution to this volume, "Music and the Hermetic Tradition," I concluded that the Hermetic path and the musical path are parallel ways to the same goal, and virtually exclusive of one another. Stockhausen and his musicians seem to me supreme examples of people committed to spiritual development and realization through music. It is alluring to speculate, along with the composer, about other worlds where such musicality is the normal mode of existence. In an infinite universe, there seems little doubt that such worlds must exist.

NOTES

1. I am grateful to the composer and to his companion, Suzanne Stephens, for giving me recordings, librettos, and copies of Stockhausen's writings.

2. K. Stockhausen, *Towards a Cosmic Music*, selected and translated by Tim Nevill (Shaftesbury, 1989), 87; original in Stockhausen's *Texte zur Musik, 1977–1984* (Cologne, 1989), 6:201. The latter will be referred to in the text as *TM*, followed by the volume and page numbers.

3. Michael Kurtz, *Stockhausen: a Biography* (London, 1992), 41.

4. *The Urantia Book* (Chicago, 1955).

5. Kurtz, *Stockhausen: a Biography*, 188, 196.

6. The anonymity of *Urantia*'s receiver was penetrated by Martin Gardner. See Gardner's *On the Wild Side* (Buffalo, 1992), 103–8.

7. K. Stockhausen, *Donnerstag aus Licht* (London, 1985), unpaginated libretto, [5, 7].

8. Ibid., [65].

9. *Urantia Book*, 234.

10. *Donnerstag*, [111].

11. Ibid., [113].

12. *Urantia Book*, 559.

13. *Donnerstag*, [115].

14. *Urantia Book*, 604.

15. Ibid., 239.

16. K. Stockhausen, "Sieben Tage aus LICHT," *Deutsches Aerzteblatt* 82, no. 37 (1985): 2.

17. *Donnerstag*, [135].

CHAPTER 18

THE NEW AGE MOVEMENT AND
THE ESOTERIC TRADITION

WOUTER J. HANEGRAAFF

Over the course of this volume, one may follow the main historical threads that lead from the Gnosticism of late antiquity, and from the Hermetic revival of the Renaissance, to various kinds of post-Renaissance developments that may be referred to as western esotericism. In Antoine Faivre's article about Renaissance Hermeticism and the concept of western esotericism, the latter concept was defined in terms of six basic characteristics; Joscelyn Godwin has discussed "musical esotericism"; and the term esotericism has appeared again and again in several other contributions. As a result, the reader of this volume may have become used by now to understanding the word in a technical sense. However, if one goes out and asks the average passerby what "esotericism" means, she or he is most likely to mention the New Age movement.

In common parlance, "New Age" and "esotericism" tend to be used interchangeably, as near or complete synonyms. It must be said that this does not make life easier for the serious student of esotericism, for she or he is forced to explain again and again the differences between the popular and the technical usage of the term. Furthermore, even when she or he successfully gets the point across, other problems follow in its wake. One may explain that "esotericism" existed far before the New Age movement, so that the two cannot be synonyms; but to account for the precise nature of the relationship between the two is far more difficult. If the New Age movement is a contemporary phenomenon historically rooted in much older esoteric traditions, then does this mean that

The research for this article was supported by the Foundation for Theology and Religious Studies in the Netherlands (SFT), founded by the Netherlands Organization for Scientific Research (NWO).

one gains an adequate idea of what esotericism is all about by imagining modern New Age beliefs and practices transposed back into an earlier period? Many students of esotericism will be horrified by such an assumption, protesting that New Age is at most a thoroughly trivialized and commercialized travesty of *real* esotericism. But what, then, is this "real" esotericism? Some authors are convinced that the Theosophical Movement was already based on a misunderstood and therefore shallow esotericism, and that the New Age movement only made matters worse. Others argue that Blavatsky is still to be taken seriously, and that the fatal process of trivialization occurred later. Similar differences of opinion exist with regard to other "intermediate links." Again and again, one finds the same thing: the extent to which students in these fields emphasize either the similarities or the differences between traditional esotericism and the New Age movement depends *not* in the first place on investigation of the historical evidence. It depends on their personal preferences and beliefs. Roughly stated: those who are positively inclined toward western esotericism but reject the New Age movement will tend to minimize the historical connection; those who feel attracted to the New Age movement will tend to maximize it.

In this article I will not discuss questions of value, profundity, or truth. I will make an attempt to bracket my own biases, and simply take a look at the historical evidence. My conclusion is predictable: obviously, traditional esotericism and the New Age movement are both similar *and* different. As in the case of romanticism, the New Age movement is a revival of something old, but it is a revival *with a difference*. Put differently: there can be no doubt about the historical continuities between "Gnosis and Hermeticism" and the New Age movement; but this continuity consists by virtue of an ongoing process of *reinterpretations*. Ideas are changed (sometimes dramatically, sometimes very subtly) according to the cultural context in which they are perceived; and over time the context itself is transformed by these changed ideas. In order to gain a balanced perspective, one has to follow the development both of the ideas and of their cultural contexts.

In this contribution, I will not be able to do more than give a very general impression of the conclusions to which such an approach may lead[1]. Firstly, I will provide a general overview of the New Age movement. Secondly, I will outline the main avenues by which New Age is connected with esotericism, with an eye to the continuities as well as the differences between both.

NEW AGE IN A RESTRICTED, GENERAL, AND IMPROPER SENSE

Speaking about a movement without founders and without an institutionalized organization, it is always precarious to mark a beginning in time. Recognizing this, it nevertheless makes sense to begin the story of the New Age movement in the 1950s. In this period one finds, both in Europe and the United States, many groups of people who were fascinated by the mystery of the UFO phenomenon. Some of these so-called flying-saucer clubs were concerned with scientific research, but many of them developed into religious cults based on an occultist belief system. Most of them held strongly apocalyptic beliefs. They believed that very soon the world would be hit by unheard-of catastrophes, such as earthquakes, floods, famines, epidemic diseases, and so on. These disasters would completely disrupt civilization. Spiritually highly evolved beings, living in higher dimensions or on other planets and knowing what would come to pass, were now trying to warn humanity. They did this by appearing in their spacecraft and communicating with human beings by paranormal means. Those who followed their teachings would be picked up by flying saucers and brought into safety. Following the apocalyptic period, they would become the pioneers of a new civilization that would be built on the ruins of the old. A New Age of peace and prosperity would begin, in which humanity would live according to the universal spiritual laws of the universe.[2] I propose to refer to these groups as a *proto-New Age movement*.

These apocalyptic UFO cults were based on the conviction that modern western society was corrupted beyond a possible cure. A similar rejection of the ruling order is to be found in the alternative countercultural communities that flowered since the 1960s. Many of these communities took over the beliefs of the UFO cults. Perhaps the best known is the Scottish Findhorn community,[3] but many more existed. Within these alternative communities, the apocalyptic expectations of the original UFO cults were slowly transformed. What emerged can be characterized as a "pioneer attitude": people tried to live "as if" the New Age had already arrived. In this way, they hoped to be a source of inspiration to others, and thus to contribute in an active way to the coming of the New Age. In other words: the emphasis gradually shifted from an attitude of passive expectation of the Big Event to an active attitude of trying to help *create* the New Age.[4] I suggest that we refer to this movement of idealistic world reformers as *New Age in a restricted sense*. In terms of its basic ideas, this movement was rooted in England rather than in the United States. Its worldview was based strongly on elements of Anthroposophy and Theosophy, with particular emphasis on the teachings of Alice Bailey. In this movement, the expectation of the New Age (or "Age of Aquarius") was of central importance: all activities and speculations revolved around this central theme. This New Age in a restricted sense still exists as a subgroup within the New Age in a general sense; but as a result of the commercialization of the latter, its representatives have increasingly tended to deny association with the label "New Age."[5] Characteristic examples of the New Age in a restricted sense are David Spangler, George Trevelyan, and the so-called Ramala community in Glastonbury, England. Some more recent New Age currents, such as the Creation Spirituality of the American priest Matthew Fox, show a certain affinity with this original, idealistic New Age movement.

The *New Age in a general sense* emerged when, by the end of the 1970s and beginning of the 1980s, more and more people began to perceive an inner connection between the various kinds of alternative ideas, initiatives, and practices that had flowered since the sixties. Marilyn Ferguson, playfully alluding to the idea of the Age of Aquarius, referred to this emerging network of like-minded individuals as the "Aquarian Conspiracy." Her book of the same title is still widely regarded as the manifesto par excellence of the New Age movement.[6] It is not superfluous, however, to remark that this is correct only to a certain extent, for the volume appeared too early (in 1980) to be a completely adequate reflection of the movement as it actually developed during the 1980s. In any case, the term "New Age" (rather than "Aquarian Conspiracy") became popular during the 1980s as a general term for the whole complex of ideas and activities approximately covered by Ferguson; the term seemed appropriate because they were all seen as ways to create new ways of living, on foundations different from those of the dominant culture. One special development was the idea, with reference to the work of the philosopher of science Thomas Kuhn, of a new holistic paradigm that would replace the outdated mechanistic paradigm of Cartesian and Newtonian science. As a whole, this New Age in a general sense has a strongly American coloring. In contrast with the original movement, Theosophical and Anthroposophical ideas are no longer particularly prominent; instead, one finds a very strong influence of the typical American so-called metaphysical movements with their transcendentalist backgrounds, including the so-called New Thought movement and a certain type of religiously oriented psychology and alternative therapies.[7] The specific expectation of an Age of Aquarius is found widely, but is not by any means as prominent and central as in the original movement. The Aquarian Age has become just one of the many themes that characterize the New Age movement in a general sense. Thus, it is possible to be a "New Ager" without being very much preoccupied with the coming of a new era. Since the second half of the 1980s, finally, the New Age in a general sense has been discovered by the business world; and the increasing commercialization of the movement has tended to undermine its original potential as a countercultural force. The American movie actress Shirley MacLaine emerged during the 1980s as perhaps its most popular representative.

Finally, mention should be made of what might be called a *New Age in an improper sense.* In common parlance, a variety of "alternative" movements and tendencies have become mixed up with and incorrectly associated with the New Age movement. Increasingly, the term "New Age" has come to be used as a highly general label for whatever is seen by outsiders as vaguely "spiritual," alternative, or "soft." Thus, new religious movements of all sorts (popularly referred to as sects or cults) are presented as "New Age," even when they have little or nothing in common with the latter's central body of ideas. Likewise, a variety of older occultist movements, such as modern Theosophy or Anthroposophy, are frequently referred to as "New Age," although it is quite clear that the undeniable influence of these movements on the emergence of the New Age movement does not imply that they are themselves part of that movement. This anachronistic use of the term New Age is connected with the tendency among some critics to dismiss the New Age movement as, actually, "old age." What is meant is that the New Age movement is merely a regressive phenomenon, characteristic of the tendency to return to old, outdated, prescientific superstitions.[8] Such an interpretation is, however, highly misleading, since it reflects a simplistic idea about the relation between tradition and innovation based on questionable assumptions about secular progress. It is true, as will be seen, that the New Age movement is rooted in traditional esoteric worldviews; but it is equally evident that many important aspects of the New Age could not possibly exist outside the specific cultural constellation of western society in the late twentieth century. It is not possible to understand the New Age phenomenon without recognizing that it is a typical western and contemporary phenomenon rooted in much older, prescientific religious traditions.

MANIFESTATIONS OF THE NEW AGE MOVEMENT

Anybody who attempts to investigate the literature currently on sale in standard New Age bookshops, in order to find out what the movement is all about, is likely to come away bewildered and confused. The apparent variety is overwhelming, and at first it may seem impossible to bring any sort of order to all the tendencies that have become associated with the label "New Age." Nevertheless, a systematic survey of New Age literature over several years has taught me that the situation is somewhat less daunting than it seems at first. All varieties of New Age religiosity fall into a few, clearly demarcated categories. Each of them may be further divided into subcategories; and a certain extent of overlap between the main ones has to be recognized. But allowing for this, what finally emerges is still a reasonably clear picture, which can help us reduce the New Age phenomenon to manageable proportions.

1. *Channeling*[9] is based the conviction that some people are able, under certain circumstances, to act as a "channel" for information from sources other than their normal everyday selves. Most typically, these sources are identified as discarnate "entities" living on higher levels of being, but the complete range of channeled sources mentioned in the literature contains almost everything to which some kind of intelligence

might be attributed. In many cases a trance state appears to be required, during which the entity takes possession of the medium's body to communicate either by the speech organs or (less usual in the New Age context) by automatic writing. However, some of the phenomena classed as channeling do not seem to involve trance at all, notably the cases of inner dictation in which the medium hears a voice dictating messages which she or he writes down in a fully conscious state. The only common denominator of all the various phenomena that New Agers refer to as "channeling" appears to be the fact that people receive information (messages) that they interpret as coming from a source other than their own normal consciousness. It might be added that this source is believed to represent a level of wisdom or insight superior to that of most humans (although it is not necessarily or even usually regarded as all-knowing and infallible). Communication with such sources is sought for the purpose of learning and guidance. In contrast, communication with spirits of the recently departed, as in classical nineteenth-century spiritualism, is uncharacteristic for New Age channeling.

The background of channeling is the widespread New Age belief in progressive rebirth, both on earth and in "higher realities." Human beings are believed to develop and evolve through a succession of earthly incarnations, until they reach a point where they pass on to higher spheres of existence. Here, too, they keep developing their innate potential, thus rising to ever higher levels of insight and wisdom. From such a superior level of spiritual evolution, they may decide to get in contact with those who are still incarnated on earth, and they do this by way of channeling. Some entities only give lectures through their channels; many others engage in discussions with their audience. The subjects covered include complicated metaphysical systems, reflections on moral issues, therapeutic advice, or predictions about the near future (of course with special attention to the coming of the New Age). In the United States in particular, channeling became a popular practice during the 1980s. Many channeling mediums work on a small scale, functioning as a kind of therapist who gives channeled advice to individuals. Others attract a larger following, and a few have become well-known media personalities. Many believe that channeling is a latent ability that in principle can be developed by anyone, and therefore publish do-it-yourself channeling guides teaching readers how to employ meditation and visualization techniques so as to get into contact with their "inner guide." It must be emphasized that the complete corpus of literature based on channeled communications represents one of the most fundamental sources of the New Age belief system. Although most New Agers would say that the only reliable source of spiritual authority is one's own inner self, the New Age movement could arguably be characterized as a religion based on revelation(s) *(Offenbarungsreligion):* a close analysis reveals that many of its central ideas can be traced to quite specific channeled sources.

2. *Healing and spiritual growth*[10] is an appropriate title for the huge and diverse field of alternative therapies, psychological theories, and medical practices that have become associated with New Age. In spite of their dazzling variety, they all have two general characteristics in common. Firstly, none of them is focused exclusively on either the physical or the mental domain, such as is the case in mainstream approaches to health. While official medical practice in the contemporary west makes a sharp distinction between physical and psychological problems, the alternative therapies regard the human being as an integral whole. Both body and psyche are aspects of one encompassing reality. In the final resort, this reality is regarded as spiritual rather than physical. For the practice of healing, this implies that psychological problems are reflected on the physical level; for example, in the form of so-called energy blockages in certain parts of the body, which result in physical dysfunctions of various kinds. Conversely, a good physical condition is regarded as a prerequisite for healthy psychological functioning. In the treatment of any kind of problem, attention must be given both to the physical and to the psychological dimension.

Secondly, all New Age therapies assume that the process of healing is directly related to the process of spiritual development. Psychological and physical problems ultimately result from a lack of spiritual harmony; and, conversely, their effect is to block the natural development toward such harmony. Healing in the broadest sense of the word is thus a necessary part of the process of spiritual development toward complete inner harmony or enlightenment; and spiritual growth leads to the resolution of psychological traumas and their physical results. The complete process of "healing and spiritual growth" takes many lives, which means that one may have to deal in one's present life with psychological or physical problems that have originated in previous incarnations. In combination with the belief in the mind as the ultimate source of healing (as well as of illness), this way of thinking frequently leads to the belief that everybody has created his or her own illnesses, and can thus "take responsibility" for his or her healing by positive thinking. One of the central concepts encountered in many of these alternative therapies is the theory of the chakras: seven "subtle" centers of energy transformation located vertically in the body. In many healing practices these chakras function as the conceptual foundation both for the unity of mind and body (because as "subtle centers" they are in between both), and for the unity of healing and spiritual growth (because successive "opening of the chakras" is synonymous with attaining enlightenment).

The more theoretical aspects of the healing and growth movement form a relatively independent domain, usually referred to as *transpersonal psychology*.[11] This psychological school emerged from humanistic psychology and is based on the conviction that an all-encompassing view of the human psyche is possible only by taking into account the wide field of so-called transpersonal experiences. These include mystical experiences, paranormal perceptions, so-called altered states of consciousness, and so forth. Transpersonal psychologists believe that these experiences represent not only autonomous, but superior levels of psychological functioning. They therefore combat the tendencies of traditional psychological schools to reduce these experiences to the status of mere subjective hallucinations.

3. *Holistic science*.[12] There is a strong interest in the New Age movement in modern developments in the natural sciences, physics in particular. New Agers generally believe that their spiritual worldview is confirmed or at least strongly supported by the newest results of scientific research and that, conversely, the natural sciences might profit from taking spiritual perspectives more seriously. Ultimately, it is believed, science and spirituality are simply different roads leading to the same goal. In this context, New Age thinkers are fascinated by modern scientific theories, quantum mechanics in particular, which seem to demonstrate that the mechanistic worldview of classical science is no longer tenable. It is assumed that when these new scientific theories become fully dominant, and their holistic implications are generally understood, this will lead to a momentous paradigm shift. The consequences for our

general culture will be no less momentous than those which resulted from the scientific revolution. Thus, the idea of the imminent "new paradigm" is the scientific parallel of the New Age idea.

Undoubtedly the best-known exponent of New Age holism is Fritjof Capra. His popular book *The Tao of Physics*[13] is an attempt to demonstrate far-reaching parallels between modern physics (especially in the form of Capra's favorite "Bootstrap Theory") and oriental mysticism. Capra believes that both point to one and the same worldview; thus, what the new physics is discovering now has been known in the East for many centuries. Very influential as well is the intellectually much more profound work of David Bohm.[14] Bohm's theory of the "implicate order," combined with theories of neurophysiologist Karl Pribram, has led to the formulation of the so-called holographic paradigm.[15] This is a holistic theory par excellence, which implies that the whole universe is mirrored in each of its smallest parts. Yet another form of New Age science focuses on formulating theories of evolution. Most important is the school associated with Nobel Prize–winner Ilya Prigogine,[16] according to which evolution takes place not gradually but by sudden, discontinuous leaps to new and higher levels of organization. Applied to western society, or even to humanity as a whole, this theory can be used to support the belief that a New Age may suddenly and unexpectedly come into existence. And finally we find several New Age theories with a predominantly biological background. Well known is Rupert Sheldrake's neovitalist theory of "morphic resonance,"[17] and James Lovelock's so-called Gaia hypothesis.[18] According to the latter, our planet earth behaves like a living, self-regulating organism; and many New Agers conclude that it therefore *is* a living, and even an intelligent, organism.

4. *New Age neopaganism.*[19] As a general term, "neopaganism" covers all those modern movements that are based on the conviction that what Christianity has traditionally denounced as idolatry and superstition actually represented a profound and meaningful religious worldview, and that a "pagan" religious practice can and should be revitalized in our modern world. Current world problems, particularly the ecological crisis, are regarded as the direct result of the loss of pagan wisdom about man's relationship to the natural world. Recovery of this wisdom is regarded as urgently needed.

The type of neopaganism associated with the New Age movement is rooted in the movement of modern witchcraft or Wicca, founded by the Englishman Gerald Gardner. Wicca spread to the United States in the 1960s, where it took on new forms, particularly under the impact of the women's spirituality movement. The resulting development is usually referred to as the "Goddess movement." While Wicca originally focused on the polarity of masculine and feminine forces in the universe, represented by the Goddess and her partner the God, the Goddess movement has focused on the feminine aspect only. Wicca originally looked for its roots to the so-called burning times: the period of the witch persecutions. Many adherents of Wicca believe that there actually existed a pagan fertility cult in those times, the members of which were victimized by the Inquisition. The Goddess movement, on the other hand, sees itself as a modern revival of an ancient matriarchate. That modern scholarship dismisses both the medieval witch cult and the pre-Christian matriarchate as romantic myths hardly affects these beliefs. For some neopagans the academic world is itself a manifestation of the patriarchate, which is why they simply refuse to take it seriously; others feel that, in the end, neopaganism is not dependent on historical roots for being "authentic."

The nature of the relation between neopaganism and the New Age movement is not undisputed. Neopaganism is a relatively autonomous subculture, even within the alternative movement as such, and some neopagans do not wish to be associated with the label "New Age" at all. In terms of basic worldviews, New Age and neopaganism are best seen as two thought complexes that may theoretically be distinct but show a very large overlap in practice. When I speak of "New Age neopaganism," what I mean is only this overlap.

5. *New Age in a restricted and a general sense.* This last category of New Age literature in fact encompasses several relatively distinct groups. As remarked earlier, the New Age in a restricted sense is still recognizable as a relatively autonomous aspect within the New Age in a general sense. For many representatives, such as David Spangler or George Trevelyan, the expectation of the New Age of Aquarius is still the center of attention. Others, such as Matthew Fox, speak less about the coming of a new era but attempt to develop a new form of spirituality that is related to the New Age in a restricted sense in terms of basic inspiration. A rather similar world-reforming idealism is also found in the group of

authors whose central concern is the development of a "new paradigm" as an alternative to the Cartesian-Newtonian paradigm that is held responsible for the current global crisis. Fritjof Capra's best-seller *The Turning Point*[20] is only the best-known example among a whole series of comparable books. Finally, there are several authors who are best characterized as representatives of the New Age in a general sense. The best-known early manifesto, as noted earlier, is Marilyn Ferguson's *Aquarian Conspiracy*; and the best-known representative of the New Age as it actually emerged during the 1980s is Shirley MacLaine.[21] A comparison between their views is instructive as to the gap between vision and reality.

In sum: in all examples belonging to this final category we have to do with people who are somehow centrally concerned with "New Age," whether in the sense of a new era that will soon begin or in the sense of a new way of life that should lead to such a new era or in the sense of a new paradigm that will change our whole view of reality, or, finally, in the sense of a convenient general label for an alternative view of life.

Unity versus Diversity in the New Age Movement

I have presented a wide spectrum of ideas and activities, all belonging to the New Age movement in a general sense. The reader might be forgiven for concluding, after this overview, that although these categories perhaps bring some *order*, the New Age movement as a whole nevertheless displays little *unity or structure*. Certainly, there is an enormous difference between, for example, Shirley MacLaine's New Age channels, crystals, and reincarnation stories, on the one hand, and David Bohm's sophisticated philosophy of nature, on the other. Likewise, a huge gap exists between the world-affirming neopaganism of a politically and socially active modern witch such as Starhawk,[22] on the one hand, and the Christianized neo-Vedanta of the channeled text "A Course in Miracles," on the other.[23] These are just some random examples. It is essential to recognize this great variety of New Age beliefs, but nevertheless there are several reasons to speak of *one* movement.

Firstly, all forms of New Age thinking are concerned with developing *alternatives* for the basic, accepted values of modern western society. Presumably, the character of the "Age of Aquarius" will be determined precisely by the ways in which it *differs* from the old culture, the "Piscean Age." In other words, the New Age movement as a whole is based on a pervasive *cultural criticism* directed against the dominant values of the modern west. Some of this criticism is formulated explicitly, some of it is implicit in New Age practices and goals. This makes it possible to define the New Age movement indirectly, i.e., in a negative sense, not in terms of what its adherents *believe* (for, again, these beliefs are very diverse), but in terms of what they *reject*.

Whatever their differences, all New Agers would agree that modern western society is dominated by two pervasive tendencies: *dualism*, on the one hand, and *reductionism*, on the other. Dualism is especially associated with the heritage of mainstream Christianity; reductionism with modern forms of scientific rationalism.

1. The most important forms of dualism assume a sharp separation between *mind and matter*, *humanity and nature*, and *humanity and God*. In each of these cases, the New Age movement asserts that the dualism in question is false and misleading. Mind and matter, firstly, are merely different manifestations of one fundamental substance. This substance is usually thought of as "spiritual" in some sense, meaning that matter is essentially one of the manifestations of "mind." Secondly, humanity is intimately connected with the whole of nature, which it itself permeated by spirit. Thirdly: nature, humanity, and God are in their deepest essence *one*. God is the source of being whose creative energy permeates and sustains all, and human beings are in their innermost being one with this source. In all three cases, dualism is an illusion that leads to alienation and that should be overcome by holistic awareness. When New Agers use the word *gnosis* (which they do rather frequently), what they mean is precisely such a profound insight into the wholeness of reality, which overcomes alienation by reuniting the human individual with the All, or God.

2. Reductionism may take at least two forms; and in both cases the New Age alternative is, again, holism. Reductionism in the sense of *materialism* means that spirit is reduced to matter and thus denied an autonomous existence. Spirit is no more than an ultimately illusory "epiphenomenon" of purely material processes. The New Age alternative is the precise opposite: ultimate reality is wholly spiritual instead of

material, and matter is a manifestation of mind instead of the reverse. According to a second aspect, reductionism manifests as a tendency toward *fragmentation*: integral wholes are reduced to separate fragments or "basic building blocks." The New Age movement, in contrast, emphasizes that wholes are not mechanic but organic. The whole of reality is more than the sum of its separate parts; and the same goes for smaller parts of this whole, such as human beings.

In sum: all forms of New Age religiosity are united in their presentation of holistic concepts as alternatives to the dualism and reductionism perceived as dominating modern western society. It must be added that although this holistic orientation is universal throughout the New Age movement, the precise *forms* of New Age holism are far from uniform. Many different proposals compete for prominence; they may share a concern with wholeness in some sense but are often very different in other respects. It must be concluded that New Age adherents are generally in agreement about their *diagnosis* of what is wrong with modern western culture, but that they suggest a wide variety of treatments. New Age "holism," in other words, should never be understood as a *theory*. At the most, it is a *vision*; and New Agers try to realize this vision by many different avenues.

NEW AGE AND WESTERN ESOTERICISM

That all expressions of "New Age" are based on a shared "culture criticism," which proposes holistic alternatives to dualism and reductionism, is one argument that supports speaking of "one" movement. But this same culture criticism also provides us with a clue to understanding the relation between New Age and traditional esotericism; and this, in turn, makes it possible to define the relative coherence of New Age religiosity with more precision.

Some years ago, G. Quispel suggested that there is a fundamental distinction between what he called the three "basic components" of the European cultural tradition, referring to them as "reason," "faith" and "gnosis."[24] Although this distinction has several potential pitfalls,[25] it can well be defended as long as it is taken in an idealtypical and heuristic sense.[26] Mainstream Christianity, as represented by the churches, is based on "faith" in divine revelation as mediated by Scripture and/or tradition. Different from this is the long-standing western tradition of rational inquiry, which goes back to ancient Greek philosophy and has culminated in an intellectual tradition that supported the emergence of modern science. Different from both "faith" and "reason," however, is the tradition that may conveniently be summarized by the term "gnosis" and that is the subject of the present volume as a whole. This third component is characterized by the primacy accorded to experience (of God and the Self) over mere reason and faith. Now, this typology is highly useful in order to put the "culture criticism" of the New Age movement into perspective. It is evident that the mainstream of western culture has been based on the two pillars of "faith" and "reason": the Christianity of the churches, on the one hand, and philosophical rationalism, on the other (and, of course, on the developments that emerged from their various combinations). The "gnosis" component, in contrast, may with justification be referred to as the traditional "counterculture" of the west. Since the early centuries it has been perceived as highly problematic, and frequently as unacceptable, from the perspectives of "faith" and "reason." As a result, it became a reservoir for all those ideas that have been felt to be incompatible with the dominant trends of western culture. It is only natural, therefore, that modern people who feel that there is something fundamentally wrong with mainstream western culture should turn to this tradition for inspiration. A first indication that this has indeed happened is the strong emphasis of the New Age movement on personal, inner experience of the "self" as the ultimate authority of truth and as the only means to understand one's true relation to the universe and God. The New Age movement has even been defined as "self-religion."[27] In this sense, the New Age movement is evidently based on "gnosis"; and this gnosis implies a rejection of at least one type of dualism discussed above: that between human beings and God, creature and Creator. For traditional gnosis, as well, referred to the discovery that human beings are in their deepest essence one with divine reality.

Adherents of New Age thinking have themselves shown an increasing interest in the Gnostic tradition; but, so far, most of their attention has been focused on the Gnosticism of late antiquity. It is significant that they have strongly emphasized the importance of "gnosis" as knowledge of the Self and of God, while largely ignoring the strong dualistic tendencies in ancient Gnosticism. Given the antidualism that I highlighted as essential to New Age religiosity, one would in fact expect a much stronger interest in the Hermetic tradition and, especially, in its "holistic" manifestations since the Renaissance period. This is, however, not (yet) the case. The explanation (apart from the romantic implications of a "peaceful and mystical" religion cruelly suppressed by "violent and dogmatic" state church) lies in the simple fact that ancient Gnosticism has enjoyed wide publicity, especially following the discovery of the Nag Hammadi codices, while Renaissance Hermeticism is still comparatively unknown even in New Age circles. There are signs that this is beginning to change; but there can be little doubt that, at this moment, few New Age adherents would recognize the names of Ficino, Bruno, or Jacob Böhme while many of them have heard of the *Gospel of Thomas* or the Cathars.

If there is a connection with western esotericism, then, New Agers themselves are still largely unaware of it. It is true that many of them will affirm that their spiritual beliefs are in line with traditions of universal wisdom that have been kept alive over the centuries by the initiates of esoteric traditions. Very few New Agers, however, have any clear idea about the nature of these traditions. However, it seems evident that the central belief systems *both* of western esotericism and of the New Age movement might technically be referred to as *holistic gnosis*. This, I will argue, is not a coincidence: New Age religiosity is actually based on ideas that are rooted in western esotericism. This does emphatically *not* mean, however, that Renaissance Hermeticists and New Age adherents share the same worldview. They do not. Even disregarding other factors, at the very least the two are separated by a deep cultural gulf known as the Enlightenment. Western esotericism flowered in the sixteenth century and is based on pre-Enlightenment assumptions. The New Age movement, on the other hand, is definitely post-Enlightenment, not just in a chronological sense but in its very way of perceiving and reflecting upon reality. In their very rejection of a narrow "Enlightenment rationality," New Agers are yet deeply influenced by the very traditions they reject.[28] Whenever they borrow traditional esoteric concepts, they interpret these from a distinctly twentieth-century, secularized perspective.

The essential watershed in this development is the period of the second half of the eighteenth century and the first decades of the nineteenth. The movements of Enlightenment, Counter-Enlightenment, and romanticism are therefore essential for understanding the emergence of New Age thinking. Very roughly, the main lines of development relevant to the New Age movement may be sketched as follows.[29]

First of all, this period saw the emergence of *occultism*. Contrary to common usage, I would argue that the terms "esotericism" and "occultism" should be clearly distinguished; and "occultism," furthermore, should not be confused with the "occult sciences." When I speak of *esotericism* I mean the cluster of traditions as defined and circumscribed by Antoine Faivre.[30] The so-called occult sciences (*magia*, alchemy, astrology) are, of course, intimately connected with esotericism in this sense. Occultism, on the other hand, should be used only for post-Enlightenment developments of esotericism. It can be defined as the product of a collision between two different and inherently incompatible worldviews: the organicist worldview of esotericism based on "correspondences" and the post-Enlightenment worldviews based on instrumental "causality."[31] What happened is very simple and, indeed, predictable. Inevitably, esotericists living in the post-Enlightenment period were themselves profoundly influenced by the new rationalism, positivism, and scientism. In defending their esoteric views they therefore used a terminology that would be understandable to contemporaries (including themselves). The result was a conflation of two systems of thought, as a result of which original esoteric ideas underwent subtle but far-reaching changes. It is to such modern adaptations of esotericism, which have flowered since the nineteenth century, that I refer to as "occultism." Of special importance with respect to the New Age movement is the Theosophical tradition (including its more "Christian" offshoots founded by Rudolf Steiner and Alice Bailey). These forms of occultism provided the basic ideas of the *New Age in a restricted sense*.

However, in many studies of the New Age movement this theosophical influence is overemphasized at the expense of a second one.[32] The *New Age in a general sense*, with its strong American flavor, cannot be accounted for by the modern Theosophical tradition only. Here, the phenomenon of transcendentalism, the most important American manifestation of romanticism, is particularly important. The general affinities between esotericism and romanticism[33] are one reason why American transcendentalism could provide a religious and philosophical context in which various occultist or quasi-occultist movements flourished. Most important in that respect is the nineteenth-century movement known as New Thought, as well as the many related phenomena that have been referred to, somewhat misleadingly, as the "metaphysical movements."[34] Several scholars have analyzed this American spiritual scene of the nineteenth century, in which transcendentalism, New Thought and metaphysical movements were closely interwoven. It is to this context that one should look in order to understand the cultural backgrounds of the New Age in a general sense.

In my two contributions to this volume I have emphasized the importance, with respect to the history of ideas, of *reinterpretation* in contrast to mere *continuity*. Ideas do not move through history unchanged: what "continues" is never simply "the original idea" but, rather, the original idea *as perceived through the eyes of later generations*. It seems to me that any study of the historical connections between esotericism and New Age should be based on that realization. The actual historical developments in question are highy complicated, and can definitely not be accounted for in terms of a simplistic "continuity" of "the esoteric tradition." The developments outlined above already demonstrate this. There are, for example, certain historical connections between esotericism, occultism, the Theosophical Society, Alice Bailey's Theosophy, and the New Age in a restricted sense. And there are such connections between esotericism, European romanticism, American transcendentalism, various kinds of American alternative movements, and the New Age in a general sense. Obviously, any such summary of the historical "chain" amounts to an extreme simplification: in each case it is only *certain* elements of each given phenomenon that are focused on by later interpreters, to the exclusion of others. Each generation not only reinterprets ideas of the past, but also makes its own personal selection while adding innovations of its own. With respect to the past, it generally selects what suits its purposes while simply disregarding the rest.

To round off this overview of the New Age movement, I want to identify three *new*, modernist developments that have been of crucial importance in this whole development of successive reinterpretations. In each case we are dealing with a factor that is *not* part of traditional esotericism, but has been added to it during the nineteenth century. Each of these additions has decisively influenced the way in which the New Age movement interprets esoteric ideas.

1. Firstly, there is the so-called *Oriental Renaissance.* During the period of romanticism, there was an increasing interest in oriental cultures and their religious beliefs. The result was a romantic vision of "the East," and of India in particular, as the homeland and treasure-house of a superior spiritual wisdom. Such romantic conceptions of oriental religions lived on in modern Theosophy as well as in various American movements.[35] Special mention must be made of Indian missionary movements, particularly the Ramakrishna mission and its best-known representative, Vivekananda, who made a great impression during the World Parliament of Religions that met at the end of the nineteenth century. The influence of oriental ideas on the ideas of the New Age movement is far from insignificant, but it is important to understand the precise nature of this influence. It is often assumed that many New Age beliefs have originated in oriental religions. This is, however, not the case. Rather, what one finds is oriental ideas *as perceived by* western esotericists, occultists, romantics, and contemporary New Agers. Throughout, oriental conceptions have been adopted *only* to the extent that they could be assimilated into already existing western frameworks. And these frameworks were either occultist or romantic in nature, i.e., they were of western origin.

2. An instructive example is the New Age idea of reincarnation, which can also be used to illustrate the second innovative factor that I want to emphasize, i.e., *evolutionism.* Although a belief in reincarnation is found already in some manifestations of eighteenth-century esotericism, it seems that the new influence of oriental religions has been the chief reason for its popularity. However, a closer look at New Age reincarnationism demonstrates a crucial difference with its oriental parallel. In the official teachings of Hinduism and Buddhism, reincarnation is essentially something negative. To reach enlightenment means that one is at last free of the tyranny of the "wheel of rebirth" and no longer needs to be reborn in the flesh. In the New Age movement,

however, as in modern Theosophy, reincarnation is a *positive* process. The prospect of many lives after this one is regarded not as a doom but as a promise. It is seen as an *attractive* alternative to the essentially static heaven or hell of traditional Christianity, because it ensures infinite possibilities of further spiritual evolution. Thus, it is true that the oriental concept of reincarnation is assimilated into occultism, but only by virtue of having been reinterpreted in the characteristically western terms of *romantic evolutionism*. In this process, reincarnation has become something very different, even antithetic to its oriental model.[36] The factor of *evolution* is the second innovative factor that I wish to emphasize here. This too, as I argued in my contribution about romanticism in the present volume, is essentially a new addition to traditional esotericism. Its influence is not restricted to contemporary western reinterpretations of reincarnation and its underlying concept of spiritual growth, but is also found, for instance, in New Age conceptions of world history culminating in the Age of Aquarius.

3. A third essential innovative factor, finally, consists of the influence of modern *psychology* on how the New Age movement has come to understand esoteric concepts. In general terms, New Age religiosity is characterized by the double phenomenon of a *psychologizing of religion combined with a sacralization of psychology*. The psychologization of religion is usually assumed to imply that religion is "all in the mind," i.e., that religious beliefs are merely subjective. Characteristic for New Age religiosity is that it indeed assumes that religion is "all in the mind," but that this does *not* lead to atheist conclusions. For, under the influence of Jungian psychology in particular, the mind itself is assumed to have a sacred dimension. Thus, New Agers concur with the characteristic modernist tendency to understand religion in psychological terms, but they do not *reduce* religion to psychology. On the contrary: the gods reappear, alive and potent as ever, from the depths of the collective psyche. To New Agers, this means that the question whether divinity is "real" or only "in the mind" is ultimately a meaningless question, because it assumes a false dualism between mind and "outer" nature. In this way, New Agers believe that, far from undermining religion, they have reached a higher and more mature perspective on the true nature of religion. Humanity has progressed to the point where divinity is no longer located outside the mind, but in it.

Now, Jung's well-known interest in Gnosticism and alchemy has of course made it particularly easy for the New Age movement to assimilate traditional esoteric elements and give them a psychological and religious meaning at the same time. Whether the Jungian interpretation of Gnosticism and alchemy—apart from being brilliant—is *correct* does not have to concern us here. It is important to note, however, that the Gnostics and alchemists themselves did certainly *not* interpret their beliefs and practices in psychological terms but in religious ones. That the alchemical process is actually a reflection of the dynamics of the unconscious may or may not be true; but the alleged connection between the two is undoubtedly an idea of the twentieth century and, as such, alien and inconceivable to the worldview of the traditional alchemists. This conclusion may be extended to the general problem of the relation between New Age and western esotericism. Traditional esotericists did not think in psychological terms; New Agers, on the other hand, find it almost impossible *not* to do so.

CONCLUSION

That there are strong and essential historical connections between various western esoteric traditions and the New Age movement is beyond question. These connections are highly instructive and they merit serious study. But the fact that the contemporary New Age movement has a mental horizon that includes the religious world of the orient, and that it interprets esotericism from distinctly modernist and secular frameworks (instrumental causality; evolutionism; psychology) means that traditional esotericism and New Age are nevertheless "worlds apart." In general, the New Age can be defined as a movement based on popular culture criticism expressed in terms of a thoroughly *secularized* esotericism.[37]

Accordingly, there is no good reason to exclude the phenomenon of New Age religion from the academic study of esotericism. This does not imply, however, that New Age is therefore simply an aspect of esotericism. The distinction is subtle; but the quality of future research into contemporary alternative spirituality will depend on the extent to which the importance of precisely such subtleties is recognized.

Notes

1. For a complete discussion, see my *New Age Religion and Western Culture: Esotericism in the Mirror of Secular Thought* (Leiden, 1996).

2. For a classic discussion of a UFO cult of the 1950s, see Leon Festinger, Henry W. Riecken, and Stanley Schachter, *When Prophecy Fails* (Minneapolis, 1956). For a recent overview of the UFO cult phenomenon, see James R. Lewis, *The Gods Have Landed: New Religions from Other Worlds* (Albany, 1995).

3. See Paul Hawken, *The Magic of Findhorn* (Glasgow, 1975); Andrew Rigby and Bryan S. Turner, "Findhorn Community, Centre of Light: A Sociological Study of New Forms of Religion," in *A Sociological Yearbook of Religion in Britain*, vol. 5, ed. Michael Hill (London, 1972); Stephen M. Clark, "Myth, Metaphor, and Manifestation: The Negotiation of Belief in a New Age Community," in *Perspectives on the New Age*, ed. James R. Lewis and J. Gordon Melton (Albany, 1992).

4. This change of attitude is described for example by the "theologian of Findhorn," David Spangler. See his *The Rebirth of the Sacred* (London, 1984), chapter 4. Spangler's early *Revelation: The Birth of a New Age* (1976, reprint, Findhorn, 1977), is a foundational source of the New Age in a restricted sense.

5. See David Spangler's attack in *The New Age* (Issaquah, 1988) and *Channeling in the New Age* (Issaquah, 1988) on the "New Age glamour" represented by figures such as Shirley MacLaine. This recent tendency of turning away from the label "New Age" is widespread. See James R. Lewis, "Approaches to the Study of the New Age Movement," in Lewis and Melton, *Perspectives*, 2.

6. Marilyn Ferguson, *The Aquarian Conspiracy: Personal and Social Transformation in the 1980s* (1980; reprint, London, 1982).

7. See, for example, J. Stillson Judah, *The History and Philosophy of the Metaphysical Movements in America* (Philadelphia, 1967); Robert C. Fuller, *Mesmerism and the American Cure of Souls* (Philadelphia, 1982); idem, *Americans and the Unconscious* (New York and Oxford, 1986).

8. Thus, for example, the German Gottfried Küenzlen, who describes the New Age as "a gnostic-esoteric amalgam, occultism, yes: obscurantism, . . . pagan-magical pieces of scenery, . . . fluttering mythologisms" ("New Age: Ein neues Paradigma? Anmerkungen zur Grundlagenkrise der Moderne," *Materialdienst EZW* 49, no. 2 [1986]: 38).

9. For overviews, see Jon Klimo, *Channeling: Investigations on Receiving Information from Paranormal Sources* (Wellingborough, 1987); Arthur Hastings, *With the Tongues of Men and Angels: A Study of Channeling* (Fort Worth, 1991); Suzanne Riordan, "Channeling: A New Revelation?" in Lewis and Melton, *Perspectives*.

10. A good introduction to the general field is provided by James A. Beckford, "Holistic Imagery and Ethics in New Religious and Healing Movements," *Social Compass* 31, no. 2/3 (1984); idem, "The World Images of New Religious and Healing Movements," in: *Sickness and Sectarianism: Exploratory Studies in Medical and Religious Sectarianism*, ed. R. Kenneth Jones (Aldershot and Brookfield, 1985). A

popular but informative introduction is Nevill Drury, *The Elements of Human Potential* (Shaftesbury, 1989).

11. See Roger N. Walsh and Frances Vaughan, *Beyond Ego: Transpersonal Dimensions in Psychology* (Los Angeles, 1980); Ronald S. Valle, "The Emergence of Transpersonal Psychology," in *Existential-phenomenological Perspectives in Psychology: Exploring the Breadth of Human Experience. With a Special Section on Transpersonal Psychology*, ed. Ronald S. Valle and Steen Halling (New York and London, 1989).

12. For a useful overview from a sympathizer's perspective, see John P. Briggs and F. David Peat, *Looking Glass Universe: The Emerging Science of Wholeness* (New York, 1984).

13. Fritjof Capra, *The Tao of Physics: An Exploration of the Parallels between Modern Physics and Eastern Mysticism* (1975, reprint, London, 1983).

14. See especially David Bohm, *Wholeness and the Implicate Order* (1980; reprint, London and New York, 1983).

15. See Ken Wilber, ed., *The Holographic Paradigm and other Paradoxes: Exploring the Leading Edge of Science* (Boston and London, 1985).

16. See especially Ilya Prigogine and Isabelle Stengers, *Order Out of Chaos: Man's New Dialogue with Nature* (1984; reprint, London 1985); and Erich Jantsch, *The Self-Organizing Universe: Scientific and Human Implications of the Emerging Paradigm of Evolution* (Oxford, 1980).

17. Rupert Sheldrake first proposed his theory in *A New Science of Life: The Hypothesis of Formative Causation,* new ed. (London, 1987).

18. J. E. Lovelock, *Gaia: A New Look at Life on Earth* (1979; reprint, Oxford and New York, 1987).

19. The best general survey is Margot Adler, *Drawing Down the Moon: Witches, Druids, Goddess-Worshippers, and Other Pagans in America Today*, 2d ed. (Boston, 1986). A brilliant anthropological analysis is T. M. Luhrmann, *Persuasions of the Witch's Craft: Ritual Magic in Contemporary England* (Cambridge, Mass., 1989).

20. Fritjof Capra, *The Turning Point: Science, Society, and the Rising Culture* (1982; reprint, Toronto, 1983).

21. Of her series of autobiographical novels, see especially *Out on a Limb* (Toronto, 1983).

22. See, for example, Starhawk, *The Spiral Dance: A Rebirth of the Ancient Religion of the Great Goddess* (1979; reprint, San Francisco, 1989).

23. *A Course in Miracles: The Text, Workbook for Students and Manual for Teachers* (1975; reprint, London, 1985).

24. G. Quispel, ed., *Gnosis: De derde component van de Europese cultuurtraditie* (Utrecht, 1988), 9.

25. See my comments with reference to Quispel in "On the Construction of 'Esoteric Traditions'," in *Western Esotericism and the Science of Religion*, edited by A. Faivre and W. J. Hanegraaff, Gnostica, vol. 2 (Louvain, 1998).

26. See my theoretical development of Quispel's suggestion, in "A Dynamic Typological Approach to the Problem of Post-Gnostic Gnosticism," *ARIES* (Association pour la Recherche et l'Information sur l'Ésoterisme) 16 (1992); and "The

Problem of 'Post-Gnostic' Gnosticism," in *The Notion of "Religion" in Comparative Research: Selected Proceedings of the Sixteenth IAHR Congress*, ed. Ugo Bianchi (Rome, 1994).

27. Paul Heelas, *The New Age Movement: Celebrating the Self and the Sacralization of Modernity* (Oxford and Cambridge, Mass., 1996).

28. See also the analyses of nineteenth-century occultism in a brilliant recent study by Joscelyn Godwin, appropriately titled *The Theosophical Enlightenment* (Albany, 1994).

29. For a complete discussion, see the third part of my *New Age Religion*.

30. See his contribution elsewhere in this volume.

31. A helpful discussion of essentially the same distinction can be found in Stanley Jeyaraja Tambiah, *Magic, Science, Religion, and the Scope of Rationality* (Cambridge, 1990), esp. 105–10.

32. Thus, for example, in the otherwise highly valuable study by Mary Farrell Bednarowski, *New Religions and the Theological Imagination in America* (Bloomington and Indianapolis, 1989).

33. See my contribution elsewhere in this volume.

34. Cf. note 7, above.

35. For modern Theosophy, helpful discussion can be found in Godwin, *Theosophical Enlightenment*, and in chapter 9 of Carl T. Jackson, *The Oriental Religions and American Thought: Nineteenth-Century Explorations* (Westport and London, 1981). For transcendentalism, see the recent definitive study by Arthur Versluis, *American Transcendentalism and Asian Religions* (New York and Oxford, 1993).

36. Here, I will disregard further aspects of the subject that further support my argument but would take too much room to discuss. In particular, it is important to recognize that in a New Age context reincarnation in a strict sense is only *part* of a much larger process of spiritual evolution in "higher worlds." In my *New Age Religion*, I explain how the New Age vision of life beyond death is derived not from Oriental models, but from eighteenth-century esotericism.

37. Cf. the conclusion of my *New Age Religion*.

LIST OF CONTRIBUTORS

PROF. R. VAN DEN BROEK is Emeritus Professor of History of Christianity at the University of Utrecht, The Netherlands. His publications include *The Myth of the Phoenix According to Classical and Early Christian Traditions* (1972) and *Studies in Gnosticism and Alexandrian Christianity* (1996).

PROF. R. EDIGHOFFER is Emeritus Professor of German Literature, University of the Sorbonne, Paris. His publications include *Rose-Croix et société idéale selon Johann Valentin Andreae* (2 vols; 1981 and 1987) and *Die Rosenkreuzer* (1995).

DR. D. VAN EGMOND is Lecturer in Philosophy at the Amsterdam Polytechnic, The Netherlands. His publications include *Body, Subject & Self: The Possibilities of Survival after Death* (1993).

PROF. A. FAIVRE is Professor of Esoteric and Mystical Currents in Modern and Contemporary Europe at the École Pratique des Hautes Études (Sorbonne), Paris, France. His recent publications include *Access to Western Esotericism* (1994) and *The Eternal Hermes: From Greek God to Alchemical Magus* (1995).

PROF. J. GODWIN is Professor of Music at Colgate University, New York. His publications include *The Theosophical Enlightenment* (1994) and *Music and the Occult: French Musical Philosophies, 1750–1950* (1995).

DR. W. J. HANEGRAAFF is Research Fellow in the Study of Religions at the University of Utrecht, The Netherlands. His publications include *New Age Religion and Western Culture: Esotericism in the Mirror of Secular Thought* (1996).

DR. J. HELDERMAN is former Lecturer in New Testament and Coptic Studies at the Free University of Amsterdam, The Netherlands. His publications include *Die Anapausis im Evangelium Veritatis* (1984).

DR. C. LEIJENHORST is Research Associate in History of Modern Philosophy at the University of Utrecht, The Netherlands. He is currently finishing his dissertation "Aristotelian Backgrounds of Thomas Hobbes's Natural Philosophy."

PROF. J.-P. MAHÉ is Professor of Armenian Studies at the École Pratique des Hautes Études (Sorbonne), Paris, France. His publications include *Hermès en haute-Egypte* (2 vols.; 1978 and 1982).

DR. J. VAN MEURS is former Lecturer in English and American Literature at the University of Groningen, The Netherlands. His publications include *Jungian Literary Criticism, 1920–1980: An Annotated, Critical Bibliography of Works in English* (1988).

DR. J. VAN OORT is Lecturer in History of Christianity at the University of Utrecht, The Netherlands. His publications include *Jerusalem and Babylon: A Study into Augustine's "City of God" and the Sources of his Doctrine of the Two Cities* (1991).

PROF. G. QUISPEL is Emeritus Professor of History of Christianity at the University of Utrecht, The Netherlands. His publications include *Gnosis als Weltreligion: Die Bedeutung der Gnosis in der Antike* (1972) and *Gnostic Studies* (2 vols; 1974).

PROF. A. VERSLUIS is Lecturer in English and American Literature at Michigan State University, U.S.A. His publications include *American Transcendentalism and Asian Religions* (1993) and *Theosophia: Hidden Dimensions of Christianity* (1994).

PROF. K.-C. VOSS is Adjunct Professor of Religious Studies at San José University, California. She has published articles in various journals.

INDEX OF NAMES

Abjesous the Teacher, 40
Abrams, M. H., 247–53, 256, 258, 265–66
Adam, A., 47
Addison, J., 243, 255
Adler, M., 381
Agrippa, H. C., 114–15, 186, 194, 273, 288
Aguzzi Barbagli, D., 141, 144
Alcott, B., 234
Aldobrandini, I., 125
Alexander of Lycopolis, 50
Allberry, C. R. C., 44, 50
Alleau, R., 194
Allen, M. J. B., 143, 146
Alveydre, S.-Y.d', 192–93, 196
Amesius, 2
Andreae, J. V., 116, 197–99, 201, 205–6, 208, 211–13
Angelus Silesius, 227, 235
Annarichos, 95
Antonaci, A., 142
Aquinas, T., 129, 199
Aristotle, 126, 128–29, 132–34, 137, 140, 143, 145–46, 243
Armstrong, A. H., 18–19
Arnold, G., 117, 121, 123, 226–27
Arnold, M., 235
Ashmole, E., 175
Ashton, D., 195
Attridge, H. W., 66–68
Atwood, M. A., 174, 181
Augustine, 46–48, 50, 93, 105, 251

Averroes, 111
Avicenna, 111
Ayrault, R., 263
Ayshford, R., 220, 234
Ayton, W. A., 326, 342–43

Baader, F. von, 118, 230–32, 235
Baarda, T., 19
Bach, J. S., 189, 357
Bacon, F., 271
Bailey, A., 362, 375–76
Balzac, H. de, 190
Baraies, 40–41
Barker, E., 382
Barthélémon, F.-H., 192
Bartók, B., 190
Barton, T., 195
Basil of Caesarea, 99, 107
Basilides, 32
Bathurst, A., 223
Baxter, R., 222, 234
Baynes, C. A., 18
Beckford, J. A., 380
Bednarowski, M. F., 382
Benz, E., 235, 263
Berg, A. 190, 191
Bergson, H. 239
Berio, L., 347
Berkeley, G., 276, 287–88, 290
Berlin, I., 267
Bernard of Clairvaux, 104

Bernoulli, R., 175–76, 178
Besant, A., 334–35, 344
Besold, C., 208
Beyer, J. H., 132
Bianchi, U., 18, 382
Biller, P., 103, 104
Blake, W., 237, 269–309
Blane, A., 236
Blavatsky, H. P., 190–92, 217, 313, 322–23, 325–27, 329–34, 336, 339, 341–45, 360
Blunden, H., 221
Boccalini, T., 211–12
Boeft, J. den, 51
Boehme, J. *See* Böhme, J.
Boer, E., 77
Böhlig, A., 47
Bohm, D., 368, 370, 381
Böhme, J., 116–17, 217–24, 226–30, 232–34, 236–37, 244–45, 251, 261–62, 266, 268–69, 72–74, 282, 284, 288, 294, 300–301, 374
Bonardel, F., 175, 181
Boulez, P., 347
Bourguignon, A., 117
Bozóky, E., 105–6
Brahe, T., 184
Brashler, J., 19, 35
Breckling, F., 225, 227
Brenon, A., 103–4, 107
Brice, E., 235
Brickman, G., 141
Briggs, J. P., 381
Britten, E. H., 192
Britton, T., 191
Brock, E. J., 267
Broek, R. van den 19, 35, 108
Bromley, T., 222–34
Brown, P., 32, 36
Brunelleschi, F., 189
Bruno, G., 114–15, 140, 142, 152, 177, 244, 374
Buddecke, W., 219, 234
Budge, E. A. W., 106
Burckhardt, T., 178
Burkitt, F. C., 50, 68

Caccini, G., 186
Cagliostro, 148
Caldwell, D. H., 341–42
Calvin, J., 211
Campagnano, A., 106
Campanella, T., 115
Capra, F., 368, 370, 381
Carlyle, T., 246
Casaubon, I., 141, 211
Castellani, N. de, 134
Castrenis, R., 162
Cavalcanti, E., 51
Champier, S., 114
Chowne, Mrs., 319–20
Chrysostom, J., 69
Cicero, 72
Cirillo, L., 49
Clark, S. M., 380
Clarke, L., 181
Cleather, A. L., 319, 341–42
Clédat, L., 107
Clement of Alexandria, 1, 4, 19, 54, 57, 217, 233
Clement VIII (pope), 125–26
Cochrane, E., 142
Colberg, E. D., 267
Coleridge, S. T., 237, 246, 257, 266, 271
Collins, M., 344
Colpe, C., 48, 50, 108
Colquhoun, I., 328, 342–43
Contarini, G., 126
Copenhaver, B. P., 18–20, 35, 66, 145–46
Corbin, H., 122, 222, 234, 267
Corregio, J. M. da, 212
Corsetti, J.-P., 233
Couliano, I. P., 72, 77, 267
Crane, R. S., 265
Cranston, S., 341
Crevel, M. van, 195
Crowley, A., 311, 337, 341, 345
Cudworth, R., 114
Cyril of Jerusalem, 95, 106

Dagens, J., 214
Damascius, 133
Dannenfeldt, K. H., 144

Dante, 188
Darnton, R., 148, 175
Darwin, C., 313
Davidson, P., 192
Davis, M., 309
Davy, M.-M., 214
Debus, A. G., 146, 175, 213, 215
Debussy, C., 190
Decret, F., 48
Dee, J., 114–15, 212, 220, 331
Deghaye, P., 217, 233–35, 268
Demetrius, 77
Democritus, 146
Denkova, L., 105
Deugd, C. de, 266
Diffey, T. J., 267
Diognetus, 36
Dionysius Areopagita, 137, 217, 233
Dirkse, P. A., 19, 35
Dodds, E. R., 18–19
Dodge, B., 48
Dondaine, A., 104
Dorn, G., 199, 200, 206, 214
Dornseiff, F., 68
Dörries, H., 107
Doutreleau, L., 67, 105

Drury, N., 381
Dubois, J.-D., 18
Dufay, G., 189
Durand of Huesca, 89, 105
Duvernoy, J., 103, 106–7

Eckhart, 217, 230, 233
Eckhartshausen, K. von, 229
Edighoffer, R., 123, 214
Ehmann, C., 235
Eklund, D., 342
Eliade, M., 147, 152, 157, 174–78, 180–81, 341
Ellebracht, M. P., 77
Ellistone, J., 221
Elsas, C., 18
Elze, M., 107
Emerson, R. W., 234, 264
Empedocles, 128, 288

Ender, C. von, 218
Enscoe, G. E., 263–65
Epiphanius of Salamis, 4, 94
Erb, P., 234–35
Erdman, D. V., 269
Evans, A. P., 103–7
Evans, C. A., 65, 68
Everard, J., 273, 309
Everwin of Steinfeld, 104

Fabre d 'Olivet, A., 192, 196
Fagiolo, M., 144
Faivre, A., 122–23, 144, 146–47, 149–50, 175–77, 179, 198, 213, 217, 229, 233, 235–36, 44, 258, 261, 263, 267–68, 341, 359, 375
Faust, A., 234
Felkin, Dr., 337
Ferguson, J. F., 179
Ferguson, M., 362, 370, 380
Festinger, L., 380
Festugière, A.-J., 17–20, 66, 145, 205, 208, 214
Fichte, J. G., 333
Ficino, M., 112–15, 125, 127–28, 133, 138–40, 146, 185–86, 212, 374
Firpo, L., 142
Flamel, N., 174
Flaxman, J., 272
Fludd, R., 114, 191, 273, 288
Flügel, G., 48
Foix de Candalle, F., 133
Foucault, M., 177
Fowden, G., 17
Fox, M., 362, 369
Francis, St., 354
Franklin, B., 148
Freher, D. A., 223, 227, 232
Frick, K. R. H., 180, 233, 267, 341, 344
Frye, N., 264
Fuller, J. O., 195
Fuller, R. C., 380

Gadon, E. W., 180
Galatino, P., 114
Galilei, G., 140

Gardner, G., 369
Gardner, M., 358
Garfagnini, G. C., 143
Garin, E., 141, 143
Gasparro, G. S., 106
Geisen, R., 344, 346
George I, 227
Gianotto, C., 36
Gibbon, E., 227
Gibbon, H., 228
Gichtel, J. G., 117, 223–28, 232, 235–36
Gilbert, R. A., 329, 342–43
Gilly, C., 123
Giorgi, F., 114–15
Giversen, S., 36, 50, 77
Gleckner, R. F., 263–65
Godet, A., 267
Gode-von Aesch, A. G. F., 263, 267
Godwin, J., 194–96, 343, 345, 359, 382
Goethe, J. W. von, 204, 237, 255, 333
Gohory, J., 115
Gombosi, O., 194
Gombrich, E., 177
Goodrick-Clarke, N., 344
Gorceix, B., 214
Gougy, C., 192
Gouk, P., 94
Graßl, H., 263
Gregory XIV (pope), 125, 129
Gregory, T., 142
Grierson, H. J. C., 263
Grobel, K., 67
Grube, G. M. A., 77
Gruenwald, I., 49
Guillaumont, A., 107
Guinet, L., 263
Gurdjieff, G. I., 193
Gwyn Griffiths, J., 180

Haeckel, E., 333
Hagman, Y., 103
Hall, M. P., 195
Halling, S., 381
Hamilton, B., 103, 105–6
Hanegraaff, W. J., 123, 195, 267–68
Harnack, A. von, 49, 67

Harper, G. M., 342–43
Hartmann, T. de, 193
Hasih, al-, 41
Hastings, A., 380
Haven, M., 180
Hawken, P., 380
Head , R., 195
Heelas, P., 382
Hegel, G. W. F., 261, 271
Heiler, F., 180
Heisler, R., 195
Helderman, J., 66–68
Henrichs, A., 39, 48
Henry of Navarre, 212
Henry, J., 145
Heraclitus, 288
Hermes, J.-P., 18
Hersey, G. L., 195
Hill, M., 380
Hippolytus, 4
Hirst, D., 269, 274, 278, 282, 309
Hölderlin, F., 271
Holmyard, E. J., 175
Holst, G., 191
Holzhausen, J., 19–20, 67
Honnecourt, V. de, 187
Hons, G., 181
Horst, P. W.van der, 51
Hotham, C., 221
Hotham, D., 221
Houten, K. van, 189, 195
Howard, M., 341
Howat, R., 195
Howe, E., 328, 337, 342–45
Hudson, A., 103–4
Hugo, V., 237
Humboldt, A. von, 230, 255
Huser, J., 218
Hutcheson, Mrs., 228
Hutin, S., 233

Irenaeus 4, 21, 29, 33, 36, 56–57, 105
Isenberg, W. W., 35

Jackson, C. T., 382
Jacobs, E., 141

James, J., 194
Jantsch, E., 381
Jennings, H., 309
Jinarâjadâsa, C. J., 342
John of Lugio, 89
Johnson, P., 313, 341
Jonas, H., 4, 17, 58, 67–68
Jones, R. K., 380
Jong, A. de, 268
Jong, A. F. de, 268
Judah, J. S., 380
Julian of Eclanum, 50
Julianus, 133, 144
Julius Cassianus, 32
Jung, C. G., 156–57, 164, 173, 178–80,
    189, 195, 213–14, 267, 302, 378–79
Justinus Martyr, 56

Kant, I., 239, 247
Kasbergen, M., 189, 195
Kayser, H., 187, 195
Keßler, E., 141, 143
Keats, J., 243
Kehl, A., 19
Kelley, D. R., 264
Kellner, C., 338, 345
Kellner, K., 338
Kellogg-Sadler, W. C., 350
Kelpius, J., 235
Kepler, J., 184–85, 194
Kerning, J. B., 336
Keynes, G., 309
Khalid ibn Yazid, 150, 162
Khunrath, H., 199, 213–14
King, F., 337, 343, 345
Kingsford, A. B., 322–23, 342
Kirchberger, N. A., 230
Kircher, A., 114, 191
Kirven, R. H., 267
Klein, A., 236
Klimkeit, H. J., 47, 49
Klimo, J., 380
Klostermann, E., 107
Kmosko, M., 107
Knorr von Rosenroth, C., 114, 323
Kober, T., 218

Koenen, L., 39, 47–49
König, P.-R., 344–45
Korzybski, A., 178
Koschorke, K., 68
Koslowski, P., 234–36
Koustaios, 40
Koyré, A., 234, 252
Krause, K. C. F., 267
Krause, M., 50, 68, 107
Kraye, J., 145
Kren, C., 122
Kristeller, P. O., 141–42, 144
Kroeger, M., 107
Kroll, J., 73, 77
Küenzlen, G., 380
Kuhlmann, Q., 227
Kuhn, T., 363
Kurtz, M., 349–50, 358

Lambert, M., 103–4
Lamprecht, F., 141
Laurant, J.-P., 123, 341
Law, W., 227–28, 234
Layton, B., 17, 68
Lazzarelli, L., 114, 144, 212
Lead, J., 117
Leade, J., 221, 223, 229
Lee, F., 223
Leeuw, G. van der, 176
Lefèvre d'Étaples, J., 212
Leijenhorst, C., 122
Lendvai, E., 195
Lentz, W., 50
Lenz, J. M. R., 264
Leo, A., 191
Leucippus, 146
Lévi, E., 325
Lévy-Bruhl, L., 260
Lewis, A. O., 141
Lewis, J. R., 380
Liessem, F., 188, 195
Lieu, S. N. C., 48
Lincoln, H., 195
Lindsay, J., 177
Liszt, F., 193
Livingstone, E., 51

Locke, J., 258, 271
Lohr, Ch., 141, 143
Lorraine, C. of, 186
Louis XIV, 186
Lovejoy, A. O., 238–43, 245–46, 248, 250–52, 254, 260–61, 263–66
Lovelock, J. E., 368, 381
Luhrmann, T. M., 381
Lully, J.-B., 186
Lupasco, S., 177
Luria, I., 229
Lütgert, W., 263
Luther, M., 208

Macarius, 100, 107
MacDermot, V., 18
MacLaine, S., 363, 370, 380

MacRae, G. W., 66
Mahe, J.-P., 17– 19, 77
Maier, M., 115, 183, 191, 194, 200–201, 213
Maitland, E., 322–23
Mammarelli, B., 142
Manget, J. J., 170
Mani, 37–46, 49–50
Mansfeld, J., 19
Marcion, 49, 56
Markschies, C., 57–58, 67
Martels, Z. R. W. M. van, 179
Maryam, 38
Mathers, M., 330
Mathers, S. L., 323–25, 327–28, 330, 332, 343
Matter, J., 118, 123
McCalla, A., 268
McIntosh, C., 235
McLean, A., 170, 172, 178–81, 195
Mead, G. R. S., 191
Medici, Cosimo de, 112–13
Medici, Ferdinando de, 186
Meinel, C., 194
Melton, J. G., 380
Menapace Brisca, L., 141
Ménard, J. E., 55, 67
Mercati, A., 142

Merkel, I., 146
Merkelbach, R., 77
Mesmer, F. A., 148
Messos, 2
Meyrink, G., 336
Miers, H. E., 267
Milton, J., 272, 286, 289
Molitor, F. J., 229
Moller, H., 344
Moneta of Cremona, 97, 106–7
Monteverdi, C., 186
Montgomery, J. W., 213–14
Morienus, 150, 162
Mosheim, J. L. von, 274, 292
Mozart, W. A., 189, 357
Mucillo, M., 141–43
Muhammad, 50
Muses, C. A., 235–36
Myerson, J., 234
Mylius, J., 201, 213

Nadim, M. I. al-, 38–41, 48
Nagel, P., 106
Nazarius, 91, 94
Needleman, J., 122–23, 175, 213, 233, 262, 268, 341
Nelly, R., 103–5, 107
Nevill, T., 358
Newsom, C., 77
Newton, I., 145, 185, 194, 257, 271, 299
Nicetas, 89
Nicolescu, B., 177–78, 234
Nicotheus, 2
Nietzsche, F., 333
Nock, A. D., 4, 17–20, 66, 145
Nono, L., 347
Norbu, N., 353
Norden, E., 77
Novalis, 237, 271

Obrecht, J., 189
Oetinger, F. C., 229, 235
Olympiodorus ,133
Oort, J. van, 48, 51
Origen, 1
Otto, R., 176

Pagel, W., 122
Pagels, E., 68
Paolini, F., 115
Paolini, L., 104
Paracelsus, 115–16, 122, 206–7, 218, 233, 251, 269, 272–73, 288, 290
Paramelle, J., 18
Parisot, I., 108
Parmenides, 132
Parrott, D. M., 19, 36
Pasqually, M. de, 229
Pasteur, L., 323
Pater, W., 263
Patrizi, F., 114, 125–46
Paul, 10, 58, 198
Pearson, B. A., 36
Peat, F. D., 381
Peckham, M., 245–47, 250, 264–65
Peladan, J., 190
Peri, J., 186
Peronelle, 174
Peter, 71
Peterson, E., 107
Petric, F., 142
Petrus Siculus, 106
Peuckert, W.-E., 233–34
Philip II, 126
Philo of Alexandria, 13, 57, 180
Philoponus, J., 126
Pico della Mirandola, G., 112–14, 127, 138, 143, 255
Plato, 1–2, 9, 12, 55, 58, 114, 127–29, 132, 134, 139, 186, 273, 291
Platvoet, J. G., 123
Plessis Mornay, P. du, 212, 214
Pletho, G. G., 133
Plotinus, 2–3, 12, 134, 248–49
Plutarch, 59, 180
Poiret, P., 227
Polotsky, H. J., 49
Pope, A., 241, 244, 255
Pordage, J., 117, 221–23, 226–28, 232, 234
Porphyry, 2, 12, 18, 217
Postel, G., 114
Poussin, N., 195
Pribram, K., 368

Prickett, S., 267
Priestley, J., 274
Prigogine, I., 368, 381
Proclus, 126, 133, 135, 217–18
Prudentius, 205
Psellus, M., 133
Pseudo-Zosimos, 183
Ptolemy, 184
Puech, H.-Ch., 18, 48, 67–68
Puli, A., 235
Puliafito Bleuel, A. L., 142, 144
Purce, J., 356
Purnell, F., 143–44
Pythagoras, 114, 141

Quispel, G., 20, 33, 36, 51, 67–68, 77, 106–8, 121–22, 145, 269, 372, 381

Raine, K., 269, 274, 278, 282, 288, 292, 294–95, 309
Read, J., 176
Regardie, I., 325, 342–43
Reitzenstein, R., 105, 144
Reuchlin, J., 114
Reuss, T., 336, 338–39, 344–45
Ricchini, Th. A., 107
Richter, G., 218
Riecken, H. W., 380
Rigby, A., 380
Rigo, A., 107
Riordan, S., 380
Ripley, G., 199
Roach, R., 223
Roberts, J., 264
Robinson, C., 272–73
Robinson, H. C., 309
Robinson, J. M., 17–18, 20, 35, 49, 55, 67, 105
Römer, C. E., 47, 49
Rose, E., 50
Rosenkreutz, C., 116, 198–200, 202–3, 206–7, 212–13, 330, 334–35
Rousseau, A., 67, 105
Rovere, G. della, 125
Rudolph, K., 17, 49, 58, 66–68
Ryan, W. F., 145

Saccaro del Buffo, G., 141
Sacconi, R., 89, 94, 106
Sachse, J., 235
Sadler, W. S., 350
Sagnard, F., 19, 66–67
Sagnard, F. M. M., 67
Saint-Germain, 192, 195
Saint-Martin, L.-C. de, 192, 195, 229–30, 232, 234
Salmaios the Ascetic, 40
Sanjek, F., 104
Santucci, J. A., 234
Satie, E., 190
Saulat, J., 170
Schachter, S., 380
Schelling, F. W. J. von, 237, 271
Schenke, H.-M., 18–19, 105
Schlegel, A. W., 230
Schmidt, C., 18, 49
Schmitt, C. B., 143, 145
Schnitzer, S., 132
Schönberg, A.,] 90–91
Scholem, G., 73–74, 77, 252
Schuhmann, K., 145
Schumaker, W., 122
Schumann, C., 192
Schuon, F., 118
Schutz, A., 345
Scott, W., 35
Scriabin, A., 190
Sebottendorf, R. von, 345
Secret, F., 122, 252
Seneca, 12
Sfondrati, N., 125
Shaftesbury, 244, 255
Shakespeare, W., 272
Sheldrake, R., 368, 381
Shelley, P. B., 244, 266, 271
Siebmacher, 213
Siémons, J.-L., 233
Simson, O. von, 187, 194–95
Sinnett, A. P., 322, 333
Sivers, M. von, 339
Skinner, Q., 143
Sladek, M., 263, 267
Socrates, 132

Soderberg, H., 103
Spangler, D., 362, 369, 380
Sparrow, J., 221
Spenser, 188
Spierenburg, H. J., 342, 344
Spiesberger, K., 345
Spitzer, L., 264
Sprengel, A., 339
Standaert, B., 67
Starhawk, 370, 381
Stavenhagen, L., 150, 161, 176, 179
Stein, C. von, 204
Steiner, F., 345
Steiner, R., 189, 193, 332–33, 335–36, 338–39, 344–46, 375
Stengers, I., 381
Stephens, S., 357–58
Stephenson, B., 194
Steuco, A., 143
Stevenson, W. H., 287, 309
Stiefenhofer, D., 107
Stirner, M., 333
Stockhausen, K., 347–85
Stockhausen, M., 357
Stroumsa, G. G., 50
Studion, S., 191
Sullivan, L. E., 175
Swedenborg, E., 190, 229, 267, 269, 273–74, 280, 292
Synesius, 133

Tambiah, S. J., 267, 382
Tardieu, M., 18, 48
Tasso, T., 126
Tatham, F., 272
Tatian, 40, 101, 107
Tatlow, R., 195
Tauler, J., 217–18, 233
Taylor, F. S., 175
Taylor, T., 273
Tegtmeier, R., 341
Telesio, B., 143
Telle, J., 122, 179
Tertullian, 32–33, 36
Thales, 128
Tharmas, 302

Theodotus, 11, 29–30, 54
Theosebeia, 174
Thomson, J., 255
Thorndike, L., 122
Thorpe, C. D., 243
Thouzellier, C., 103–5, 107
Thune, N., 233, 235
Till, W. C., 19, 105
Timotheos, 40
Toletus, F., 144
Tongerloo, A. van, 48, 51, 77
Torrens, R. G., 325, 342
Trevelyan, G., 362, 369
Tsjaikowski, P. I., 69
Tuckett, C., 65, 68
Turgot, 148
Turner, B. S., 380
Tuveson, E. L., 253–56, 262, 267

Ueberfeldt, 224
Unnik, W. C. van, 67

Valentine, B., 178
Valentinus, 31–33, 35, 56–58, 60–61, 65–66
Valiero, A., 125
Valle, R. S., 381
Valori, B., 141
Vasoli, C., 140–42, 144, 146
Vaughan, F., 381
Vaughan, T., 214
Venckeleer, Th., 104, 107
Vergil, 72
Verheule, A. F., 48
Vermaseren, M. J., 19, 108
Versluis, A., 123, 234–35, 382
Viatte, A., 237, 263
Vicaire, M.-H., 103
Visotsky, B., 49
Vivekananda, Swami, 377
Völker, W., 67–68
Voss, A., 194
Voss, K.-C., 123, 175–76, 178–79

Wachtmeister, C., 343
Wagner, R., 189, 348

Waida, M., 179
Waite, A. E., 180
Wakefield, W. L., 103–7
Waldschmidt, E., 50
Waldstein, M., 105
Walker, D. P., 122, 143, 194
Walsh, R. N., 381
Walter, B., 218
Webb, J., 313, 341, 344
Webb, R. L., 68
Webern, A., 190–91
Weeks, A., 234
Weinfurter, K., 345
Wellek, R., 242–45, 250, 264–65
Wellesz, E., 194
Welling, G. von, 229
Westcott, W. W., 320, 323–24, 326–30, 343
White, E., 350
Whitman, W., 255
Whittaker, M., 107
Wiebe, R. A., 68
Wießner, G., 49
Wilber, K., 381
Williams, C., 274
Wilmott, M., 142, 145
Wisse, F., 27, 105
Woodford, A. F. A., 324
Woodman, W. R., 324, 328
Wordsworth, W., 243, 246, 250–51, 255, 258, 271
Wright, C., 195

Xenocrates, 132

Yates, F. A., 122, 197–98, 212, 214, 252, 267
Yeats, W. B., 269, 326

Zalewski, P., 343
Zambelli, P., 142
Ziegler, L., 236
Zimmermann, R. C., 263, 266–67
Zinzendorf, 235
Zirkoff, B. de, 318
Zosimos, 163, 174, 206

INDEX OF SUBJECTS

Abel, 33
Abraham, 128, 143, 210, 276
Achamoth, 33
Adam, 14, 19, 45, 92, 100, 206, 210, 292
Adam Kadmon, 282, 329
Aeons, 8
Afrahat, 108
Albedo, 157–59, 204
Albion, 296, 304–7
Alchemy, 74, 110–11, 115, 218–19, 224,
    235, 251, 254, 259, 261, 273–74,
    289, 322, 326, 31, 375, 379
  and causality, 152–53, 176
  and energy, 176
  and music, 183, 194
  and subject/object relation, 152–53,
    176
  and time, 152–53, 160–61, 176
  in Rosicrucianism, 198
  Material alchemy, 151–52, 176
  Spiritual alchemy, 147–81, 221
Allogenes, 2, 6, 13
Altered States of Consciousness, 367
Ammon, 5
Ana, 40
Anapausis, 66
Androgyny, 14-16, 27, 32, 82, 160, 266,
    277, 284, 294, 300
Angelic Brethren, 225–26, 228
Angels, 27, 41, 74, 77, 83, 111, 115, 131,
    171, 222, 284, 353

Anonymous Treatise, 89
Anthropos, 277, 282
Anthroposophy, 332–40, 362–63
Antitypes, 2
Aphrahat, 101
Apocalypticism, 361
Apocatastasis, 223
Apocryphal Letter of James, 71
Apocryphon of John, 6–8, 13–15, 92–93,
    105–6
Apollo, 59
Apolytrosis, 96
Apsu, 165
Aquarius, Age of, 362–63, 369–70, 378
Architecture and Hermeticism, 186, 188
Arion, 186
Aristotelianism, 111, 125–27, 129–31, 143
Arithmology, 115
Art of Memory, 259
Ascensio Isaiae, 88
Asclepius, 5, 12, 23–24, 69–77, 113, 128,
    202, 206, 210, 212
Astral fatality, 81
Astrology, 109–10, 115, 138, 192, 331, 375
    and music, 184
Aurora consurgens, 199, 206, 209
Aurora Sapientiae, 220–21, 234
Automatic writing, 365

Bahir, 112
Baptism, 74

Basilianism, 103
Begotten Intellect, 80–82
Beulah, 302
Bhagavad Gita, 274
Body, 10, 12, 96
Bogomils, 87–89, 91, 93, 95, 98–99
Book of Crates, 199
Book of Two Principles, 89–90
Bootstrap theory, 368
Borborians, 94–95
Boule, 13
Buddha, 45, 48
Buddhism, 231, 340, 377

Cain, 33
Cambridge Platonists, 244, 255
Cathars, 87-108, 374
    and dualism, 87–95
Causality, 375, 379
Cedars (in Rosicrucianism), 199
Chakras, 224, 267, 321, 333
Chaldeans, 133–35, 137–38, 146
Channeling, 364–66
Child of the Work, 160–61, 167
Christ, 27–29, 44, 90–91, 93–95, 100, 139,
    167, 178, 200, 202, 204, 209, 223,
    225, 288, 292, 306, 350, 352
Circuitous journey (Romanticism), 250
Coincidentia oppositorum (alchemy),
    158–59, 161, 174
Cologne Mani-Codex, 39
Communities, Christian Theosophic, 228
Concordance, Practice of, 120
Concordia philosophorum, 127, 143
Concorezza, 89–91
Confessio Fraternitatis, 116
Coniunctio, 159, 164, 173–74, 204
Consolamentum, 87–88, 96–102, 104
Consubstantiality, 64
Contemplation, 7, 10, 79, 83–84
Corpus Hermeticum, 5, 9, 54, 74, 109, 113–
    14, 117, 126, 128, 135–37, 141, 146,
    198, 202, 205, 207–8, 210–11, 252,
    256, 259, 273, 277, 292, 294
    Patrizi's edition, 133

Correspondences, 111, 119, 185, 235, 253,
    258, 262, 349, 375
Cosmic consciousness, 255–56
Cosmos, 9–10
Counter-Enlightenment, 375
Course in Miracles, A, 370
Creation, 117, 129, 241, 277
    good/bad, 90
    according to Patrizi, 136–37, 139
    according to Steuco, 143
Cross, 65
Cupid, 203

David, 276
Death & rebirth, 246–47, 250
Definitions of Hermes Trismegistus to
    Asclepius, 74
Deism, 271
Demiurge, 9–10, 14, 56, 59–60, 68, 92,
    106, 294, 351, 356
    according to Blake, 273, 277, 292, 294,
    296
Devil, 65
Diatessaron, 40
Disciplina arcani, 118
Diversitarianism, 240–42, 250, 260
Doceticism, 94
Donar, 351
Donnerstag aus Licht (Stockhausen), 347
Dove (in alchemy), 200
Dream of Scipio, 72
Dualism, 371–74
    absolute, 89
    moderate, 89, 91
    See also under Cathars
Dynamic organicism, 245–47
Dynamism, 239–41
Dzogchen, 353

Ecological crisis, 368
Ecumenism, 231
Elchasaites, 41, 44
Elia, 210
Elohim, 274, 300, 307
Emanation, 117, 241, 248–49

Empiricism (in study of Esotericism), 121, 123
Empyreum, 131, 135, 138
Enitharmon, 278, 301
Ennoia, 8
Enoch, 210
Enuma elish, 165
Ephrata (Christian Theosophic community), 228, 235
Epistle to Diognetus, 23
Esotericism
    according to Abrams, 251–52
    concept of, 117–22, 149–51, 244, 359–60, 375
    relation to New Age Movement, 359, 372–79
Esoterism, 118
Ethics, Gnostic and Hermetic, 21–35
Eucharist, Greek, 70–71
Eurhythmy, 193
Eve, 45, 92
    according to Stockhausen, 349
Evolution(ism), 239, 241–42, 245, 249–50, 260–62, 368, 377–79
    distinct from Process, 261, 263
    evolution of consciousness, 249, 255
Exiles, 2
Experience, Primacy of, 150, 163–64, 217, 221, 231, 275, 312, 373
Ezekiel, 15, 282, 300, 307
Ezra, 272

Fall of Lucifer, 291
Fall of Man, 197–98, 210, 224
Fama Fraternitatis, 116, 330
Fihrist, 38–39
Findhorn, 361, 380
Fluor (Patrizi), 138
Fortunate fall, 248
Fragmentation, 372
Free will, 34
Freemasonry, 189, 255
    and Steiner, 333, 335–36, 338–39
Freie Hochschule für Geisteswissenschaft, 340

Friends of God, 228
Futtuq, 38

Gaia hypothesis, 368
Genesis, 204, 218, 273
Geomancy, 331
Gnosis, 1, 4, 6, 9, 11, 21–27, 30–31, 42, 45, 53, 57, 88, 118–20, 149, 151, 157, 205, 210, 231, 249–50, 258, 275, 352, 357, 371–74
Gnosticism, 2–4, 112, 133, 379
    and New Age movement, 373–74
God
    according to Gnosticism and Hermetism, 7–9
    invisible, 80
    according to Patrizi, 136
Goddess movement, 369
Goetia, 138
Golden Dawn, Hermetic Order of the, 311, 320, 322–32, 337–38
Golden Fleece, 202
Golden Section, 187, 190
Golgonooza, 278, 305
Gospel of Philip, 34
Gospel of the Hebrews, 95
Gospel of Thomas, 374
Gospel of Truth, 53–68
Grace, 33–35
Great Chain of Being, 241
Green Lion (alchemy), 201
Guénonianism, 118

Ham, 128
Healing, 366
Healing & Spiritual Growth movement, 366–67
Hekhaloth, 77
Helen (companion of Simon Magus), 174
Heliopolis, 81
Hell, 25
Hermes, 6, 109, 122, 202, 351, 355
    as Cupid, 203
    as Green Lion, 201
    as "healing medicine," 201, 209

Hermes *(continued):*
  Hermes Criophorus, 202
  Hermes Hodegos, 200
  Hermes Trismegistus, 5–6, 22–24, 27,
    79–81, 83–85, 109–10, 113–14, 122,
    127, 132–33, 136–38, 140–41, 143,
    146, 161, 163, 178, 198–99, 202,
    205, 208, 210–12, 277–78, 292
  Hermes-Mercurius, 109–10, 178, 180,
    198–202, 204, 206, 209
  Mercurius sagittarius, 203
Hermetic Brotherhood of Luxor, 192,
  325, 338, 343, 345
Hermetic Definitions, 5, 16
Hermetic Society, 323
Hermetica, 109, 113
Hermeticism, 109–23, 245, 374
Hermetism, 5–6, 26, 109–11, 113–14,
  198
Hermopolis, 81
Hieros gamos, 157, 161, 164–65, 167,
  172–73, 179, 204
High-grade Masonry, 313, 332
Hinduism, 377
Historical consciousness, 248, 261–62
Holism, 370–72
Holographic paradigm, 368
Holy Spirit, 97–102
Homer, 62
Horos, 31
Horus, 59, 180
Hosea, 199
Hostia, 70
Humanistic psychology, 367
Hyle, 59–60
Hylici, 56
Hymns, 71, 73, 76–77
  in hermetism, 75–76, 80
  in Merkabah mysticism, 73, 75–76

Idealism, German, 237
Ignorance, 57–58
Illness, 367
Illuminism, 237
Imagination, 119–20, 243–44, 250–51,
  256, 258–62

  according to Blake, 275–77, 287–88,
    290, 301, 305–6
Initiation, 27, 79, 83, 85
Innaios, 40
Interrogatio Johannis, 91, 93–95, 106
Isaiah, 30–31, 202, 272
Isidor, 32
Isis, 23, 59–60, 180
Islam, 50

Jacob, 180
Jacob's ladder, 171–72, 180
Jesus, 27–28, 44–45, 65, 71, 95, 168, 207,
  214, 276, 288, 300, 306–7, 315, 334–
  35, 350
Jupiter, 351

Kabbalah, Christian, 110, 112–14, 122,
  198, 229, 288
Kabbalah, Jewish, 111–14, 132, 144, 190,
  217–18, 228–29, 231, 251, 273–74
Kabbalah, Occultist, 322–23, 326, 329,
  335
Khnoum, 23
Koot Hoomi (theosophical Master), 334
Koran, 95
Kundalini, 321, 339, 342

Ladder, Symbolism of the, 180
Law, Jewish, 41
Light (Patrizi), 134–35, 138
Light on the Path, 334
Logikos, 75
Logos, 22, 294
  according to Patrizi, 135, 137
Los, 278, 294, 296, 301, 305–6
Love, 25
Lucibel, 89
Lucifer (Stockhausen), 349
Lutheranism and Rosicrucianism, 197,
  213
Luvah, 302

Macrocosm/Microcosm, 119, 312, 332,
  349
Madrigal and Ficino, 186

Magi, 128, 140, 144
Magia, 110–11, 113–14, 119, 138–39, 375
Magic, 12, 218, 229, 259–60, 311, 319, 325–26, 329
and music, 185–86
Mammon, 28
Man (according to Gnosticism and Hermetism), 11–12
Manichaeism, 37–51, 87, 93, 98–99, 105, 107–8
Maria, 163
Marianites, 94
Marmaryam, 38
Marriage, 32
Mary, 28, 94–95, 106, 167
Mass, Roman, 69–70, 72–77
Masters (Modern Theosophy), 313, 317–18, 320–23, 325, 327, 333, 336, 342–43
Materialism, 371
Mays, 38
Mediations, 119–20
Medinet Madi, 43
Meditation, 80
Memphis & Misraim order, 337
Mercurius, 110
Mercury (alchemy), 154, 156–60, 165, 167, 172, 178–79, 199, 201, 203
Merkabah mysticism, 73, 76
Mesmerism, 148
Messalianism, 98–102, 107
Messina Conference, 1966 4
Metanoia, 219
Metaphysical movements, 363, 376
Michael, 95
Michael (Stockhausen), 349
Miracles, 225
Mithras, 72
Mithrasliturgy, 73
Mondeva, 354
Montanism, 94
Morphic resonance, 368
Morya (Master), 334
Moses, 113–14, 127–28, 138, 140, 163, 198, 204, 210, 212
Mughtasilah, 38, 41

Mundus imaginalis, 115, 259, 267
Music and Hermeticism, 115, 183–96
Mutus liber, 170–73
Mysteria Mystica Aeterna, 311, 332–40
Myth, 243–44
in Gnosticism and Hermetism, 12–17
Manichaean, 44–46

Nag Hammadi, 2, 4, 17, 54, 374
discovery of library, 54
Nature, 3, 15, 111–14, 118–20, 148, 163, 197–98, 207, 209–12, 221, 223, 243–44, 245, 53, 258
Negative theology, 7
Neopaganism, 368–69
Neoplatonism, 244, 248, 251–52, 272–74
relation to Hermeticism, 253
status in Esotericism, 252–53
New Age movement, 191, 264–65, 359
and culture criticism, 371–73, 379
New Age in a general sense, 362–63, 370, 375–76
New Age in a restricted sense, 361–62, 369–70, 375–76, 380
New Age in an improper sense, 363
Proto-New Age movement, 361
New Thought, 363, 376
Nigredo, 157–58, 203
Noah, 128
Nous, 3, 7, 15, 22, 41, 44, 46

Oblatio rationalis, 70
Occult Sciences, 375
Occulta philosophia, 110, 113–15, 117, 122
Occultism, 311, 375–76
Ogdoad and the Ennead, The, 5–6, 24, 27, 79–85
One, the (Plotinus), 3
Opera and Hermeticism, 186
Ophites, 105
Orc, 296, 301
Ordo Rosae Rubeae et Aureae Crucis, 330
Ordo Templi Orientis, 337–40, 344–45
Organicism, 239–42, 250, 256–58, 261–62

Origenism, 103
Original sin, 46–47
Orpheus, 114, 127–30, 132, 141, 146, 186
Orphic Hymns, 132
Orphism, 131, 146
Osiris 23, 59, 180
    as son of Ham 128

Palingenesia, 205
Panentheism, 255–56, 267
Paracelsianism, 115, 199, 206–7, 210, 219, 237
Paradigm, New, 363, 368, 370
Passions, 29–31
Paulicianism, 87, 93, 95, 98–99, 102, 106
Perennialism, 114, 120
Perfect Discourse, 24–25
Perfecti, 96
Perfection, 30
Philadelphians, 221, 223–24, 228, 231, 235
Philosopher's Stone, 156–60, 180, 201
Philosophia perennis, 114, 117–18, 120, 127, 129, 143
Pietism, 226
Piety, 25, 27
Pisces, Age of, 371
Plane, 54, 58–60, 65, 68
Planets, 9, 13–15, 71–74, 81
Platonism, 1, 5, 12, 111, 114, 125, 127, 129, 133, 138, 140, 240–42, 248, 277, 289, 291, 94
Pleroma, 8–10, 13
Pneumatici, 53, 56, 65–66, 99
Poimandres, 5–6, 8, 10, 13–16, 54, 75, 82, 209, 288
Positive thinking, 367
Prayer, 24, 79, 83, 224
Pre-Socratics, 132–33
Prisca theologia, 127–29, 134, 139, 143
Procreation
    according to Gnosticism, 27–28
    according to Hermetism, 26–27
Progress, 248
Prometheus, 291
Prophets, 128

Psychic body, 14
Psychici, 56
Psychology and New Age movement, 378–79
Puffers, 151
Pythagoreanism, 112, 127–28, 133, 183, 186–87, 193

Ramakrishna mission, 377
Ramala community, 362
Realized eschatology, 68
Rebirth, 74–75, 83, 219, 225
Reductionism, 371–72
Reformation, Second, 198, 212–13
Regeneration, 82–85, 204–5, 208–10
Reincarnation, 117
    and the Cathars, 104
    in the New Age movement, 365–66, 370, 377–78, 382
Reintegration, 198
Religionsgeschichtliche Schule, 39
Repentances, 2
Resurrection, 30, 96
Revelation, 5–6
Revelations of Morienus to Khalid ibn Yazid, 161–64
Rhea, 59
Ritual, 83–85
Romanticism, 237–68, 360, 375–78
    positive versus negative, 246
Rosarium Philosophorum, 164–68, 172
Rosicrucianism, 116, 197–215, 235
    and Christian Theosophy, 235
    and Hermeticism, 202–10
    and Hermetism, 198–202
    and music, 191
    in occultism, 323, 326, 332–33, 335–38
Rubedo, 157, 159, 161, 204–5

Sabbath, 41
Saint-Félix, Cathar meeting at, 89
Salvation, 6, 21–22, 32, 35, 66, 82, 96, 98
Sanctus, 75
Satan, 89, 91–92, 286, 289, 296, 300–301, 352
Satanael, 89

Scholasticism, 129–30
Science and the New Age movement, 367–68
Scientific revolution, 197, 212
Secret Chiefs, 320, 324, 327–28, 330, 343
Self-Begotten Intellect, 80–84
Sepher Yetzirah, 112
Serapis (Master), 344
Serpens mercurialis, 204
Seth, 33
Seventh Day Adventists, 350
Sex
    according to Gnosticism, 27–28, 31–32
    according to Hermetism, 26–27
Sex-magic, 338–39, 343
Sexual desire, 16, 46–47
Shamanism, 219
Sibyls, 114
Signatures, 355
Simon Magus, 174
Simonians, 32
Sirius, 348, 356
Societas Rosicruciana in Anglia, 323–24, 327, 343
Sola Gratia, 205, 211
Solomon, 199, 206, 210
Solomon's Temple, 189
Son of God (in Rosicrucianism), 207
Sophia, 8–9, 14, 31, 56, 60, 217, 221–22, 225–26, 231–32, 235, 355
Soul
    good/bad soul, 33–34
    according to Patrizi, 131, 133–34, 137
Speculative music, 183
Spiritualism, 314, 365
Spiritus Paracliticus, 97
Spiritus Principalis, 97
Spiritus Sanctus, 97
Stella Matutina, 337
Stoa, 5, 10, 12, 112, 133
Sufism, 217, 222, 231
Symbols, 243–44, 259
Systems, 247
Syzygos (Mani's), 41–42, 46

Tabula smaragdina, 172, 290

Tantra, 166, 174, 325, 340, 353, 355
Tariqah, 228
Tarot, 331
Tat, 5, 85, 128
Teleology, 247
Temporalism, 260–62
Testimony of Truth, 27, 31
Theatrum chemicum, 201
Theosophia (term), 217
Theosophy, Christian, 110, 116, 117–237
    and Rosicrucianism, 235
    and science, 232
    Iconography of, 232
Theosophy, Modern, 190, 217, 311, 322–27, 329–30, 332–33, 335–36, 338–39, 360, 376–78
    and New Age, 362–63, 375
    Esoteric School of the Theosophical Society, 311–22
    Hermetic Lodge, 323
Theurgy, 115
Thor, 351
Thoth, 81, 109
Tiamat, 165
Timaeus (Plato), 111
Tractatus aureum, 168–70
Trance, 365
Transcendentalism, 234, 264, 363, 375–76
Transmission (of esoteric knowledge), 120
Transmutation, 120, 149–51, 203, 259, 261–62
Transpersonal psychology, 367
Trinity, 97–98, 130, 139, 199, 202
    in Alchemy, 180
    in Christian Kabbalah, 112
    in *Rosarium Philosophorum*, 167
    according to Patrizi, 129–37, 139, 146
Turfan, 43

UFO-cults, 361, 380
Ulro, 302, 304
Una voce, 70, 72–73, 77
Unbegotten God, 24
Unbegotten Intellect, 80–84
Untitled Treatise of the Codex Brucianus, 2

Urantia Book, 350–51, 355, 358
Urizen, 294, 296, 299, 301
Urthona, 301

Vala, 302, 304
Valentinianism, 21, 29–35, 96, 105, 355
Venus, 199, 202–3
Visions, 80, 83–84

Waldenses, 87, 93
Way, the (concept in *Gospel of Truth*), 53
Wicca, 369

Women's spirituality, 369
World Soul, 3, 137
World, the (according to Gnosticism and
    Hermetism), 9–11

Zeus, 173
Zoas, 300–302, 307
Zohar, 112
Zoroaster, 2, 45, 87, 114, 127–33, 137–38,
    140–41, 143, 146
Zoroastrianism, 39
Zostrianus, 2–3, 6, 13